I

LOVE

LOS ANGELES

GUIDE

I

LOVE

LOS ANGELES

GUIDE

THIRD EDITION

Edited by Marilyn J. Appleberg
Text by Yvette Lodge and Francis Morgan

Illustrations by Albert Pfeiffer

COLLIER BOOKS
Macmillan Publishing Company
New York

Maxwell Macmillan Canada • Toronto
Maxwell Macmillan International • New York • Oxford • Singapore • Sydney

Collier Books
Macmillan Publishing Company
866 Third Avenue
New York, NY 10022

Maxwell Macmillan Canada, Inc.
1200 Eglinton Avenue East
Suite 200
Don Mills, Ontario M3C 3N1

Macmillan Publishing Company is part of the Maxwell Communication Group of Companies.

Library of Congress Cataloging-in-Publication Data
Lodge, Yvette.
I love Los Angeles guide / edited by Marilyn J. Appleberg; text
by Yvette Lodge and Francis Morgan; illustrations by Albert Pfeiffer.
p.   cm.
Includes index.
ISBN 0-02-097242-3
1. Los Angeles (Calif.)—Guidebooks.   I. Appleberg, Marilyn J.
II. Morgan, Francis.   III. Title.
F869.L83L63   1993
917.94′940453—dc20   93-20200

Macmillan books are available at special discounts for bulk purchases for sales promotions,
premiums, fund-raising, or educational use. For details, contact:

Special Sales Director
Macmillan Publishing Company
866 Third Avenue
New York, NY 10022

10 9 8 7 6 5 4 3 2 1

Printed in the United States of America

CONTENTS

FOREWORD

There is nowhere on earth quite like LA. Sinfully rich and carefree, Los Angeles is a warmhearted city bathed in sunshine and alive with opportunity, freedom, and early-morning energy. It's a hodgepodge of culture and coarseness, softened by swaying palm trees and balmy evenings. It's a city people love to hate, yet hate to leave. Both tasteful and tasteless, it's the ultimate in plastic and stucco, enviably decadent, smiling, affluent, and creative. Surprising.

This all-inclusive guide has been carefully compiled to bring together everything that is LA—the services, the sights, and the pleasures. Each entry is clearly detailed with an individual heading and map reference for quick and easy location. Sixteen pages of maps, plus dozens of fine illustrations, make this the most complete guide to Los Angeles ever written.

Using This Guide

General categories are listed in the table of contents; for more specific information refer to the index. Due to the vast size of Los Angeles, certain sections (ACCOMMODATIONS, RESTAURANTS, and Art Galleries in MUSEUMS & GALLERIES) have been split into geographical areas to assist both visitors and residents.

To obtain full use of this book, please read the introductory notes at the beginning of chapters.

Map References

Map 1 (page 54) shows Greater Los Angeles with all freeways (major thoroughfares) marked. It has nine shaded areas, which represent maps 2 through 10. Each entry in the book that lies within the confines of map 1 has a map reference. A separate map is provided for Day Trips on page 38 and there are detailed maps for the Walking Tours on pages 31—35.

Telephones

Numbers with the prefix (800) are toll-free. Overseas visitors should note: when dialing outside your present area code, always start by dialing 1—for example, 1-714-123-4567, or 1-800-123-4567.

Symbols

Symbols are used to indicate prices and services. They are explained on the following pages:
Accommodations, page 10.
Restaurants, page 150.
Tours, page 26.

Credit Cards

AE	American Express
CB	Carte Blanche
D	Discover
DC	Diners' Club
MC	MasterCard
V	Visa

In 1769, Spanish explorer Gaspar de Partolá, then-governor of Baja California, discovered a small Indian village on a river he called Porciuncula in the region of Alta California. The village was renamed Pueblo de Nuestra Señora la Reina de los Angeles de Porciuncula. In short, Town of Our Lady Queen of the Angels of Porciuncula, known today simply as Los Angeles. In 1822, California passed from Spanish to Mexican rule, and in 1845 was taken by the Americans in a final battle, fought in the San Fernando Valley. California was admitted to the Union as the 31st state in September 1850.

The discovery of gold, good agricultural land, oil, and the opening of a cross-country railroad contributed to the growth of the area. But Los Angeles experienced its biggest boom when pioneers of the motion picture industry chose the city as a perfect location for making movies. The section known as Hollywood became synonymous with movie stars, glamour, luxury, and opulence. Los Angeles, affectionately known as LA, is still a city of dreams.

Southern California enjoys a Mediterranean climate with mild winters and warm, dry summers. Annual rainfall averages only 14 inches, falling mainly in winter.

Los Angeles County (California's largest) covers 4,900 square miles and in 1985 had a population of 8 million. It is a huge, sprawling coastal metropolis, surrounded by mountains. The close proximity of the mountains makes it possible to swim in the Pacific and ski in the snows of the Sierras on the same day.

There is no real center or area that could be called typical. Los Angeles is made up of 95 different communities that have grown outward rather than upward. This was partly due to an earthquake clause limiting buildings to a height of 150 feet. In 1957, with new construction techniques, the restriction was lifted, and the skyline has since changed. Today, huge skyscrapers strike a vivid contrast to the low, flat-topped homes of the 1940s.

Los Angeles boasts the most extensive freeway system in the world. Ironically, the millions of vehicles using the system each day contribute substantially to smog pollution—that thorn in LA's side. (Please don't confuse coastal mist or early-morning haze with the real thing!) However, welcome desert winds often blow across the LA basin and clear the smog layer to expose breathtaking views of snow-capped mountains.

The warm climate encourages a relaxed, casual atmosphere and outdoor activities are abundant. Angelinos are friendly, helpful, and outgoing. Their city provides excitement, fascination, and fantasy for millions who visit year-round.

BASIC
INFORMATION

GEOGRAPHY & WEATHER

Los Angeles County is 70 miles long and over 70 miles wide, rising from sea level along the west side to 10,064 feet at Old Baldy in the San Gabriel Mountains. Metropolitan Los Angeles sprawls across the LA basin—a huge plain surrounded and divided by mountain ranges. The San Gabriel Mountains, to the northeast, stand between Los Angeles and the vast Mojave Desert. To the northwest, the Santa Monica Mountains form a ridge between the city and the San Fernando Valley. The Santa Ana Mountains trail away from Los Angeles to the south.

California's mountains were formed by the uplifting movements of huge landmasses. A drive through the local ranges best illustrates how the land has been folded and rippled to form beautiful canyons. The LA basin is a relatively flat bed of sandstone, shale, and ocean sediment resting on a deep shelf known as the Pacific Plate. This meets the North American Plate at a point called the San Andreas Fault, which crosses the desert northeast of Los Angeles. The two landmasses are continually in motion and pass each other at a rate of two inches a year. Occasionally this natural movement is halted by the plates' locking against each other. When enough force builds up they jolt free, resulting in what we know as an earthquake. Earthquakes occur frequently throughout California but only a few are felt. Major damage is rare thanks to strict building codes.

Temperatures within LA County vary greatly. Beach area temperatures are generally 10°F cooler than Downtown, but beach cities experience a smaller change in temperature from day to night. The farther inland the location, the more extreme the temperature change—for example, the San Gabriel Valley can reach 100°F in the daytime and drop to 40°F at night.

The mountain areas of San Gabriel and San Bernardino, farther east, enjoy seasonal winter weather and numerous ski resorts offer a variety of sporting activities.

Los Angeles is vulnerable to fire and flood. After a long dry summer, huge brush fires, fanned by warm desert winds, can burn thousands of acres in a matter of hours. Rainfall may average only 14 inches a year, but sometimes it seems to arrive in one burst, causing flash floods and chaotic road conditions.

With such a diversity of landscapes, Angelinos can enjoy sunny beaches, alpine forests, canyons, lakes, and vast desert regions at any time of year. Although temperatures can be extreme in desert and mountain areas, the LA basin remains warm and sunny year-round.

GETTING AROUND LA

Los Angeles developed along with the automobile, and without a car it can be difficult to enjoy the city to its fullest. With one of the most extensive and best-designed freeway systems in the world, motorists can reach any point in this huge, sprawling metropolis quickly and easily. To maintain a safe and even flow of traffic on LA's 700 miles of freeways, remember that the maximum speed limit is 55 miles per hour. In business or residential districts the speed limit is 25 mph unless otherwise posted. Stopping is not permitted on any freeway except in cases of emergency. Slower vehicles are expected to use traffic lanes on the right. In case of breakdown, pull across to the right-hand shoulder and use one of the emergency telephones provided (one free call is permitted). With most freeway traffic moving at an even speed, lane changing can be difficult. Strangers to the area should watch signs carefully and allow plenty of time to change lanes before exiting.

It is generally permissible to turn right against a red light, providing the vehicle has been brought to a full stop and the route is clear.

Parking facilities throughout the city are above average and most businesses provide adequate customer parking.

In January 1993, part of the core line of LA's first subway, the Metro Red Line, opened, ushering in a new era in modern transportation in this car-dependent region. Now covering 4.4 miles, the Red Line when completed will cover 17.4 miles from Union Station in downtown to North Hollywood via the mid-Wilshire district, Hollywood Boulevard, and Universal City. When the entire project is completed, the resulting commuter rail system will cover 400 miles throughout LA County. For details on the subway see TRANSPORTATON & VACATION INFORMATION, Bus & Metro Rail Services.

Auto rentals, airport, airline, taxi, train, bus, and Metro Rail services are all detailed under TRANSPORTATION & VACATION INFORMATION.

Fitness-conscious travelers may prefer other means of transportation. Bicycle, roller skate, and roller blade rental facilities are plentiful, and bike paths are provided throughout beach and park areas (see SIGHTSEEING, Bicycle Trails). It is also possible to rent motorcycles, mopeds, boats of all kinds, recreational vehicles, and even small aircraft (see SPORTS & RECREATION, Sporting Activities, and SHOPPING & SERVICES, Specialty Shopping, Rentals).

Hitchhiking is definitely not recommended. In recent years a lot of serious crime has been committed against, and by, hitchhikers. This form of "transportation" is not safe in Los Angeles.

Visitors are often confused when obtaining directions. An Angelino may advise you to "go north to Pico, then east to Westwood." To explain briefly: Los Angeles, like most American cities, was built on a grid system with most streets running north-south or east-west. Once you have a mental picture of a few main streets (two good ones to remember are Sepulveda Boulevard, running north-south, and Wilshire

Boulevard, east-west), it becomes very simple to get around. A good method is to picture the coastline as a line going north-south and as being the most westerly edge of the city.

CAUTION

Street crime is a sad fact of life in every major city and public awareness is important. Generally speaking, it is best to avoid parks and beaches after dark. Crime is more prevalent in run-down areas (which can easily be avoided). Police in Los Angeles do not normally patrol on foot, but you'll see plenty of patrol cars, and daytime bicycle and mounted horse patrols are now a common sight along the beaches.

TELEPHONE SERVICES

(*See also* SHOPPING & SERVICES, Complaints & Consumer Services.)
Emergency: Fire, police, ambulance: 911
Beach & surf conditions: (310) 451-8761
Better Business Bureau: (213) 251-9696
Catholic information: (213) 627-4861
Customs information: (310) 514-6030
Directory assistance (information): 411
Federal Information Center: (213) 894-3800
Forest Service information: (818) 790-1151
Gay Community Center: (310) 464-7400
Highway conditions: (213) 628-7623
Islamic Center: (213) 384-5783
Jewish Federation Council: (310) 852-1234
LA County Parks Service: (213) 744-4211
LA Public Library: (213) 612-3200
Legal Aid Foundation: (213) 487-3320
Long distance information: 1 + Area
  Code + 555-1212
National Parks Service: (818) 888-3770
Operator assistance: 0
Postal Service: (213) 586-1467
Senior Citizens Information: (213) 485-4851
Smog forecast: (800) 242-4022
State Parks Service: (213) 620-3342
Tel-Med: (310) 825-9921
Time: (213) 853-1212
Traveler's Aid Society: (213) 625-2501
Visitors & Convention Bureau: (213) 689-8822
Weather report: (213) 554-1212
Woman's Building: (213) 221-6161

INFORMATION CENTERS

(*See also* ANNUAL EVENTS, Visitors Information)
LA Convention & Visitors Bureau   **7-C3**
685 S. Figueroa St, LA. (213) 689-8822.
Anaheim Visitors & Convention Bureau   **1-F8**
800 W. Katella Ave, Anaheim. (714) 999-8999.

Beverly Hills Visitors & Convention Bureau
       5-E8
239 S. Beverly Dr, Beverly Hills. (310) 271-8174.
Buena Park Visitors & Convention Bureau
       3-B6
6280 Manchester Blvd, Suite 103, Buena Park. (714) 994-1511.
Hollywood Chamber of Commerce   **6-C6**
6290 Sunset Blvd, Suite 525, Hollywood. (310) 469-8311.
Long Beach Convention & Tourism Bureau
       1-G5
World Trade Center, Suite 300, Long Beach. (310) 436-3645.
LA County Public Information Office   **7-B4**
500 W. Temple St, LA. (213) 974-1311.
Marina Del Rey Visitors Center   **3-A2**
4701 Admiralty Way, Marina del Rey. (310) 305-9545.
Pasadena Convention & Visitors Bureau
       8-C3
171 S. Los Robles, Pasadena. (818) 795-9311.
Riverside Visitors & Convention Bureau
3443 Orange St, Riverside. (714) 787-7950.
Ventura Visitors & Convention Bureau
89-C S. California St, Ventura. (805) 648-2075.
City of LA Dept of Parks & Recreation
  Main office: (213) 485-5515
  Metropolitan area: (213) 485-1310
  Municipal sports: (213) 485-4871
  Swimming pools: (213) 485-2844
  Camp information: (213) 485-4853
LA County Dept of Parks & Recreation
  Main office: (213) 738-2995
  Beaches: (310) 305-9545

PUBLIC TRANSPORTATION

See TRANSPORTATION & VACATION INFORMATION.

NEWSPAPERS & MAGAZINES

Newspapers

Los Angeles Times   **7-C4**
202 W. 1st St (Times Mirror Sq), LA. (213) 237-5000. Major daily of Southern California. Sunday edition includes a weekly TV guide and a calendar section listing local events and forthcoming attractions. Free tours. (*See also* SIGHTSEEING, Tours.)
LA Opinion   **7-E3**
411 5th St, LA. (213) 622-8332. Daily Hispanic newspaper.
The Outlook   **4-B4**
1920 Colorado Ave, Santa Monica. (310) 829-6811. Daily Santa Monica-area newspaper.
The Daily Breeze   **1-F4**
5215 Torrance Blvd, Torrance. (310) 772-6281.

Daily; distribution covers South Bay beach cities.

The Daily News   **1-B3**
14539 Sylvan St, Van Nuys. (818) 713-3131. Daily morning paper serving greater Los Angeles and outlying valley communities.

Independent Press-Telegram   **1-G5**
644 Pine Ave, Long Beach. (310) 436-3676. Daily, covering Long Beach and adjacent communities.

Star-News   **8-D3**
525 E. Colorado Blvd, Pasadena. (818) 578-6300. Daily Pasadena-area newspaper.

Los Angeles Sentinel   **1-D5**
1112 E. 43rd St, LA. (213) 232-3261. Weekly newspaper catering to LA's black population.

Recycler   **1-C5**
2898 Rowena Ave, LA. (213) 660 8900. A weekly comprised entirely of classified ads. Private party ads are published free. (Five editions: Los Angeles, San Fernando Valley, South Bay, San Gabriel Valley, and Orange County.)

Free Papers

Many free weekly neighborhood newspapers and shopping guides are available at supermarkets, bookstores, record shops, etc. The following papers cover greater Los Angeles.

LA Weekly   **6-C7**
2140 Hyperion Ave, LA. (213) 667-2620. Best publication for listings of weekly entertainment in LA. A "must" for those interested in music and movies. Radical editorials.

Reader   **6-G4**
12224 Victory Blvd, N. Hollywood. (818) 933-0161. Weekly reviews and listings on entertainment and events in LA. Good, in-depth topical features.

Trade Papers

These famous papers cater to LA's large entertainment industry.

Daily Variety   **6-D5**
1400 N. Cahuenga Blvd, Hollywood. (213) 857-6600. Daily Monday to Friday. (NOTE: The *Variety* published in New York is a weekly, available each Wednesday.)

The Hollywood Reporter   **6-C5**
6715 Sunset Blvd, Hollywood. (213) 464-7411. Daily Monday to Friday.

Magazines

Los Angeles Magazine   **5-E7**
1888 Century Park East, Suite 920, LA. (310) 557-7592. A big, glossy monthly packed with interesting information focusing on LA events, amenities, and personalities. Comprehensive restaurant guide. Good, light reading.

International Newsstands

Al's Newsstand   **6-E3**
370 N. Fairfax Ave, LA. (213) 935-8525. Domestic, French, Israeli, and English newspapers and magazines.

Sherman Oaks Newsstand   **1-B2**
14500 Ventura Blvd, Sherman Oaks. (818) 995-0632. Large selection of foreign and domestic fashion magazines, design publications, and newspapers.

Universal News Agency   **6-B5**
1655 N. Las Palmas Ave, Hollywood. (213) 467-3850. Selection of newspapers and magazines from major European countries and the U.S. *OPEN 7am-midnight.*

World Books & News   **6-C5**
1652 N. Cahuenga Blvd, Hollywood. (213) 465-4352. Excellent selection of newspapers and magazines from around the world. *OPEN 24 hours.*

GUIDEBOOKS

Available at most bookstores.

A Guide to Historic Places in Los Angeles County
Kendall Hunt Publishing Company. Details of more than 400 historic places to visit in LA County.

Around the Town with Ease
Junior League of Los Angeles Inc. Special information for those with physical limitations.

LA on Foot
David Clark, Camaro Publishing. Twelve walking tours in different areas of LA.

Los Angeles, the Architecture of Four Ecologies
Reyner Banham; Pelican Books. Architectural study of the city.

This Is Hollywood
Kenneth Schessler; Gresha Publications. Over 600 exciting and unusual places to visit, including stars' homes, hangouts, graves, and scenes of murders and suicides.

Only in LA
Roni Sue Malin and Judy Ruderman; Chronicle Books. A guide to exceptional services.

All Night LA
John Pashdag, Jim Woller, and Gary Krueger; Chronicle Books. A guide to activities and services available after dark.

The Blue Book
Payne Publications. A guide to gay and lesbian LA, published three times a year.

Where Can We Go This Weekend?
George Lowe; J. P. Tarcher Inc. One-, two-, and three-day travel adventures in Southern California.

CALIFORNIA STATE LAWS

Drinking

The legal age is 21 years to purchase alcoholic beverages. The sale of alcohol is prohibited between 2am and 6am. One quart of alcohol may be imported or transported into the state.

Driving

The minimum age for obtaining a license to drive an automobile is 16 years with authorized drivers' training, 18 without (*see also* Getting Around LA).

Arrest Information

If signaled by police while driving, pull over, wind down the window, and place both hands on the steering wheel. Always keep both hands in plain view whenever stopped by a police officer. The officer may have been alerted to apprehend someone of similar description. The police may frisk for weapons and will check identification. Do not offer any resistance. If arrested, you must give your name and address but need not answer any other questions. Arrestees are allowed two phone calls at their own expense. Contact a lawyer or public defender for advice immediately.

—Public Defenders

Los Angeles County: (213) 974-2811

Drugs

Possession of following drugs without a prescription is illegal throughout the state: cocaine (including "crack" and "rock"), opium, morphine, codeine, heroin, sedatives, barbiturates, Quaaludes, LSD, and amphetamines. Other illegal drugs include THC, angel dust (PCP), and marijuana. NOTE: Drug laws vary from state to state and penalties for possession can be extreme.

Gambling

Gambling is generally illegal in the state of California, but there are some exceptions. In 1978, bingo was legalized, with prizes given in goods, not cash. A state lottery was introduced in 1986. Betting on horse races is permitted at the track, and since 1936, poker and panguingue (a form of gin) have been allowed by public option in certain cities. (*See also* SPORTS & RECREATION, Sporting Activities, Gambling.)

Sales Tax

A tax of 8.25% is added to all sales and services, with the exception of food purchased in a store. Labels and advertisements show prices before the addition of sales tax.

Dogs

There are pet restrictions in every Los Angeles community. Dogs must be leashed on all city streets and parks. In Santa Monica, dogs are prohibited on beaches and in parks. A license is required for all dogs over four months old. For license information, call (213) 893-8420.

BANKS

Normal banking hours are Monday to Thursday from 10am to 3pm and Friday from 10am to 6pm. Some banks are open on Saturday. Many convenience stores and supermarkets have automatic teller machines that will dispense up to $300 in cash. Foreign exchange services are listed in TRANSPORTATION & VACATION INFORMATION, Foreign Exchange.

POST OFFICE INFORMATION

For general information, call (213) 586-1737. Normal hours are Monday to Friday from 8:30 am to 5pm. Some main offices are open Saturday from 8:30am to noon. Mail collection times vary; latest pickup at main offices is generally Monday to Friday at 6:00pm and weekends at 2pm.

ZIP Code Information

Los Angeles: (213) 586-1737
Beverly Hills: (310) 274-3400
Culver City: (310) 391-6374
Santa Monica: (310) 576-2626
San Fernando Valley: (818) 908-6737

Postal Rates

To any point within the U.S. or Canada, first class (12 ounces or less) is 29 cents for the first ounce, 23 cents for each additional ounce. Postcards are 19 cents. All offices provide specialized services, including special delivery, special handling, and insurance.

Overseas Mail: Rates vary; for information, call (213) 586-1467
Express Mail: (310) 337-8845 or -8911
Federal Express (for nearest office): (213) 687-9767
United Parcel Service (for nearest office): (213) 626-1551

Freight Forwarding

A.F.L. International Shipping
Los Angeles: (310) 352-4161
American Export Lines
Call for nearest location: (800) 777-2888
Express International Forwarding
San Fernando Valley: (818) 966-3340
Nedrac Inc.
(800) 366-1204
Omega Shipping, Inc.
4375 Sheila Street, LA. (213) 264-2644

Telegrams

Western Union   **7-D3**
Call for nearest location: (800) 638-1131

Singing Telegrams

Messengers, dressed in various costumes, will sing or recite special greetings in person. They will also deliver singing messages by phone.
Live Wires
(213) 462-3111
Monkey Business Singing Telegrams
(310) 641-8867

LA MISCELLANY

Personalized License Plates
For a $25 fee, Californians can select any combination of seven letters and/or numbers for an individualized automobile license plate (providing it does not offend public decency and is not a duplication). Keep an eye out for inventive license plates or for cars of the stars:

BORG 9	Ernest Borgnine
FIRM UP	Health club founder Jack La-Lanne
KILLER	Comedian Flip Wilson
360 GUY	Johnny Carson (all-around guy)
RATS 1	Valerie Perrine (it spells STAR backwards)
Y NOT SUE	Anonymous attorney
8A UNIS A	French expatriate

The Goodyear Blimp
The blimp is a huge, gas-filled airship stationed at Long Beach. It can often be seen elegantly cruising the skies above Los Angeles. At night, brightly lit patterns and messages flash across its sides.
Skywriting
Up to five jets will fly in formation, releasing smoke in a computerized pattern to form words. In advertising, the sky may be the limit!
Banner Towing
On summer weekends, along the beaches, low-flying airplanes trail banners displaying messages ranging from suntan lotion ads to personal birthday greetings.

SPANISH PLACE NAMES

Los Angeles was founded by the Spanish and the Mexicans and has retained many of its original place names. The following list explains their meanings.

Agua	water
Alamo	poplar tree
Alta	high ground, elevated
Arroyo	creek bed
Bodega	wine vault
Bonito	pretty, cute
Brea	pitch, tar
Buena Vista	good view
Calabasas	pumpkin, squash
Caliente	hot
Camino	road
Camino Real	royal highway
Carbon	coal
Casa	house
Centinela	sentinel
Cerritos	little hills
Cienega	swamp, marsh
Cisco	broken coal, coal dust
Colorado	red
Cruz (cruce)	cross (crossing)
Del Mar	from the ocean
Del Rey	from the king
Del Sur	from the south
Diego	James (a given name)
Dos Rios	two rivers
El Dorado	golden, land of gold
El Paso	the pass
El Toro	the bull
Encino	oak tree
Ensenada	bay
Escondido	hidden, concealed
Feliz	happy
Flores	flowers
Fontana	fountain, spring
Granada	pomegranate
Hermosa	beautiful
Hondo	deep
Laguna	lake, pond
La Jolla	the hollow
La Joya	the jewel
La Mesa	tableland
La Mirada	the view
La Paz	peace
La Playa	the beach
Las Vegas	the meadows, plains
Lobos	wolves
Loma	hill
Los Angeles	the angels
Los Banos	the baths
Los Gatos	the cats
Madera	wood, lumber
Mariposa	butterfly
Merced	mercy
Miramar	ocean view
Modesto	modesty, chastity
Mojave	three mountains
Nuevo	new, just started
Oro	gold

Palo Alto	tall tree, stick	Redondo	round
Palos Verdes	green sticks	San, Santa	saint
Paraiso	paradise	Soledad	loneliness, solitary
Pescadero	fishing grounds	Sur	south
Pico	California's last Mexican governor, Pio Pico (also a beak or a bill)	Tejon	badger
		Tiberon	shark
		Tonto	stupid
		Vacaville	cow town
Pinos	pines	Ventura	luck, fortune
Portillo	little gate, way in or out	Vista	view
Presidio	prison		

ACCOMMODATIONS

Beverly Hills Hotel

As Los Angeles caters to thousands of visitors year-round, it is advisable to make hotel reservations well in advance. Listed in this chapter are hotels and motels to suit every pocketbook (including some famous and unusual places to stay) plus campus, hostel, and campground facilities.

BUDGET ACCOMMODATIONS

Budget-conscious travelers may enjoy the following services.

Campus Lodging
Fourteen California institutions offer a variety of lodgings at low cost. Call the UCLA information office for nearest location: (310) 825-4321.

Rent-A-Room International   **1-F8**
1153 Varna St, Garden Grove, CA 92640. (714) 638-1406. Accommodations in private homes at rates lower than most motels. (Three-day minimum.)

YMCA
For referral to inexpensive hotel accommodations, call (213) 380-6448.

YWCA   **7-B3**
306 Loma Dr, LA, CA 90017. (213) 483-5780. Low-cost accommodations, includes food. Private rooms.

Campgrounds
For a listing of campgrounds and RV parks in and around Los Angeles, see Campgrounds & RV Parks.

American Youth Hostels   **4-B3**
For information on locations and costs: 1434 2nd St, Santa Monica, CA 90401. (310) 393-3413.

Fullerton Hacienda Hostel   **1-E8**
1700 N. Harbor Blvd, Fullerton, CA 92635. (714) 738-3721. Spanish-style, hilltop house 5 miles from Disneyland. Low cost. 15 beds.

Los Angeles International Hostel   **1-G5**
3601 S. Gaffey St, Building 613, LA, CA 90731. (310) 831-8109. Close to Queen Mary. Low cost.

ABBREVIATIONS

Due to price fluctuations it is impossible to show exact rates. Use the code below as a guideline for one room for one night (double occupancy) without breakfast and excluding the California sales tax of 6.5%.

$	Under $30
$$	$30-$60
$$$	$60-$90
$$$$	$90-$130
$$$$$	Over $130

ac	Air-conditioning in room
H	Special facilities for the handicapped

Credit Cards

AE	American Express
CB	Carte Blanche
D	Discover
DC	Diners' Club
MC	MasterCard
V	Visa

NOTE: Long-distance phone calls from hotels are often surcharged up to 200%.

Accommodations are listed in alphabetical order according to the following geographical areas: Airport Area, Anaheim, Beverly Hills & Century City, Downtown, Hollywood, Pasadena, San Fernando Valley, Santa Monica & Marina del Rey, Westwood & West Los Angeles, and Wilshire District. Hotels and motels are listed separately for each area. A listing of bed-and-breakfast and campground accommodations follows the hotel/motel listings. All (800) numbers are free to the calling party.

AIRPORT AREA

Hotels

Airport Century Inn   **3-D8**
5547 W. Century Blvd, LA, CA 90045. (310) 649-4000; (800) 421-3939. Fax (310) 649-0311. Large, full-service hotel. Families welcome. Banquet facilities, restaurant, lounge with entertainment, 24-hour coffee shop. Olympic-size pool.

Free airport transportation (24 hours). 150 rooms.

$$$ ac H   AE CB D DC MC V

Airport Marina   **3-B4**

8601 Lincoln Blvd, LA, CA 90045. (310) 670-8111; (800) 421-0041. Fax (310) 337-1883. Ten stories. Banquet facilities, restaurant, lounge with entertainment, dancing. Pool; golf course and tennis courts close by. 50% discount for AAA members. Free airport transportation. Multilingual staff. 752 rooms.

$$$ ac H   AE CB D DC MC V

Barnabey's Hotel   **2-A7**

3501 Sepulveda Blvd, Manhattan Beach, CA 90266. (310) 545-8466; (800) 552-5285. Fax (310) 545-8621. Very "British" establishment, complete with Rosie's Pub. Expensively appointed throughout with leaded glass, imported Victoriana, authentic canopied four-poster beds, and antiques. Restaurants, romantic dining, garden fountains. Piano bar and dancing in the pub. Pool, Jacuzzi, steam saunas. Wheelchair ramps. Free transportation to beaches and airport. Complimentary buffet breakfast. 126 rooms.

$$$$$ ac H   AE CB DC MC V

Crown Sterling Suites   **3-E5**

1440 E. Imperial Ave, El Segundo, CA 90245. (310) 640-3600. Fax (310) 322-0954. Large, new, all-suites hotel—excellent value for money. Each two-room suite has living room (with sofa bed), two TVs, two phones, wet bar, refrigerator, private bedroom. Complimentary breakfast, cocktails, airport transportation, and parking. Conference facilities; restaurant. Pool, sauna, whirlpool, steam room. Reduced rates Friday and Saturday. 350 suites.

$$$$$ ac H   AE CB D DC MC V

Hacienda   **3-F6**

525 N. Sepulveda Blvd, El Segundo, CA 90245. (310) 615-0015; (800) 421-5900. Fax (310) 615-0217. Half the rooms overlook the pool. Coffee shop, restaurant, lounge, banquet facilities. Nightly entertainment. Pool, Jacuzzi. Free airport transportation (24 hours). Multilingual staff. 635 rooms.

$$$ ac H   AE CB D DC MC V

Holiday Inn—Airport   **3-D8**

9901 La Cienega Blvd, LA, CA 90045. (310) 649-5151; (800) 465-4329. Fax (310) 670-3619. Close to airport. Meeting facilities, lounge, restaurant. Daily tours to LA attractions. Pool, free movies on cable TV, rent-a-car service, gift shop. Multilingual staff. Over 400 rooms.

$$$ ac H   AE CB D DC MC V

Holiday Inn—Crowne Plaza   **3-D7**

5985 W. Century Blvd, LA, CA 90045. (310) 642-7500; (800) 465-4329. Fax (310) 417-3608. Luxurious Holiday Inn with excellent business facilities. Exercise room, pool, Jacuzzi, sauna. Concierge, gift shop, two restaurants. Banquet facilities, meeting rooms, ballroom. Free airport transportation. 615 rooms.

$$$$$ ac H   AE CB D DC MC V

Hyatt at Los Angeles Airport   **3-D6**

6225 W. Century Blvd, LA, CA 90045. (310) 672-1234; (800) 233-1234. Fax (310) 216-9334. Luxury high-rise hotel with extensive conference facilities, soundproofed rooms, health club. Live entertainment nightly. Restaurants, takeout bakery. Pool, sauna. Push-button information service listing LA events, weather, church services, legal and medical facilities, and beach conditions. Free airport transportation. 600 rooms.

$$$$$ ac   AE CB D DC MC V

Los Angeles Airport Hilton and Towers 3-D7

5711 W. Century Blvd, LA, CA 90045. (310) 410-4000; (800) 445-8667. Fax (310) 410-6250. Plush, newer high-rise with the largest hotel convention facilities in LA. Soundproofed rooms. Fitness and racquetball club, pool, Jacuzzis. Gift shop. Three restaurants, two lounges, 24-hour coffee shop. Rooftop gardens. Special VIP section (Towers) with luxury suites, private club, and security. Free airport transportation. Free bus service to Manhattan Beach Mall. 1,309 rooms.

$$$$ ac H   AE CB DC MC V

Los Angeles Marriott   **3-D7**

5855 W. Century Blvd, LA, CA 90045. (310) 641-5700; (800) 228-9290. Fax (310) 337-5358. One of LA's most luxurious airport hotels. Pool with swim-up bar, Jacuzzi. Seven restaurants and lounges. Live entertainment, dancing. Babysitting service. Plainclothes police patrol. Free airport transportation. Low weekend rates. 1,015 rooms.

$$$$$ ac H   AE CB D DC MC V

Pacifica   **1-D4**

6161 Centinela Ave, Culver City, CA 90230. (310) 649-1776; (800) 541-7888. Fax (310) 649-4411. Spanish-style, deluxe hotel with excellent facilities, including health club, Jacuzzi, pool, conference facilities, restaurant, and lounge. Shops, entertainment, baby-sitting service. Free airport transportation. 375 rooms.

$$$$ ac H   AE D DC MC V

Quality Inn—Airport   **3-D7**

5249 W. Century Blvd, LA, CA 90045. (310) 645-2200; (800) 228-5151. Fax (310) 641-8214. Inexpensive accommodations close to LAX. Restaurant, deli, lounge, banquet facilities. No-smoking floor. Free airport transportation. 8 suites; 274 rooms.

$$ ac H   AE CB D DC MC V

Radisson Plaza   **2-A7**

1400 Park View Ave, Manhattan Beach, CA 90266. (310) 546-7511; (800) 333-3333. Fax (310) 546-7520. Luxurious new hotel in trendy Manhattan Beach. Landscaped grounds include lakes and a nine-hole golf course. Top-quality restaurants, discotheque, three lounges. Gym, sauna, pool, Jacuzzi. Baby-sitting service. Conference facilities. Free airport transportation. 10 suites; 400 rooms.

$$$$ ac H   AE CB D DC MC V

Ramada Inn Culver City   **1-D4**

6333 Bristol Pkwy, Culver City, CA 90230. (310) 670-3200; (800) 228-2828. Fax (310) 641-8925. Large conference hotel close to freeways and convenient to beaches, shops, and Hollywood Park racetrack. Restaurant; pool, full use of

nearby racquetball club. Free airport transportation. 260 rooms.
$$$ ac H   AE CB D DC MC V

Ramada Inn LAX   3-C7
9620 Airport Blvd, LA, CA 90045. (310) 670-3200; (800) 228-2828. Fax (310) 216-6681. Larger airport hotel. Pool; coffee shop. 505 rooms.
$$$$$ ac H   AE CB D DC MC V

Sheraton Los Angeles Airport Hotel   3-D6
6101 W. Century Blvd, LA, CA 90045. (310) 642-1111; (800) 325-3535. Fax (310) 645-1414. New luxury hotel. 24-hour room service. Shops; pool. No-smoking rooms. Braille markings for the blind. Conference facilities, secretarial service. Free airport transportation. Multilingual staff. 807 rooms.
$$$$$ ac H   AE CB D DC MC V

Skyways Airport Hotel   3-C7
9250 Airport Blvd, LA, CA 90045. (310) 670-2900. Fax (310) 410-1787. Colorful rooms and kitchen apartments. Pets allowed. Restaurant, two pools, sightseeing tours. Free airport transportation. Multilingual staff. 98 rooms.
$$ ac   AE CB DC MC V

Viscount International   3-C7
9750 Airport Blvd, LA, CA 90045. (310) 645-4600; (800) 255-3050. Fax (310) 216-7029. Formerly the largest TraveLodge in California, now a Trusthouse Forte hotel—renovated at a cost of $5.5 million. Good airport location. Pool. Coffee shop, steakhouse dinner restaurant, piano lounge. Convenience gift shop. Free airport transportation. 571 rooms.
$$$ ac H   AE CB D DC MC V

Westin Hotel Los Angeles Airport   3-D7
5400 W. Century Blvd, LA, CA 90045. (310) 216-5858; (800) 228-3000. Fax (310) 670-1948. Built as a Stouffer Hotel in 1986 at a cost of $87 million, it's the most sumptuous of the airport hotels. Large, light, airy atmosphere. Fully-soundproofed rooms with minibar and airline information on closed-circuit TV. Extensive facilities; 7 conference suites, 37 meeting rooms, executive boardrooms; ballroom, large theater, lounges; spa and fitness center, pool; cafes and first-class restaurant. Airline bookings and car rental desks, complimentary airport transportation. Free daily newspaper, coffee, wake-up call, and continental breakfast. 21 of the 68 suites have outdoor patios with Jacuzzis. 750 rooms.
$$$$ ac H   AE CB D DC MC V

Motels

Caesar's Motel   1-E4
4652 W. Century Blvd, Inglewood, CA 90304. (310) 671-6161. Reliable motel, near racetrack. Convenient to bus routes for major attractions.
$ ac   AE MC V

Courtesy Inn   3-B8
901 W. Manchester Blvd, Inglewood, CA 90301. (310) 649-0800; (800) 231-2508. Fax (310) 649-3837. Close to Hollywood Park racetrack and

convenient to airport. Pool; restaurant. Free airport transportation. 47 rooms.
$$ ac   AE MC V

Howard Johnson Motor Lodge   1-D4
5990 Green Valley Circle, Culver City, CA 90230. (310) 641-7740; (800) 654-2000. Deluxe accommodations. Close to Fox Hills shopping mall. Cocktail bar, restaurant. Pool. Free airport transportation. 200 rooms.
$$$ ac H   AE CB D DC MC V

Vista   1-D4
4900 Sepulveda Blvd, Culver City, CA 90230. (310) 390-2014. Small motel, 10 minutes from airport and beaches. Cable TV. Maid service. 19 rooms.
$$ ac

ANAHEIM

Hotels

Anaheim Marriott   1-F7
700 W. Convention Way, Anaheim, CA 92802. (714) 750-8000; (800) 228-9290. Fax (714) 750-9100. Deluxe hotel. Extensive banquet and convention facilities. Three lounges, two restaurants. Games room, health club with Jacuzzi, indoor/outdoor pool. Adjacent to Anaheim Convention Center and close to Disneyland. 1,065 tastefully furnished rooms, including 74 suites.
$$$$$ ac H   AE CB DC MC V

Anaheim Plaza Hotel   1-F7
1700 S. Harbor Blvd, Anaheim, CA 92802. (714) 772-5900; (800) 228-1357. Fax (714) 772-8386. Large, two-story, luxury hotel. Many rooms with balconies. Restaurant. Gift shop. Olympic-size pool. 300 rooms.
$$$$ ac H   AE CB DC MC V

Disneyland Hotel   1-F7
1150 W. Cerritos Ave, Anaheim, CA 92803. (714) 778-6600. Fax (714) 956-6597. World's largest hotel. Across from Disneyland and connected to it by monorail. Luxury accommodations, gourmet restaurant, lounges, entertainment, coffee shops. Freshwater marina with paddleboats and evening "Dancing Waters" shows. Baby-sitting service. Tennis courts, three pools. Clothing stores, gift shops, a waterfront bazaar—Seaports of the Pacific—features arts, crafts, and marine equipment. 1,131 rooms.
$$$$$ ac H   AE CB DC MC V

Embassy Suites   1-F7
7762 Beach Blvd, Buena Park, CA 90620. (714) 739-5600; (800) EMBASSY. Fax (714) 521-9650. New all-suites hotel close to Knott's Berry Farm. Each tastefully furnished, two-room suite has living room (with sofa bed), private bedroom, two phones, two TVs, wet bar, refrigerator. Restaurant. Pool, Jacuzzi. Gift shop. Rates include cocktails and full breakfast. 203 suites.
$$$$ ac H   AE CB D DC MC V

Hilton at the Park   1-F7
1855 S. Harbor Blvd, Anaheim, CA 92802. (714)

750-1811; (800) 445-8667. Fax (714) 971-3626. Close to Anaheim Convention Center and Disneyland. Dancing nightly to big-band sounds. Restaurant, coffee shop. Pool. 1,000 luxurious rooms
$$$$ ac H AE CB D DC MC V

Holiday Inn   **1-F7**
1850 S. Harbor Blvd, Anaheim, CA 92802. (714) 750-2801; (800) HOLIDAY. Fax (714) 971-4754. Facing Disneyland—good views of evening fireworks displays. Restaurant, coffee shop, lounge. Pool. 312 rooms.
$$$ ac H AE CB D DC MC V

Howard Johnson Hotel   **1-F7**
1380 S. Harbor Blvd, Anaheim, CA 92802. (714) 776-6120; (800) 654-2000. Fax (714) 533-3578. Across from Disneyland, close to all Buena Park attractions. Tour pickups for all LA attractions. Restaurant. Two pools, Jacuzzi. 320 rooms.
$$$ ac H AE CB DC MC V

Quality Inn   **1-F7**
616 Convention Way, Anaheim, CA 92802. (714) 750-3131; (800) 221-2222. Fax (714) 750-9027. Just two blocks to Disneyland. Suites available. Pool; beauty salon. Near bus lines. Reliable. 284 rooms.
$$$ ac H AE CB D DC MC V

Ramada Inn   **1-F7**
1331 E. Katella Ave, Anaheim, CA 92805. (714) 798-8088; (800) 228-2828. Fax (714) 937-5622. Popular with businesspeople. Close to all attractions. Restaurant, lounge; pool, Jacuzzi, sauna; laundry facilities. 240 rooms.
$$$ ac H AE CB D DC MC V

Sheraton-Anaheim Hotel   **1-F7**
1015 W. Ball Rd, Anaheim, CA 92802. (714) 778-1700; (800) 325-3535. Fax (714) 535-3889. Five minutes from Disneyland. Luxury rooms. Restaurant and bistro, cocktail lounge, coffee shop, delicatessen. Pool. 491 rooms.
$$$$ ac H AE CB D DC MC V

Stoval Inn   **1-F7**
1110 W. Katella Ave, Anaheim, CA 92802. (714) 778-1880; (800) 854-8175. Fax (714) 778-3805. Mid-size, quality hotel two blocks from Disneyland. Pool, Jacuzzi, sauna; gift shop. Two restaurants. 300 rooms.
$$$ ac H AE CB D DC MC V

Motels

Aloha TraveLodge   **1-F7**
505 W. Katella Ave, Anaheim, CA 92802. (714) 774-8710; (800) 255-3050. Just one block to Disneyland. Suites available. Baby-sitting service; pool. Near bus lines. 50 rooms.
$$$ ac H AE CB D DC MC V

Alpine   **1-F7**
715 W. Katella Ave, Anaheim, CA 92802. (714) 535-2186; (800) 772-4422. Fax (714) 535-3714. Across from Convention Center, walk to Disneyland. Above average. Fully-refurbished rooms. Adjacent restaurant. Pool. 41 rooms.
$$ ac AE CB DC MC V

Lincoln Palms   **1-F7**
1600 E. Lincoln Ave, Anaheim, CA 92805. (714) 772-0200. Fax (714) 776-3413. Excellent value. Maid service, direct phones, satellite TV, kitchenettes. Pool, spa. Coin laundry. 88 rooms.
$$ ac H MC V

Magic Lamp   **1-F7**
1030 W. Katella Ave, Anaheim, CA 92802. (714) 772-7242; (800) 422-1556. Fax (714) 772-5461. Opposite Disneyland and close to Convention Center. Good value. Pool; coin laundry. 76 rooms.
$$ ac H AE CB DC MC V

BEVERLY HILLS & CENTURY CITY

Hotels

Hotel Bel-Air   **1-B3**
701 Stone Canyon Rd, Bel-Air, CA 90077. (310) 472-1211; (800) 648-1097. Fax (714) 476-5890. Gorgeous Bel-Air hostelry—quiet, luxurious, and expensive. Beautiful gardens. Banquet facilities, room service, romantic restaurant, piano lounge. Some suites have private Jacuzzis, some have fireplaces. Oval-shaped pool, Jacuzzi. A 1984 renovation added 26 suites in a "California-modern" decor, making this beautiful hostelry a little less exclusive. 92 suites.
$$$$$ ac H AE CB DC MC V

Beverly Comstock   **5-E6**
10300 Wilshire Blvd, LA, CA 90024. (310) 275-5575; (800) 800-1234. Fax (310) 278-3325. (Will accept collect calls for reservations.) Deluxe one- and two-bedroom suites. Near country club, close to best shops and restaurants. Small restaurant; 24-hour convenience shop. Free security parking. Pool. 73 units.
$$$$$ ac AE CB DC MC V

Beverly Crest   **5-E7**
125 S. Spalding Dr, Beverly Hills, CA 90212. (310) 274-6801; (800) 247-6432. Fax (310) 273-6614. Small and comfortable with luxurious accommodations. Restaurant; pool. 52 rooms.
$$$$ ac AE CB DC MC V

Beverly Hillcrest   **5-G8**
1224 S. Beverwil Dr, LA, CA 90035. (310) 277-2800; (800) 252-0174. Fax (310) 203-9537. Large, beautifully furnished rooms, each with a private balcony and refrigerator. Also lobby restaurant *OPEN 6:30am-10pm*. Pool. 150 rooms.
$$$$ ac AE MC V

Beverly Hills Hotel   **5-C7**
9641 Sunset Blvd, Beverly Hills, CA 90210. (310) 276-2251; (800) 283-8885. Fax (310) 271-0319. A pink palace frequented by famous personalities. The beautiful grounds contain private bungalows. Pool, tennis courts. Three quality restaurants offer full menus, late supper served nightly from 10:30pm to 1am; comfortable coffee shop; famous Polo Lounge (*see* RESTAURANTS, Beverly Hills & Century City, Continental). Expensive boutiques; convenience shop; beauty salon, barber shop; florist. Relaxed atmosphere, excel-

lent service. 268 rooms, including 21 bungalows.
$$$$$ ac H   AE CB DC MC V

Beverly Hills St. Moritz   **5-E8**
120 S. Reeves Dr, Beverly Hills, CA 90212. (213)
276-1031. Fax (213) 276-9251. Small, clean,
modest, and inexpensive. Courteous staff.
$$ No cards.

Beverly Hilton   **5-E7**
9876 Wilshire Blvd, Beverly Hills, CA 90210.
(310) 274-7777; (800) 922-5432. Fax (310) 285-
1313. For 24-hour reservations, call (800) 445-
8667. Large complex. Excellent services. Con-
cierge can arrange everything, from theater
tickets to sightseeing tours. Unusual theme
lounges. First-class restaurants: L'Escoffier and
Trader Vic's (*see* RESTAURANTS, Beverly Hills
& Century City, French *and* Polynesian). Confer-
ence facilities. Pool. Convenience shop and ex-
clusive gift and clothing boutiques. Multilingual
staff. 625 rooms.
$$$$$ ac H   AE CB D DC MC V

Beverly Pavilion   **5-E8**
9360 Wilshire Blvd, Beverly Hills, CA 90212.
(310) 273-1400; (800) 441-5050. Fax (310) 859-
8551. Central Beverly Hills location. Completely
and tastefully refurbished in 1986. Quiet, sophis-
ticated yet unpretentious. Heated rooftop pool.
Acclaimed restaurant Colette (*see* RESTAU-
RANTS, Beverly Hills & Century City, French).
Tour pickups. Gift shop. Over 100 deluxe rooms,
including 5 minisuites.
$$$$$ ac H   AE CB DC MC V

Beverly Rodeo   **5-E8**
360 N. Rodeo Dr, Beverly Hills, CA 90210. (310)
273-0300; (800) 356-7575. Fax (310) 859-8730.
Luxury hotel, superior location. Good restaurant
and lively bar. European atmosphere. 100
rooms, including 6 suites.
$$$$$ ac H   AE CB D DC MC V

Beverly Wilshire   **5-E8**
9500 Wilshire Blvd, Beverly Hills, CA 90212.
(310) 275-5200; (800) 427-4354. Fax (310) 859-
9232. Some truly luxurious suites. Deluxe, distin-
guished, and deserving of its first-class status.
Impeccable service. Fine restaurants. Ballroom,
conference, and banquet facilities. Pool, health
spa; shopping mall. Tour pickups arranged. Air-
port limousine service. 300 rooms.
$$$$$ ac H   AE CB D DC MC V

Century Plaza Hotel & Tower   **5-F7**
2025 Avenue of the Stars, LA, CA 90067. (310)
277-2000; (800) 228-3000. Fax (310) 551-
3355. Large, luxurious five-star hotel. Well-
decorated rooms with patios and excellent
views. Four restaurants; huge ballroom; nightly
entertainment. Conference facilities. Pools,
sauna, Jacuzzi. Shops. Access from ABC en-
tertainment complex and Century City shop-
ping mall. Multilingual staff. The Tower is the
ultra-luxurious addition with stunning marble
lobby with a million dollars' worth of antique art.
Every room has a balcony. No-smoking floors.
750 rooms, including penthouse suites. Tower:
322 rooms.
$$$$$ ac H   AE CB D DC MC V

Hotel Del Flores   **5-D8**
409 N. Crescent Dr, Beverly Hills, CA 90210.
(310) 274-5115. (No fax.) Excellent value—
popular with European students. Clean, friendly,
close to shops and restaurants. Patio. 37 rooms.
$$ MC V

L'Ermitage   **5-D8**
9291 Burton Way, Beverly Hills, CA 90210. (310)
278-3344; (800) 421-4306. Fax (310) 278-8247.
Elegant   and   expensive,   this   luxurious,
European-style hotel is the only hotel on the West
Coast to receive Mobil's five-star rating and
AAA's five-diamond rating. All rooms have pri-
vate terraces, fireplaces, safes, and wet bars.
Full security. Excellent restaurant. Pool, Jacuzzi.
105 suites.
$$$$$ ac H   AE CB DC MC V

Ramada Inn   **5-F8**
1150 S. Beverly Dr, LA, CA 90035. (310) 553-
6561; (800) 228-2828. Fax (310) 277-3739.
Close to shops and business district. Restaurant, coffee shop, delicatessen, banquet facilities, lounge. Pool. Baby-sitting service. 260
rooms.
$$$$ ac H   AE CB D DC MC V

Motels

Beverly Terrace Motor Hotel   **6-E1**
469 N. Doheny Dr, Beverly Hills, CA 90210.
(310) 274-8141; (800) 421-7223. (No fax.) Good
location—near shops and entertainment. Restaurant; pool, sundeck. 37 rooms.
$$$ ac   AE DC MC V

DOWNTOWN

Hotels

Alexandria   **7-D4**
501 S. Spring St, LA, CA 90013. (213) 626-7484.
(No fax.) Restored to its former Edwardian ele-
gance. Reasonably priced and within walking
distance of Downtown attractions. (*See also* HIS-
TORIC LA, Buildings & Landmarks.) Banquet fa-
cilities, restaurant. 500 rooms.
$$ ac H   AE CB DC MC V

The Biltmore   **7-C4**
506 S. Grand Ave, LA, CA 90013. (213) 624-
1011; (800) 245-8673. Fax (213) 612-1545.
Huge, impressive, historic, and luxurious. A $41
million renovation placed this 1923 landmark
firmly back at the top of the luxury hotel list. Gorgeous, classical decor. Restaurants, lounges,
entertainment. Conference facilities. Shops.
Shuttle bus to airport. (*See also* HISTORIC LA,
Buildings & Landmarks *and* RESTAURANTS,
Downtown, French: Bernard's.) Over 707 rooms,
35 suites.
$$$$$ ac H   AE CB DC MC V

Figueroa   **7-D3**
939 S. Figueroa St, LA, CA 90015. (213) 627-
8971; (800) 421-9092. Fax (213) 689-0305. Cen-

The Biltmore Hotel

tral Downtown location. Older building, full of character. Hourly express bus to airport. Tours. Pool, Jacuzzi. Restaurant, 24-hour coffee shop, bar. 285 rooms.
$$$ ac AE DC MC

Holiday Inn—Convention Center 7-D3
1020 S. Figueroa St, LA, CA 90015. (213) 748-1291; (800) 525-2793. Fax (213) 748-6028. Across from LA Convention Center, close to freeways. Restaurant, lounge, banquet facilities. 193 rooms.
$$$$ ac H AE CB D DC MC V

Holiday Inn—Downtown 7-C3
750 Garland Ave, LA, CA 90017. (213) 628-5242; (800) HOLIDAY. Fax (213) 628-1201. Convenient for shopping and sightseeing. Restaurant, lounge; pool. 201 rooms, 3 suites.
$$$ ac H AE CB D DC MC V

Howard Johnson 7-C8
1640 Marengo St, LA, CA 90033. (213) 223-3841; (800) 654-2000. Fax (213) 222-4039. Close to Chinatown and other sightseeing attractions. Restaurant, lounge; pool. 126 rooms.
$$ ac H AE CB D DC MC V

Hyatt Regency Los Angeles 7-C3
711 S. Hope St, LA, CA 90017. (213) 683-1234; (800) 233-1234. Fax (213) 629-3230. Impressive hotel in the Broadway Plaza shopping center. Spacious rooms with views. Close to Downtown attractions. Conference facilities. Two restaurants, coffee shop. Health club. Multilingual staff. 500 rooms.
$$$$$ ac H AE CB DC MC V

Industry Hills & Sheraton Resort 1-C8
One Industry Hills Pkwy, City of Industry, CA 91744. (818) 965-0861; (800) 325-3535. Fax (818) 964-9535. Focal point of new, 650-acre, recreational complex. Luxury resort hotel (just 10 miles from the heart of Downtown LA) surrounded by landscaped grounds containing an equestrian center with 15 miles of trails (horse rentals available), 17 tennis courts, two 18-hole golf courses, and an Olympic aquatic center. Hotel facilities are extensive, with three health spas; three restaurants, three lounges (including a piano bar), 24-hour room service. Auto rental. Gift and sporting-goods shops. One mile from Puente Hills shopping mall. 300 rooms.
$$$$ ac H AE CB D DC MC V

Los Angeles Hilton 7-C3
930 Wilshire Blvd, LA, CA 90017. (213) 629-4321; (800) 445-8667. Fax (213) 612-3977. Central location, convenient to business district and shops. Meeting and banquet facilities. Restaurants, lounges; fitness center, pool. Multilingual staff. 1,200 luxury rooms, including 65 suites.
$$$$$ ac H AE CB D DC MC V

Milner 7-D3
813 S. Flower St, LA, CA 90017. (213) 627-6981; (800) 521-0592. (No fax.) Basic, no frills. Across from Broadway Plaza shopping center. Restaurant. 175 rooms.
$$ ac AE MC V

New Otani 7-C5
120 S. Los Angeles St, LA, CA 90012. (213) 629-1200; (800) 421-8795. Fax (213) 472-0429. Impressive, modern luxury hotel in Little Tokyo, close to Civic Center and freeways. Unique Garden in the Sky rooftop patio with excellent Japanese restaurant (*see* RESTAURANTS, Downtown, Japanese: A Thousand Cranes). Also American and continental restaurants. Sauna, Jacuzzi. Meeting facilities. In-room refrigerators and alarm clocks. Shopping mall with Japanese boutiques. Multilingual staff. 440 rooms.
$$$$$ ac H AE CB DC MC V

Sheraton Grande 7-C3
333 S. Figueroa St, LA, CA 90071. (213) 617-1133; (800) 325-3535. Fax (213) 613-0291. New, large, luxurious, and very well staffed. Close to Music Center and all Downtown attractions. Nightclub, lounges, two restaurants. Butler

on every floor. Baby-sitting service; shopping facilities. Outdoor pool, full use of LA Racquet Club
(health spa and tennis club). Airport bus service. Multilingual staff. 470 rooms.
$$$$$ ac H AE CB D DC MC V

University Hilton   **7-G1**
3540 S. Figueroa St, LA, CA 90007. (213) 748-
4141; (800) 872-1104. Fax (213) 746-3255. Luxury hotel near USC and Exposition Park, only
minutes from all Downtown attractions. Meeting
facilities. Restaurant, coffee shop, lounge; pool,
Jacuzzi. Airport shuttle bus. 241 rooms.
$$$$ ac H AE CB D DC MC V

Westin Bonaventure   **7-C3**
404 S. Figueroa St, LA, CA 90071. (213) 624-
1000; (800) 228-3000. Fax (213) 612-4800.
Spectacular architectural feat. Huge, space-
age complex containing impressive restaurants
(Top of Five on the 35th floor has citywide
view), lounges (including a revolving one on
the roof), and six levels of shops. Pool. 1,474
rooms.
$$$$$ ac H AE CB DC MC V

Motels

Best Western InnTowne Hotel   **7-D3**
925 S. Figueroa St, LA, CA 90015. (213) 628-
2222; (800) 528-1234. Fax (213) 687-0566.
Large, modern motel near Convention Center.
Restaurant, coffee shop; pool. 170 rooms.
$$$ ac AE CB D DC MC V

City Center Motel   **7-C3**
1135 W. 7th St, LA, CA 90017. (213) 628-7141.
(No fax.) Convenient to shops, freeways, busi-
ness district. Quiet rooms. Tours; pool. 42 rooms.
$$ ac MC V

Westin Bonaventure Hotel

Comfort Inn Wilshire   **7-A1**
3400 W. 3rd St, LA, CA 90020. (213) 385-0061;
(800) 266-0061. Fax (213) 385-8571. Modern
motel, close to shops. Coffee shop; pool. 120
rooms, 10 apartments.
$$ ac AE CB D DC MC V

Kent Inn Motel   **7-D3**
920 S. Figueroa St, LA, CA 90015. (213) 626-
8701. (No fax.) Quality motel near Convention
Center. Restaurant, lounge; pool. In-room refrig-
erators. 91 rooms.
$$ ac H AE CB D DC MC V

Motel de Ville   **7-C3**
1123 W. 7th St, LA, CA 90017. (213) 624-8474.
Fax (213) 624-8474. (A Friendship Inn.) Central
Downtown location. Tours; pool. 61 rooms.
$ ac AE CB DC MC V

Oasis   **7-C1**
2200 W. Olympic Blvd, LA, CA 90006. (213) 385-
4191. Fax (213) 480-1628. Close to Little Korea,
near the Coliseum. Restaurant across the street.
Pool, sundeck; in-room refrigerators. 69 rooms.
$$ ac H AE CB D DC MC V

HOLLYWOOD

Hotels

Le Bel Age   **6-D1**
1020 N. San Vicente Blvd, W. Hollywood, CA
90069. (213) 854-1111; (800) 424-4443. Fax
(213) 854-0926. (A L'Ermitage hotel.) Very
grand and impressively sumptuous with the
ambience of a French country chateau.
Museum-quality art appears on every floor.
Large salons, ballroom, exclusive boutiques. A
gorgeous rooftop pool is surrounded by a
sculpture-enhanced garden. Breathtaking city
views. 200 suites.
$$$$$ ac H AE CB DC MC V

Best Western Hollywood Plaza Inn   **6-B5**
2011 N. Highland Ave, Hollywood, CA 90068.
(213) 851-1800; (800) 232-4353. Fax (213) 851-
1836. Minutes to Hollywood Bowl and other at-
tractions. Restaurant, bar; pool. 82 rooms.
$$$ ac H AE CB D DC MC V

Beverly Plaza   **6-E1**
8384 W. 3rd St, LA, CA 90048. (213) 658-6600;
(800) 62-HOTEL. Fax (213) 653-3464. Small,
comfortable, all-suites hotel close to the Beverly
Center. Tastefully decorated in Italian Provincial
style. Bathrooms are thoughtfully stocked. Attractive restaurant. Pool, Nautilus. Baby-sitting
service. Complimentary limousine (5-mile radius
of hotel). No-smoking rooms. 97 suites.
$$$$ ac H AE CB DC MC V

Chateau Marmont   **6-C2**
8221 Sunset Blvd, Hollywood, CA 90046. (213)
656-1010; (800) 242-8328. Fax (213) 655-
5311. Resembling a rambling, Norman castle
perched on the hillside above Sunset Boulevard, this quiet, elegant hotel has been a favorite with movie stars since the 1920s. Jean

Harlow once lived in a third-floor apartment. Greta Garbo, Errol Flynn, and Howard Hughes also lived here at one time. Still popular with avant-garde artists (Oldenburg, Stella, Hockney) who come here seeking solitude. Tony Randall used one bungalow for five years while starring in "The Odd Couple" TV series. Luxury suites with balconies and views across LA. Room service; pool. 62 suites.

$$$$$ ac AE CB DC MC V

Le Dufy 6-E1
1000 Westmount Dr, W. Hollywood, CA 90069. (213) 657-7400; (800) 424-4443. Fax (213) 854-6744. (A L'Ermitage hotel.) Named for the renowned French painter Raoul Dufy, this is a soft, dreamy retreat from the bustle of Hollywood. Gorgeous original art (includes four Dufy paintings). Rooftop pool and Jacuzzi, sauna. Restaurant. All suites are exquisitely decorated and have fireplaces. Free limousine service within 3 miles. Multilingual staff. 135 suites.

$$$$$ ac AE CB DC MC V

Four Seasons Hotel 6-E1
300 S. Doheny Dr, LA, CA 90048. (310) 273-2222; (800) 332-3442. Fax (310) 859-3824. A large, European-style hotel overlooking Beverly Hills. Expensive, luxurious accommodations. Three restaurants, including Gardens, which offers upscale California cuisine. Lounge with piano entertainment; banquet and meeting facilities. Terraced pool, Jacuzzi, massage. Licensed baby-sitters. Multilingual staff. Free limousine service to Rodeo Drive. 285 rooms, including 106 suites.

$$$$$ ac H AE CB DC MC V

Hallmark House Motor Hotel 6-C4
7023 Sunset Blvd, Hollywood, CA 90028. (213) 464-8344; (800) 346-7723. Fax (213) 962-9748. Close to Hollywood attractions. Rooms have kitchenettes. Pool, sundeck. Coffee shop. Underground parking. Weekly rates. 74 rooms.

$$ ac AE CB DC MC V

Holiday Inn—Hollywood 6-B5
1755 N. Highland Ave, Hollywood, CA 90028. (213) 462-7181; (800) HOLIDAY. Fax (213) 466-9072. Large, comfortable hotel. Revolving restaurant and lounge atop 23 stories; entertainment. Meeting facilities. Pool; tours. Safeboxes in all rooms. Airport transportation. 500 rooms.

$$$$ ac H AE CB DC MC V

Hollywood Roosevelt 6-C4
7000 Hollywood Blvd, Hollywood, CA 90028. (213) 466-7000; (800) 950-7667. Fax (213) 462-8056. Impressive Hollywood hotel. Popular with movie stars during the 1930s and 1940s. Renovated to its original splendor—all rooms, completely refurbished, original moldings and tilework painstakingly uncovered. Photographic history of Hollywood (mezzanine level). Poolside villas in garden setting. The two-story Gable & Lombard Suite is so named because it was reportedly a favorite of Gable and Lombard. Junior and senior suites. Eight banquet rooms. Entertainment in the Cinegrill. Theodore's restaurant (named for Teddy Roosevelt). Jacuzzi with trop-

ical bar. Gift shop. Japanese-, Spanish-, and French-speaking staff. 450 rooms.

$$$$$ ac H AE CB D DC MC V

Hyatt on Sunset 6-C1
8401 Sunset Blvd, Hollywood, CA 90069. (213) 656-4101; (800) 228-9000. Fax (213) 650-7024. This high-rise hotel on Sunset Strip is popular with rock stars. Rooftop pool. Bar, restaurant, entertainment. Gift shop. 70 rooms.

$$$$$ ac H AE CB D DC MC V

Mondrian 6-C2
8440 Sunset Blvd, Hollywood, CA 90069. (213) 650-8999; (800) 525-8029. Fax (213) 654-5804. A large, geometrical splash of color—resembling a Mondrian canvas—towers over the already colorful Sunset Strip. Unlike much of the strip, the Mondrian really is a work of art—and it's filled with 2,000 contemporary paintings. Spacious modern suites, decorated in bold blocks of color, follow high-style fashion. Already perched on a hillside, this tall hotel offers stunning views of the city. Restaurant, lounge; entertainment. Fitness center, gym, pool, Jacuzzis. Multilingual staff. 224 suites.

$$$$$ ac H AE CB DC MC V

Le Parc 6-E2
733 N. West Knoll Dr, W. Hollywood, CA 90069. (310) 855-8888; (800) 424-4443. Fax (310) 659-7812. (Another successful L'Ermitage hotel—one of five in a ten-block area.) Le Parc has an informal, unhurried atmosphere. Lovely Impressionist paintings add serenity to the relaxed pace. Cafe le Parc (for guests only) offers healthy (low-fat, low-salt) cuisine. Pool, Jacuzzi; rooftop tennis court. Free limousine service within 3 miles. Multilingual staff. 150 suites.

$$$$$ ac AE CB DC MC V

Sunset Marquis 6-D1
1200 Alta Loma Rd, W. Hollywood, CA 90069. (310) 657-1333; (800) 858-9758. Fax (310) 652-5300. Bordering Beverly Hills, this hotel is popular with people in the arts and entertainment industries. Attractive garden setting. Health spa, Jacuzzi, pool. Room service, laundry, kitchenettes. 118 rooms, including 4 luxury villas.

$$$$$ ac AE CB D DC MC V

Wilshire Dunes Motor Hotel 6-G6
4300 Wilshire Blvd, Hollywood, CA 90010. (213) 938-3616; (800) 443-8637. Fax (213) 469-1962. Between Beverly Hills and central Hollywood, it's convenient to all attractions. Pool; kitchenettes. 63 rooms.

$$$ ac AE CB DC MC V

Motels

Dunes 6-C7
5625 Sunset Blvd, Hollywood, CA 90028. (213) 467-5171; (800) 443-8637. Fax (213) 469-1962. Near TV and recording studios. Coffee shop, lounge. 54 rooms.

$$$ ac AE CB DC MC V

Hollywood Downtowner 6-C7
5601 Hollywood Blvd, Hollywood, CA 90028. (213) 464-7191. (No fax.) Near Hollywood Free-

way. Pool; kitchenettes. Spanish- and German-speaking staff. 30 rooms.
$$ ac AE CB D DC MC V

Hollywood Premier   **6-C7**
5333 Hollywood Blvd, Hollywood, CA 90027. (213) 466-1691. (No fax.) Small, inexpensive. Pool; kitchenettes. 45 rooms.
$$ ac AE CB D DC MC V

Hollywood Travel Inn   **6-C4**
7370 Sunset Blvd, Hollywood, CA 90046. (213) 876-0330; (800) 876-0330. Formerly a Travel-Lodge. Near restaurants, shops, and studios. Pool. 40 rooms.
$$ ac H AE CB D DC MC V

Ramada—West Hollywood   **6-D1**
8585 Santa Monica Blvd, LA, CA 90069. (310) 652-2135; (800) 845-8585. Fax (310) 652-2135. Close to Hollywood and Beverly Hills. Popular with touring rock bands. Outdoor heated pool; poolside apartments. Lively coffee shop. No-smoking rooms. 67 rooms.
$$ ac H AE DC MC V

Saharan   **6-C4**
7212 Sunset Blvd, Hollywood, CA 90046. (213) 874-6700. Fax (213) 876-2625. Central location. Pool. Kitchenettes; stereo music. Most pets allowed. 62 rooms.
$$ ac H AE CB DC MC V

Sunset La Brea TraveLodge   **6-C4**
7051 Sunset Boulevard, Hollywood, CA 90028. (213) 462-0905; (800) 255-3050. Fax (213) 465-6088. Convenient to all major attractions. A dozen restaurants within two blocks. Pool. 43 rooms.
$$ ac AE CB DC MC V

PASADENA

Hotels

Embassy Suites   **1-B7**
211 E. Huntington Dr, Arcadia, CA 91006. (818) 445-8525; (800) EMBASSY. Fax (818) 445-8548. Tastefully decorated, all-suites hotel near Santa Anita Park (horse racing). Each two-room suite has living room (with sofa bed), private bedroom, two TVs, two phones, wet bar, and refrigerator. Pool, Jacuzzi, steam, sauna. Good restaurant—Velvet Turtle. Free transportation to Burbank airport. Rates include cocktails and full breakfast. 194 suites.
$$$$ ac H AE CB D DC MC V

Holiday Inn—Pasadena   **8-C3**
303 E. Cordova St, Pasadena, CA 91101. (818) 449-4000; (800) 238-8000. Fax (818) 548-1390. Adjacent to Convention Center. Soundproofed rooms. Restaurant, bar, lounge. Tennis courts, pool. Dry cleaning and laundry. 318 rooms.
$$$$ ac H AE CB D DC MC V

Pasadena Hilton   **8-C3**
150 S. Los Robles Ave, Pasadena, CA 91101. (818) 577-1000; (800) 445-8667. Fax (818) 584-3140. Short distance from Rose Bowl. Deluxe

accommodations with good views from higher floors. Pool. Baby-sitting service. Most pets allowed. Limousine service to Burbank and LAX airports. 291 rooms.
$$$$$ ac H AE CB D DC MC V

Ritz-Carlton Huntington   **8-E4**
1401 S. Oak Knoll Ave, Pasadena, CA 91106. (818) 568-3900; (800) 325-3535. Fax (818) 568-3700. Famous resort hotel. (*See* HISTORIC LA, Buildings & Landmarks: Huntington [Ritz-Carlton] Hotel.) Large rooms with views; 23 acres of private gardens. Restaurant, lounge. Pool, tennis courts. Gift shop. 383 rooms.
$$$$$ ac H AE CB D DC MC V

Motels

Pasadena Motor Hotel   **8-C6**
2131 E. Colorado Blvd, Pasadena, CA 91107. (818) 796-3121; (800) 255-3050. Fax (818) 793-4713. Downtown location, close to restaurants and shops. Pool. 48 rooms.
$$ ac H AE D DC MC V

SAN FERNANDO VALLEY

Hotels

Beverly Garland   **9-F4**
4222 Vineland Ave, N. Hollywood, CA 91602. (818) 980-8000; (800) BEVERLY. Fax (818) 766-5230. Deluxe resort hotel that's convenient to all attractions. Restaurant, lounge; gift shop. Tennis courts, pool, putting greens. Attractive gardens. Children's playground. 254 rooms.
$$$$ ac H AE CB D DC MC V

Holiday Inn—Mid-San Fernando Valley 1-B3
8244 Orion Ave, Van Nuys, CA 91406. (818) 989-5010; (800) 465-4329. Fax (818) 781-6453. Convenient for Universal Studios, shops, and freeways. Tours to all major attractions. Conference facilities. Pool, work-out room; lounge, restaurant. 130 rooms.
$$$ ac H AE CB D DC MC V

Mission Hills Inn   **1-A3**
10621 Sepulveda Blvd, Mission Hills, CA 91345. (818) 891-1771; (800) 528-1234. Fax (818) 891-6921. (A Best Western Hotel.) All rooms have garden patios. Lovely setting near San Fernando Mission and Brand Park. Convenient for Magic Mountain and Universal City. Coffee shop, restaurant; pool. Multilingual staff. (Do not confuse with Mission Inn—Riverside.) 120 rooms.
$$ ac AE CB D DC MC V

Radisson Valley Center   **10-F4**
15433 Ventura Blvd, Sherman Oaks, CA 91403. (818) 981-5400; (800) 248-0446. Fax (818) 981-3175. Large, luxury hotel (formerly a Hilton property) near freeways and convenient to shops and major attractions. Most rooms have balconies. Banquet facilities, continental restaurant, dancing. Pool, sundeck. 215 rooms.
$$$$ ac H AE CB D DC MC V

Safari Motor Hotel　　　　　　**1-B4**
1911 W. Olive Ave, Burbank, CA 91506. (818)
845-8586; (800) 782-4373. Fax (818) 845-0054.
Attractive accommodations. One mile to freeways and close to studios. Rooms with kitchenettes and suites available. Italian restaurant.
Pool, Jacuzzi. 107 rooms.
$$$　ac H　AE CB DC MC V

Sheraton Universal　　　　　　**9-G5**
333 Universal Terrace Pkwy, Universal City, CA
91608. (818) 980-1212; (800) 325-3535. Fax
(818) 985-4980. Great location—on the Univer-
sal Studios lot. Deluxe accommodations with ex-
cellent views. Extensive convention and banquet
facilities. Restaurants, lounges; pool. Multilingual
staff. 446 rooms, 22 suites.
$$$$$　ac H　AE CB D DC MC V

Sportsmen's Lodge　　　　　　**9-E1**
12825 Ventura Blvd, Studio City, CA 91604.
(818) 769-4700; (800) 821-1625. Fax (818)
877-3898. Enchanting garden setting with fish
and duck ponds. Well-furnished rooms with
private patios. Excellent service. Banquet
facilities. Above-average restaurant, good
lounge, entertainment. Pool. Baby-sitting ser-
vice. Free transportation to Burbank airport.
195 rooms.
$$$$　ac　AE CB D DC MC V

Universal City Hilton and Towers　　**9-G5**
555 Universal Terrace Pkwy, Universal City, CA
91608. (818) 506-2500; (800) 445-8667. Fax
(818) 509-2058. Even more luxurious than the
neighboring Sheraton Universal (*see above*). An
architecturally gorgeous building that utilizes sil-
vered glass, chrome, and mauve paneling.
Three restaurants; lounges. Pool, Jacuzzis, gym.
Gift shop. Valet and butler service. Airport trans-
portation. 450 rooms.
$$$$$　ac H　AE CB D DC MC V

Warner Center Marriott　　　　　**1-B2**
21850 Oxnard St, Woodland Hills, CA 91367.
(818) 887-4800; (800) 228-9290. Fax (818) 347-
0907. Attractive hotel close to Promenade Mall.
Everything centers around a luxurious sunken
lobby. Grand ballroom, extensive conference fa-
cilities. Restaurants; gift shop. Gym, indoor/
outdoor pool, Jacuzzi. 473 rooms.
$$$$　ac H　AE CB D DC MC V

Motels

Chalet Lodge　　　　　　　　　**1-B2**
19170 Ventura Blvd, Tarzana, CA 91356. (818)
345-9410; (800) 347-9410. (No fax.) Good
location—close to shops and attractions. Heated
swimming pool. 46 rooms.
$$　ac H　AE CB D DC MC V

Heritage Motel　　　　　　　　**10-F4**
15485 Ventura Blvd, Sherman Oaks, CA 91403.
(818) 981-0500. Fax (818) 907-8050. Mid-size
motel close to freeways and attractions. Japanese restaurant. Rooms with kitchenettes; laundry. French- and Spanish-speaking staff. 70
rooms.
$$　ac　AE CB DC MC V

TraveLodge—Burbank　　　　　**9-C6**
1112 N. Hollywood Way, Burbank, CA 91505.
(818) 845-2408; (800) 255-3050. Fax (818) 846-
7801. Close to all studios and minutes from Hol-
lywood Boulevard. Pool. Most pets allowed. 28
rooms.
$$$　ac　AE CB DC MC V

SANTA MONICA & MARINA DEL REY

Hotels

Best Western Jamaica Bay Inn　　**4-F6**
4175 Admiralty Way, Marina del Rey, CA 90292.
(310) 823-5333; (800) 538-1234. Fax (310) 823-
1325. Attractive setting overlooking marina. All
rooms have balconies. Pool. Mexican restaurant
next door. 42 rooms.
$$$$　ac　AE CB D DC MC V

Doubletree　　　　　　　　　　**4-F6**
4100 Admiralty Way, Marina del Rey, CA 90292.
(310) 301-3000; (800) 528-0444. Fax (310) 301-
6890. Newest luxury hotel in the marina. A curving, nine-story structure overlooking the harbor.
The large, tree-filled lobby echoes with music
from a grand piano. Decor is California contemporary, and light pastel tones are reflected
throughout. Two restaurants (one gourmet),
rooftop lounge with entertainment, 24-hour room
service. Pool. Gift shop. Free airport transportation. 350 rooms.
$$$$$　ac H　AE CB D DC MC V

Holiday Inn　　　　　　　　　　**4-C3**
120 Colorado Ave, Santa Monica, CA 90401.
(310) 451-0676; (800) HOLIDAY. Fax (310) 393-
7145. Convenient location across from Santa
Monica Pier. Near shops and beach. Restaurant;
pool. 300 rooms.
$$$　ac H　AE CB D DC MC V

Holiday Inn—Bay View Plaza　　**4-C4**
530 Pico Blvd, Santa Monica, CA 90405. (310)
399-9344; (800) HOLIDAY. Fax (310) 399-2504.
Luxury hotel four blocks from beach. Impressive
lobby area with lounge. Most rooms have balco-
nies and ocean views, some have private out-
door Jacuzzis. Conference facilities. Penthouse
ballroom; entertainment; coffee shop. Pool, exer-
cise room. 309 rooms.
$$$$　ac H　AE CB D DC MC V

Huntley House　　　　　　　　**4-C2**
1111 2nd St, Santa Monica, CA 90403. (310)
394-5454. (800) 333-3333. Fax (310) 458-
9776. Center of town, five minutes to beach.
Quiet, comfortable rooms. Rooftop bar and res-
taurant with panoramic views of Santa Monica
Bay; coffee shop. Conference facilities. Beauty
salon and gift shop. Multilingual staff. 209
rooms.
$$$$　ac H　AE CB D DC MC V

Marina del Rey Hotel　　　　　**4-G7**
13534 Bali Way, Marina del Rey, CA 90292.
(310) 822-1010; (800) 421-8145. Fax (310) 301-

8167. Beautiful location: right at the water's edge, in the center of the marina. Over half the rooms have balconies. Restaurant, coffee shop, garden patio. Pool, putting green, bike rental. Comfortable. Complimentary airport transportation. 160 rooms.
$$$$$ ac H AE CB DC MC V

Marina International   **4-F6**
4200 Admiralty Way, Marina del Rey, CA 90292. (310) 822-1010; (800) 421-8145. Fax (310) 301-6687. Large, deluxe hotel with balconies to all 25 suites. Restaurant. Pool, Jacuzzi. Free airport transportation. 135 rooms.
$$$$ ac H AE CB DC MC V

Marina Marriott   **4-F7**
13480 Maxella Ave, Marina del Rey, CA 90292. (310) 822-8555; (800) 228-9290. Fax (310) 823-2996. Deluxe, five-story hotel in the attractive Villa Marina shopping and entertainment center. Restaurant; pool. 284 rooms.
$$$$ ac H AE CB D DC MC V

Marina Pacific   **4-F5**
1697 Pacific Ave, Venice, CA 90291. (310) 399-7770; (800) 421-8151. Fax (310) 452-5479. Deluxe rooms and apartments, close to the beach. Informal atmosphere. Indoor/outdoor cafe. Weekly rates. 99 rooms
$$$ ac AE CB D DC MC V

Miramar Sheraton   **4-C3**
101 Wilshire Blvd, Santa Monica, CA 90401. (310) 576-7777; (800) 325-3535. Fax (310) 458-7912. Luxury hotel overlooking the ocean. Conveniently located for beaches and shops. Banquet facilities. Restaurant, lounge with live entertainment, coffee shop. Heated pool. Gift shops. Tours. 303 rooms, 61 suites.
$$$$$ ac H AE CB D DC MC V

Pacific Shore   **4-D3**
1819 Ocean Ave, Santa Monica, CA 90401. (310) 451-8711; (800) 622-8711. Fax (310) 394-6657. Modern deluxe hotel with beautiful ocean views. Restaurant, bar, coffee shop. Sauna, Jacuzzi, pool. Baby-sitting service. 168 rooms.
$$$$ ac AE CB DC MC V

Shangri-La   **4-C2**
1301 Ocean Ave, Santa Monica, CA 90401. (310) 394-2791; (800) 345-7829. Fax (310) 451-2351. A quiet, stylish, art deco hotel overlooking Santa Monica Bay. This place was meant for artists and writers. There is a respectable tranquility that alludes to a private club. Room decor follows the art deco theme. A breakfast room is also open for afternoon tea (no other meals). Most rooms have kitchens or wet bars. Airport shuttle service. 42 suites, 12 studios.
$$$$ AE CB D DC MC V

Sovereign Hotel   **4-B2**
205 Washington Ave, Santa Monica, CA 90403. (310) 395-9921; (800) 331-0163. Fax (310) 458-3085. Hotel/apartment complex close to beaches and shops. Most rooms have kitchenettes; 24-hour desk. 82 rooms.
$$$ AE CB DC MC V

Motels

Encore   **4-E7**
13432 Washington Blvd, Marina del Rey, CA 90292. (310) 823-5066. (No fax.) Small, adult motel featuring water beds and X-rated movies. 17 rooms.
$$ MC V

Jolly Roger   **4-F6**
2904 Washington Blvd, Marina del Rey, CA 90291. (310) 822-2904; (800) 822-2904. Fax (310) 801-9461. Budget Marina del Rey! Bright rooms at reasonable rates. Pool, sundeck, two Jacuzzis, recreation rooms. 84 rooms.
$$$ ac H MC V

Pacific Sands   **4-C3**
1515 Ocean Ave, Santa Monica, CA 90401. (310) 395-6133. (No fax.) Near Santa Monica Pier. Lively; popular with young adults. Pool. 50 rooms.
$$ H AE CB D DC MC V

Santa Monica TraveLodge   **4-C3**
1525 Ocean Ave, Santa Monica, CA 90401. (310) 451-0761; (800) 255-3050. Fax (310) 393-5311. Close to beach, park, and shopping. Pool. 29 well-appointed rooms.
$$$ ac H AE CB D DC MC V

WESTWOOD & WEST LOS ANGELES

Hotels

Best Western–Royal Palace   **4-A8**
2528 S. Sepulveda Blvd, W. LA, CA 90064. (310) 477-9066; (800) 528-1234. Fax (310) 478-4133. Each of the minisuites has a terrace and full kitchen. Acclaimed worldwide. Quiet and refined. Beautifully furnished. Excellent value. Pool, sauna, tennis nearby. 32 mini-suites.
$$$ ac AE CB DC MC V

Century Wilshire   **5-E5**
1077 Wilshire Blvd, LA, CA 90024. (310) 474-4506; (800) 421-7223. Fax (310) 474-2535. Close to Westwood theaters, restaurants, shops, and UCLA. Luxury rooms, suites, and bachelor apartments. Pool. Multilingual staff. 66 rooms.
$$$$ ac AE CB DC MC V

Del Capri   **5-E5**
10587 Wilshire Blvd, LA, CA 90024. (310) 474-3511; (800) 44-HOTEL. Fax (310) 470-9999. Luxury rooms and kitchenette suites. Complimentary continental breakfast. Pool. Limousine service to Westwood and Century City. 80 rooms.
$$$$ ac H AE CB DC MC V

Holiday Inn—Brentwood   **5-D2**
170 N. Church Lane, Sunset Blvd, LA, CA 90049. (310) 476-6411; (800) 465-4329. Fax (310) 472-1157. Circular landmark next to the 405 Freeway. Convenient location for UCLA, shops, and attractions. Spacious, well-furnished rooms.

Rooftop restaurant with great views. Pool, health club. Tour pickups. 211 rooms.
$$$$ ac H AE CB D DC MC V

The Radisson Bel-Air 5-E2
11461 Sunset Blvd, LA, CA 90049. (310) 476-6571; (800) 421-6649. Fax (310) 471-6310. Renovated luxury hotel in Brentwood. Transportation to Beverly Hills. Restaurant, lounge. Pool, workout room, tennis court, putting green. Babysitting service. Most pets allowed. Multilingual staff. 162 rooms.
$$$$ ac H AE CB D DC MC V

Westwood Marquis Hotel & Gardens 5-E5
930 Hilgard Ave, LA, CA 90024. (310) 208-8765; (800) 421-2317. Fax (310) 824-0355. Westwood's most luxurious hotel with each suite individually decorated. European elegance, quiet location. Restaurant, lounge, entertainment. Pool, sauna, Jacuzzi. Baby-sitting service; beauty salon, florist. Free limousine service to Beverly Hills and Century City. 250 suites.
$$$$$ ac H AE CB DC MC V

Westwood Plaza 5-E5
10740 Wilshire Blvd, LA, CA 90024. (310) 475-8711; (800) 472-8556. Fax (310) 475-5220. (A Holiday Inn.) Close to Westwood Village shops and theaters. Convenient for UCLA. Meeting facilities. Restaurant; pool, Jacuzzi. 296 rooms.
$$$$ ac H AE CB D DC MC V

Motels

Brentwood Motor Suites 5-D2
199 N. Church Lane, LA, CA 90049. (310) 476-6255; (800) 235-8990. Fax (310) 471-4285. Attractive all-suites inn next to San Diego Freeway. Most suites have kitchens and private patios. Pool, Jacuzzi, sauna. Free continental breakfast and newspaper. 59 suites.
$$$ ac H AE CB D DC MC V

Los Angeles West TraveLodge 5-F5
10740 Santa Monica Blvd, LA, CA 90025. (310) 474-4576; (800) 255-3050. Fax (310) 470-3117. Inexpensive accommodations in convenient location. Pool. 55 rooms.
$$$ ac H AE CB D DC MC V

Royal Westwood 5-G5
2352 Westwood Blvd, LA, CA 90064. (310)475-4551. (No fax.) Quiet, clean, and comfortable. Complimentary morning coffee. 26 rooms.
$$ ac AE MC V

St. Regis Motor Hotel 5-G2
11955 Wilshire Blvd, W. LA, CA 90025. (310) 477-6021. (No fax.) Convenient for beaches, shops, and UCLA. Pool. Multilingual staff. 49 rooms.
$$ ac AE CB DC MC V

Westwood Inn 5-E4
10820 Wilshire Blvd, LA, CA 90024. (310) 474-3118. Fax (310) 475-9844. Within walking distance of Westwood Village, 5 minutes from UCLA campus. 20 rooms.
$$ ac D MC V

WILSHIRE DISTRICT

Hotels

Executive Motor Inn—Mid-Wilshire 6-G8
603 S. New Hampshire Ave, LA, CA 90005. (213) 385-4444; (800) 528-1234. Fax (213) 380-5413. (A Best Western hotel.) Centrally located. Excellent facilities, including Jacuzzi, sauna, indoor pool, gymnasium. In-room refrigerators. Good value. 90 rooms.
$$ ac AE CB D DC MC V

Los Angeles Midtown 6-E8
400 N. Vermont Ave, LA, CA 90004. (213) 662-4888; (800) 950-4458. Fax (213) 662-2974. Elegant hotel close to the Hollywood Freeway. Decor is Orient-inspired, using Chinese artwork and calm peach tones. Conference facilities. Continental and Chinese restaurants. Pool, Jacuzzi, health club. Gift shop. 201 rooms.
$$$$ ac H AE CB D DC MC V

Sheraton Town-House 7-B1
2961 Wilshire Blvd, LA, CA 90010. (213) 382-7171; (800) 325-3535. Fax (213) 487-7148. Luxurious resort hotel with conference facilities. Attractive gardens. Two restaurants. Tennis courts, Olympic-size pool, sauna. Multilingual staff. 272 rooms.
$$$$ ac H AE CB DC MC V

The Wilshire Koreana 6-G8
3515 Wilshire Blvd, LA, CA 90010. (213) 381-7411; (800) 382-7411. Fax (213) 386-7379. Convenient for freeway travel and all major attractions. Luxurious rooms and suites. Convention facilities. Restaurant, cafe; nightclub. Pool. Multilingual staff. 396 rooms.
$$$ ac H AE CB D DC MC V

Motels

Bevonshire Lodge 6-E4
7575 Beverly Blvd, LA, CA 90036. (213) 936-6154. (No fax.) Quiet, family motel near Farmer's Market. Pool. 24 rooms.
$$ ac AE CB DC MC V

Farmer's Daughter 6-F3
115 S. Fairfax Ave, LA, CA 90036. (213) 937-3930. (No fax.) Across from Farmer's Market and CBS Studios. Pool. Tour pickups, TV show tickets. 66 rooms.
$$ ac H AE D MC V

BED & BREAKFAST

NOTE *to European visitors: Bed & breakfast accommodations in the United States are far more luxurious than those in Europe, and the prices are therefore much higher than may be expected.*

Anaheim Country Inn 1-F8
856 S. Walnut St, Anaheim, CA 92802. (714) 778-0150; (800) 755-7801. (No fax.) Built in 1910, this friendly and welcoming inn is filled

with turn-of-the-century antiques. Close to Disneyland and convention center. Jacuzzi. Full breakfast. 8 rooms.

$$$ AE MC V

Eastlake Inn   **7-A3**
1442 Kellam Ave, LA, CA 90026. (213) 250-1620. (No fax.) A beautifully furnished Victorian house, built in 1887. Located next to historic Carroll Avenue. Complimentary champagne, hors d'oeuvres, flowers. Unusual weekend packages can include a ride in a hot-air balloon. Full breakfast. 9 rooms.

$$$ AE MC V

Gull House
344 Whittley Ave, Avalon, Catalina Island, CA 90704. (310) 510-2547. (No fax.) Just two large suites—each with its own private entrance. No more than two persons per suite allowed. Patio, pool, Jacuzzi. Continental breakfast served outdoors. Two-night minimum. Reserve ahead (personal checks accepted).

$$$$ No cards

La Maida House   **9-D5**
11159 La Maida St, N. Hollywood, CA 91601. (818) 769-3857. (No fax.) Gorgeous villa with bungalows set in landscaped grounds, which include a rose garden, herb garden, and water garden. There's a pond and the owners grow their own fruit for homemade preserves. Close to studios. Romantic suites with canopied beds. Jacuzzis in two rooms. Full service includes breakfast, daily newspaper, shoe shine, laundry. 11 rooms, including 4 suites.

$$$$ ac H   MC V

Venice Beach House   **4-F5**
15 30th Ave, Venice, CA 90291. (310) 823-1966. (No fax.) A 1911 California craftsman home with sunny verandas and flower gardens, just half a block from (the quiet end of) Venice beach. One full suite has a fireplace and one room has a double Jacuzzi. Continental breakfast, evening wine and cheese. 9 rooms.

$$$$ AE MC V

CAMPGROUNDS & RV PARKS

Circle X Ranch   **1-C1**
12896 E. Yerba Buena Rd, Malibu, CA 91361.

(310) 457-6408; (818) 597-9192. (No fax.) Rustic parkland. 600 campsites. Archery range, pool, volleyball courts. Tents okay.

Good Sam Park   **1-E7**
311 N. Beach Blvd, Anaheim, CA 92801. (714) 821-4311. (No fax.) Pool, laundry, showers, playground. No tents.

H   MC V

KOA—Anaheim   **1-F8**
1221 S. West St, Anaheim, CA 92802. (714) 533-7720. (No fax.) Pool, Jacuzzi; laundry, showers; store. Tents okay.

H   AE D MC V

KOA—San Fernando Valley
15900 Olden St, Sylmar, CA 91342. (818) 362-7785. Olympic-size pool, games room, laundry, full facilities, store. Tents okay.

H   MC V

Leo Carrillo State Beach
Pacific Coast Hwy, Leo Carrillo, CA 90265. Reserve ahead from March to September (*see* State Parks *below*), the rest of year it's first come, first served. Two sites. Tents okay.

H   AE D MC V

Malibu Beach RV Park   **1-D1**
25801 Pacific Coast Hwy, Malibu, CA 90265. (310) 456-6052. (No fax.) Large site. Showers, laundry. Tents okay.

H   MC V

State Parks
Reservations for state campgrounds can be made through Mistix. To charge (MasterCard or Visa), call (310) 444-7275; for nearest Mistix outlet, call (800) 952-5580. Reservations accepted according to season and up to eight weeks in advance (but not less than 48 hours).

Traveler's World   **1-F8**
333 W. Ball Rd, Anaheim, CA 92805. (714) 991-0100. (No fax.) Pool, showers, laundry, store. Tents okay.

MC V

Vacationland RV Park   **1-F8**
1343 S. West St, Anaheim, CA 92802. (714) 533-7270. (No fax.) Pool, showers, laundry, playground, store. Tents okay.

AE DC MC V

SIGHTSEEING

Hollywood Sign, Hollywood Hills

VIEWPOINTS & SCENIC DRIVES

Breathtaking views of Los Angeles may be enjoyed from locations within the city or from surrounding mountains both by day and by night. The scenic drives included in this section cover areas of exceptional interest, and specific attractions are listed after each entry.

Viewpoints

City Hall   **7-C5**
200 N. Spring St, LA. (213) 485-2121. An observation deck is located on the 27th floor of this impressive building, which is *OPEN to the public Mon-Fri 9am-5pm.* Excellent views of the city. (*See also* HISTORIC LA, Buildings & Landmarks.)

Griffith Park Observatory   **6-A8**
2800 E. Observatory Rd, Griffith Park. (213) 664-1181. The view from here on a clear night is unforgettable. There is a winding balcony on each side of the observatory and small telescopes are provided along the outside terraces. Huge solar telescopes on the roof are *OPEN to the public from 7:30pm-9:45pm.* (*See also* HISTORIC LA, Buildings & Landmarks.)

The Hollywood Sign   **9-G8**
This famous sign can be seen from many parts of the city, but a short hike is necessary to get close to it. Exit the Hollywood Freeway at Beachwood Drive and travel uphill turning left on Ledgewood Drive, then right on Deronda Drive to the end. Park here; go through the gate near

the water tower and walk up. Built on the south slope of Mount Lee, the sign is 50 feet high and 450 feet long. (*See also* HISTORIC LA, Buildings & Landmarks.)

LAX (LA International Airport)   **3-C5**
First impressions linger, and if you are flying into Los Angeles after dark you may enjoy a startling bird's-eye view of the city. Driving away from LAX (if your destination is on the west side) Lincoln Boulevard north is a pleasant alternative to freeway travel. Just past the Airport Marina Hotel, at the corner of Manchester Avenue, the road drops down to the basin where the city is spread out before you.

Airplane buffs may enjoy an end-of-runway view of gigantic jumbo jets taking off above their heads. This location is on Pershing Drive (**3-D3**) between Manchester Avenue and Imperial Highway. A more placid view of airport operations can be enjoyed from the 135-foot-high Theme Building, which dominates the central terminal area. There is a lounge, restaurant, and observation deck for visitors.

Lookout Mountain   **6-A1**
Take Laurel Canyon Boulevard to Lookout Mountain Avenue and drive to Appian Way for spectacular panoramic views from Downtown to Malibu. Particularly beautiful at sunset.

Mount Wilson Observatory   **1-A6**
Although only 30 miles north of Los Angeles, allow a full day for a visit to Mount Wilson. The Angeles Crest Highway (2) starts at the Foothill Freeway just northwest of Pasadena. This is a beautiful scenic highway that winds up the mountain, affording splendid views along the

left at light out of parking
structure go thru light and
enter 55 no. Approx 1 mile
exit on your right at
Baker. At the bottom of
the exit turn left and
go thru one light to the
next light which is Bristol
turn left and go approx.
1 mile and hotel on right.

405 no. to Santa Monica
Blvd turn right - go approx.
5 miles left on LaCienega
right on Holloway store is
on left park in back

way. At about 5,000 feet, Mount Wilson Road will take you to the observatory, which is close to the peak (5,710 feet). For observatory information, call (818) 577-1122. NOTE: Snow can be a hazard during winter, call for road conditions: (818) 440-1131; U.S. Forest Service (818) 790-1151.

Rooftop Lounges
Several high-rise buildings have lounges on their top floors; exciting views may be enjoyed while dining or just sipping cocktails. These are a few.

Castaway   **1-B4**
1250 Harvard Rd, Burbank. (818) 848-6691. Perched on top of the De Bell golf course, this interesting hideaway bar and restaurant overlooks the whole San Fernando Valley. Especially impressive at night.

Huntley House Hotel   **4-C2**
1111 2nd St, Santa Monica. (310) 394-5454. Top-floor lounge and restaurant with beautiful ocean views.

Monty's   **5-F5**
1100 Glendon Ave, Westwood. (310) 208-8787. A 21st-floor restaurant with good views of Westwood and Hollywood.

The Tower   **7-D3**
1150 S. Olive St, LA. (213) 746-1554. Beautiful French restaurant with a 360° view of LA from one of Downtown's tallest buildings. (*See also* RESTAURANTS, Downtown, French.)

Westin Bonaventure Hotel   **7-C3**
404 S. Figueroa St, LA. (213) 624-1000. Lounge (34th floor) and restaurant (35th floor). The lounge, which revolves, giving a 360° view of the city, is especially romantic at night.

Scenic Drives

Malibu/Mulholland Scenic Drive
This particularly scenic drive takes in much of LA's rugged backcountry. Begin at Malibu Canyon (**1-D1**) just north of Pepperdine University and follow the crest of the Santa Monica Mountains. Turn right onto Mulholland Highway and right again onto Mulholland Drive—an open scenic wilderness that provides a sharp contrast to the city below. There are countless viewpoints and hiking trails, and the abundance of wildlife is surprising. Mulholland Drive is unpaved for approximately 9 miles between Canoga Avenue and Encino Hills Drive. Do not negotiate this stretch in wet weather unless you have a four-wheel-drive vehicle. The road becomes paved again before crossing the San Diego Freeway and continues a winding scenic route through the Hollywood Hills, ending at the Hollywood Freeway (**1-B4**). This drive can be reversed or taken as two shorter trips from either Hollywood or Malibu. *Allow 2½ hours.* Malibu Creek State Park and Topanga State Park (*see* PARKS & GARDENS, Nature Centers & Trails).

Palisades Coast Highway Scenic Drive
Coastal drives are always refreshing and this one begins at Santa Monica Pier (**4-C3**), at the heart of the Santa Monica Bay. Drive north from the pier passing Palisades Park and descend to Pacific Coast Highway, which traces the coastline and is bordered by miles of wide public beaches. Past Topanga Canyon Boulevard (5½ miles), where Malibu Point juts out to meet the ocean, the terrain becomes quite rugged. The beach here is a favorite of surfers. The largest headland along this stretch is Point Dume (about 15 miles from Santa Monica) beyond which lies Leo Carrillo Beach, popular with divers and an area of great scenic beauty. Point Mugu State Park covers an expanse of rolling hills opposite Leo Carrillo and is a perfect resting point before journeying back to Santa Monica. *Allow 2 to 4 hours.* Point Mugu State Park (*see* PARKS & GARDENS, Nature Centers & Trails), J. Paul Getty Museum (*see* HISTORIC LA, Buildings & Landmarks, *and* MUSEUMS & GALLERIES, Museums, General Art), Self-Realization Fellowship Lake Shrine (*see* PARKS & GARDENS, Parks), and Beach Cities (*see* HISTORIC LA, Main Districts).

Palos Verdes Scenic Drive
The Palos Verdes Peninsula is a lush, green, rugged area dotted with impressive homes, riding establishments, and a handful of beautiful beaches. Palos Verdes Drive West takes up the coastal route where Pacific Coast Highway turns inland. It begins at Palos Verdes Estates (**1-F4**). The well-maintained route travels to Point Verdes Drive South and passes the site of the old Marineland before merging into 25th Street. Turn right on Western Avenue to reach Point Fermin Park and the Cabrillo beach recreation area. The road soon leads to San Pedro's Pacific Avenue, which heads toward Los Angeles Harbor. From here, visitors not wishing to retrace their steps may take the Harbor Freeway north to join the San Diego Freeway for Los Angeles. *Allow 2 to 4 hours.* South Coast Botanic Gardens (*see* PARKS & GARDENS, Botanical Gardens), Wayfarer's Chapel (*see* HISTORIC LA, Churches), Ports O' Call Village (*see* Tours), Cabrillo Marine Museum (*see* MUSEUMS & GALLERIES, Museums, Science).

San Diego Freeway Scenic Drive
What is often a tedious journey for commuters can be a scenic drive to a visitor. Join the San Diego Freeway (405) northbound at Venice Boulevard (**1-D3**). Between here and Sunset Boulevard are good views of Century City and Westwood to the right; Santa Monica and West Los Angeles to the left. Past Sunset Boulevard the freeway climbs through Sepulveda Canyon, crossing Mulholland Drive. From the highest point, panoramic views of the San Fernando Valley, edged by the San Gabriel Mountains, can be enjoyed as the road descends to meet the Ventura Freeway (**10-E4**). Here the journey may be reversed to give great views across Los Angeles from the north. Daytime visibility depends on weather conditions but nighttime views are always good. *Allow 1 hour. Avoid during rush hours.* Century City (*see* HISTORIC LA, Main Districts), Mormon Temple (*see* HISTORIC LA,

Churches), Westwood (*see* HISTORIC LA, Main Districts: West Los Angeles & Westwood), San Fernando Valley (*see* HISTORIC LA, Main Districts).

Sunset Boulevard Scenic Drive
Sunset runs from the heart of the city to the edge of the ocean and tells a story about many aspects of Los Angeles. The drive can begin at Topanga State Beach (**1-C2**), or in reverse from the Civic Center, Downtown (**7-C4**). Starting from the beach, Sunset Boulevard winds up into the foothills of the Santa Monica Mountains through the affluent communities of Brentwood, Bel Air, and Beverly Hills. Having passed luxurious mansions, the brashness of the Sunset Strip is quite startling. The route progresses through Hollywood, taking in the TV studios and some seedier sections that are now a fact of life in LA. This famous street continues to Downtown Los Angeles (passing Echo Park and the Harbor Freeway) and ends at Hill Street, close to City Hall. *Allow 2 hours. Avoid during rush hours.* Will Rogers State Historic Park (*see* PARKS & GARDENS, Parks), UCLA (*see* HISTORIC LA, Schools), City Hall (*see* HISTORIC LA, Buildings & Landmarks), Downtown (*see* HISTORIC LA, Main Districts).

Topanga Canyon Scenic Drive
Follow Pacific Coast Highway north from Santa Monica (**4-C3**) to Topanga Canyon Boulevard (5½ miles). Turn right and climb the winding canyon road through massive rock formations to the country community of Topanga 10 miles ahead. In another 5 miles one sees the summit, with its breathtaking views of the San Fernando Valley and surrounding hills. You may return via the same route or continue east to join the Ventura Freeway (101) for Los Angeles. *Allow 1½ hours.* Topanga State Park (*see* PARKS & GARDENS, Nature Centers & Trails). NOTE: Topanga Canyon may be closed to through traffic during heavy rainfall.

TOURS

The following tours will appeal to a variety of interests. As agendas change from season to season, it is impossible to quote exact operating hours and admission costs. Always phone ahead for up-to-the-minute information.

Price code (where applicable)
$ under $6 admission
$$ $6-$12
$$$ $12-$18
$$$$ over $18

Art Tours of Los Angeles
(213) 870-2549. Informative, well-organized, half-day tours of Los Angeles art galleries and gallery districts, specializing in contemporary art. Price includes breakfast, lunch, and transportation. $$$$

Burbank Studios   9-F7
4000 Warner Blvd, Burbank. (818) 954-1744. Make reservations three or four days in advance for a technical tour of the Columbia/Warner Brothers complex. This 2-hour tour is particularly recommended for people interested in filmmaking. Burbank is the only studio that allows visitors to watch movies being made. Visits to the technical departments involved in TV and movie production are highlights of the tour. Children under age 10 not admitted. (*See also* HISTORIC LA, Motion Picture Studios.) Tours *Mon-Fri 10am & 2pm.* $$$

California Parlor Cars Tours   6-C4
7000 Hollywood Blvd, LA. (800) 227-4250. (In the Hollywood Roosevelt Hotel.) Tours of three, four, and six days, exploring the beautiful country between LA and San Francisco. Tours can include the Hearst Castle, Solvang, or scenic Highway 1. (*See also* Hearst Castle; Day Trips: Solvang; *and* Weekend Trips: Highway 1.) Prices include all transportation, sightseeing, hotels, meals, and tips. Reservations are required.

Catalina Cruises   1-G6
320 Golden Shore Blvd, Long Beach. (310) 436-5006. The boat trip to Avalon on Catalina Island takes 1 hour, 45 minutes. For tours of the island, call the Tourist Bureau in Avalon, (310) 510-1520 (east to remember: 5, 10, 15, 20) or the Visitors Bureau, (310) 510-2500. Various tours are available including scenic drives. (*See also* HISTORIC LA, Main Districts: Beach Cities.) Boats depart Monday to Friday at 9am and 2:45pm; Saturday at 9am, 11am, 2:45pm, and 4:45pm; and Sunday at 11:30am and 1:45pm. With additional daily departures in summer. Round trip. $$$

Charter Concepts   4-G4
3137 Barkentin Rd, Rancho Palos Verdes. (310) 306-9600. Yachts, with full staff and personal chefs, are available for luxurious, private cruises of local marinas and coastal islands. Comfortable for up to ten people for a weekend. Let the champagne flow! $$$$

Descanso Gardens Tour   1-C5
1418 Descanso Dr, La Canada. (818) 952-4400 (recorded) or 952-4401. A 45-minute drive from central LA. Beautiful ornamental plants, running streams, live oaks, dozens of species of birds. Walks and tram hours. Teahouse and picnic facilities. No radios or pets allowed. Children under age 18 must be accompanied by an adult. Tram tours (45 minutes) *Tues-Fri 1, 2 & 3pm; Sat & Sun 11am, 1, 2 & 3pm.* Gardens OPEN *7 days 9am-4:30pm.*

Gray Line Bus Tours   7-C3
4800 Staunton Ave, LA. (213) 856-5910. Escorted tours in air-conditioned buses. Many fares include admission to attractions. Multilingual guides available. Reservations are essential (phone at least 24 hours in advance) and can be made at hotels or at Gray Line offices. Departures are from numerous hotels throughout the city—call Gray Line for most convenient pickup point. Limousine service also available

(for additional fee). The following is a selection of Gray Line Tours in and around LA.:

Beverly Hills, Hollywood, and LA by day
Catalina Island
Disneyland—afternoon and evening
Disneyland—brief tour
Disneyland—by night
All-day Disneyland—guided tour
All-day Disneyland—self-guided
Hollywood-stars' homes, Beverly Hills
Knott's Berry Farm
LA City
LA by night
Las Vegas
Magic Mountain
Movieland Wax Museum
NBC Studios & Lawry's Center
Pasadena, Huntington Gallery, and Forest Lawn
Queen Mary
San Diego and San Juan Capistrano
San Diego and Sea World
San Diego Zoo
Santa Barbara Mission and Ojai
Tijuana Shopping

Greystone Mansion & Park   **5-B8**
Loma Vista Dr and Doheny Rd, Beverly Hills. Formerly the estate of the Doheny oil family, this 55-room mansion is situated in 18 acres of landscaped parkland. Although the mansion is usually closed to the public, tours of the grounds are offered by the Department of Recreation & Parks. For schedule, call (310) 285-2537. (*See also* HISTORIC LA, Buildings & Landmarks.) Grounds *OPEN 7 days 10am-5pm.*

Hearst Castle
Off Highway 1, San Simeon. (805) 927-2000; reservations (800) 444-7275; wheelchair bookings (805) 927-2020. Hearst Castle is a State Historic Monument situated high on a hill overlooking the rugged Pacific coastline. Although 5½ hours northwest, it is a very popular day trip for visitors to LA (bus tours are available). Four varied tours are offered of this magnificent mansion, which was built over a period of 30 years (but never fully completed) by the late William Randolph Hearst—once one of the richest men in America. His colorful and controversial life is reflected in the extravagant excesses of style and taste within the castle. Tours are well organized, interesting, informative, and last approximately 2 hours. Tickets are available through Ticketron (*see* ENTERTAINMENT, Tickets, Ticket Agencies) and are bookable up to 60 days in advance. It is advisable to book one week in advance during peak summer months. $$

Jet Propulsion Laboratory   **8-C8**
4800 Oak Grove Dr, Pasadena. (818) 354-8594. Two-hour general tours of the laboratory detailing activities and accomplishments. Reserve in advance. Fascinating for the science buff, young or old.

Lawry's California Center   **1-C5**
570 W. Ave 26, LA. (213) 225-2491. Garden setting in 12 acres of El Pueblo de Los Angeles

State Historic Park (*see* PARKS & GARDENS, Parks). A variety of restaurants offer lunch and dinner—all enhanced by Lawry's famous seasonings. A special guided tour shows how Lawry's products are made. Interesting mission-style architecture. Gift and wine shops. Lawry's popular Fiesta Dinner occurs May to September, 7 days a week. Tours *Mon-Fri 11:30am, 12:30 & 1:30pm.* Center *OPEN 7 days.* Good Sunday brunch.

The Los Angeles Conservancy   **7-D4**
727 W. 7th St, Suite 955, LA. (213) 623-2489. The Los Angeles Conservancy aims to preserve the urban heritage of the city through "action, assistance, and awareness." The following tours are interesting and enlightening.

"Would You Believe LA?" Self-guided or docent-led tour of the Broadway Theater District, Spring Street, and Pershing Square.

"Would You Believe Hollywood Boulevard?" Self-guided tour concentrating on the architectural heritage of this famous street.

"Discover North University Park." A self-guided tour that reveals the Los Angeles of 1900, showing beautiful Craftsman and Victorian homes.

"Cruisin' LA." A 2½-hour driving or guided bus tour featuring programmatic architecture (structures made to resemble everyday objects), freeway and building design, neon signs, billboards, and vintage cars.

Guided tours of Downtown (four different tours) are arranged each Saturday ($5 fee for nonmembers). Call the Conservancy for reservations. Brochures for self-guided tours are available for a small fee and are free to members. For information, call (213) 623-2489. $

Los Angeles State & County Arboretum 1-B7
301 N. Baldwin Ave, Arcadia. (818) 821-3222. Less than one hour from central LA. Over 125 acres of plants are featured in different theme gardens. Over 200 peacocks roam the grounds. Demonstration gardens provide new ideas in home landscaping. There are streams, lagoons, a bird feeding area, greenhouses, terraces, and historic buildings. (*See also* HISTORIC LA, Buildings & Landmarks: Queen Ann Cottage.) Gift shop, refreshments, no pets, no bicycles, no radios or musical instruments. Guided tram tours every 45 minutes, *Mon-Fri 12:15-3pm; Sat & Sun 10am-4pm.* Arboretum *OPEN 7 days 9am-5pm. CLOSED Christmas.* $

Los Angeles Times   **7-C5**
1st & Spring Sts, LA. (213) 626-2323; (213) 237-5000; (800) LATIMES. See a newspaper in the making. Public tours begin at the 1st Street lobby *Mon-Fri 11:15am & 3pm.* No reservations necessary. FREE.

Malibu Creek State Park   **1-C1**
Las Virgines Rd (off Mulholland Hwy), Agoura. (818) 706-8809; (818) 533-PARK. Until 1976 this was the Century Movie Ranch. The outdoor scenes for the TV series "M*A*S*H" were also filmed here. A man-made lake now attracts an assortment of wild birds. A guide is available to

take groups on educational walks through the flower-filled park on Saturdays and Sundays at 10am. (Weekday tours by appointment only.) Low parking fee. Visitors center. FREE.

Mission San Fernando Rey de Espana   1-A3
15151 San Fernando Mission Blvd, Mission Hills. (818) 361-0186. A beautiful reconstruction of the historic San Fernando Mission, set in 7 acres of well-kept grounds. Tours *7 days 9am-4:15pm.* (*See also* HISTORIC LA, Churches.) $

Olvera Street Tour   7-B5
El Pueblo de Los Angeles State Historic Park, LA. (213) 628-3562. The birthplace of Los Angeles (1781) and still a colorful, bustling, Mexican market street. The Avila Adobe (No. 10) was built in 1818 and is the oldest house in LA. Guided tours begin at the visitors center (south side of the Plaza) *Tues-Sat 10 & 11am, noon, 1pm.* No reservations necessary except for groups. (*See also* Walking Tours: The Plaza & Chinatown *and* HISTORIC LA, Main Districts: Downtown.) FREE.

George C. Page Museum   6-G3
5801 Wilshire Blvd, LA. (213) 857-6311. Museum tours including laboratories and extinct animal exhibits are given from Tuesday to Sunday at 2pm. (Admission free second Tuesday of each month.) (*See also* MUSEUMS & GALLERIES, Museums, Historic.) $

Police Headquarters   7-C5
Parker Center, 150 N. Los Angeles St, LA. (213)

485-3281. Group tours for ten or more people, Monday to Friday. A tour of the academy is followed by a tour of the jail and the crime lab. Call for appointment. FREE.

Ports O' Call Village   1-G5
Berth 77, San Pedro. Information (310) 831-9930; management (310) 831-0287. Special group tours include harbor cruise, lunch, and a bottle of California wine. Ports O' Call Village contains a collection of interesting crafts shops and restaurants. Reserve in advance. $$

***Queen Mary* Tour   1-G5**
Pier J, Long Beach. (310) 435-4747. One of the world's largest, and best-loved, ocean liners. Much of the inner structure has been removed to house exhibits that demonstrate how the ship looked during different periods in her history. In the Grand Salon, and in many of the cabins and social rooms, efforts have been made to restore the old *Queen* to her original 1930s art deco splendor. The ship also houses a first-class hotel.

Guided and self-guided tours of the liner *Mon-Fri 10am-4pm; Sat & Sun 10am-4:30pm.* (*See also* HISTORIC LA, Buildings & Landmarks: *Queen Mary.*) $$ Rates lower for children.

San Antonio Winery   7-A6
737 Lamar St, LA. (213) 223-1401. Self-guided tours of the oldest producing winery in Los Angeles show the different stages of wine-making and bottling. Guided tours, for 15 people or

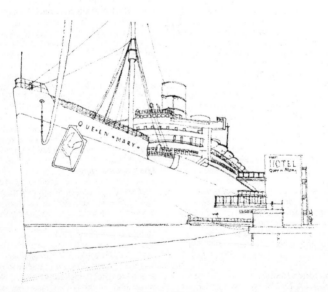

Queen Mary

South Coast Botanic Gardens   **1-C4**
26300 Crenshaw Blvd, Palos Verdes. (310) 377-0468. A lake, streams, and a bird sanctuary are included in 87 acres of landscaped gardens. Pleasant picnic area but no refreshment facilities. Children under age 18 must be accompanied by an adult. Tram tours lasting 45 minutes are available on weekends. *OPEN 7 days 9am-5-m. (See also* PARKS & GARDENS, Botanical Gardens.*)* $

Starline Tours   **6-C5**
6845 Hollywood Blvd, Hollywood. (213) 856-5900. Conducted tours of Hollywood, Universal Studios, and other attractions in small, 14-passenger buses or larger coaches. A nightclub tour (groups of eight or more) that includes dinner and drinks takes visitors to a club where dancers, singing waiters, comedians, and song-and-dance acts provide entertainment. Complimentary pickup from hotel or motel if required. Charter buses and limousines also available. Sightseeing tours leave from the Greyline/Starline offices daily, on the hour. No reservations necessary. Prices vary.

UCLA Tours   **5-E5**
405 Hilgard Ave, W. LA. (310) 206-8147. The University of California, Los Angeles, became a 419-acre campus in 1929. It was built (on a beanfield) in the rural area now known as Westwood. Walking tours of the campus are available Monday to Friday from 10:30am to 1:30pm by reservation. All-day parking $5. Tours are FREE.

Universal Studios   **9-G5**
100 Universal City Plaza, Universal City. (818) 508-9600 or -5444. This is the world's largest, busiest motion picture studio. The blockbuster movie *Jaws* and hundreds of other exciting productions were made here. Universal offers the public the best-organized and longest (5 hours if you take in everything) studio tour available in Los Angeles. With entertaining attractions and excellent facilities, this is a "must" for every visitor (it's second only to Disneyland in popularity).

Much of the 420-acre lot is viewed from the tram ride, which winds its way through some surprising situations! There is a visit to a star's dressing room, a demonstration of special effects, a look at the "Bionic Testing Center," and a genuinely scary trip through the "King Kong" exhibit. The Entertainment Center presents exciting live shows throughout the day. See a real Western stunt show, incredible performing animals, get spooked in Castle Dracula, visit the World of Woody Woodpecker, or be a star in the Screen Test Comedy Theater and see yourself in an instant replay.

Gift shops and refreshment centers are plentiful. The guides at Universal are all budding actors or comedians—and don't be surprised if Frankenstein or the Incredible Hulk creeps up behind you!

OPEN 7 days. CLOSED Christmas & Thanksgiving. (See also HISTORIC LA, Motion Picture Studios.*)* Tours *Sept-June Mon-Fri 10am-3:30pm, Sat & Sun 9:30am-4pm; July & Aug 7 days 8am-5pm.* Allow a full day.

Van Nuys Airport   **10-A2**
Manager's Office, 16461 Sherman Way, Suite 300, Van Nuys. (818) 785-8828. Informative tours of this busy San Fernando Valley airport are available for groups of ten or more. Not suitable for small children. Reserve in advance.

Whale Watching   **1-G5**
Catalina Cruises, Berths 95/96, end of the Harbor Fwy (11). Whale-watching tours, aboard a 700-passenger ship, are available late winter and early spring. The graceful gray whales can be sighted as they migrate to warmer waters off Mexico to spawn. As many as 80 whales have been counted sounding their way south. Tickets usually available through Ticketron (*see* ENTERTAINMENT, Tickets, Ticket Agencies). Tours last 3 hours. $$

Additional whale-watching tours are available from Fisherman's Wharf Boat Dock, 13759 Fiji Way, Marina del Rey. (310) 822-3625. (**4-G7**) Daily departures. Group rates available. $$

AMUSEMENT PARKS

NOTE: *Although directions are given for those wishing to drive, the following amusement parks are all accessible by bus or organized tours. (See also* Tours: Gray Line Bus Tours.*)*

Disneyland   **1-F8**
1313 S. Harbor Blvd, Anaheim. (213) 626-8605; (714) 999-4000. Whatever your age, a trip to Southern California is not complete without experiencing the magic of Disneyland. Most first-time visitors find it larger, cleaner, less commercial, and more fun than expected.

Disneyland, California's most popular attraction, is a fairy-tale world made up of six "lands": Adventureland, New Orleans Square, Bear Country, Frontierland, Fantasyland, and Tomorrowland. Allow at least one full day and form a plan of action. If possible, avoid school holidays and weekends. Arrive early and enjoy the most popular rides (listed below) before the crowds gather. Ticket booths are located near the main gate. Some areas are closed during winter months for repair or renovation; so to avoid disappointment, call in advance or check listings posted on the ticket booths.

Main Street USA, an American shopping street of the 1890s, forms Disneyland's theme entrance. Baby strollers, camera rentals, and cash checking facilities are available here together with a grand assortment of tempting gift items. Leave shopping until later and walk through to the major attractions. Much of the fun at Disneyland is in anticipating the surprises hidden around every corner. Rides not to be missed are

Pirates of the Caribbean and the Haunted Mansion (New Orleans Square); Space Mountain, Star Tours, and Captain EO (Tomorrowland); Matterhorn Bobsleds (Fantasyland); and Big Thunder Mountain (Frontierland). NOTE: There are minimum height requirements for some of the more hair-raising rides. Small children will especially enjoy Fantasyland (which was completely rebuilt in 1983) and Bear Country.

After sunset on summer evenings the atmosphere changes. Music fills the air, fireworks light up the sky, and the Electric Parade winds its way through the park. One of Disneyland's newest attractions also takes place in the pm. FANTASMIC! is a unique extravaganza, mixing magic, music, 51 live performers, and state-of-the-art special effects, just one of which—the giant mist screens—is so dazzling as to allow film projections to appear on water. The screens are placed in such a way as to permit thousands of people in Frontierland and New Orleans Square to see them (the main stage is in front of the Cider Mill on Tom Sawyer Island). The 22-minute presentation takes place three times an evening during the summer season.

Disneyland has several theme restaurants and dozens of refreshment centers. (Don't expect to find gourmet treats here—fast food is generally the order of the day.) The Blue Bayou restaurant (serving Creole-style food) in New Orleans Square has a patio next to the Pirates of the Caribbean ride—watch boats of excited visitors descend a waterfall to face the pirates! Western-style barbecued food is served outdoors at the Big Thunder Ranch in Frontierland.

NOTE: Disneyland prohibits alcohol within the park. Also, gate attendants have the right to refuse admission to any person they consider unsuitably attired (their judgment is generally conservative so leave the punk T-shirts at home!). No pets are allowed but kennels are available.

Budget approximately $25 per person (for admission and light refreshments). *OPEN mid-June-Oct, 7 days 8am-1am; rest of year Mon-Fri 9am-midnight, Sat & Sun 8am-1am.*

Knott's Berry Farm   1-F7
8039 Beach Blvd, Buena Park. (714) 220-5200; (714) 827-1776. Mrs. Knott opened her farm to the public in 1934 when she started selling her (now famous) chicken dinners to earn a little extra income. The farm is now a grand amusement park—the oldest independent theme park in the world—and it's still run by the family.

Knott's provides 150 acres of fun, featuring 165 different attractions in five main theme areas. The Old West Ghost Town is complete with a gold mine, stage coach, train rides, and an Indian village. Fiesta Village has a Mexican theme and contains the scary Montezuma's Revenge ride. The Roaring Twenties goes back to the days of the Charleston, with big bands and a music hall. The popular Knott's Airfield contains the Sky Jump—a 20-story parachute drop. Camp Snoopy has 30 rides set into a mountain-

like area. The Pacific Pavilion features aquatic shows, including Snoopy's Diving Doggies. Knott's newest attraction is Kingdom of the Dinosaurs, which features 30 animated dinosaurs and an erupting volcano. There are plenty of thrill rides at Knott's, such as the Double-Loop Corkscrew, the Timber Mountain Log Ride, and the Dragon Boat—a huge Viking ship that swings back and forth reaching a 70° arc.

Knott's is popular with teenagers. Evening entertainment throughout the park includes live rock music shows (featuring well-known bands), celebrity shows, Studio K discotheque, dancing, and fireworks displays. Rates for teenagers are lowered after 8pm on weekend evenings. Everyone will enjoy the Knott's Good Time Theater, where ice-show extravaganzas are often presented. (Check local press or call for information.)

There are several fast-food centers and restaurants in the park. The famous Chicken Dinner Restaurant, located in Knott's Marketplace, was one of the first attractions at Knott's when it was still a thriving berry farm in the 1930s—the food here is definitely superior and thoroughly recommended. Admission to Knott's Marketplace, which is separate from the park, is free.

Allow a full day. *OPEN summer Sun-Thurs 9am-midnight, Fri & Sat 9am-1am; winter Sun-Tues 10am-6pm, Fri & Sat 10am-10pm. CLOSED winter Wed & Thurs.*

Raging Waters
111 Raging Waters Dr, San Dimas. (714) 592-6453 or -8181. East on Interstate 10 to Interstate 210 junction. Exit freeway and follow signs. Approximately 20 miles west of LA, this 30-acre aquatic park features incredible water amusements for all ages. Travel at speeds of up to 40 miles an hour on Fast Flumes, a 50-foot water tower; slide down four other water slides or go to the Wave Pool where 24-foot waves crash onto a sandy beach area. There is a special place for children under age 8, called Splash Palace. There are 40 lifeguards on duty to ensure safety. Good refreshment facilities, changing area, gift shop, and complete food service. Season passes available. Lower rates for children and seniors; children under age 4 free. For other splashy locations, see Water Slides listed below. *OPEN late May-mid-Oct, 7 days 10am-9pm* (season may be extended depending on climate; call in advance).

Six Flags Magic Mountain
Magic Mountain Pkwy, Valencia. (805) 255-4111. Drive north on the San Diego Freeway (405), or the Golden State Freeway (5), exit Magic Mountain Freeway. Located 35 miles northwest of Los Angeles, people come here to ride Colossus—the world's highest, scariest, wooden roller coaster—and over 100 other fun rides. There's Freefall, the world's first total free-fall ride; Roaring Rapids, a thrilling white-water raft ride; and Shock Wave, a first-of-its-kind stand-up roller coaster. The Grand Centennial Trainride takes visitors into America's past as it

chugs through countryside filled with buffalo and longhorned cattle. Its final stop is Spillikin Junction, a crafts village where traditional skills are demonstrated. Dolphin and sea lion shows are presented in the Aqua Theatre. Animal Farm has friendly animals for children to pet, and little ones will love Bugs Bunny World—6 acres of fun with scaled-down rides created for kids under 4 feet 8 inches.

Live bands perform daily at Magic Mountain and big-name rock bands are featured each week. There is a large outdoor dance floor where everyone can join in the fun. Fireworks displays are presented nightly.

Fast-food centers are located throughout. The Four Winds restaurant has a full menu and good views across the park.

New attractions are added each year. Magic Mountain is a fun world for all the family.

Allow a full day. Reduced rates for seniors and children under 4 feet. *OPEN end of May-early Sept 7 days; rest of year, weekdays & holidays only. Hours vary—call in advance.*

Universal Studios **9-G5**
100 Universal City Plaza, Universal City. (818) 508-9600 or -5444. Take the Hollywood Freeway (101), exit Lankershim Boulevard, and follow the signs for Universal. Not strictly an amusement park but certainly amusing—for all age groups. Visit the studios and have fun at the entertainment center, which offers an assortment of live shows. Board the tram ride for an entertaining jaunt through movie history, and see movies in the making. (*See* Tours.)

Water Slides
Water playgrounds are the latest, most fun way to stay cool during the long, dry summer months. Raging Waters listed above is highly recommended. The following are among other noteworthy parks near Los Angeles. Season and rates vary—call in advance.

Camelot Golf Land **1-F8**
3200 Carpenter Ave, Anaheim. (714) 630-3343. Four 50-foot-long twisting tubes.

Wild Rivers
8770 Irvine Center Dr, Irvine. (714) 768-9453. Large water park with over 40 water rides and attractions. There are water rapids, five-story slides with twists, a scary ride through a mountain, and a six-lane gradual slide. Several of the wild rides are scaled down for children in a special adventure playground. Showers, lockers, refreshments, gift shop.

WALKING TOURS

It is often said that the best way to see a city is to walk its streets. Angelinos are lost without their cars and the suggestion of walking more than a block may evoke looks of horror. However, the following walking tours would surprise even the

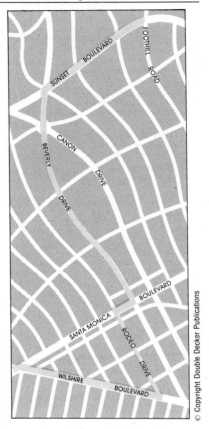

Beverly Hills

most avid auto addict. Each illustrates a different part of LA's character and history without being too exhausting—for feet or wallet. (Please remember to wear comfortable shoes.) Map references in this section indicate suggested starting points. All starting and finishing points are accessible by bus. For free maps and information see TRANSPORTATION & VACATION INFORMATION, Bus Services.

Beverly Hills **5-C7**
Begin with a short walk west on Sunset Boulevard from the corner of Foothill Road. Stroll past fabulous homes to the Beverly Hills Hotel (*see* ACCOMMODATIONS, Beverly Hills, Hotels), where a visit to the Polo Lounge for a champagne cocktail would be quite pleasant. Walk south along Beverly Drive through Beverly Hills' most affluent residential neighborhood and cross Santa Monica Boulevard, diagonally to the right, to enter Rodeo Drive (*see* SHOPPING &

SERVICES, Shopping Centers). Here you may spot famous personalities shopping for clothes or enjoying a low-calorie lunch. Wilshire Boulevard crosses Rodeo Drive where the impressive Beverly Wilshire Hotel (*see* ACCOMMODATIONS, Beverly Hills, Hotels) dominates the landscape. A right turn here will direct you to luxurious department stores and to some popular eateries. Wilshire Boulevard soon meets Santa Monica Boulevard at the Beverly Hilton (*see* ACCOMMODATIONS, Beverly Hills, Hotels). Bus stops are located nearby. (*See also* HISTORIC LA, Main Districts: Beverly Hills.) Tour length approximately 2 miles.

Century City   5-E7
From Santa Monica Boulevard walk south along Century Park East to enter the space-age Century City complex where the twin triangular office towers stand majestic. Walk between these imposing buildings and continue to the Shubert Theatre and the impressive Century Plaza Hotel (*see* ACCOMMODATIONS, Beverly Hills, Hotels). Here, at Avenue of the Stars, turn right. Once past Constellation Boulevard, cross the street to enter the Century Square shopping area, where you'll find restaurants, fine stores, and boutiques. Bus stops are located on Santa Monica Boulevard. (*See also* HISTORIC LA, Main Districts.) Tour length approximately 1 mile.

Exposition Park Area   7-F2
Start at St. Vincent de Paul Roman Catholic Church (*see* HISTORIC LA, Churches) at the

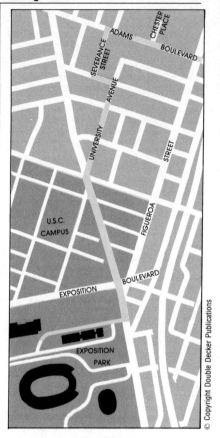

Exposition Park Area

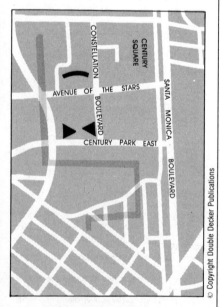

Century City

corner of Adams Boulevard and Figueroa Street. A short walk west to Chester Place will lead to the Doheny Mansion (*see* HISTORIC LA, Buildings & Landmarks). Backtrack to Adams and continue west to Severance Street. Turn left here and continue in a southerly direction through the campus of USC. From University Avenue you will see the impressive Shrine Auditorium (*see* HISTORIC LA, Buildings & Landmarks). The famous University of Southern California boasts impressive and historic buildings and is bordered by Exposition Park. Cross Exposition Boulevard to the Los Angeles County Museum of Natural History and the California State Museum of Science and Industry (*see* MUSEUMS & GALLERIES, Museums, Historic *and* Science). The Exposition Park Rose Garden (*see* PARKS & GARDENS, Botanical Gardens) is perfect for a quiet rest before heading home. Bus stops are located at the corner of Exposition Boulevard and Figueroa Street. Tour length approximately 1¼ miles.

Hollywood Boulevard

Hollywood Boulevard   6-C6

Hollywood Boulevard has become sadly tarnished in recent years. "Ladies of the night" are now a common daytime sight and many local businesses look tired and shabby, but don't be deterred. The street is still colorful and vibrant and certainly worth a visit. Begin at the famous intersection of Hollywood and Vine. The circular landmark just north is the Capitol Records Tower (*see* HISTORIC LA, Buildings & Landmarks) and slightly east is the gorgeous Pantages Theatre (*see* HISTORIC LA, Buildings and Landmarks). Proceed along Hollywood Boulevard in a westerly direction and notice the pink marble stars embedded in the sidewalk. This is the "Walk of Fame" designed to pay tribute to performing artists and talented personalities of yesterday and today. At Ivar Avenue look right to see the Knickerbocker Hotel, once one of Hollywood's finest. It was the temporary home of Bette Davis, Gloria Swanson, and Frank Sinatra. Where Ivar Avenue continues on the south side of Hollywood Boulevard is the USO (United Service Organization). Farther along the boulevard is the Pacific Theater, where Carol Burnett once worked as an usherette. You will soon reach Misses Janes School (No. 6541) where the Janes sisters taught child stars and stars' children in the 1920s

and 1930s. Across the street one block ahead is Frederick's of Hollywood, famous for exotic lingerie. Opposite is Musso & Frank's Grill (*see* RESTAURANTS, Hollywood & Wilshire District, Continental), frequented by famous personalities, who in the past included W. C. Fields, Ernest Hemingway, and Steve McQueen. One block farther, look across to the decorative Egyptian Theatre (*see* HISTORIC LA, Buildings & Landmarks). Walk on to the Hollywood Wax Museum (*see* MUSEUMS & GALLERIES, Museums, Entertainment Industry). Cross Highland Avenue and continue to Mann's Chinese Theatre (*see* HISTORIC LA, Buildings & Landmarks), where you can match footprints with the stars. A little farther, at the corner of Sycamore Avenue, is C. C. Brown's Ice Cream Parlor, unchanged since 1929 and frequented by Bob Hope, Dinah Shore, and Perry Como. In the 1930s, Brown's was also a favorite of Mary Pickford and Harold Lloyd. The Roosevelt Hotel opposite was Hollywood's most elegant hotel in the 1920s and 1930s, and has since entertained the likes of Marilyn Monroe, Gary Cooper, Rudy Vallee, and Joan Crawford. It is rumored that the ghost of a bugle-playing Montgomery Clift can sometimes be heard in the early morning hours. Bus stops are located all along Hollywood Boulevard. (*See also* HISTORIC LA, Main Districts: Hollywood.) Tour length approximately 1 mile.

The Plaza & Chinatown   7-C5

Union Station (*see* HISTORIC LA, Buildings & Landmarks) is an interesting starting point for a tour of LA's historic birthplace. From the station, cross Alameda Street and walk to Olvera Street (*see* Tours: Olvera Street) for bargains and refreshments. Visit the Avila Adobe (*see* HISTORIC LA, Buildings & Landmarks), and continue through to the Plaza, which is bordered by

The Plaza & Chinatown

Main Street. The nearby Pico House, Merced Theater, Old Plaza Firehouse (see HISTORIC LA, Buildings & Landmarks), and Plaza Church (see HISTORIC LA, Churches) are within El Pueblo State Historic Park. These preserved buildings reflect the city's multiethnic origins. Proceed northward along Main Street to Macy Street and turn left to Spring Street. Turn right into the area known as China City, which was created in the 1930s as a tourist attraction. Turn left on Ord Street and finally right on Broadway to reach New Chinatown. Gin Ling Way forms the entrance to Chinatown, a collection of authentic shops and restaurants. The RTD MiniBus service covers this whole area. (See also HISTORIC LA, Main Districts: Chinatown and Downtown.) Tour length approximately 1 mile.

Sunset Strip   6-C2

Near the corner of Crescent Heights on Sunset Boulevard is the site of Schwab's Pharmacy, a nostalgic starting point for a tour of the Sunset Strip. Frequented by movie stars for decades, Schwab's lunch counter fed many famous faces, some of whom lived across the street at the Garden of Allah (now Great Western Savings). Ex-Garden of Allah residents include David Niven, Humphrey Bogart, Errol Flynn, and F. Scott Fitzgerald. Countless others stayed at the nearby Chateau Marmont (see ACCOMMODATIONS, Hollywood, Hotels), which still caters to celebrities. Look for today's screen idols in the limousines that come and go. Continue west to the Comedy Store (see NIGHTLIFE, Comedy & Magic). Previously Ciro's nightclub, it was popular with Hollywood's top stars. Across the street up ahead is Chez Denis, established by Dean Martin, who operated the club as Dino's. This was the site for the old TV series "77 Sunset Strip." Past La Cienega Boulevard is Sunset Plaza. Two restaurants here, Le Dome (see RESTAURANTS, Hollywood & Wilshire District, French) and Cyrano are frequented by famous celebrities. Where Sunset meets Holloway Drive the colorful facade of Tower Records (see SHOPPING & SERVICES, Specialty Shopping, Records) advertises the latest in popular music. Famous rock stars can often be seen browsing the aisles. Around the next bend a famous music venue, The Whiskey, once hosted rock stars from Little Richard to the Rolling Stones. Walk on to the Roxy. Notice the huge billboards that tower over the street. The pop music industry has two more famous showcases nearby, the Rainbow (see NIGHTLIFE, Discos & Dance Clubs) and Gazzari's (see NIGHTLIFE, Rock). Bus stops are located nearby. Tour length approximately 1¼ miles.

Venice & Ocean Front Walk   4-D3

Begin in Santa Monica with a stroll along the pier (see KIDS' LA, Children's Entertainment). The carousel used in the movie The Sting, a fortune teller, and amusement arcades provide family fun. At the foot of the pier is Ocean Front Walk. Head south past the Pritikin Longevity Center and alongside wide sandy beaches to Ocean

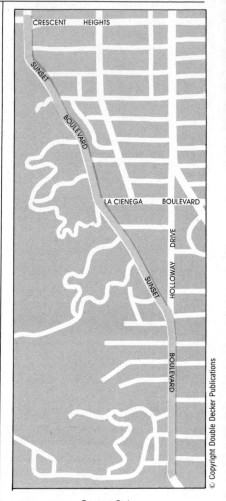

Sunset Strip

Park. Lick Pier and Ocean Park Pier once jutted out from this beach and were great centers of entertainment. The big bands of Jimmy Dorsey and Lawrence Welk played to fashionable socialites here in the 1930s. Heritage Square (see HISTORIC LA, Buildings & Landmarks) and Main Street (see SHOPPING & SERVICES, Shopping Centers) are a short detour inland. At Rose Avenue, Venice begins to take shape. On weekends, Ocean Front Walk has a fairground atmosphere (see HISTORIC LA, Main Districts: Beach Cities). No. 625 Ocean Front Walk was once owned by actor Peter Lawford. His former brother-in-law President Kennedy stayed here on several occasions. No. 705 was the final

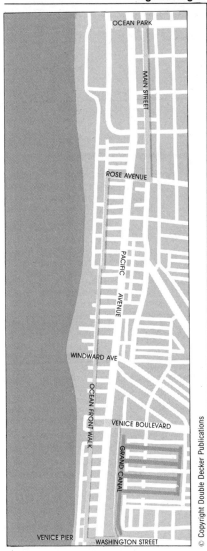

Venice & Ocean Front Walk

bridges. Grand Canal leads to Venice Boulevard. Turn left to return to the beach, or take a bus back to Santa Monica Pier from Pacific Avenue. Tour length approximately 2½ miles.

Vine Street   **6-C6**

The Hollywood Plaza Hotel, now a retirement community, stands near the renowned intersection of Hollywood and Vine. The hotel was a gathering place for the likes of Bing Crosby and Bob Hope. Clara Bow once owned the adjoining bar, which she named the It Room. Across the street is the site of the old Brown Derby. W. C. Fields often sat at the bar here and (so the story goes) would frequently fall off his stool. Walk south past the James A. Doolittle Theatre (*see* ENTERTAINMENT, Theater) to Selma Avenue. The American Savings and Loan building on the corner was once the site of Lasky Studios and a plaque commemorates the "Birthplace of Motion Pictures." Lasky went on to co-found Paramount Pictures (*see* HISTORIC LA, Motion Picture Studios). Cross Selma to the Celebrity Theater, home of the "Merv Griffin Show," then walk to Sunset Boulevard. Where Home Savings now stands was the famous NBC Radio building. The Aquarius Theatre, across on Sunset Boulevard, was once a notorious nightspot. Back on Vine Street, continue south to the ABC Theatre, famous for the "Steve Allen Show." The Hollywood Ranch Market, a little farther along, has served many a famous customer in its day. Santa Monica Boulevard is a short distance from here, and bus service is frequent. Tour length approximately ¾ mile.

home of Douglas Fairbanks, Sr. He died of a heart attack in this house in 1939. Continue to Windward Avenue and turn left toward Pacific Avenue. On the left a huge mural shows a mirror image of the street, and the columned arcades are a reminder of Venice's former glory. Backtrack to Ocean Front Walk and continue south to Venice Pier. Turn left on Washington Street and walk to Grand Canal. Here, a narrow pathway to the left allows you to enjoy a little of old Venice, with pretty cottages, wild ducks, and arched

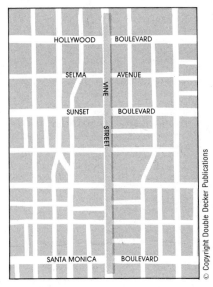

Vine Street

BICYCLE TRAILS

A desire for physical fitness has encouraged thousands of Californians to take to the bike paths in recent years. Bicycle rentals are usually inexpensive; see the Yellow Pages for bike rental nearest you. Map references in this section indicate suggested starting points. See also SPORTS & RECREATION, Sporting Activities, Bicycling.

Arcadia Trail   **1-B6**
A well-marked bikeway in the San Gabriel Valley that takes in the Los Angeles State and County Arboretum (*see* PARKS & GARDENS, Botanical Gardens) and Santa Anita racetrack (*see* SPORTS & RECREATION, Sporting Activities, Horse Racing). Suggesting starting point: Huntington Drive and Baldwin Avenue, Arcadia.

Beach Bike Path   **4-D3**
Stretching south from Sorrento Beach (below Pacific Palisades) to Palos Verdes Estates, this path winds along the beach following the coastline. It gets crowded on summer weekends, especially between Santa Monica and Marina del Rey. Suggested starting point: Santa Monica Pier.

Burbank Trail   **1-B4**
A marked bike path starts at the intersection of Alameda Avenue and Mariposa Street. Enjoy mountain views, local parks, and the NBC and Disney studios.

Griffith Park   **1-B5**
An interesting, although energetic, ride along Griffith Park Drive to Travel Town (*see* MUSEUMS & GALLERIES, Museums, Transportation), then along Zoo Drive to the Los Angeles Zoo (*see* PARKS & GARDENS, Zoos & Aquariums) and back through the golf course to the ranger station. Suggested starting point: Ranger Station, Crystal Springs Drive.

Los Angeles River Trail   **1-E5**
A flat, traffic-free ride to Long Beach. Peaceful cycling on well-paved paths, shared with the occasional equestrian. Suggested starting point: Long Beach Freeway and Rosecrans Boulevard, Compton.

Kenneth Newell Bikeway   **8-A1**
Scenic bike path following the Arroyo Seco Canyon and circling the Rose Bowl. Suggested starting point: Brookside Golf Course, Pasadena.

Newport Beach Trails
Although Newport's beach bike path is popular, there is another marked trail along the bluffs. Suggested starting point: Newport Dunes Aquatic Park, Backbay Drive, Newport Beach.

San Gabriel River Trail   **1-D7**
A marked path follows the river from Whittier to Long Beach, through Santa Fe Springs. Bicyclists and equestrians only. Suggested starting point: 3700 block, San Gabriel River Parkway, Whittier.

San Vicente   **5-G3**
Join the joggers on a trip to the beach through pleasant residential areas. Downhill all the way (there). Suggested starting point: San Vicente Boulevard and Wilshire Boulevard, Westwood.

Santa Ana River Trail   **1-F8**
From Disneyland to the Pacific along a well-marked, traffic-free bikeway. Suggested starting point: Katella Avenue, Anaheim.

Whittier Narrows Recreation Area
A beautiful recreation area with many points of interest. Suggested starting point: Durfee Road parking lot, Whittier. (*See* also PARKS & GARDENS, Parks.)

DAY TRIPS

Directions and distances in this section are from central Los Angeles. NOTE: *Temperatures can drop sharply in mountain areas, so take appropriate clothing—especially in winter. When making time estimates, remember that curving mountain roads take longer to negotiate. Also, in winter snow chains may be required (for road conditions in mountain areas call the U.S. Forest Service Information Center, [818] 574-5200, for the Angeles National Forest and [714] 383-5588 for the San Bernardino National Forest). It is safe to estimate covering 50 miles per hour on freeways. Rest areas, food outlets, and gas stations are plentiful along California's freeways, but be sure to "top-up" before entering a wilderness area. Many of the following locations can be reached by bus. (See also Tours: Gray Line Bus Tours and Weekend Trips.)*

Big Bear
Accommodations (24-hour service) (714) 866-5877 or -4601. The Pacific Crest National Scenic Trail passes through this district of the San Bernardino National Forest. With their pine forests, mountain trails, campgrounds, cabins, picnic facilities, and winter ski resorts, Lake Arrowhead and Big Bear Lake are two of the most popular recreational areas near Los Angeles.

Big Bear's Goldmine Recreation Area has the area's longest and highest chairlift, which is open during summer for a 20-minute scenic trip rising to 8,600 feet. Moonridge Animal Park (*OPEN 7 days 8am-4pm*) is filled with local wildlife, including the once abundant black bear—almost wiped out of these mountains by miners and hunters. The area also has facilities for boating, fishing, skating, horseback riding, and tennis. A drive up to Big Bear via the Rim of the World Highway affords splendid views of local mountain ranges. Take Interstate 10 east to Interstate 15E (this is 15 miles past Interstate 15); exit Sierra Way leading to California Highway 18 (Waterman Canyon), which winds up the mountain to Crestline, Running Springs, and Big Bear Lake. Approximately 200 miles round-trip.

Castaic Lake
(805) 257-4050. A scenic setting in Angeles National Forest. This is the main reservoir for the California Water Project and provides recreational facilities within a short distance of the

city. The large lake has waterskiing and fishing access and a smaller lake is reserved for sailing and rowing; there is a roped-off area for swimmers. Take Interstate 5 north to the Lake Hughes exit. Approximately 90 miles round-trip.

Catalina Island
(310) 510-2500. Travel by sea or air from the Catalina Terminals in Long Beach and San Pedro (*see* TRANSPORTATION & VACATION INFORMATION, Boat Services). Catalina is a picturesque island with many points of interest, including the famous Avalon Casino (*see* HISTORIC LA, Buildings & Landmarks), wild buffalo, water sports, and botanical gardens. Inland excursions are available from Avalon. A 66-mile inland tour takes visitors to Pirate's Cove and Wrigley's El Rancho Escondido, where Arabian horses are still raised. The 1921 Wrigley mansion has been converted into a luxury hotel—The Inn on Mount Ada (for reservations, call 510-2030). Boat excursions from Catalina include a flying-fish tour or a cruise in a glass-bottom boat. (*See also* HISTORIC LA, Main Districts: Beach Cities.)

Dana Point
(714) 496-1555. Dana Point was once the major port between Santa Barbara and San Diego. Today it is a quiet harbor town where the emphasis is on relaxation, sailing, swimming, shopping, and picnicking. Take Interstate 5 south to Pacific Coast Highway (Camino Las Ramblas) and follow the signs for Dana Point. Approximately 110 miles round-trip.

Del Mar
In addition to its popular racetrack, Del Mar boasts picturesque beaches, interesting shops, and fine restaurants. A train journey from Los Angeles takes 2 hours each way and is a pleasant alternative to driving. Amtrak, (213) 624-0171, has eight departures daily to Del Mar. By road, take Interstate 5 south to Via del la Valle. Approximately 196 miles round-trip.

Desert Hot Springs
(619) 329-6403. A 20-minute drive from Palm Springs, Desert Hot Springs is a rapidly growing desert town with six mineral-water spas open to the public. For golfers, the Lakes Country Club has a fine 18-hole course, and for historians, Cabot Yerxa's Old Indian Pueblo Museum shows how one man and his mule started the whole thing. Take Interstate 10 east to the Palm Drive/ Desert Hot Springs exit. Approximately 220 miles round-trip.

Devil's Punchbowl
At a point where the San Andreas Fault runs through the San Gabriel Mountains, the rocks have been turned and pounded for millions of years. The resulting formations are startling evidence of nature's power. There are pleasant picnic grounds and an easy hiking trail, suitable for all ages. The elevation is 4,750 feet and the temperature generally cool. Take Interstate 5 north to California Highway 14; northeast to Highway 138—Pearblossom; south to 131st Street. Follow

Punchbowl signs from there. Approximately 140 miles round-trip.

Fort Tejon
(805) 248-6692. Founded in 1854, Fort Tejon had the only camel cavalry in the U.S. Today, mock battles, with authentically dressed troops firing muzzle-loading cannons, are staged the third Sunday of each month from April to October. The fort is located at the edge of the Tehachapi Mountains. Take Interstate 5 north to Fort Tejon. Approximately 150 miles round-trip. (*See also* Mount Pinos *below*.)

Glen Ivy Hot Springs
25000 Glen Ivy Rd, Corona. (714) 277-3529. Fax (714) 277-8700. A day-use hot springs resort (near Lake Elsinore) that is better than most in Palm Springs. A therapeutic pool, whirlpools, saunas, mud pool, children's pool, massage, blanket wraps, sunning decks, full-size swimming pool, and best of all a friendly, unpretentious staff. The pools and hot tubs have been thoughtfully designed in a garden setting amid citrus orchards and swaying palm trees. The spa was established in 1890 and has maintained its country charm. Good restaurant with wholesome food, beer, and wine. Picnic facilities. Take Interstate 5 south to California Highway 91; east to Interstate 15; south 8 miles to the Temescal/Glen Ivy exit—turn right, hot springs are 1½ miles ahead. (*See also* Lake Elsinore *below*.) Approximately 120 miles round-trip.

Idyllwild
(714) 659-3259. Reminiscent of a Swiss mountain paradise, Idyllwild has remained unspoiled since the Cahuilla Indians used it as a favorite hunting ground and as a retreat from the hot desert below. Hiking and artistic pursuits are the most popular activities. Take Interstate 10 east to Banning; California Highway 243 southeast to the village. Approximately 225 miles round-trip.

Joshua Tree
This unusual desert area was made a National Monument in 1936 and is home to many species of wildlife, including reptiles, amphibians, birds, and desert animals. Wildflowers and cacti cover the area and bloom during spring and early summer, when the desert is at its most beautiful. There is a visitors center at the monument— (619) 367-7511. Take Interstate 10 east to California Highway 62; north to Joshua Tree and Twenty-nine Palms. Approximately 280 miles round-trip. Note: Bring a canteen or bottles of water.

Julian
(619) 765-1857. A historic gold-rush town, now the apple capital of San Diego County. Julian was founded in 1870 and still has its original Town Hall and drugstore, complete with soda fountain. The beautifully restored Julian Hotel, originally owned by two freed slaves, shows General Grant on its register. Two local gold mines are open to the public and a Frontier Museum is located in the old blacksmith's shop. Take Interstate 5 south to California Highway 78;

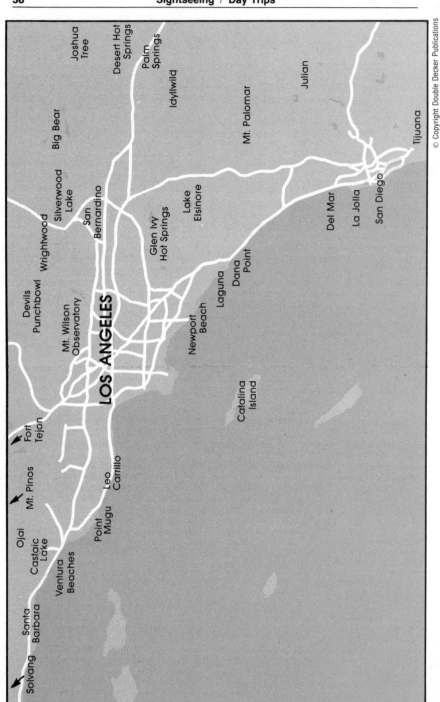

Day Trips

east to Julian. Approximately 290 miles round-trip.

Laguna
(714) 494-1018. This scenic, art lover's paradise is beautiful year-round but is especially interesting during February and July when the winter and summer arts festivals are held (see ANNUAL EVENTS, Calendar, February and July). Laguna welcomes visitors and caters to their needs with unusual shopping areas, oceanfront restaurants, and delightful beaches. Take Interstates 5 or 405 south to California Highway 133, east to Laguna (Laguna Canyon Road). Approximately 110 miles round-trip.

La Jolla
(619) 454-1444. La Jolla's stretch of rugged coastline includes the Torrey Pines State Reserve, an 887-acre protected wilderness area, outstanding in natural beauty and interest. La Jolla (pronounced "la-hoya"; derived from the Spanish joya, meaning jewel) is popular with surfers, hang gliders, swimmers, and picnickers. The cliff-top Torrey Pines Municipal Golf Course hosts an annual celebrity Open in February. The famous Scripps Institute of Oceanography is located just north of the town and is open daily. Admission free. At Scripps Pier, visitors get a diver's view of the La Jolla Underwater Park via underwater TV cameras. For information on Torrey Pines State Reserve, call (619) 755-2063. Take Interstate 5 south to La Jolla Village Drive. Approximately 200 miles round-trip.

Lake Elsinore
(714) 674-2577. A popular inland resort within easy reach of LA and San Diego. Recreational facilities at Lake Elsinore include camping, boating (usually speed boats), windsurfing, waterskiing, and even sport parachuting. Glen Ivy Hot Springs (see above) is nearby. Two routes from Los Angeles may be taken: either Interstate 10 east to Interstate 15 south, or the coast/mountain route of Interstate 5 south to California Highway 74 (Ortega Highway) east to Lake Elsinore. Approximately 180 miles round-trip.

Leo Carrillo
(818) 706-1310. A beach area of unusual beauty, Leo Carrillo is popular with divers, surfers, and fishermen. Good kelp beds attract sea life and wild birds. There are campgrounds and nature trails. Take Interstate 10 west to Pacific Coast Highway; north to Leo Carrillo. Approximately 55 miles round-trip.

Mount Palomar Observatory
(619) 742-2119. In the heart of the old Palo Indian country, Mount Palomar rises to 6,126 feet. Atop the mountain is a giant telescope 200 inches in diameter and 12 stories high. A gallery and exhibit hall are open to the public. Take Interstate 5 to Oceanside; California Highway 76 east; follow signs to observatory. Approximately 225 miles round-trip.

Mount Pinos
Mount Pinos (Pine Mountain) is the highest point in the Los Padres National Forest. It is a popular recreation area with campgrounds, hundreds of hiking trails, and an abundance of wildlife. During winter, chains are usually required—these can be rented at the foot of the mountain in the town of Frazier Park. Take Interstate 5 north to the Frazier Park exit. Approximately 140 miles round-trip. (See also Fort Tejon above.)

Mount Wilson Observatory
A beautiful mountain drive of approximately 60 miles round-trip (see Viewpoints & Scenic Drives, Viewpoints).

Newport Beach
(714) 644-8211. The harbor here is crammed with every type of sailing craft imaginable and is a haven for pleasure-boat enthusiasts. Craft may be rented and there is a ferry service to nearby Balboa Island, with its landmark Victorian pavilion and newly renovated Fun Zone amusement park. Newport is a fashionable beach town with wealthy residents and expensive homes. It is a shopper's paradise and has some excellent restaurants with seafood an obvious specialty. A short drive south, along a scenic section of Pacific Coast Highway, leads to the particularly beautiful Corona del Mar State Beach. Take Interstate 5 or 405 south to California Highway 55; southwest to Newport Beach. Approximately 80 miles round-trip.

Ojai
(805) 646-8126. The beautiful Ojai Valley, covered in orange groves, is home to many artists, and every Sunday a dozen or so will gather in the center of the small town of Ojai to show and sell their work. The valley was once the territory of the peaceful Chumash Indians. Ojai (pronounced "oh-hi") is Chumash for "the nest." Two annual music festivals, featuring classical music and jazz, are held in June and August, and a Shakespeare festival is presented around the summer solstice. The road from Interstate 5 to Ojai is especially picturesque as it passes through the Valencia orange groves. The oranges are harvested from April to November. Take Interstate 5 to Castaic Junction; California Highway 150 north of Ojai. Approximately 160 miles round-trip.

Orange Harvests
Between May and November the Valencia oranges are harvested along the valleys of the Santa Clara River. (Follow directions to Ojai, above.) Navel oranges are harvested from November to April and the most attractive groves are around East Highlands. Take Interstate 10 east to Redlands; Orange Avenue north to 3rd Street and East Highlands. Approximately 140 miles round-trip.

Palm Springs Aerial Tramway
(619) 325-1391. Aside from the obvious attractions of sunshine, spas, resort hotels, and affluence, Palm Springs has a family attraction that offers "the ride of your life." The Aerial Tramway climbs 8,516 feet in 18 minutes to Long Valley on Mount San Jacinto. Here, mule rides are available in summer and skiing is popular in winter. There is also an alpine restaurant—Ride 'n Dine

tickets, which include tram fare, may be purchased at the base. Views from the mountain are magnificent and there are miles of hiking trails. NOTE: Temperatures from the hot desert floor to the summit can drop 40°. Take Interstate 10 east to California Highway 111; southeast to the Tramway sign. Approximately 210 miles round-trip. (*See also* Weekend Trips: Palm Springs.)

Point Mugu State Park
(818) 706-1310. Point Mugu State Park sits on the western edge of the Santa Monica Mountains and is bordered by the Pacific Ocean. The Chumash Indians lived here for 6,000 years and named the area Muwu, meaning "beach." Inland nature trails lead to areas of unspoiled natural beauty, filled with a variety of wildlife. Camping (there are two campgrounds), hiking, swimming, and fishing are favorite pastimes. Take Interstate 10 west to Pacific Coast Highway, then north to Point Mugu. Approximately 80 miles round-trip.

San Bernardino County Regional Parks
Eleven regional parks offer every possible recreational facility in San Bernardino County, the largest county in the U.S. Parks close to Los Angeles are: Prado (near Chino), Cucamungi Guasti (near Ontario), Glen Helen (near San Bernardino), and Mojave River Forks (near Lake Silverwood). For information, call the Regional Parks Department, (714) 387-2594.

San Diego
The first permanent Spanish settlement on California's coast was San Diego, and the city's "Old Town" traces that history. San Diego is full of historical and cultural interests with added attractions such as its world-famous zoo, Sea World, the Wild Animal Park, and Cabrillo National Monument. Balboa Park contains excellent museums, the zoo, and the Old Globe Shakespeare Theatre. San Diego Bay is home to a large portion of the U.S. Navy. The harbor is an attraction in itself, with the resort area of Seaport Village, historic ships (which are open to visitors), and sightseeing cruises. Amtrak ([213] 624-0171) has train services to San Diego. By road take Interstate 5 south; follow the Zoo-Museum signs from the freeway. Approximately 250 miles round-trip.

Santa Barbara
A hundred miles north of Los Angeles the Santa Ynez mountains rise sharply from the Pacific Ocean. The attractive Spanish-style community of Santa Barbara is built on sheltered foothills and overlooks a scenic yacht harbor. The town is full of color and history. Its famous mission has been in the hands of Franciscan padres since 1786, and the County Courthouse has been rated the most beautiful public building in North America. The recently renovated Stearns Wharf invites visitors to dine on fresh seafood or shop for souvenirs. Unspoiled beaches, good restaurants, cozy accommodations, and a quiet, calming atmosphere make this a popular getaway for Angelinos. Of the fairs and festivals held year-

Sea World, San Diego

round, the celebration of Old Spanish Days (in August) is the most spectacular. The scenic coastal drive to Santa Barbara is especially beautiful. The Chamber of Commerce provides a complete schedule of events, for information, call (805) 965-3021. Take Interstate 10 west to Pacific Coast Highway; north to Santa Barbara. Or take California Highway 101 west to Ventura, then north to Santa Barbara. Approximately 200 miles round-trip.

Silverwood Lake
(619) 389-2281. This man-made lake has created a new habitat for thousands of wild birds. It is stocked with fish and facilities are provided for boating, swimming, and fishing, with a separate area for camping and waterskiing. Located in the San Bernardino National Forest, the elevation at Lake Silverwood is 3,378 feet. Take Interstate 10 east to Interstate 15, then north to California Highway 138 and east to the lake. Approximately 180 miles round-trip.

Solvang
(805) 688-3317. Denmark in the heart of Santa Ynez Valley. Founded in 1911 by Danish immi-

grants, Solvang contains a unique collection of shops, restaurants, bakeries, and authentic provincial architecture that is almost more Danish than Denmark itself. The picturesque countryside has been described as the Shangri-La of the West. During recent years, vineyards have been established and the area has developed into a notable wine-producing region. The neighboring communities of Buellton (famous for its pea soup) and Ballard are also worth a visit. Take Interstate 5 north to California Highway 101, then west to Ventura, through Santa Barbara to Buellton and east on California Highway 246 to Solvang. Approximately 280 miles round-trip.

Tijuana
For a taste of Mexico, Tijuana, commercial though it might be, is within easy reach. The city is quite a culture shock from neighboring San Diego. Lack of housing, poor sanitation, and poverty are evident to the visitor. It is nevertheless a colorful, bustling, duty-free marketplace packed with bargains for souvenir hunters, providing they remember that it is customary to barter! A facelift has transformed a nine-block stretch of the main thoroughfare into a tree-lined shopping plaza where buses and taxis are banned. The old river basin has been reclaimed and a brand-new shopping center built over it. There is also a cultural center with a theater, concert hall, and museum as well as lively nightlife popular with students and U.S. Navy personnel. People driving to Tijuana should remember to buy Mexican auto insurance (available for one day or longer). Call the Tijuana Visitors Bureau in San Diego for information, (800) 522-1516. Newcomers may find a Gray Line Bus Tour (*see* Tours) the best way to visit Tijuana. By road take Interstate 5 south through San Diego. Approximately 275 miles round-trip. Note: Remember to carry U.S. identification or a valid passport.

Tule Elk State Reserve
(805) 765-5004. This surviving herd of the rare California Tule Elk can be seen most frequently between April and October. A viewing area with picnic facilities is provided. Take Interstate 5 north to Stockdale Highway exit, then west on Morris Road and follow Elk Reserve signs. Approximately 240 miles round-trip.

Ventura State Beaches
(805) 654-4611. Emma Wood, McGrath, and San Buena Ventura form Ventura County's beach playgrounds. Sand dunes and offshore rocks make the area a haven for wild birds. Extensive camping facilities. Activities include fishing, surfing, and hiking. Take Interstate 5 north to California Highway 101, then west to Ventura. Or take the coastal route: Interstate 10 west to Pacific Coast Highway, then north past Oxnard. Approximately 110 miles round-trip.

Wild Flowers
Palm Springs, Joshua Tree, Idyllwild—all mentioned in this chapter—are excellent places to see wildflowers during spring, but it is the Antelope Valley that has the most breathtaking views. The Wildflower Information Center, 44811 Sierra Highway, Lancaster, opens for the season at the beginning of April. For information, call (805) 724-1180 or (805) 948-4518. Take Interstate 5 north to California Highway 14, then northeast to Lancaster. Approximately 100 miles round-trip.

Closer to home, wildflowers can be seen at Malibu Creek State Park and Placerita Canyon Park (*see* PARKS & GARDENS, Nature Centers & Trails).

Wrightwood
(619) 249-4320. Best known for winter sports facilities at Mountain High, this interesting mountain town is lovely during summer, when hiking, backpacking, fishing, and horseback riding are favorite pastimes. Take Interstate 5 north to California Highway 14, then northeast to Highway 138 Palmdale, and east through Pearblossom to the Wrightwood exit. Approximately 150 miles round-trip.

WEEKEND TRIPS

Los Angeles is a perfect base from which to make trips to mountain resorts, lakes, rivers, the desert, beautiful beaches, and to a variety of towns of scenic and historic interest. Most of the following locations have camping facilities in addition to hotel/motel accommodations. Book in advance for peak summer months. For campground reservations see ACCOMMODATIONS, Campgrounds & RV Parks. For travel tips see also Day Trips.

Anza-Borrego
This is the nation's largest state park, covering nearly half a million acres of scenic desert. At its center is the friendly town of Borrego Springs. Surrounded by colorful mountains, this desert park has 700 miles of trails bordered by cacti and over 600 species of flowering plants. Each weekend, park rangers guide special tours (either by car or on foot). Campsite spaces may be reserved in advance (*see* ACCOMMODATIONS, Budget Accommodations). For other accommodations, call (619) 767-5555. Approximately 360 miles round-trip.

Baja California
Southern Californians often take a trip to Baja for sunshine, sport, and relaxation, which they can enjoy in an unhurried Latin atmosphere. Ensenada, 65 miles south of Tijuana, is a popular fishing resort. Mexicali, although a border town, is not a tourist trap and is perhaps more typical of Mexico. Baja has dozens of unspoiled beaches from which to swim, dive, or fish. The best beaches are around the Sea of Cortez. Remember that laws are stricter south of the border, but crime is more prevalent. Do not take unnecessary valuables and never leave vehicles unlocked. For information, call (800) 522-1516; also the Mexico Tourist Office (619) 231-8414. Approximately 400 to 600 miles round-trip, de-

pending on destination. The tip of Baja—Cabo San Lucas—is 1,300 miles from Los Angeles. (*See also* Day Trips: Tijuana.)

Big Sur
See Highway 1 (*below*).

Calico
(619) 254-2122. The old ghost town of Calico is now a regional park. In 1882 a big silver strike attracted prospectors, who numbered 3,500 by 1885. When silver prices dropped in the 1890s, the town declined. Several old buildings have now been restored and the Maggie Mine is open to the public. The town has restaurants, shops, and a campground. Nearest lodgings are in Barstow (7 miles away). Approximately 300 miles round-trip.

Carmel
See Highway 1 (*below*).

Colorado River
The mighty Colorado forms a natural boundary between California and Arizona. Low desert regions edged by mountains make this whole border popular with vacationers. Boating, fishing, and waterskiing are favorite pastimes, especially at Parker Dam and Lake Havasu, two major recreational areas. Boat and equipment rentals are available. Lake Havasu is now home to London Bridge, which was shipped (in pieces) 10,000 miles from England's River Thames to this unusual desert setting where it was meticulously reassembled. An "English" village adds atmosphere. Approximately 650 miles round-trip.

Death Valley
Despite its name, this is one of America's most popular national monuments. Covering 3,000 square miles, Death Valley's topography—with sand dunes, salt flats, harsh peaks, and volcanic craters—is amazing. It also contains the lowest area in the Western Hemisphere, 282 feet below sea level (near Badwater). In sharp contrast, nearby Telescope Peak rises 11,000 feet above sea level. Summertime temperatures can be unbearably hot. The region obtained its unenviable name from an early pioneer who upon leaving the area, turned and said, "Good-bye, death valley," in remembrance of a friend who died along the way. Today, the valley may be enjoyed at leisure and accommodations are available in Furnace Creek and Stove Pipe Wells. A remarkable attraction is Scotty's Castle, an eccentric 1920s ranch. For information, call the Death Valley Visitor Center (619) 786-2331. Approximately 600 miles round-trip.

Grand Canyon
Although too far for a weekend drive from Los Angeles, visitors going to Nevada may wish to visit America's greatest natural wonder by driving from the world's greatest unnatural wonder, Las Vegas! (Tours and excursions are available from Las Vegas.) Approximately 550 miles round-trip from Las Vegas.

Highway 1
California's Highway 1, from San Luis Obispo north to San Francisco, passes through some of the state's most breathtakingly beautiful areas. Spring and autumn are the best times to enjoy the scenic splendor and avoid summer mists and winter rains farther north. Traveling northwest from San Luis Obispo, Highway 1 meets the ocean at Morro Bay, the center of California's abalone industry. Morro Rock, rising 576 feet from the ocean, is one of several volcanic outcroppings in the area. The road through the picturesque towns of Cayucos and Cambria to San Simeon was a familiar route to many of Hollywood's stars during the 1930s. High on a hill above San Simeon, millionaire William Randolph Hearst built a fabulous castle where he entertained celebrities in grand fashion. North of Hearst Castle lies Jade Cove, which contains unknown quantities of semiprecious stones beneath dangerous bluffs and strong currents. Building the road through this stretch of rugged coastline was a remarkable feat of engineering. It took 18 years to build, using convict labor. Lucia is a good resting point along sparsely populated Highway 1. Lodgings, food, and gas are available.

The scenery becomes even more beautiful as the highway enters Big Sur, with its artistic community and attractive resorts. Sea lions, sea otters, and even whales (in early spring) are a common sight along this stretch, where the California Redwoods meet the ocean. On to Point Lobos, where gnarled, sturdy cypress trees jut out from the cliff tops, silhouetting themselves against the sunset. Sea lions cluster and call from the rocks off this headland, which was named after them (Los Lobos del Mar means "Sea Wolves"). Robert Louis Stevenson called Point Lobos, now a nature preserve buzzing with wildlife, "the most beautiful meeting of land and sea." The enchanting community of Carmel-by-the-Sea lies ahead. It is easy to see why this area became so popular with artists and writers and more recently with golfers. The world-famous Pebble Beach is located along 17 Mile Drive, between Carmel and Monterey. A golfer's paradise, the Monterey Peninsula is known as the Circle of Enchantment. Monterey is full of history. The Old Fisherman's Wharf and Cannery Row attract thousands of visitors. The city was the first capital of California and the original site of the Carmel Mission, founded in 1770. Approximately 1,100 miles round-trip to Monterey (those traveling the full distance to Monterey may wish to return via California Highway 101). (*See also* TRANSPORTATION & VACATION INFORMATION, Trains.)

Lake Tahoe
Beautiful Lake Tahoe lies 80 miles northeast of Sacramento and spans the California-Nevada border. If time is limited to two or three days, it is advisable to travel by air from Los Angeles. Some of the world's best snow skiing can be enjoyed at Lake Tahoe's resorts during winter and early spring. In the summer, the lake is perfect for boating, fishing, and camping. Luxurious hotels with glittering casinos and lavish

dinner theaters featuring world-famous stars make Tahoe an interesting alternative to Las Vegas. The South Lake Tahoe Visitors Bureau provides an excellent information package covering accommodations, services, entertainment, and transportation. For information, call (916) 544-0300. Approximately 1,100 miles round-trip.

Las Vegas

Las Vegas is the ultimate tourist attraction. A fantasyland in the desert, as glittery and glamorous as every visitor had hoped. Accommodations and restaurants are surprisingly inexpensive, especially midweek. (It is advisable to book in advance for weekend reservations.) Stage shows are unsurpassed for quality, entertainment, and pure magic. Las Vegas is alive 24 hours a day, every day. The sound of money spilling in and out of slot machines is incessant and all too attractive to the novice gambler.

A distance of almost 350 miles (one way) may not seem overly grueling, but when a large portion of that journey is through the blistering desert, the motorist may want to consider an alternative means of transport. Excellent tours and weekend packages are offered by several Los Angeles bus companies (*see* Tours). Amtrak (*see* TRANSPORTATION & VACATION INFORMATION, Trains) offers a relaxing train excursion aboard *The Desert Wind*. Four local airlines serve Las Vegas with daily flights from LAX, Ontario, Orange County, and Hollywood-Burbank airports. PSA airlines will arrange three-day/two-night vacations at very low rates (contact your travel agent). The Las Vegas Reservation Center in Los Angeles will help with hotel and show bookings, call (213) 933-9321. Approximately 700 miles round-trip.

Los Alamos

A hundred years ago this sleepy little town thrived as a bustling railroad stop. Farmers from the surrounding valley brought their produce here for shipment aboard the Pacific Coast Railroad. Los Alamos was also a stagecoach stop and boasted seven saloons. Today, the Old Union Hotel, (805) 344-2744, has been restored, antique shops line the main street, and the neighboring farmland boasts nine wineries (all open to the public). North on Highway 101, near Santa Maria. Approximately 300 miles round-trip.

Mammoth

(619) 934-6611 or -2505. A vast area of outstanding beauty, Mammoth is perhaps the favorite playground of Southern Californians. Mammoth Mountain ski area (elevation 10,000 feet) enjoys perfect skiing conditions well into spring (*see also* SPORTS & RECREATION, Sporting Activities, Skiing). Waterfalls, hot springs, volcanic craters, unusual geological formations, and over 30 lakes attract vacationers year-round. Approximately 600 miles round-trip.

Mojave Desert

The most famous part of this amazing desert is Death Valley, but several areas closer to LA are unusually interesting. Burton's Tropico Goldmine, near Rosamond, was the last operating gold mine in Southern California (1956) and is now open to the public. Apple Valley, east of the Mojave River, and Antelope Valley, surrounding Lancaster, contain some of the state's most attractive desert scenery. The Mojave (pronounced "mo-haa-ve") is true Indian country and there is still evidence of native culture throughout the desert. Approximately 100 to 500 miles round-trip, depending on destination.

Palm Springs

(619) 770-9000. Hotel referral service: (619) 778-8418. Sun-worshiping and refined sporting activities (primarily golf) are the major pastimes in this world-famous desert oasis. A quiet, uncluttered city of low buildings, silent limousines, sumptuous boutiques, and manicured gardens. Palm Springs has been a fashionable winter resort since the 1930s and has retained a certain mystique. The world's beautiful people still flock to the luxury hotels and spas that rest quietly along just two main streets. In case you were wondering, Palm Springs has 10,000 palm trees on city property alone. (*See also* Day Trips: Palm Springs Aerial Tramway; Desert Hot Springs; *and* Joshua Tree.) Approximately 210 miles round-trip.

Pismo Beach

(805) 773-4382. California's beach paradise for campers. The wide, flat sands of Pismo State Beach, famous for its (now scarce) clams, are open to motor vehicles. There are several good campgrounds with full facilities. Motel accommodations are also available. Rent a dune buggy or motorbike and explore 850 acres of sand dunes. Rent horses, or fish from the pier. Approximately 400 miles round-trip.

Salton Sea

This saltwater lake in the Colorado Desert was created by accident when a dam on the Colorado River burst and water flowed into a huge salt basin 234 feet below sea level. The lake is stocked with ocean fish and is actually saltier than the ocean. The Salton Sea Recreation Area has year-round facilities for waterskiing, fishing, sailing, and camping. Nearby mineral pools and beautiful desert flora can add to a pleasant and unusual weekend. Approximately 300 miles round-trip.

San Diego

Although a perfect distance for a day trip from Los Angeles, San Diego has so much history and such a wealth of attractions that visitors may wish to spend more time exploring the city. A hotel/motel guide is available from the Convention and Visitors Bureau, 1200 3rd Avenue, Suite 824, San Diego, CA 92101, or call (619) 236-1212. (*See also* Day Trips.) Approximately 250 miles round-trip.

San Francisco

San Francisco is obviously too far for a leisurely weekend drive, but it can be reached in an hour by air from Los Angeles. Amtrak's *Coast Starlight* train travels the scenic coastal route, but as the one-way journey takes almost a day, allow extra time. Romantic San Francisco is definitely worth a trip, by whatever means. Cable cars, Fisherman's Wharf, Golden Gate Bridge, Chinatown, countless beautiful buildings, and a colorful history attract thousands of visitors each year. The combination of generally excellent, though expensive (remember to book in advance), accommodations, first-class restaurants, and lively nightspots to suit all tastes make this city a "must" for any visitor to California. For information, write to the Visitors Bureau, 201 3rd Street, Suite 900, San Francisco, CA 94103-3185, or call (415) 974-6900. Approximately 1,200 miles round-trip.

Santa Barbara
Quiet, restful, and full of history, picturesque Santa Barbara is a perfect weekend retreat. Accommodations are excellent, and in recent years European-style bed and breakfasts have become very popular. For information, call the Santa Barbara Visitors Center at (805) 965-3021. (*See also* Day Trips.) Approximately 200 miles round-trip.

Sequoia and Kings Canyon
These two adjoining mountain parks are the home of California's giant sequoia trees. The largest living thing in the world is the General Sherman Tree, said to be approximately 2,750 years old. Mount Whitney (highest mountain in the U.S. outside Alaska) is located in Sequoia National Park. The scenery is spectacular, with lakes, caves, an abundance of wildlife, and huge, rugged mountains covered with majestic redwoods. The area's natural beauty is almost overwhelming. Numerous campgrounds are located throughout both parks, there are also cabins and motel rooms available. For information, call (209) 561-3314. Approximately 450 miles round-trip.

Solvang
See Day Trips. In the Danish language Solvang means "sunny valley" and this enchanting village, with its windmills and Scandinavian influence, is an idyllic vacation spot. For information, call (805) 688-3317. Approximately 280 miles round-trip.

Yosemite National Park
Yosemite is California's biggest natural attraction. It's a scenic wonderland made up of glacial rocks, breathtaking waterfalls, redwood forests,

Solvang Windmill

and alpine meadows. Every effort has been made to preserve the natural beauty of this monumental park. The Visitors Center in Yosemite Village is packed with information on all facilities, accommodations, and activities. For information, call (209) 372-0265. Approximately 600 miles round-trip.

ANNUAL EVENTS

Tournament of Roses Parade Float

CALENDAR

Holidays, sporting events, shows, and festivals celebrated annually in and around Los Angeles are listed. As exact dates can fluctuate, it is advisable to check the local press, especially the Calendar section of the Los Angeles Times, *Sunday edition. Telephone numbers for local visitor information centers are listed after the calendar section.*

January

Public Holiday
New Year's Day, January 1.

Tournament of Roses Parade   **8-D2**
Pasadena streets, New Year's Day. Initiated in 1890 to display California's favorable climate. Millions of flowers are fashioned into spectacular structures that all follow a given theme. Dozens of floral floats are accompanied by marching bands, horses, entertainers, and celebrities. Spectators camp out on Pasadena sidewalks to ensure good viewing positions and millions worldwide watch the parade on TV. There is a charge for grandstand seating—reserve well in advance. For information write the Tournament of Roses Association, 391 S. Orange Grove Boulevard, Pasadena, CA 91184, or call (818) 449-4100.

Rose Bowl Football Game   **8-A1**
1001 Rose Bowl Dr, Pasadena. (818) 793-7193. Following the Tournament of Roses Parade on

New Year's Day. Contest between the winning teams of the Pacific Coast Conference and the Big Ten Conference.

Disney on Ice   **7-G1**
Sports Arena, 3939 S. Figueroa St, LA. (213) 748-6131. Ice-skating spectacular featuring all the Walt Disney characters.

Greater Los Angeles Auto Show   **7-D3**
LA Convention Center, 1201 S. Figueroa St, LA. (213) 748-8531. "A complete auto show. A supermarket of cars and trucks." Also shown are competition cars, antiques, and accessories.

Anaheim Sports, Vacation & RV Show   **1-F8**
Anaheim Convention Center, 800 W. Katella Ave, Anaheim. (714) 999-8900. Huge display, from small trailers to gigantic motor homes. Luxury on wheels. Vacation planning, film shows, sporting goods, and accessories.

William Shakespeare Film Festival   **5-G4**
Royal Theater, 11523 Santa Monica Blvd, W. LA. (310) 477-5581. Acclaimed films of Shakespearean productions featuring such stars as Laurence Olivier and Elizabeth Taylor.

Whale Watching
Next three months. (*See also* SIGHTSEEING, Tours.)

Sunkist Track & Field Invitational   **7-G1**
Sports Arena, 3939 S. Figueroa St, LA. (213) 748-6131; (213) 747-7111. Top-class international track meet.

February

Public Holiday
Presidents' Day, third Monday.

Holidays
Valentine's Day, February 14.
Chinese New Year Celebrations   7-B5
Chinatown. Chinese Chamber of Commerce, 977 N. Broadway, LA. (213) 617-0396. Traditional, colorful street parade with dragons, lanterns, firecrackers, music, and dancing. FREE.
Southern California Boat Show   7-D3
LA Convention Center, 1201 S. Figueroa St, LA. (213) 748-8531. Over 600 craft in all classes. Accessories and water sports equipment. Children under age 6 free.
Laguna Beach Winter Festival
Festival Grounds, 650 Laguna Canyon Rd, Laguna Beach. (714) 494-1018. Popular winter festival featuring arts and crafts, theater, horse show, surfing contest.
Long Beach Marathon   1-G5
Starts at Long Beach Convention Center, 300 E. Ocean Blvd, Long Beach. (310) 494-2664. Full marathon—26.2 miles.
International Folk Dance Festival   7-B4
LA Music Center, 135 N. Grand Ave, LA. (213) 972-7211. Colorful and lively dance displays ranging from flamenco to Highland Scottish, interspersed with performances by magicians and jugglers.
Antiques Show & Sale   4-C3
Santa Monica Civic Auditorium, 1855 Main St, Santa Monica. (310) 393-9961. Best antiques show on the West Coast. Dozens of dealers. Group discounts; children under age 12 free.
Annual Heart Ball   6-G8
3550 Wilshire Blvd, Beverly Hills. To benefit the Heart Association. Celebrity orchestra, raffle for new Cadillac. For information, call (310) 385-4231.
Pismo Beach Clam Festival
(805) 773-4382. Clam-digging contests, sand castles, arts and crafts. (*See also* SIGHTSEEING, Weekend Trips.)
LA City Schools Basketball Finals   7-G1
Sports Arena, 3939 S. Figueroa St, LA. (310) 748-6131; (310) 747-7111.

Chinatown

National Date Festival
Indio, near Palm Springs. (619) 347-0676. Camel races, amusement fair, food, and fun.
Kennel Club of Beverly Hills Dog Show 7-G1
Sports Arena, 3939 S. Figueroa St, LA. (310) 748-6131; (310) 747-7111. Demonstrations, films, nutritional advice, and championship-level competition.
LA Open Golf Tournament   1-C2
Riviera Country Club, 1250 Capri Dr, Pacific Palisades. Admission packages available, including clubhouse privileges and grounds passes. Reservations taken. For information, call (310) 454-6591.
Harness Racing   1-F7
Los Alamitos Raceway, 4961 Katella Ave, Los Alamitos. (310) 431-1361. Harness racing: February to April.
Whiskey Flats Days
Kernville. (619) 376-2629. The Old West is brought to life.

March

Holiday
St. Patrick's Day, March 17.
Beverly Hills St. Patrick's Day Parade   5-D8
Rodeo Dr, Beverly Hills. (310) 271-8126. This extravagant, zany, star-studded parade travels along Rodeo Drive (carpeted in green for the occasion) to Wilshire Boulevard, and ends on Little Santa Monica Boulevard. There is a charge for grandstand seats.
Long Beach Grand Prix   1-G6
Streets of Long Beach. (310) 437-0341. Famous international formula-one auto race. Sponsored by Toyota, the events include a charity golf tournament and a 10k run.
Return of the Swallows
Mission San Juan Capistrano. (714) 493-1111. Each March 19, the swallows return to nest in the old church ruins. Celebrations include a parade, dancing, and art exhibition. (*See also* HISTORIC LA, Churches: Mission San Juan Capistrano.)
Los Angeles Marathon   7-G1
For information, call (213) 747-7111; (213) 748-6131. Starts at LA Memorial Coliseum, 3911 S. Figueroa Street.
Azalea Festival   1-D5
South Gate. For information, call (213) 567-1203 or -1331.
Wild Flower Festival
Lancaster. (805) 948-4518. (*See* SIGHTSEEING, Day Trips: Wild Flowers.)
Western Fishing Tackle & Fishing Boat Show   1-G5
Long Beach Convention Center, 300 E. Ocean Blvd, Long Beach. (310) 436-3636.
Southern Sierra Loggers
Kernville. (619) 376-2629.
National Mime Week
Touring shows around the city. Closing parade, end of month, in Venice.
Town Fair Bazaar   7-C5
317 S. Crocker St, LA. (213) 626-4611. Huge

variety of brand-new goods, donated by merchants and manufacturers, are sold at discount prices to raise money for the City of Hope.

Camellia Show. **1-B7**
LA State & County Arboretum, 301 N. Baldwin Ave, Arcadia. (818) 821-3222. Over 2,000 flowers are exhibited, including some new varieties. Reduced admission for children under age 17, seniors, and students. (See also SIGHTSEEING, Tours: Los Angeles State & County Arboretum.)

Santa Monica Pier Spring Kite Festival 4-C3
Santa Monica beach, north of the pier. (310) 396-KITE. Everyone can bring his favorite kite to fly. No rules, fees, or competition. (March/April)

Academy Awards Presentations **7-B4**
LA Music Center, 135 N. Grand Ave, LA. (213) 972-7211. Glittering evening, when Hollywood's stars really come out and shine. Bleacher seating is set up outside for the public to watch luminaries arrive.

April

Holiday
Easter.

Easter Sunrise Service **6-A5**
Hollywood Bowl, 2301 N. Highland Ave, Hollywood. (213) 850-2000. Religious service at dawn with music and prayer.

Blessing of the Animals **7-B5**
Olivera St, LA. (213) 628-3562. Reenactment of an ancient tradition (held in front of the Plaza Church) followed by festivities. Some zoo animals are usually present.

Filmex (LA International Film Exposition)
(213) 856-7707. Cultural, two-week, noncompetitive celebration of film. New releases, retrospectives, and foreign films. Some free films.

Thoroughbred Racing **1-D4**
Hollywood Park, 1050 S. Prairie Ave, Inglewood. (310) 419-1500. Racing season: April to July and November to December.

Renaissance Pleasure Faire **1-B1**
2555 Devore Rd, Devore, CA 92407. (415) 892-0937. An Elizabethan festival/extravaganza staged in a simulated medieval village with no visible signs of the 20th century. Over 3,000 actors, dancers, musicians, jugglers, and artisans. Visitors are encouraged to come dressed in period costume. Outdoor kitchens serve up giant ribs, poultry, and good grog. Check local press for admission discounts.

California Angels Baseball **1-F8**
Anaheim Stadium, 2000 State College Blvd, Anaheim. (714) 634-2000. Baseball season: April to September.

LA Dodgers Baseball **7-A5**
Dodger Stadium, 1000 Elysian Park Ave, LA. (213) 224-1500. Baseball season: April to September.

LA March of Dimes Superwalk
Numerous, sponsored walks throughout the LA area.

Ramona Outdoor Pageant
Hemet. (714) 658-3111. Located 35 miles south-

east on Riverside. Colorful, outdoor theatrical extravaganza. Indian rituals, music, and dancing.

Los Alamitos Spring Championship **1-F7**
Los Alamitos Raceway, 4961 Katella Ave, Los Alamitos. (310) 431-1361. Top-class race for 3-year-old pacers.

Affaire in the Gardens **5-D8**
Santa Monica Garden Pkwy, Beverly Hills. (310) 271-8126; (310) 550-4816. Semiannual outdoor exhibition of works by over 200 artists and craftspeople.

May

Public holiday
Memorial Day, last Monday.

Holidays
Cinco de Mayo, May 5; Mother's Day, second Sunday.

Cinco de Mayo Celebrations **7-B5**
Celebration commemorating Mexico's victory over the French. Dancing, street festivities, mariachi bands, food, arts and crafts. Several locations including Olvera Street, LA. For information, call (213) 628-0605. Or Belvedere Park, 4914 E. Brooklyn Avenue, LA; (213) 268-7264 (**1-C6**).

Strawberry Festival **1-F8**
Village Green, 72762 Main St, Garden Grove. (714) 638-0981. Parade, amusements, and pie-eating contest.

Quarter Horse Racing **1-F7**
Los Alamitos Raceway, 4961 Katella Ave, Los Alamitos. (310) 431-1361. Quarter horse racing season: May to December.

Student Art Award Show **1-B4**
Los Angeles Valley College, 5800 Fulton Ave, Van Nuys. (818) 781-1200.

UCLA Mardi Gras **5-D4**
UCLA Athletic Field, Sunset Blvd at Westwood Blvd, LA. (310) 825-4321. Fireworks, games, rides, music, dancing, fun house, horror house, and laserama. Proceeds go to charity.

Children's Horse Show **1-A5**
Flintridge Riding Club, 4625 Oak Grove Dr, Flintridge. (818) 952-1233. Hospital benefit with competition in equitation, hunt teams, jumping, and cross-country.

Pierce College Rodeo **1-B2**
621 Winnetka Ave, Woodland Hills. (818) 719-6401. Contestants from western colleges. Steer wrestling, bronc riding.

Boy Scout Council Runs **1-B7**
Santa Anita Park, 285 W. Huntington Dr, Arcadia. (818) 574-7223. Two runs—a 10k and a 5k—around the Santa Anita golf course and race track.

Mule Days
Bishop. (619) 873-8405. Mule show and sale, shoeing contest, barbecue, and other festivities. (See also Weekend Trips: Mammoth.)

Memorial Day Classic Horse Show **1-B4**
Griffith Park Equestrian Center, 500 Riverside Dr, Burbank. (818) 840-9063. A six-day event featuring grand-prix jumping. Riders from U.S. and

Canada compete for a purse of over $15,000. Qualifying events for World Cup competition.

Spring Tour of Carroll Avenue   **7-A4**
Carroll Avenue, LA. (213) 623-2489. Tour of well-preserved Victorian homes—all private residences. (*See also* HISTORIC LA, Buildings & Landmarks: Carroll Avenue.)

**President's Invitational Golf
Tournament**   **9-F6**
Lakeside Country Club, Valleyspring Lane, Toluca Lake. (818) 984-0601; (213) 877-1310. Sponsored by former President Gerald Ford to benefit the Children's Bureau of Los Angeles.

Venice Art Walk   **4-E4**
Antioch University, 300 Rose Ave, Venice. (310) 392-8630. Visit 28 studios and galleries and meet some of the area's internationally known artists. Bus transportation, art fair, silent auction (usually expensive). Proceeds benefit the Venice Family Clinic.

June

Holidays
Flag Day, June 14; Father's Day, third Sunday.

All City Outdoor Arts Festival   **6-C8**
Barnsdall Park, LA. Outdoor festivities include puppet shows, music, arts and crafts. (*See also* PARKS & GARDENS, Parks: Barnsdall Park.)

In-the-Water Boat Show   **4-G7**
Burton Chase Park, Mindanao Way, Marina del Rey. (310) 821-0555. Variety of craft and boating accessories.

Santa Monica Art & Craft Show   **4-C3**
Santa Monica Mall. (310) 393-9825. Outdoor exhibition of works by dozens of local artists.

Greek Theatre Summer Concerts   **6-A8**
4730 Crystal Springs Dr, Griffith Park. (213) 665-5188; (213) 665-5857. A season of outdoor concerts from classical to rock 'n' roll, June to September.

Playboy Jazz Festival   **6-A5**
Hollywood Bowl, 2301 N. Highland Ave, LA. (213) 850-2000. For additional information, call (213) 450-9040. All star performers.

**Los Angeles Philharmonic Summer
Concerts**   **6-A5**
Hollywood Bowl, 2301 N. Highland Ave, LA. (213) 850-2000. Summer season of classical concerts.

Folk Art Festival   **7-G1**
LA County Museum of Natural History, 900 Exposition Blvd, LA. (213) 744-3466 or -3414. Demonstrations of arts and crafts, folk dancing, music, ethnic foods. Exhibits both inside and outside museum.

Watts Summer Games   **1-C6**
Junior Chamber of Commerce. (213) 482-1311. Over 10,000 high schoolers compete in 21 events. Sports celebrities supervise.

Manhattan Beach Art Festival   **2-B6**
Joslyn Community Center, 1601 Valley Dr, Manhattan Beach. (310) 545-5313. Two shows—one for professionals, one for amateurs.

Old Globe Festival
Old Globe Theatre, Balboa Park, San Diego. (619) 239-2255. Famous festival continuing through September. Top stage actors perform classic Shakespearean plays on the Festival Stage. Beautiful setting. Book in advance. (*See also* SIGHTSEEING, Day Trips: San Diego.)

**Los Angeles Public Parks Tennis
Championship**
Various locations. (213) 485-4871.

Ojai Music Festival
Festival Bowl, Libbey Park, Ojai. (805) 646-2094. Classical music and jazz concerts, beautifully performed in one of California's most picturesque valleys. (*See also* SIGHTSEEING, Day Trips.)

Country Bluegrass Festival   **1-G6**
Long Beach Veteran's Stadium, Clark Ave at Carson, Long Beach. (310) 426-6773.

**Santa Monica Pier Summer Kite
Festival**   **4-C3**
Santa Monica beach, north of the pier. Everyone can bring his own kite to fly. No rules, fees, or competition.

Bel-rey 500 U.S. Grand Prix of Motocross
Carlsbad Raceway, Carlsbad. (619) 727-1171.

Variety Show & Auction
South Coast Repertory Theater, 655 Town Center Dr, Costa Mesa. (714) 957-2602. Fund-raising dinner, live and silent auctions, flea market of theater memorabilia, theatrical performances.

Shakespearean Revels
Ojai. (805) 646-8126. Summer solstice celebrations include performance of *A Midsummer Night's Dream* and a crafts fair. (*See also* SIGHTSEEING, Day Trips: Ojai.)

Love Your Heart 10k Run   **2-F7**
Redondo Beach. For information, call the American Heart Association at (213) 385-4231.

July

Public Holiday
Independence Day, July 4.

Fireworks
Displays on the Fourth at Dodger Stadium, LA Coliseum, the Rose Bowl, Santa Monica Pier, Hollywood Bowl, Anaheim Stadium, Avalon (Catalina Island), Disneyland, and other locations. For information, call the local chamber of commerce. (*See* Visitors' Information.)

Laguna Beach Arts Festival
Festival grounds, 650 Laguna Canyon Rd, Laguna Beach. (714) 494-1145. Displays by local artists and craftspeople. The Pageant of the Masters, presented nightly at 8:30pm, is a re-creation of works of art with living models. For Pageant ticket information, call (714) 494-1146 or -1147. Other exhibits include stained glass, leatherwork, graphics, watercolors, oils, acrylics, jewelry, and ceramics. The festival lasts for six weeks. Park in town and take tram service to festival grounds.

Malibu Summer Festival & Art Show   1-C1
Malibu Civic Center, 23545 Civic Center Way, Malibu. (310) 456-9025. Arts, crafts, entertainment, and specialized exhibits.

Sawdust Festival
935 Laguna Canyon Rd, Laguna Beach. (714) 494-1018 or -3030. Exhibition and sale of arts and traditional crafts held in a 3-acre eucalyptus grove. Wide variety of entertainment and food. Admission, children under age 12 free.

Southland Home & Garden Show   1-F8
Anaheim Convention Center, 800 W. Katella Ave, Anaheim. (714) 999-8900. Latest concepts in home and garden design, displayed by almost 600 exhibitors. New ideas for home improvements and refurbishing. Beautiful displays, including landscaped gardens with rock pools and fountains. Live entertainment.

Orange County Fair
Orange County Fair and Exhibition Center, 88 Fair Dr, Costa Mesa. (714) 751-3247. Carnival, amusements, rodeo, horse fair, arts and crafts. Nightly entertainment in the fairground amphitheater.

Catalina Dixieland Jazz Jamboree
(310) 510-1520. The jamboree begins aboard boats leaving from San Pedro, Newport Beach, Long Beach, and Oceanside and continues on the crossing to Catalina with jazz bands leading a parade from the boats to Avalon Casino. Musicians are encouraged to bring their own instruments and jam. *Depart 8am, return 9:30pm.*

U.S. Lifesaving Association Championship
At various locations each year. For information, call (714) 494-1018. Over 450 lifeguards from around the world compete. Swimming, running, and surf ski racing.

Grove Shakespeare Festival   1-G8
Festival Amphitheater and Gem Theater, Garden Grove. (714) 638-7950. A month-long season of classic Shakespearean plays.

Los Angeles Shakespeare Festival
Several locations. See local press for details.

Topanga Banjo & Fiddle Contest   5-D4
UCLA Athletic Field, Westwood. (310) 825-4321. Hundreds of musicians compete in this fun-filled contest. Fancy fiddle players, clog dancers, square dancing, and Scottish dancing are included in a variety of entertainment. Large grassy field allows for picnicking.

Marina del Rey Arts and Crafts Fair   4-G7
Admiralty Way, Marina del Rey. (310) 821-0555. Dates vary. Local craftspeople display and sell their work. Mimes, musicians.Scenic harbor setting.

Summer Festival of Arts and Crafts   1-E6
Town Center Hall, 11740 E. Telegraph Rd, Santa Fe Springs. (310) 868-0511. Local artists and craftspeople display their work.

Laguna Beach Open Volleyball
Pacific Coast Hwy & Laguna Canyon Rd, Laguna Beach. (714) 494-1018. Part of the Pro Beach Tournament. Finals are held in Redondo Beach in September. Two-man teams compete on sand courts.

Hollywood Bowl Open House   6-A5
Hollywood Bowl, 2301 N. Highland Ave, LA. (213) 850-2000. Performing arts festival for children. (*See* KIDS' LA, Learning.)

Superbowl of Motocross   7-G1
LA Coliseum, 3911 S. Figueroa St, LA. (213) 747-7111. Motorcycles race over ridges and jumps, through trenches and sand pits.

Ringling Brothers & Barnum & Bailey Circus
Various locations include the Sports Arena (**7-G1**), Anaheim Convention Center (**1-F8**), and Long Beach Stadium (**1-G6**). See local press for details. Opening night is generally a charity benefit with TV and movie celebrities participating.

World Frisbee Championships
La Mirada Park, 13701 S. Adelfa Dr, La Mirada. (310) 943-6978. International field of over 150 competitors. Each ticket holder gets a free Frisbee. Children under age 12 free.

August

Nisei Week   7-C5
Little Tokyo, 1st & 2nd Sts between Los Angeles & Alameda Sts, LA. (213) 628-2725; (213) 687-7193. Celebration of Japanese traditions. (Nisei is the word for "Japanese born in America.") Grand parade with Japanese dancers, music, and floats. Crafts demonstrations, tea ceremonies, martial arts. Most events are free. Schedules and maps are available from businesses in Little Tokyo.

International Surf Festival
Various South Bay Beaches. (310) 545-5313.

Ojai Jazz Festival
Festival Bowl, Libbey Park, Ojai. (805) 646-8126. An enchanting setting for open-air jazz. Diverse program of top-name performers.

Long Beach Sea Fest
This ten-day event includes international ski race, pro beach volleyball, catamaran racing, sailboat regatta, fishing rodeo, sand sculpture contest. For information, call (310) 436-3636.

Old Spanish Days
Various locations in and around Santa Barbara. (805) 962-8101; (805) 965-3021. Heritage celebration. Five-day festival with historical parade. Colorful costumes, fiesta, California crafts. (*See* SIGHTSEEING, Day Trips: Santa Barbara.)

Old Miner's Days
Big Bear Lake. (714) 866-5877 or -4601. Old West festival with burro races, dancing, and parades. (*See* SIGHTSEEING, Day Trips: Big Bear.)

Santa Monica Sports & Arts Festival   4-C3
Palisades Park, Santa Monica. (310) 458-8311. Arts and crafts exhibits, swimming, boating, fishing, and lawn-bowling contests.

Jewish Summer Festival   5-G3
West Los Angeles Civic Center Mall, Purdue Ave at Santa Monica Blvd, W. LA. (310) 828-3433. Arts and crafts, games, rides, entertainment, refreshments, and an auction. All proceeds go to the Bay Cities Jewish Community Center.

San Fernando Valley Fair **1-A2**
Devonshire Downs, 18000 Devonshire St,
Northridge. (818) 373-4500. Extremely popular
three-day event. Four stages of live entertainment, arts and crafts village, livestock exhibits,
carnival rides, bake-offs, music of all kinds. Miss
LA County Beauty Pageant, banjo contests, and
all the fun of the fair. *OPEN Thurs & Fri 12 noon-
10pm; Sat & Sun 10am-10pm.* Reduced rates for
students and seniors.

Newport Harbor Character Boat Parade
Newport Beach. (714) 673-5070. Third Sunday
in August. Over 100 craft festively decorated.
Crews dress in costume.

Karate Championships **1-G5**
Long Beach Arena, 300 E. Ocean Blvd, Long
Beach. (310) 436-3661. Top international and
American athletes compete in this two-day com-
petition. Entrants are ages 5 to 50.

Los Angeles Rams Football **1-F8**
Anaheim Stadium, 2000 State College Blvd, Anaheim. (714) 535-7267. Football season: August
to December.

Los Angeles Raiders Football **7-G1**
LA Memorial Coliseum, 3911 S. Figueroa St, LA.
(213) 747-7111. Football season: August to December.

Venice Beach Rathayatra Festival **4-G5**
Ocean Front Walk, Venice. Three giant chariots
resembling Buddhist temples, each brightly
decorated and weighing 5 tons, make their way
along the boardwalk from Santa Monica to
Venice, accompanied by music and chanting
followers who throw flowers to the crowds. Parade ends with an ethnic festival of Eastern music, dance, and exotic foods. FREE.

**Westwood Sidewalk Arts and Crafts
Show.** **5-E4**
Streets of Westwood Village, W. LA. (310) 475-
4574. Excellent annual show featuring artists
from all over Southern California. The *October*
show concentrates on the Christmas market,
with a huge variety of handmade gifts and unusual crafts. FREE.

San Bernardino County Fair
14800 7th St, Victorville. (619) 245-6506. Home
arts and crafts, gem and mineral exhibits, carnival, entertainment, livestock auction, and
rodeo.

September

Public Holiday
Labor Day, first Monday.

Los Angeles County Fair
County Fairgrounds, Interstate 10, Pomona.
(714) 623-3111. Largest traditional county fair in
the U.S. Livestock, including horses, cattle,
goats, and rabbits. Butter-churning, horse-
shoeing, and wood-carving competitions. Bluegrass banjo championships. Fine-art pavilion,
wine tastings, produce exhibits. Flower and garden festival. Rodeo, horse racing, carnival rides,
amusement park, special events with guest celebrities.

Danish Days
Solvang. (805) 688-3317. Celebration of Den-
mark's independence. Costumed dancers, mu-
sic, and singing. Food and merriment. (*See*
SIGHTSEEING, Day Trips *and* Weekend Trips:
Solvang.)

Greek Festival **1-B7**
Santa Anita Racetrack, 285 W. Huntington Dr,
Arcadia. (818) 574-7223. Authentic Greek
foods, music, and dancing. Small donation suggested.

Arts and Crafts by the Sea **2-E6**
Pier & Hermosa Aves, Hermosa Beach. (310)
376-0951. Art show with strolling musicians.
Face painting, puppet shows. FREE.

Los Angeles City Birthday Party **7-C5**
El Pueblo de Los Angeles State Historic Park.
(213) 680-2525. Annual festive celebration with
music, dancing, and singing.

Championship Volleyball Finals **2-G7**
King Harbor Seaside Lagoon, Redondo Beach.
(310) 379-3636. Two-man double-elimination
contest.

Beverly Hills Affaire in the Gardens **5-D8**
Santa Monica Blvd at Rodeo Dr, Beverly Hills.
(310) 271-8126. Over 200 craftspeople display
their work, much of which is for sale. Special
entertainment for children.

Santa Monica Cat Club Show **4-D3**
Santa Monica Civic Auditorium, 1855 Main St,
Santa Monica. (310) 393-9961. Organized by
Pet Pride, the national humane society for cats.
All breeds are shown and celebrities present
awards.

**Harvest Festival & Christmas Crafts
Market** **7-D3**
LA Convention Center, 1201 S. Figueroa St, LA.
(213) 748-8531. Arranged in the style of a 19th-
century village fair. Hundreds of craftspeople
and entertainers, all in costume. Decorative and
traditional arts, crafts, and decorations for the
upcoming holiday season.

Portuguese Bend National Horse Show **1-F4**
Empty Saddle Club, 39 Empty Saddle Rd, Rolling Hills Estates. (310) 377-8111. Full program
of junior and adult events. Two rings, demonstrations, trophies, and money prizes. Food booths,
country and western music, and barbecue. Proceeds go to the Children's Hospital of Los Angeles.

Great Western Fair
LA County Fairgrounds, Interstate 10, Pomona.
(714) 623-3111. Huge selection of antique and
modern firearms. Military, Western, and Indian
artifacts. Buy, sell, or trade.

October

Holidays
Columbus Day, second Monday; Halloween,
October 31.

Oktoberfest **1-F4**
Alpine Village, 833 W. Torrance Blvd, Torrance.
(310) 327-4384. Traditional celebration in the

German beer garden with yodelers, brass bands, and plenty of beer drinking.

Big Bear Oktoberfest

Big Bear Lake. (714) 866-5877 or -4601. Everyone in this delightful mountain resort celebrates in a traditional German way. Street dancing, brass bands, food, and festivities. (*See also* SIGHTSEEING, Day Trips: Big Bear.)

ArtExpo   **7-D3**

LA Convention Center, 1210 S. Figueroa St, LA. (213) 748-8531. Over 250 exhibitors from around the world. Paintings, etchings, sculpture, lithographs, posters, and photographs. Renowned artists and unknowns.

Los Angeles Philharmonic   **7-B4**

Music Center, 135 N. Grand Ave, LA. (213) 972-7200. The Philharmonic returns to its winter home after a summer season at the Hollywood Bowl.

Los Angeles Lakers Basketball   **1-D4**

The Forum, Manchester Blvd & Prairie Ave, Inglewood. (310) 419-3100. Basketball season: October to April.

Los Angeles Kings Ice Hockey   **1-D4**

The Forum, Manchester Blvd & Prairie Ave, Inglewood. (310) 419-3100. Ice hockey season: October to April.

Thoroughbred Racing   **1-B7**

Santa Anita Racetrack, 285 W. Huntington Dr, Arcadia. (818) 574-7233. Racing season: October to November.

Calico Days

Calico Ghost Town, Yermo. (619) 254-2122. The Old West revived with mock gunfights and greased-pig contests. (*See* SIGHTSEEING, Weekend Trips.)

Equestrian Day   **1-C2**

Will Rogers State Historic Park, 14253 Sunset Blvd, Pacific Palisades. (310) 454-8212. (*See also* PARKS & GARDENS, Parks: Will Rogers State Historic Park.)

Knott's "Scary" Farm   **1-F8**

Knott's Berry Farm (*see also* SIGHTSEEING, Amusement Parks). A haunted maze (with monsters to chase the children) is added for a special Halloween night of entertainment.

November

Public Holiday

Thanksgiving, fourth Thursday of month.

Holiday

Veteran's Day, November 11.

Hollywood Christmas Parade   **6-B6**

Sunset & Hollywood Blvds, Hollywood. (213) 469-8311 or -2337. Internationally famous parade with marching bands and floats carrying dozens of celebrities of TV and movie fame—plus, of course, Santa Claus. Normally held the Sunday following Thanksgiving.

Parade of Masks   **6-G3**

Wilshire Blvd, from Crescent Heights Blvd to Curson Ave, LA. Always held November 1 at noon. Final celebration of the Festival of Masks. Participants include winners from the Masked

Ball, civic artists, and museum workshop students. Parade ends with a festival in Barnsdall Park. FREE.

Doo Dah Parade   **8-2C**

(818) 796-2591. Antithesis of the Rose Parade—it has no theme, no judges, no motorized vehicles. A zany assemblage of such groups as the Dull Men's Club and the Garbage Can Drum Corps parade the revered streets of Pasadena. Starts at Colorado Boulevard and Fair Oaks Avenue.

Death Valley Encampment Days

Various Death Valley locations. (619) 786-2331. Western festivities, square dancing, cookouts.

Orange County Fall Fair

Los Alamitos Raceway, 4961 Katella Ave, Los Alamitos. (310) 431-1361. Theme exhibits relating to the seasonal holidays. Entertainment.

Manufactured Housing & Recreational Vehicle Show   **7-A5**

Dodger Stadium, 1000 Elysian Park Ave, LA. (213) 224-1400. Large exhibition of multipurpose vehicles and motor homes. Reduced admission for children age 6 to 16; under age 6 free.

Los Angeles Antiques Show

Locations vary. (213) 937-5566. Dealers from Europe and U.S. exhibit museum-quality antiques.

Winston Western 500

Riverside International Raceway, 22255 Eucalyptus Ave, Edgemont. (714) 653-1161. 500k stock car races at speeds of up to 200 mph.

December

Public Holiday

Christmas Day, December 25.

American Indian Festival   **7-G1**

LA County Museum of Natural History, 900 Exposition Blvd, LA. (213) 744-3414. Traditional Indian crafts—including pottery, weaving, and basketry—are demonstrated. Tribal dancing, films, and photographic displays. Children under age 5 free.

Las Posadas   **7-C5**

Olvera St, LA. (213) 625-5045. Nightly at 8pm, from December 16 to December 24. Candlelight procession reenacting the journey of Mary and Joseph.

Lighted Boats Parades

All types of craft, decorated with festive lights, parade around local harbors and beaches in celebration of Christmas. For information call:

    LA Harbor: (310) 437-0041   **1-G5**

    Marina del Rey (main channel): (310) 821-7614   **4-G6**

    Dana Point Harbor: (714) 496-1555

    Long Beach: (310) 435-5911   **1-G5**

    Newport Harbor: (714) 644-8211

    Oxnard Channel Islands Harbor: (805) 485-8833

The Nutcracker Suite   **7-C4**

Los Angeles Ballet, Music Center, 135 N. Grand Ave, LA. (213) 972-7211. This traditional Christmas ballet can usually be seen from December 26 to January 2. Performances of this same ballet, performed by Ballet West and the Long Beach Symphony, are held in Long Beach's Terrace Theater ([310] 436-3661) from December 4 to December 6.

Long Beach Christmas Water Parade   1-G5
Naples Canals, Long Beach. (310) 436-3645. A choir sings as decorated boats wander through the canals.

Long Beach Kennel Club Dog Show   1-G5
Long Beach Convention Center, 300 E. Ocean Blvd, Long Beach. (310) 436-3645. All-breed dog show. Twelve show rings. Reduced admission for seniors and children under age 12.

Beverly Hills Perrier 10k Run   5-E7
Beverly Hills High School, 241 S. Moreno Dr, Beverly Hills. (310) 550-4816. Run is through the streets of Beverly Hills. Other events include unusual competitions in which local celebrities participate. Roller-disco run, newscasters' challenge race. Free to spectators.

Feast of Lights   1-G5
Long Beach City College, Long Beach. (310) 420-4353. Traditional English cathedral Christmas service (two days).

Festival of Lights   6-F3
Fairfax Ave between Melrose Ave & Beverly Blvd, LA. (213) 857-1255. One-day fair and carnival.

Arthritis Run-a-Thon   6-A8
Griffith Park, LA. (213) 665-5188. A 10k run for charity. Runners include TV and film celebrities.

Christmas Craft Faire   1-C5
Heritage Square, 3800 N. Homer St, LA; (213) 222-3150. And Santa Monica Civic Auditorium, 1855 Main St, Santa Monica; (310) 393-9961 (**4-D3**). Unusual and traditional gifts and accessories befitting the Christmas season. Attractions for children include puppet shows, magic, and mime. Reduced admission for children.

Holiday Look-in House Tour
Pasadena. (818) 798-7988. Four homes of different architectural styles are decorated for the holiday season. American colonial, Mediterranean, contemporary, and country cottage.

Holiday on Ice   1-F8
Anaheim Convention Center, 800 W. Katella Ave, Anaheim. (714) 999-8900. Seasonal skating spectacular.

Candlelight Caroling Ceremonies   1-F8
Disneyland. (714) 999-4565.

Winterfair   7-F1
Shrine Exposition Hall, 649 W. Jefferson Blvd, LA. (213) 749-5123. Grand shopping bazaar. Food, entertainment, handcrafted holiday gifts. Benefit for noncommercial radio.

Dickens Downtown Christmas Celebration   7-C4
ARCO Plaza (*see* HISTORIC LA, Main Districts: Downtown), Broadway Plaza, and the Biltmore

Hotel (*see* HISTORIC LA, Buildings & Landmarks). Choirs sing traditional Christmas carols daily from December 1 to December 24.

VISITORS INFORMATION

Agoura: (818) 889-3150
Anaheim: (714) 758-0222; (714) 999-8999
Bakersfield: (805) 861-2367
Beverly Hills: (310) 271-8126 or -8174
Big Bear Lake: (714) 866-5652
Bishop: (619) 873-8405
Buena Park: (714) 994-1511
Catalina Island: (310) 510-2500 or -1520
Century City: (310) 553-2222
Chinatown: (213) 617-0396
Escondido: (619) 745-4741
Garden Grove: (714) 638-7950
Goleta: (805) 967-4618
Hollywood: (213) 469-8311
La Jolla: (619) 454-1444
Laguna Beach: (714) 494-1018
Lake Arrowhead: (714) 337-3715
Long Beach: (310) 436-1251
Los Angeles: (213) 629-0711
Malibu: (310) 456-9025
Mammoth Lakes: (619) 934-2505
Manhattan Beach: (310) 545-5313
Marina del Rey: (310) 821-0555
Newport Beach & Harbor: (714) 644-8211; (714) 729-4400
Oceanside: (619) 722-1534
Ojai: (805) 646-8126
Orange County: (714) 634-2900
Oxnard: (805) 485-8833
Palm Springs: (619) 778-8418
Palos Verdes: (310) 377-8111
Pasadena: (818) 795-3355
Pismo Beach: (805) 773-1661
Redondo Beach: (310) 376-6911
Ridgecrest: (619) 375-8331
Riverside: (714) 683-7100
San Bernardino: (714) 885-7515
San Diego: (619) 276-8200
San Fernando: (818) 361-1184
San Pedro: (310) 832-7272
Santa Barbara: (805) 965-3021
Santa Monica: (310) 393-9825
Solvang: (805) 688-3317
Venice: (310) 827-2366
Ventura: (805) 648-2075
West Hollywood: (213) 654-9213
West Los Angeles: (310) 475-4574

NOTE: *Datelines Newsletter* (published by the Los Angeles Visitors and Convention Bureau) is a monthly publication detailing recreational, cultural, and festive events in Los Angeles. (*See* BASIC INFORMATION, Information Centers, *for locations of visitors bureaus.*)

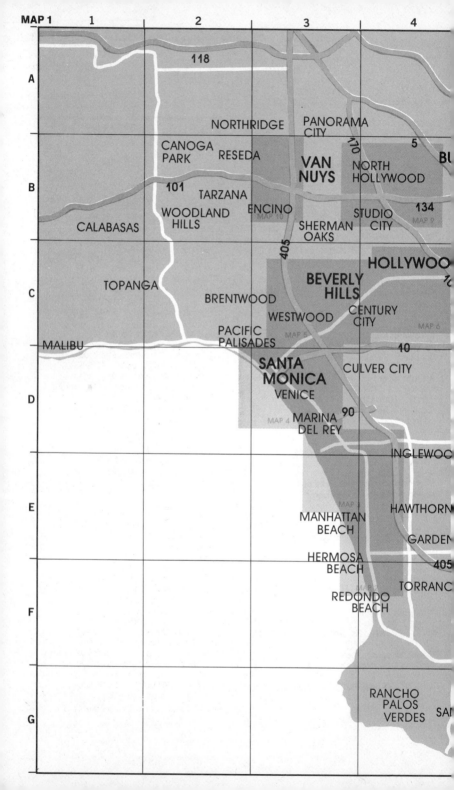

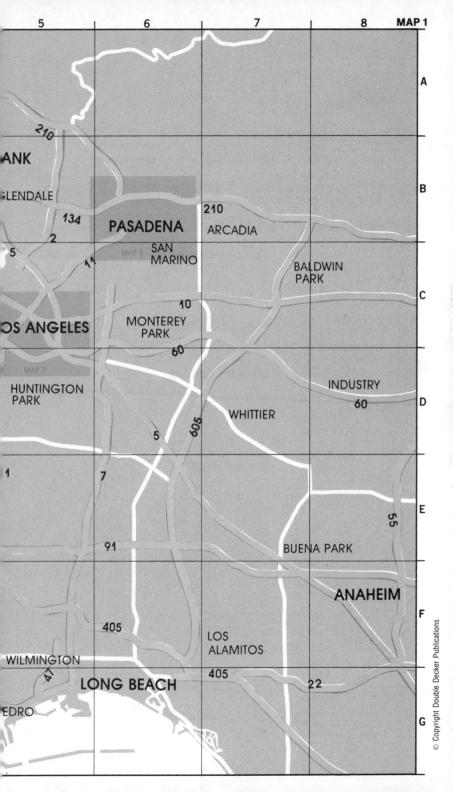

AREA MAPS OF LOS ANGELES

MAP 2

5   6   7   8

ROSECRANS AVENUE

A

MARINE AVENUE

MANHATTAN BEACH

B

BEACH BOULEVARD

BOULEVARD

MANHATTAN BEACH

HIGHLAND

MANHATTAN

AVENUE

SEPULVEDA

BOULEVARD

AVIATION

C

ARTESIA BOULEVARD

D

STRAND

HERMOSA

PACIFIC

HERMOSA BEACH

HERMOSA BEACH

PIER AVE

COAST

E

PACIFIC OCEAN

AVENUE

HIGHWAY

CATALINA AVE

BERYL

STREET

F

HARBOR DRIVE

KING HARBOR

REDONDO BEACH

G

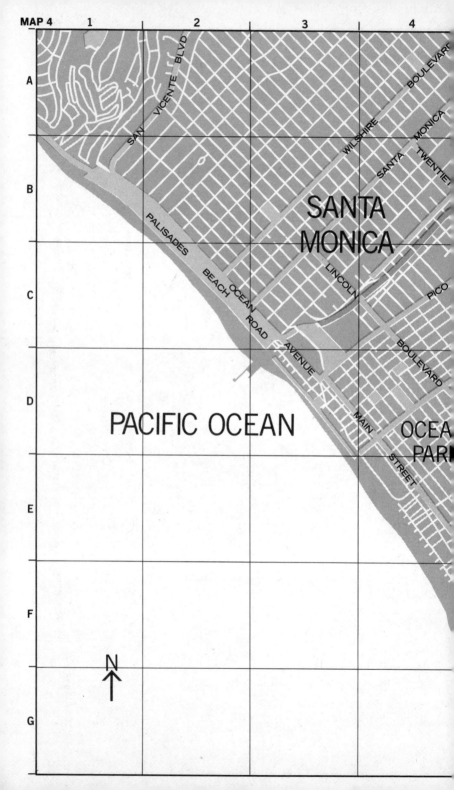

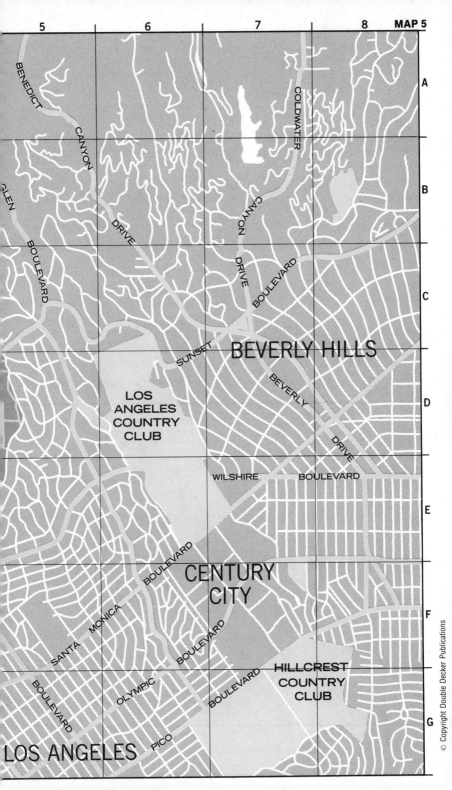

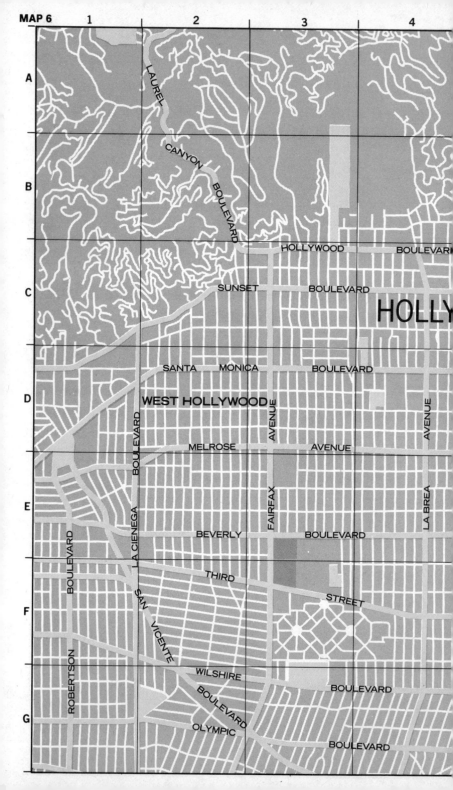

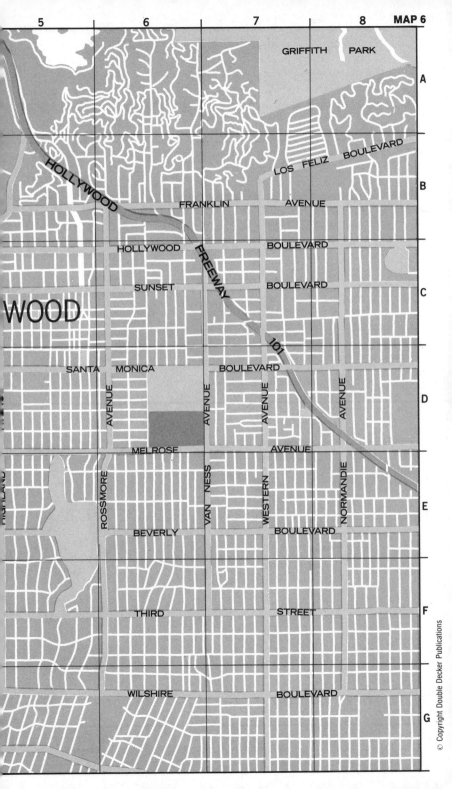

MAP 7

5　　　　6　　　　7　　　　8

ODGER
'ADIUM

PASADENA FREEWAY 11

NORTH   BROADWAY

A

MARENGO

5 FREEWAY

NORTH SPRING STREET

NORTH

MAIN   STREET

ROAD

VALLEY BLVD

B

MISSION

STREET

OWN

SANTA   ANA

GOLDEN   STATE

SAN   BERNARDINO   FREEWAY

WABASH AVE

C

STREET
REET

FREEWAY

BROOKLYN   AVENUE

FIRST

STREET

STREET

D

STREET

FOURTH

5

10

STREET

BOYLE   HEIGHTS

SIXTH   STREET

WHITTIER

SOTO

EUCLID   AVENUE

E

ALAMEDA

AVENUE

BOULEVARD

10

POMONA   FREEWAY 60

F

MONICA   FREEWAY

SANTA FE

OLYMPIC

EIGHTH

STREET

LORENA

STREET

BOULEVARD

WASHINGTON

BOULEVARD

G

© Copyright Double Decker Publications

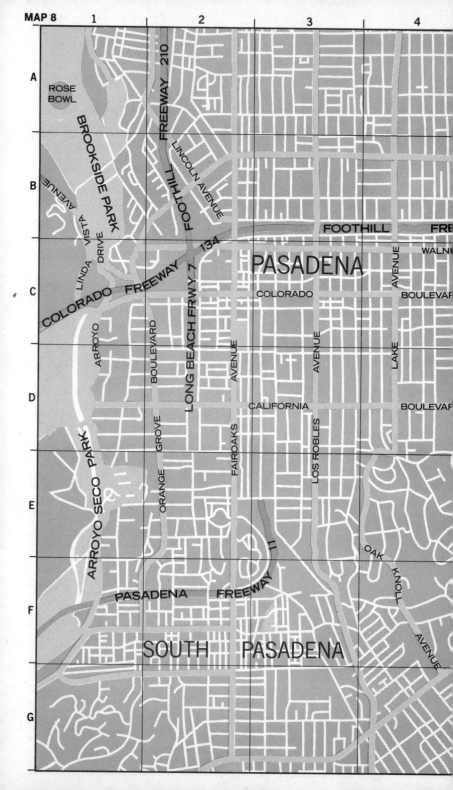

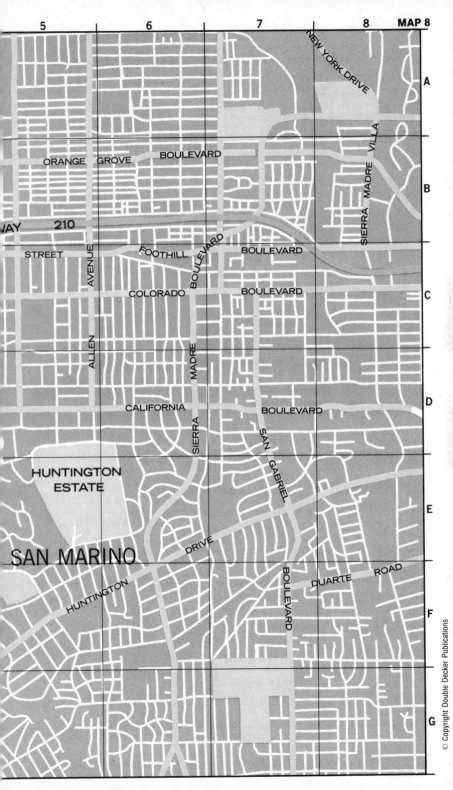

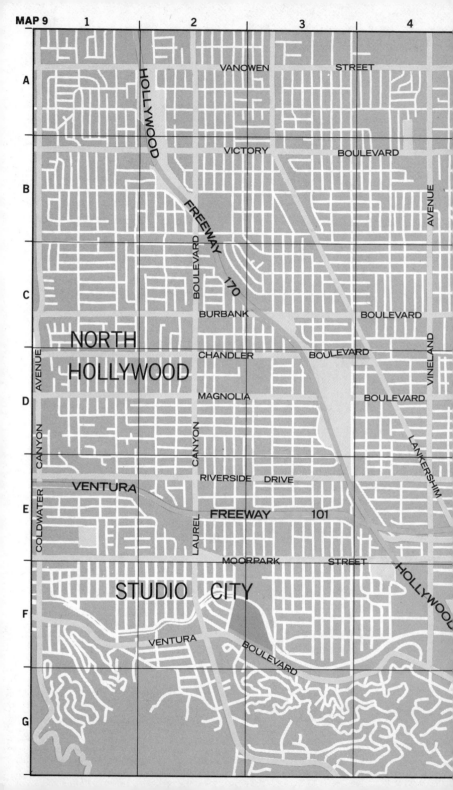

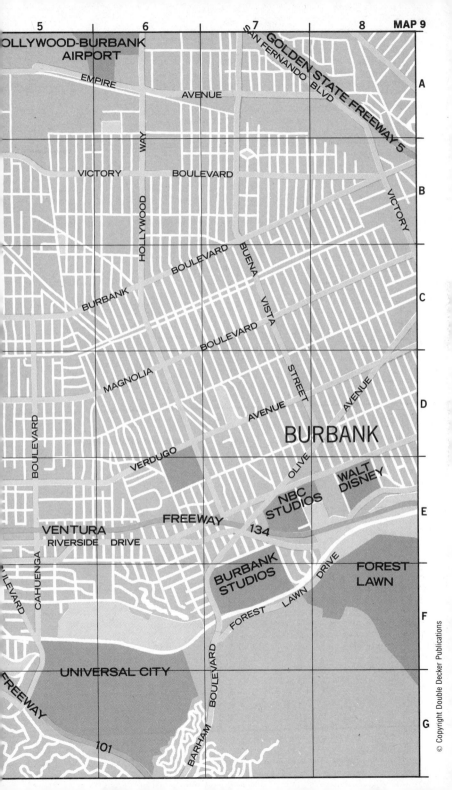

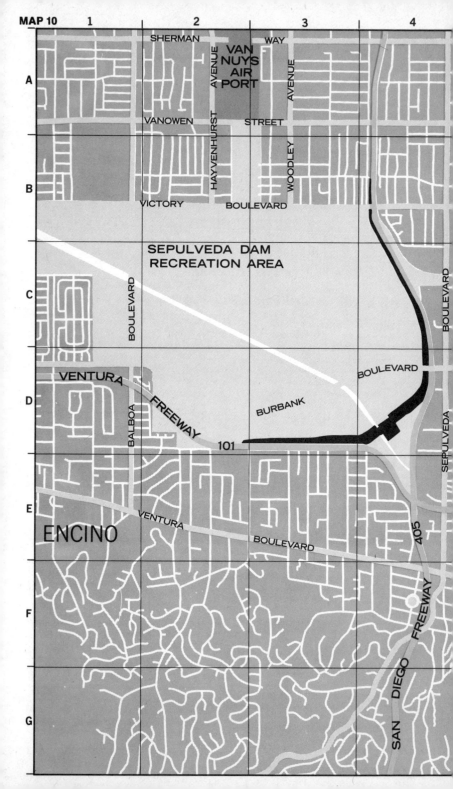

HISTORIC LA

Los Angeles City Hall

MAIN DISTRICTS

The following districts (listed alphabetically) contain a variety of communities, each with its own personality, yet all melting together to form a very different city—Los Angeles. (For information services, see BASIC INFORMATION, Information Centers.)

Anaheim   **1-F8**
A colony established in 1857 by German wine makers on the north banks of the Santa Ana River. At that time the round-trip to Los Angeles (35 miles northwest) took two days. Within 30 years Anaheim had become the wine capital of the country. Unfortunately that status was short-lived. A plant virus swept the Santa Ana Valley, destroying the grapevines, and by 1890 the vineyards had been replaced by orange groves and the rich farming area of Orange County was formed. An industrial revolution and the discovery of oil rapidly changed Anaheim's appearance as technology began to replace agriculture. An even bigger change came with the opening of Disneyland in 1955. Tourism exploded and today Anaheim is most famous for its visitor attractions, including nearby Buena Park, and for the huge Anaheim Stadium.

Beach Cities
Spreading south from Point Mugu to Long Beach are beach cities large and small. The beaches between Point Mugu and Malibu are sparsely populated and excellent for swimming, fishing, surfing, and picnicking. The ocean is relatively clean along this stretch and good kelp beds attract a variety of marine creatures. Camping facilities are provided at **Leo Carrillo** and **Point Mugu State Park**, where there are interesting trails into the foothills. The roads into the canyons above Malibu wind through beautiful rugged mountains with spectacular views across the Santa Monica Bay (*see also* SIGHTSEEING, Viewpoints & Scenic Drives, Scenic Drives: Malibu/Mulholland Scenic Drive.)

Malibu (**1-D1**), once the property of the Chumash Indians (*malibu* is a Chumash word meaning "where the mountains meet the sea"), was taken by the Spanish and later purchased by a young Frenchman named Leon Victor Prudhomme. In 1857, Monsieur Prudhomme sold Malibu for ten cents an acre! Today, with much of its beachfront occupied by private homes (whose rear entrances line Pacific Coast Highway), the area is often a disappointment to tourists. Malibu's famous residents enjoy their privacy and (understandably) do not advertise their wealth. Malibu is especially popular with surfers and a section of Malibu Surfrider State Beach is reserved exclusively for them. Along the stretch of Pacific Coast Highway between Malibu and Santa Monica are several good restaurants, interesting bars, and boutiques.

Santa Monica, perhaps the most popular of the Beach Cities, is covered separately in this section.

Each of LA County's beach communities has an interesting history, but perhaps the most amazing is that of **Venice** (**1-D3**). Founded by Abbott Kinney in 1904, Venice was to be a simulation of Venice, Italy. Canals were built, and expensive attractions, including a huge amusement park and gorgeous bathing facilities, brought droves of visitors. Venice became a true resort. Sadly, through bad planning, bad luck, and opposition from adjoining communities, Venice was all but destroyed. A few of the original canals and interesting buildings remain and recent renovations have begun to reestablish Venice's charm. So once again it is a fashionable neighborhood with real estate values skyrocketing. During the 1950s and 1960s, Venice was considered very bohemian. Claiming to be the birthplace of the beatnik, it still houses an artsy, offbeat community. Well-known painters, writers, and producers have moved to the area—over 2,000 artists live in Venice today. Venice's popular boardwalk has become a "must-see" for thousands of visitors. The atmosphere is cosmopolitan, creative, and colorful. (*See also* SIGHTSEEING, Walking Tours: Venice & Ocean Front Walk.)

The largest man-made harbor for pleasure boats along the Pacific coast is **Marina del Rey** (**1-D3**). Over 6,000 craft, from small sailboats to square-rigged schooners, can be seen in a clinically clean environment. Many famous personalities have boats moored here. Tours of the Marina are available and all kinds of craft can be rented or chartered. The community is affluent, and there are good restaurants and first-class hotels close to the waterfront. Fisherman's Village is a reproduction of a Cape Cod village and houses gift shops and restaurants. The atmosphere is relaxed and romantic.

Beneath the takeoff points at LA International Airport is a huge expanse of golden sands called **Dockweiler State Beach** (**1-E3**). Parking and barbecue facilities are provided and the bike path that started in Santa Monica winds on through here to **Manhattan** and **Hermosa beaches** (**1-E3**). These two beach cities are overflowing with young, suntanned, and fun-loving residents. Apartments and houses are built (almost on top of each other) along steep-sided streets running down to the ocean. Parking facilities are very limited; it is advisable to

park early in the day in one of the municipal parking areas along the beach.

There was a flurry of land speculation at the beginning of the century, with railroad magnate Henry Huntington selling lots at **Redondo Beach** (**1-F4**) to buyers who were anxious to capitalize on property next to the new railroad system. Beach property was divided into smaller and smaller lots and by 1920 the area was overcrowded. Redondo today has a beautiful marina complex in King Harbor, which has a variety of restaurants, theme bars, and interesting shops plus extensive boating and fishing facilities. In 1907, California's first surfers took to the waves at Redondo Beach and today the sport is more popular than ever. Early-morning surfers frequent this stretch of beach every day of the year, rain or shine.

The city of **Torrance** (**1-F4**) has its own county beach, which runs into the rocky peninsula of **Palos Verdes** (**1-G3**). A beautiful scenic drive can be enjoyed through this rugged and peaceful headland. (*See* SIGHTSEEING, Viewpoints & Scenic Drives, Scenic Drives: Palos Verdes Scenic Drive.)

The city of **Long Beach** (**1-G5**) was originally a strip of sandy land set aside for trading between mainland Indians and those who came across from Catalina Island in canoes. When Henry Huntington extended his famous Pacific Railroad to Long Beach, people quickly moved homes and businesses into the area. After the discovery of oil at Signal Hill in 1921, the population exploded to 100,000—a jump of 50,000 from 1890. Today, Long Beach is a major port, an important naval base, an international trade center, and a magnet for tourists. Each March the famous Long Beach Grand Prix attracts motor racing celebrities from around the world. There is a well-protected beach along the innerside of the harbor for safe swimming, waterskiing, and yachting. The most publicized attraction in recent years has been the famous ocean liner *Queen Mary* (*see* SIGHTSEEING, Tours: *Queen Mary* Tour), whose immediate fate is uncertain. The port of Los Angeles and the Port of Long Beach combine to make the world's largest man-made harbor. Fort MacArthur in San Pedro near the entrance to the harbor was built for protection and is now an important center for air defense. The quaint Ports O' Call Village (*see* SIGHTSEEING, Tours) is a local attraction. A variety of craft leave San Pedro daily for **Catalina Island.** A 20-minute plane journey or 2-hour boat crossing may be made to the city of Avalon.

Catalina was originally occupied by Gabrieleno Indians (who were wiped out mainly by Russian sea otter hunters) but later became a hideout for smugglers, fur traders, and bootleggers. In 1850 the island was bought for $10,000 by Jose Convarrubias, who sold it three years later for just $1,000 to San Franciscan Albert Packard. The island was sold and resold until a major interest was finally acquired by the Wrigley family (of chewing gum fame). William Wrigley, Jr., was responsible for building the circular casino in 1929. Clear waters, nature preserves, and a bird sanctuary make Catalina a haven for divers and naturalists. Visitors are restricted to tour buses and designated camping areas, ensuring the preservation of this unspoiled area. Buffalo, shipped across for a Hollywood movie entitled *The Vanishing American*, multiplied and still roam freely on the island. The town of Avalon has many attractions including a beautiful natural harbor. Festivals, art shows, and sporting events are held year-round. Amazingly, Catalina remains virtually traffic-free (*see* SIGHTSEEING, Day Trips).

Beverly Hills   1-C3
Named after Beverly, Massachusetts, Beverly Hills was purchased by the Rodeo Land and Water Company in 1906—at the time it was a lima bean plantation. The famous Beverly Hills Hotel (*see* ACCOMMODATIONS, Beverly Hills, Hotels) was one of Beverly Hills's first buildings, constructed in 1912. With the movie industry explosion in the 1920s, many stars moved to new homes in Beverly Hills and later to the exclusive area of Bel-Air. An independent community, Beverly Hills has never been annexed to Los Angeles and the early movie stars fought relentlessly to preserve that status. (*See* Outdoor Sculpture: Monument to the Stars.) In 1919, Mary Pickford and Douglas Fairbanks built their famous home, Pickfair. Their neighborhood was to become one of the richest communities on earth.

Beverly Hills is surprisingly small (under 6 square miles) but contains huge mansions and open expanses of manicured gardens along wide, tree-lined streets. Rodeo Drive is famed for beautiful, expensive boutiques and nearby Wilshire Boulevard has impressive department stores such as Neiman-Marcus and Saks Fifth Avenue. Everything is presented with elegance—even window displays are works of art. Celebrities are often seen in Beverly Hills, especially at their favorite dining spots, such as La Scala, The Bistro, or Chasen's. Two famous hotels, the Beverly Hills Hotel and the Beverly Wilshire Hotel, cater to wealthy visitors ranging from oil tycoons to the world's nobility.

It is difficult to view luxurious homes in most areas of LA, but along Sunset Boulevard, between Canon Drive and Hillcrest Drive, several interesting mansions can be seen from the road, typifying the elegance and wealth of Beverly Hills. (*See also* SIGHTSEEING, Walking Tours.)

Burbank   1-B4
Burbank is the center of today's movie and television industry. Once dominated by the Warner Brothers' empire, its studio backlot was second home to such movie greats as Humphrey Bogart, Lauren Bacall, Errol Flynn, and James Cagney. Considering the movie magic produced there, Burbank does not look glamorous, as one might expect. It is more a center of industry, housing several great studios (Warner Brothers/ Columbia, NBC, Disney, and others). The Hollywood-Burbank airport is one of the busiest in Southern California. (*See also* Motion Picture Studios: Burbank Studios *and* Walt Disney; *and* Television Studios: NBC Television Network.)

Century City   1-C3
Tom Mix, famous cowboy of the early screen, once owned a ranch on the land that is now Century City. His ranch became the backlot of the 20th Century-Fox studios, where a multitude of great movies were made (*see* Motion Picture Studios). Much of the lot was sold for development as Century City in 1961.

Century City was a phenomenal venture. It was designed by world-famous architects whose combined talents blended to produce a city of tomorrow. The expertly planned area is dominated by two gleaming, triangular office buildings, Century Plaza Towers. The complex includes the Century Plaza Hotel (*see* ACCOMMODATIONS, Beverly Hills, Hotels) and the ABC Entertainment Center. Buildings are varied and impressive with good landscaping and ample parking. Excellent restaurants and a huge shopping center cater to thousands of office workers and nearby residents of Beverly Hills and Century City's plush new condominiums. Live, outdoor entertainment is featured regularly in the plaza area. Century City is an example of urban planning at its best. (*See also* SIGHTSEEING, Walking Tours.)

Chinatown   1-C5
Los Angeles's original Chinatown was located close to Olvera Street. The new Chinatown, off N. Broadway, opened in 1939 with an emphasis on tourism. Shopping is a major pastime and most stores are open in the evening. For authentic Chinese markets and restaurants, North Spring Street is worth a visit. There is also a Chinese cinema.

Although small in comparison to Chinatown in San Francisco, the LA version is just as lively and colorful, especially in February during the celebration of the Chinese New Year, when traditional parades take to the streets and the sounds of music and firecrackers fill the air as dragons wind their way along.

Culver City   1-D4
The MGM (Metro-Goldwyn-Mayer) studio—now Lorimar Telepictures—is Culver City's main claim to fame. The motion picture industry controlled the economy of Culver City during the 1920s and 1930s and is still operating on a large scale (*see* Motion Picture Studios: Culver Studios *and* Lorimar Telepictures). Howard Hughes, who played his own part in the development of motion pictures (he once owned RKO-Pathé), established Hughes Aircraft in Culver City and set up an industrial complex that still provides jobs for thousands. An excellent shopping center, Fox Hills Mall, serves a growing residential population as many people move to the area to work in technology and electronics.

Downtown   1-C5
Olvera Street, known as the birthplace of Los Angeles, stands in El Pueblo de Los Angeles State Historic Park in the heart of Downtown LA.

The area was originally settled by Mexican Americans, but as the city grew, Downtown became home for immigrants of all nationalities and the cosmopolitan atmosphere remains.

Although this is the oldest settlement in Los Angeles, few buildings of historical interest remain. During the past 25 years the Downtown Bunker Hill area has been virtually rebuilt. High-rise office buildings and new hotels are interspersed with preserved buildings such as the Biltmore Hotel and the Bradbury Building (for both, see Buildings & Landmarks). The beautiful Music Center (see Buildings & Landmarks), which opened in 1965, houses three fine theaters. The Bunker Hill project also contains the Museum of Contemporary Art (MOCA), which is stunning both architecturally and in content (see MUSEUMS & GALLERIES, Museums, General Art).

The University of Southern California (USC), the largest private coed university on the West Coast, is located close to Exposition Park, which contains the California State Museum of Science and Industry and the Los Angeles County Museum of Natural History (see MUSEUMS & GALLERIES, Museums, Science and Historic). USC opened in 1880 with only 55 students; enrollment today is well over 20,000. The Los Angeles City Hall (see Buildings & Landmarks), now dwarfed by new high rises, has always been a landmark and the nearby Civic Center complex has an impressive array of public buildings.

The Greater Los Angeles Visitors and Convention Bureau is located Downtown in the Atlantic Richfield Shopping Plaza, 505 South Flower Street. Known as ARCO Plaza, it is a huge shopping mall containing fashion boutiques, galleries, and an impressive display area for artistic events. Because of scant and expensive parking facilities, the best way to get around the Downtown area is to use the RTD Downtown MiniBus service (Route 202). The small striped buses run every 10 minutes and cover Olvera Street, Chinatown, Little Tokyo, City Hall, and all points of interest. (See also SIGHTSEEING, Tours: The Los Angeles Conservancy and Walking Tours: Exposition Park and The Plaza & Chinatown.) The new, long-awaited Metro Rail system (still under construction) should ease traffic considerably in the Downtown area.

Hollywood   **1-C4**
Hollywood was officially "born" in 1886 when developer Harvey Wilcox applied to the LA County recorder's office to sell parcels of land. Wilcox's wife named the land Hollywood after an estate of the same name near Chicago.

Before Hollywood became part of the city of Los Angeles in 1910 it was a quiet, rural, fruit-producing community. Claiming to be free of crime, there was no jail. In 1906, Otis M. Gove and George Van Guysling combined their photographic talents to make a motion picture. Their location was a ranch in a quiet rural area—Hollywood. In the same year the city was annexed to LA, two English brothers opened the Nestor Film Company, and Hollywood was really on its way.

By 1940, Hollywood was responsible for over 90% of all films produced in the U.S., and the once quiet community exploded into a maze of wooden houses and apartment buildings. Hollywood still boasts famous attractions, such as Mann's Chinese Theatre (see Buildings & Landmarks) and the Sunset Strip, but sadly today's "Tinsel Town" has a rather tarnished image. Famous nightclubs and celebrity hangouts have diminished along with the number of movie studios. Some of the famed and historic sights remain, and walking tours of both Sunset Boulevard and Hollywood Boulevard are definitely recommended for true nostalgia buffs. Organized tours are also highly recommended. (See SIGHTSEEING, Tours: Grey Line Bus Tours and Starline Tours.)

Nightspots in Hollywood are now geared toward the popular music industry. Rock clubs dot the Sunset Strip and recording stars frequent local restaurants and bars. (See SIGHTSEEING, Walking Tours: Sunset Strip, Hollywood Boulevard, and Vine Street; and NIGHTLIFE, Cabaret, Discos, and Rock.)

Little Tokyo   **1-C5**
The largest Japanese community outside Japan (over 110,000) happens to be in Los Angeles. The Japanese-American population grew rapidly between the world wars but was drastically reduced by forced evacuation during World War II. Little Tokyo was gradually resettled and is today a center for Japanese cultural arts.

Buddhist temples reflect traditional architectural styles. Shops, galleries, and restaurants abound. During Nisei Week (nisei is the Japanese word for "born in the U.S.") in August, the community celebrates its cultural heritage with parades, dancing, tea ceremonies, and demonstrations ranging from karate to flower arranging.

Pasadena   **1-B6**
Pasadena, "Crown of the Valley" in the language of the Chippewa Indians, was settled in the late 1880s by colonists from Indiana. Extensive development caused rapid growth as the city became popular with writers and artists and attracted a fashionable vacation crowd. It was a favorite winter resort for East Coast millionaires, whose lavish mansions still stand along Orange Grove Avenue.

Pasadena has first-rate museums and fine art galleries (see MUSEUMS & GALLERIES, Museums, General Art: Norton Simon Museum of Art; and Historic: Pasadena Historical Society Museum), and the city's early architecture has been well preserved. The Tournament of Roses Parade and Rose Bowl football game on New Year's Day have made Pasadena world famous (see ANNUAL EVENTS, Calendar, January).

San Fernando Valley   **1-A3**
Named after the Mission San Fernando Rey de Espana but originally known as Encino Valley, this was the site of the victorious battle that ended the American conquest of California in 1845.

The Valley, as it is known to Angelinos, now houses over one-third of LA's residents. Its first town, Toluca—now called North Hollywood—was home to personalities from the motion picture industry. Over a century ago Calabasas was a stagecoach stop and still holds much of its old charm. Gold was first discovered in California in what is now Newhall. In 1848 a shepherd pulled wild onions for his lunch and found gold nuggets clinging to the roots.

The San Fernando Valley became a rich, wheat-producing agricultural area, but it was not destined to remain so. In 1874 the Southern Pacific Railroad arrived and housing development began as immigrants flocked to the West Coast. The San Fernando Valley was annexed to Los Angeles in 1915 (shortly after the Owens River Aqueduct brought water to the city). Property values rose as middle-class families moved in to build their homes and realize the American dream. The Valley is full of historical sites detailing its growth since the mission was founded.

San Gabriel Valley   **1-C6**
This eastern valley at the foot of the San Gabriel Mountains contains a wealth of history and culture. The first people to settle in the Los Angeles area were the founders of the Mission San Gabriel Archangel (see Churches) in 1771. The mission became a resting place for people journeying to the Pueblo de Los Angeles.

Under Mexican rule the San Gabriel Valley was divided into huge ranchos, the largest being Rancho Santa Anita, where the Santa Anita Racetrack now stands. Ranchers used the peaceful Gabrieleno Indians to work the fertile land, which was perfect for citrus crops. Two wealthy businessmen, Henry E. Huntington and E. J. "Lucky" Baldwin, contributed substantially to the area's cultural development—the Huntington Library, Art Gallery, and Botanical Gardens (see MUSEUMS & GALLERIES, Museums, General Art) contain a breathtaking collection of rare and priceless specimens, and "Lucky" Baldwin's estate is now the Los Angeles State and Country Arboretum (see SIGHTSEEING, Tours). Despite a huge population growth that has merged its cities into a long surburban sprawl, the San Gabriel Valley has retained a certain country ambience. NOTE: It is possible to visit the San Gabriel Mission, the Huntington collections, and the Arboretum all in one day, at a total cost of less than $5 per person admission.

Santa Monica   **1-D3**
In 1542, Juan Rodriguez Cabrillo discovered the "Bay of Smokes," so named because of rising smoke from Indian campfires. The bay was later named Santa Monica, in honor of the mother of St. Augustine. A new town was started (with one hotel and several bathhouses) from plans laid out by Senator John P. Jones and Col. Robert Baker. In 1875, lots measuring 60 feet by 150 feet were sold for $300. With a new railroad from central Los Angeles, excursionists flocked to the coast.

Santa Monica Pier

Growing as quickly as the motion picture industry in Hollywood, Santa Monica became a favorite place for movie stars to build their beach homes. Reminiscent of the Mediterranean, the city attracted many visitors. Tourism is still a major industry. Recreation facilities abound; beaches are extensive and never overcrowded; and shopping and parking areas are excellent.

To get a true feeling of Santa Monica, walk. The pier has several attractions, including the carousel used in the movie *The Sting*. Fishing from the pier is free and boat trips are available. On a weekend morning, stroll along the boardwalk to the adjacent community of Venice and enjoy a carnival atmosphere among musicians, jugglers, bodybuilders, and skaters. Beachside merchants sell everything from antique clothes to potted plants. Restaurants with outdoor patios and refreshment stands are plentiful along Ocean Front Walk. Visit nearby Main Street; once a canal, it's now a chic shopping, dining, and browsing area. Santa Monica has a large British population, apparent by several pubs that offer imported beers, darts, and fish 'n' chips.

A clean, friendly city with a casual air, Santa Monica is a perfect vacation spot for all ages. The Chamber of Commerce has a tourist information center in Palisades Park, (310) 393-9825. (See also SIGHTSEEING, Walking Tours: Venice & Ocean Front Walk.)

West Los Angeles & Westwood   **1-C3**
Westwood Village was developed during the 1920s. Shortly after World War II the university campus at UCLA was enlarged to the tune of $160 million. The influx of students attracted new businesses and entertainment facilities.

West Los Angeles expanded with the growth of the automobile and became a fashionable residential district for the first commuters. It is a rather indefinable area with quiet, residential sections, smart shopping districts, and ultra-modern high-rise buildings. Westwood's plush, new condominium complexes represent some of the most expensive real estate in the world. The large Veterans Administration Facility on Wilshire Boulevard is an impressive reminder of recent wars, which seem so far removed from this sunny, peaceful region.

Greatly influenced by the young university students, Westwood Village is lively, innovative, and charming. A variety of interesting shops are interspersed with good restaurants, friendly bars, and a concentration of cinemas showing first-run movies. Some shops stay open late into the evening and theatergoers are entertained by strolling artists. A semiannual arts and crafts show is among the best in Southern California. The university hosts a variety of fairs, festivals, and concerts throughout the year.

The Federal Building on Wilshire Boulevard, close to the San Diego Freeway, offers free parking to those wishing to avoid the nightmare of parking in Westwood Village. An inexpensive minibus service runs between the Federal Building and the entertainment areas of the village on Friday evenings and all day Saturday (Sunday until 2am). (*See also* SHOPPING, Shopping Centers: Westwood Village.)

BUILDINGS & LANDMARKS

Despite the many jokes made about it, Los Angeles has a surprisingly wealthy cultural heritage. The following section describes a wide variety of fine architecture and buildings of local historical interest, plus some of the more colorful and flamboyant structures that make LA unique. Although several notable hotels are listed, see ACCOMMODATIONS *for detailed information on services. For further information on LA's architectural treasures contact:*

The Los Angeles Conservancy   7-D4
727 W. 7th St, Suite 955, LA. (213) 623-2489. The Conservancy publishes walking guides and arranges tours. (*See* SIGHTSEEING, Tours.)

The Cultural Affairs Board   7-C4
433 S. Spring St, 10th Floor, LA. (213) 485-6793. The board provides information on historical monuments, cultural events, and societies.

Alexandria Hotel   7-D4
501 S. Spring St, LA. (213) 626-7484. (John Parkinson) Built in 1906, the Alexandria has provided luxury accommodations for U.S. presidents and celebrities. The Palm Court, with its huge stained-glass ceiling and decorative paneling, is the hotel's main attraction.

Automobile Club of Southern California 7-F2
2601 S. Figueroa St, LA. (213) 741-3111. (Hunt & Burns, 1923) This Spanish-colonial structure contains a domed rotunda with an ornate gold ceiling. The club sells useful publications on Southern California (available to AAA members only).

Avalon Casino
Airport Rd, Avalon, Catalina Island. (Weber & Spaulding) Built between 1927 and 1929, the Mediterranean-style circular casino cost $2 million (at a time when the whole island was valued at only $6 million). Beautifully decorated, the ca-

sino still features big-band sounds in its famous ballroom. The building also contains a theater, museum, and art gallery. Gambling is prohibited.

Avila Adobe   7-B5
10 Olvera St, LA. (213) 628-1274. The oldest house in Los Angeles. It was built in 1818 by Francisco Avila, once mayor of the pueblo. *OPEN Tues-Sat.* FREE. (*See also* SIGHTSEEING, Walking Tours: The Plaza & Chinatown.)

Banning Residence Museum   1-F5
401 East M St, Wilmington. (310) 548-7777. In 1876, "transportation king" Gen. Phineas Banning brought the Southern Pacific Railroad to Los Angeles. His mansion, built in 1864 using local Indian labor and skilled shipwrights, is a fine example of the Greek revival style with its use of marble and colored glass. The mansion is located in an attractive 20-acre park and is filled with elegant period furniture. *CLOSED Mon & Fri.* Tours *12:30, 1:30 & 2:30 p.m.; also 3:30pm on Sat & Sun.* Small donation requested.

Susana Machado Bernard Residence   7-C1
845 S. Lake St, LA. (John Parkinson) (Private residence.) This 1902 art nouveau/gothic mansion has been beautifully restored.

Beverly Hills City Hall   5-D8
455 N. Rexford Dr, Beverly Hills. (310) 285-1000. An exceptionally decorative structure with a colored tile dome. Designed by William Gage in 1932 in the Spanish baroque style. Recently renovated and very much a part of Beverly Hills Civic Center.

Beverly Hills Hotel   5-C7
9641 Sunset Blvd, Beverly Hills. (310) 276-2251. (Elmer Grey, 1912) Internationally famous as the hotel for celebrities, this sugar-pink mission-style building was completed in 1912, two years before the City of Beverly Hills was officially

Beverly Hills City Hall

founded. Its 12 acres of tropical grounds contain 21 individual bungalows.

Beverly Wilshire Hotel   **5-E8**
9500 Wilshire Blvd, Beverly Hills. (310) 275-5200. (Walker & Eisen) Hernando Courtwright's prestigious hotel was opened in 1928. The new wing, added in 1971, was designed by Welton Becket and is separated from the main complex by a private road that features cobblestones and gas lamps imported from Edinburgh, Scotland. Catering to the world's nobility, the hotel contains only the very best in furnishings and amenities.

Biltmore Hotel   **7-C4**
506 S. Grand Ave, LA. (213) 624-1011. (Schultze & Weaver) Dominating Pershing Square since 1923, the Biltmore is as impressive inside as one would expect. No expense was spared on the decor, which includes impressive wall and ceiling murals, fine wrought-iron decorations, and a beautiful Spanish-style lobby. A $41 million renovation was completed in 1986.

Bonnie Brae Street   **7-C2**
800 & 1000 Blocks, S. Bonnie Brae St, LA. Beautifully preserved Victorian residences (privately owned) adorn two blocks of S. Bonnie Brae Street near MacArthur Park. Most homes were built in the 1890s.

Bradbury Building   **7-C4**
304 S. Broadway, LA. (213) 626-1893. One of LA's most unique and most photographed edifices is still in use as an office building. It was designated a historic cultural monument in 1962. Louis L. Bradbury commissioned the building, which was designed by George Herbert Wyman (then a junior draftsman) in 1893. The exterior is overly plain compared to the building's interior of ornate ironwork, open stairways, decorative railings, and wood paneling, all illuminated by natural light that filters through a glass roof. The Los Angeles Conservancy includes the Bradbury Building lobby in a tour of Downtown LA. (*See also* SIGHTSEEING, Tours: The Los Angeles Conservancy.)

Brand Library   **1-B5**
1601 W. Mountain St, Glendale. (818) 548-2051. A multistory mansion in the Glendale foothills built in 1904. The Saracenic architecture, with minarets and domes, combines Moorish and Indian styles. Leslie C. Brand donated the estate to the city of Glendale with a provision that it should be used as a public library and park. *CLOSED Sun and Mon.* FREE.

Broadway Theater District   **7-D4**
Between 3rd & 9th Sts, Downtown. Theaters dating back to 1910 are scattered along this stretch of Broadway, LA's original theater district. Hollywood's first movie epics opened here in the early 1920s to excited crowds. The Tower Theater, 802 Broadway, was designed specifically to show the first talkies. The Doremus Building, at the corner of 9th Street, is a successful combination of art deco and moderne styles and has an impressive clock tower. The Cameo Theater,

at 528, opened in 1910 and admission was just five cents (an original nickelodeon). In 1918 the Million Dollar Theater, at 307, was opened by Sid and D. J. Grauman. The decorative interior (by A. C. Martin) is particularly impressive. The Bradbury Building, at 304, is listed separately above. Unfortunately, the Broadway theaters no longer show first-run movies. Selections are most often Spanish-language films attracting a neighborhood audience. Tours are arranged by the Los Angeles Conservancy (*see* SIGHTSEEING, Tours).

The Brown Derby   **6-G8**
Wilshire Blvd at Alexandria, LA. (Original shell, interior is new.) This was the famous Brown Derby restaurant that was constructed in 1926. It glowed with early movie celebrities and became one of LA's most famous landmarks. Preservationists fought relentlessly for its survival. The restaurant was built in the shape of a derby hat, a style known as programmatic architecture.

Bullocks Wilshire Building   **7-B1**
3050 Wilshire Blvd, LA. (310) 382-6161. (John & Donald Parkinson) Now an I. Magnin store this is still one of LA's most elegant department stores and is a tribute to art deco. Designated a historic cultural monument in 1968, this store has catered to LA's affluent society since 1929, when it opened as the city's first suburban department store. A six-story, copper-crested tower, with a beacon, rises above the main structure, making the building visible for miles.

Campo de Cahuenga   **9-F5**
3919 Lankershim Blvd, N. Hollywood. This six-room abode is a 1923 replica of the 1845 house (constructed by Thomas Feliz) that saw the signing of the treaty to end the Mexican-American War in 1847. Documents relating to the signing are on display together with other historical memorabilia. *OPEN Mon-Fri 8am-3pm.* FREE.

Capitol Records Tower   **6-B6**
1750 Vine St, Hollywood. (213) 462-6252. (Welton Beckett) Thought to be the first circular office tower ever built, the design of this well-known landmark, built in 1954, is said to resemble a stack of records.

Carroll Avenue   **7-A3**
1300 Block, Carroll Ave, Angelino Heights. Magnificent Victorian mansions constructed during the 1800s have been lovingly restored to make this section of Carroll Avenue a famous architectural landmark in Los Angeles. Movie crews are often seen filming in this area, which has changed little since the 1890s.

Case Study Houses   **4-A1**
205 & 219 Chautauqua Blvd, Pacific Palisades. (Charles Eames, Eero Saarinen & Richard Neutra) These private residences are fine examples of modern architecture. Built in 1948 and 1949, using the latest techniques and materials available, they were quite futuristic in their design.

Chateau Marmont   **6-C2**
8221 Sunset Blvd, Hollywood. (310) 656-1010. This nostalgic hostelry resembles a Norman castle. Built in 1927, it has been popular with Holly-

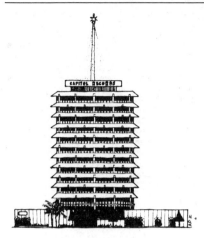

Capitol Records Tower

wood's elite ever since. It has always been frequented by artists and writers, and several screenplays have been written here, including *The Music Man, Butch Cassidy and the Sundance Kid*, and *The Day of the Locust*. There is nothing very social about the Chateau; its attraction is its promise of privacy. Greta Garbo once lived here. John Belushi died here.

Cinerama Dome   **6-C6**
6360 Sunset Blvd, Hollywood. (213) 466-3401. Its impressive white cellular structure makes this theater a Hollywood landmark. (*See also* ENTERTAINMENT, Cinema, Select Theaters.)

The Citadel   **1-D6**
5675 Telegraph Rd, City of Commerce. (Morgan, Wall & Clements) A former Uniroyal tire plant, built in 1930, it looks rather like an impregnable fortress but is really a facade. This imposing structure is 1,700 feet long and was designed to resemble an ancient Assyrian palace.

City Hall   **7-C4**
200 N. Spring St, LA. (213) 485-2121. (Austin, Parkinson, Martin & Whittlesey) The Los Angeles City Hall was completed in 1928 and for many years was the highest visible structure in the city. An imposing building featuring a collection of architectural styles, it is easily recognized by its jagged, pyramidlike tower. Inside, the domed rotunda is decorated with tile patterns showing various government services. Short tours are given on weekdays and an observation deck on the 27th floor allows visitors impressive views of the city. *OPEN Mon-Fri 9am-5pm.*

Clifton's Silver Spoon Cafeteria   **7-D3**
515 W. 7th St, LA. (213) 485-1726. Clifton's Caf-

eterias are a Los Angeles institution. This location (designed by Plummer, Wurdeman & Becket in 1935) is in an ornate Victorian building (circa 1900) and contains exhibits showing Clifton's history. A meditation room offers "food for thought." Visit in daylight only.

Coca-Cola Building   **7-F4**
1334 S. Central Ave, LA. (213) 746-5555. (Robert V. Derrah) A bottling plant that was completed in 1937. The unusual but attractive structure resembles an ocean liner, complete with portholes and a curved superstructure.

Crossroads of the World   **6-C6**
6671 Sunset Blvd, LA. 463-5611. (Robert V. Derrah) Originally designed as a shopping center, this unusual complex has a European village theme. A central ship design suggests transportation to foreign ports. Built in 1936, it was once a major tourist attraction but today houses offices.

Doheny Mansion   **7-E2**
8 Chester Pl, LA. (213) 746-0405; (310) 476-2237. (Theodore Eisen & Sumner Hunt) Chester Place is an exclusive residential park containing 13 fine houses, of which Doheny Mansion is the most impressive. Completed in 1900, the residence was later sold to oil magnate Edward L. Doheny. It sustained damage in the 1933 earthquake and was beautifully remodeled in the French rococo style. Today the mansion is occupied by the Sisters of St. Joseph of Carondolet. Tours may be arranged by appointment.

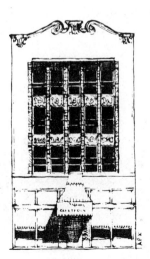

Clifton's Silver Spoon Cafeteria

Do-Nut Hole   **1-C8**
Junction of Elliot Ave & Amar Rd, San Gabriel. A 1958 fantasy structure of two oversized dough-nuts. It is a local attraction, serving calorie-laden creations 24-hours a day.

Dunbar Hotel   **1-D5**
4225 S. Central Ave, LA. The Dunbar opened in 1928 as the Hotel Somerville, named after its builder, Dr. John Alexander Somerville. It was the first hotel in America built specifically for black people. The Dunbar was recently reno-vated into a senior residence as well as a mu-seum.

Eames House   **4-A1**
203 Chautauqua Blvd, Pacific Palisades. (Pri-vate residence.) Internationally famous indus-trial designer Charles Eames built this house for himself in 1949. Its stark modern design was revolutionary for the time. Eames also had an influence in the construction of the nearby Case Study Houses (*see above*) initiated by Jean Entenza, editor of *Arts and Architecture* magazine.

Egyptian Theatre   **6-C5**
6712 Hollywood Blvd, Hollywood. (213) 467-6167. A decorative Hollywood cinema fash-ioned after an Egyptian palace. The concept of Sid Grauman, whose Chinese Theatre along the boulevard is now world famous. (*See also* ENTERTAINMENT Cinema, Select Theaters.)

Ennis-Brown House   **6-A8**
2607 Glendower Ave, LA. Built in 1924, this is one of Frank Lloyd Wright's most impressive Mayan-style houses. It has been featured in sev-eral Hollywood movies, including *The Day of the Locust* and *Blade Runner*. Though a private res-idence, tours are available the second Saturday of odd-numbered months throughout the year. Call (213) 660-0607 for reservations and fee schedule.

Fleetwood Center   **1-B2**
19611 Ventura Blvd, Woodland Hills. (Matlin & Dvoretzky, 1987) A pink stucco office building,

built to resemble the front of a 1970 Fleetwood Cadillac, it is an appropriate salute to the motor car on this very busy thoroughfare.

Freeway Stack   **7-E2**
Carrying 400,000 vehicles per day, "The Stack" is a feat of modern engineering located in Downtown LA: Three freeways (the Pasadena, Santa Monica, and Harbor) meet and cross each other. A good view of the stack is from Wilshire Boulevard as it crosses the Harbor Freeway (**7-C3**).

Gamble House   **8-B1**
4 Westmoreland Place, Pasadena. (818) 793-3334. A beautiful Craftsman-style bungalow built in 1908 for Mr. and Mrs. David Gamble (of Procter & Gamble). Architects Charles and Henry Green took great care to utilize natural elements that complemented their design and blended with regional characteristics. Their de-sign is influenced by Japanese architecture, but the outcome is a perfect example of "California Bungalow." Tours available, times vary—phone for information.

J. Paul Getty Museum   **1-C2**
17985 Pacific Coast Hwy, Malibu. (310) 458-2003. A replica of a Roman seaside villa that was buried during an eruption of Mount Vesuvius in A.D. 79, the Getty Museum overlooks the Pacific Ocean from a Malibu hillside. Completed in 1974, the villa contains 38 galleries where price-less Greek and Roman works of art, European paintings, and French decorative arts are dis-played. Outdoors, decorative walkways with mo-saics, statues, and Roman-style landscaping border a central pool. The Getty Museum was recently pronounced the most richly endowed museum in the world. Paul Getty himself never saw it completed. Pleasant resting areas and a tearoom are provided for visitors. Lunch is avail-able from 11am to 2:30pm. Phone at least one week in advance for parking reservations. (*See also* MUSEUMS & GALLERIES, Museums, Gen-eral Art.)

Gamble House

Greystone Mansion **5-B7**
501 N. Doheny Rd, Beverly Hills. This European-style mansion, completed in 1928, was designed by architect Gordon B. Kaufman for oil magnate Edward L. Doheny. Fittings include marble floors and hand-carved oak banisters. The huge mansion is surrounded by beautiful gardens that have been made into a public park.

**Griffith Park Observatory &
Planetarium** **6-A8**
2800 E. Observatory Rd, Griffith Park. (213) 664-1191. (John C. Austin & F. M. Ashley) An architectural landmark high above the city. This 1930s moderne structure contains the Planetarium Theater and Hall of Science. (*See also* SIGHT-SEEING, Viewpoints & Scenic Drives, Viewpoints.)

Heritage Square, Highland Park **1-C5**
3800 N. Homer St, Highland Park. When redevelopment began in the Downtown area of LA during the 1960s, several fine old Victorian buildings were threatened with destruction. The Cultural Heritage Foundation had them moved to Homer Street for preservation. The collection includes a small railway depot that was built in 1886.

Heritage Square, Santa Monica **4-D4**
Jones House, 2612 Main St, Santa Monica. (310) 392-8537. (Sumner P. Hunt) Santa Monica's Heritage Square is a three-story house that was built in 1894 and moved from 1007 Ocean Avenue to this location in 1978. The building contains a small museum and period rooms.

Hollyhock House **6-C8**
Barnsdall Park, 4800 Hollywood Blvd, LA. (213) 662-7272. Built in 1921 and designated a historic cultural monument in 1963, Hollyhock House is a superb example of Frank Lloyd Wright's California Romanza period. The Barnsdall Park cultural complex, bordered by olive trees, contains several unusual buildings and is the setting for many art-related activities during summer. (*See* PARKS & GARDENS, Parks: Barnsdall Park; *and* MUSEUMS & GALLERIES, Art Galleries, Central Los Angeles: Barnsdall Municipal Art Gallery.)

Hollywood Bowl **6-B5**
2301 N. Highland Ave, Hollywood. (213) 850-2000. (Lloyd Wright, 1922) This huge famous amphitheater was built into a natural depression in the hillside. Lloyd Wright designed the present, acoustically perfect dome in 1928. It has seen performances by world celebrities from Bernstein to the Beatles. Extensive alterations were made in 1969 during which the Bowl's seating capacity was extended to over 17,000. The area was originally known as Daisy Dell and is today a 116-acre park filled with trees and wildlife, with the world-famous Bowl as a centerpiece. (*See also* ENTERTAINMENT, Theater.)

The Hollywood Sign **9-G8**
Mount Lee. In 1923, real-estate developers erected a sign to promote the sale of lots in Beechwood Canyon. The sign spelled "Hollywoodland" and was illuminated by 4,000 light bulbs. There was even a caretaker who lived in a small cabin behind the first "L." In 1945, long after the land had been sold off, the dilapidated sign was repaired by the Hollywood Chamber of Commerce and reduced to read Hollywood, thus creating an advertisement for the city During the next 30 years vandalism and the elements took their toll, and in 1978, after much publicity, campaigning, and fund-raising by Hollywood celebrities, a new sign was erected. (*See also* SIGHTSEEING, Viewpoints & Scenic Drives, Viewpoints.)

Higashi Hongwangi Temple **7-C5**
8505 E. 3rd St, Little Tokyo. A Japanese Buddhist temple with a stunning gold altar and a brilliantly crafted lattice ceiling constructed the traditional way—no nails were needed. *OPEN Sun.*

Hotel Green **8-C2**
50 E. Green St, Pasadena. (Frederick Roehrig) Hotel Green, originally known as the Webster, opened in 1890 and was one of Pasadena's grandest inns. The hotel was immensely popular with wealthy vacationers who loved the unusual Moorish/Roman-style architecture. A portion of the original structure was demolished in 1924. The remaining section, now a retirement community, is known as Castle Green Apartments.

Huntington (Ritz-Carlton) Hotel **8-F4**
1401 S. Oak Knoll Ave, Pasadena. (818) 568-3900. One of Southern California's loveliest hotels. The Huntington was built in 1907 and was purchased by Henry E. Huntington, the railway tycoon, 1913. Through thoughtful planning on the part of the original owner-designer, Gen. Marshall C. Wentworth, every room received direct sunlight. Rooms were tastefully decorated and the beautiful gardens are still carefully maintained. Earthquake safety codes caused closure of the main building in 1986, but an exact replica of the original building was reopened in 1989 as the Ritz-Carlton.

La Miniatura **8-A1**
645 Prospect Crescent, Pasadena. Another Frank Lloyd Wright gem in the Mayan style. This residence, built in 1923, is around the corner from the famous Gamble House.

Los Angeles Central Library **7-C4**
433 S. Spring St, LA. (213) 612-3200. (Bertram Goodhue & Carleton Winslow, Sr.) A distinctive Los Angeles landmark, the library is easily recognizable by its colorfully tiled pyramid tower. Completed in 1926, the building shows Roman and Egyptian architectural influences. Contents include fine murals and sculpture as well as excellent library facilities.

Los Angeles Herald Examiner Building **7-D3**
1111 S. Broadway, LA. Built for newspaper magnate W. R. Hearst. The design influence of Julia Morgan is evident in this building, completed in 1912. She had worked on Hearst's famous San Simeon estate, and the familiar Spanish mission

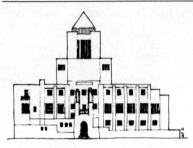

Los Angeles Central Library

style is repeated here. The newspaper is now defunct.

Los Angeles Times Building　　7-C4
Times Mirror Sq, LA. (213) 237-5000. (Gordon Kaufmann, 1935) An imposing moderne-style building is HQ for the Times Mirror Company, which publishes the *LA Times.* (*See* SIGHT-SEEING, Tours.)

Lovell House　　1-C5
4616 Dundee Dr, LA. (Private residence.) Considered by some to be architecturally the most important house in Los Angeles, it was designed by Richard Neutra in 1929 but looks surprisingly modern today.

Lummis Home (El Alisal)　　1-C5
200 E. Ave 43, Highland Park. (213) 222-0546.

Charles F. Lummis designed and constructed his unusual boulder and cement house over a period of 13 years, from 1898 to 1910. Lummis was the first city editor of the *LA Times.* He loved natural surroundings and native Indian culture, and stood strongly in defense of the Indians of the Southwest, one of whom was his only assistant in the building of this house.

Mann's Chinese Theatre　　6-C4
6925 Hollywood Blvd, Hollywood. (213) 464-8111. (Meyer & Holler) Opening in 1927 with Cecil B. De Mille's *King of Kings,* the Chinese Theatre has remained a major attraction throughout Hollywood's history. Built and financed by realtor C. E. Toberman for movie-theater king Sid Grauman (whose name can be seen many times in the famous cement prints across the forecourt), the colorful and ornate theater resembles a Chinese temple. The decorative embellishments and grand scale of the interior make a visit to the movies a real occasion. (*See also* ENTERTAINMENT, Cinema, Select Theaters.)

Max Factor Salon　　6-C6
1666 N. Highland Ave, Hollywood. (213) 463-6164. The swanky art deco salon opened in 1935 to the delight of Hollywood's movie community. Max Factor designed the first makeup used for both black-and-white and color television. A complete makeover can still be obtained today—by appointment only.

Melrose Design Center　　6-E2
8500 Melrose Ave, W. Hollywood. (Robert R. Murrin) A zebra-striped, sawtoothed structure made of black granite and white marble. Its fit-

Max Factor Salon

tingly eye-catching design is perfect for fashionable Melrose Avenue. All showrooms have pink-framed windows overlooking the street and a pink circular staircase ascends to a second level.

Merced Theater   **7-C5**
418 N. Main St, LA. (Ezra Kysor) The Merced was LA's first theater building and was constructed in 1870, adjacent to Pico House (*see below*). Now a State Historic Landmark, the theater has a colorful background, having been used as a saloon, an armory, and a church.

Monica's on Main   **4-D4**
2640 Main St, Santa Monica. (310) 392-4956. A 1906 Victorian home built for the mayor of Santa Monica. It was moved here from its original location on Ocean Avenue, was formerly the Chronicle restaurant, and now accommodates Monica's on Main restaurant.

Music Center   **1-G4**
135 N. Grand Ave, LA. (213) 972-7211. (Welton Beckett & Associates) An impressive group of three fine theaters: the Dorothy Chandler Pavilion, Mark Taper Forum, and Ahmanson Theatre (*see* ENTERTAINMENT, Theater). Dorothy Chandler's efforts to provide Los Angeles with a first-rate cultural center resulted in this magnificent complex designed by Welton Beckett and completed in 1969.

Old Plaza Firehouse   **7-B5**
Paseo de la Plaza, LA. (213) 628-1274. Built in 1884, this was LA's first fire station. Now a museum, it is a part of El Pueblo de Los Angeles State Historic Park. (*See also* SIGHTSEEING, Walking Tours: The Plaza & Chinatown.)

One Bunker Hill   **7-C3**
Corner of Grand Ave & 5th St, LA. (Alison & Alison, 1930) A 12-story office building, built in the zigzag moderne style. The entryway is richly paneled and the main lobby is a feast for the eyes: 17 types of marble were used to create an intricately patterned floor and the ornate ceiling is etched in gold.

Oviatt Building   **7-D4**
617 S. Olive St, LA. (Walker & Eisen, 1927) Decorative zigzag paving in the art deco style, together with Lalique glass and ornate grillwork, makes this one of LA's most glamorous buildings.

The Ozzie & Harriet House   **6-B4**
1822 Camino Palmero Dr, Hollywood. (Private residence.) This is where the real Nelson family (of the popular TV show "The Adventures of Ozzie & Harriet") lived. The house was so suited to the family that their TV house was actually modeled after it. Harriet sold the house soon after Ozzie's death in 1975.

Pacific Design Center   **6-E1**
8687 Melrose Ave, Hollywood. (310) 657-0800. A gigantic blue glass building, designed by Cesar Pelli in 1975 to house outlets for the interior design trade. It dominates the area and glows at night, earning the nickname "Blue Whale."

Pacific Design Center

Pan Pacific Auditorium   **6-E3**
7600 Beverly Blvd, LA. (Walter Wurdeman & Welton Beckett) The nation's last remaining major example of streamline moderne. This beautiful building suffering years of neglect, but ongoing renovation has given it a new lease on life. Construction, completed in 1935, took just six weeks. The building was well used as a large exhibition space and is a fine example of 1930s futuristic architecture. Trivia enthusiasts may enjoy learning that this was the scene of the West Coast premiere of the up-and-coming Elvis Presley.

Pantages Theatre   **6-C6**
6233 Hollywood Blvd, Hollywood. (310) 216-6666. (B. Marcus Priteen) One of Hollywood's finest old movie theaters. A beautiful building, constructed in 1929, the theater is now used for live performances. It is a magnificent example of art deco style. The fabulous interior was designed by Anthony Heinsbergen. (*See also* ENTERTAINMENT, Theater.)

Paramount Ranch   **1-C1**
2813 Cornell Rd, Malibu. (818) 889-0781. Stroll through a mock Western town that has been used for hundreds of movies. TV shows and commercials are still filmed here. The ranch is part of the Santa Monica Mountains Recreation Area and guided nature walks are available most weekends. *OPEN 7 days, dawn to dusk*. FREE.

Pasadena City Hall   **8-B3**
100 N. Garfield Ave, Pasadena. (818) 405-4124. (John Bakewell & Arthur Brown) With a style described as Spanish neo-baroque, Pasadena City Hall, completed in 1927, dominates the civic center group. It has a beautiful domed tower and fountain courtyard.

Pickfair   **5-B6**
1143 Summit Dr, Beverly Hills. (Wallace Neff) Originally a hunting lodge, this house was purchased in 1919 by Mary Pickford and Douglas Fairbanks. Extensive remodeling transformed the lodge into a fine colonial-style mansion. The press of the day invented the name Pickfair by combining the stars' names. Lively celebrations were often held at the house during the 1920s and the couple encouraged many famous people to move to Beverly Hills.

Pico Adobe   **1-A3**
10940 Sepulveda Blvd, Mission Hills. (818) 365-7810. The Pico Adobe belonged to Governor Pio Pico's brother Andreas. It was built in 1834 and is the second oldest house in Los Angeles. Today it is HQ for the San Fernando Historical Society. *OPEN Wed-Sun 1-4pm.*

Pico House   **7-C4**
420 N. Main St, LA. (213) 628-1274. (Ezra Kysor) Commissioned in 1869 by Governor Pio Pico, this building was LA's first major three-story hotel. Now part of the Plaza area, it has been designated a State Historic Landmark. (*See also* SIGHTSEEING, Walking Tours: The Plaza & Chinatown.)

Queen Anne Cottage   **1-B7**
301 N. Baldwin Ave, Arcadia. (818) 821-3222. (A. A. Bennett) "Lucky" Baldwin, a lively tycoon (silver mining), once owned a huge portion of the San Gabriel Valley. He had Queen Anne Cottage constructed in 1881 solely for the entertainment of his guests. The cottage is located in the grounds of the LA State and County Arboretum (*see* PARKS & GARDENS, Botanical Gardens), once part of Baldwin's ranch. This highly decorative cottage has been fully restored and is furnished with period antiques and Baldwin memorabilia.

Queen Mary   **1-G5**
Pier J, Long Beach. (310) 435-4747. Britain's most beloved ocean liner. The *Queen Mary* carried thousands of stylish travelers across the world's oceans from 1936 to 1967. King George V called her "the stateliest ship." As a troopship during World War II, she escaped the wrath of German U-boats despite a huge bounty placed on her by Adolf Hitler. Her interior was a work of art, and although much of it has been removed

the fine art deco lines, gorgeous wood-paneled walls, and impressive stairways conjure images of her former majesty. The wedding chapel is still in operation (for those wishing to tie a nautical knot), and there is a very British captain who lives on board. (*See also* SIGHTSEEING, Tours.)

Virginia Robinson Estate   **5-C7**
1008 Elden Way, Beverly Hills. (Nathaneal Dryden) Accepted as the first modern residence in Beverly Hills, the 1911 estate was originally surrounded by fields. Though still a private residence, the impressive entrance may be viewed from the street.

Royce Hall   **5-D5**
UCLA, Hilgard Ave, LA. 825-4338. (Allison & Allison) Josiah Royce Hall is part of the original UCLA quadrangle, which was completed in 1929. The building is Romanesque and Byzantine in style and contains a 2,000-seat auditorium as well as classrooms and offices.

Shrine Auditorium   **7-F1**
665 W. Jefferson Blvd, LA. (213) 749-5123. (Al Malikah Temple) For many years the Shrine was the largest theater in the nation, seating 6,500. The architecture is Moorish influenced and Spanish colonial in style. Built in 1925, it has a templelike appearance with tall arches and an interior ceiling resembling a canopied tent.

Southern Pacific Railroad River Station 7-A6
Between N. Broadway & N. Spring St., LA. Freight yards, dating back to 1876, are still in use today. Cobblestones, warehouses, tracks, and switch houses remain. The station was designated a historic cultural monument in 1971.

Tail o' the Pup   **6-E1**
San Vicente Blvd, W. Hollywood. (Milton Black) An example of programmatic architecture (in which the shape of the structure describes

Tail o' the Pup

the merchandise sold within), this giant hot dog was designed in 1938 and is a Hollywood landmark.

Temple House   **1-C3**
231 N. Rockingham Ave, Brentwood. (John Byers & Edla Muir) (Private residence.) An attractive, scaled-down, European-style farmhouse designed in 1936 for famous child-star Shirley Temple.

Vincent Thomas Bridge   **1-G5**
Toll Plaza, Terminal Island. (213) 831-0641. Clearing the water by 185 feet, this elegant suspension bridge was completed by 1963 and links San Pedro with Terminal Island. It offers panoramic views of Los Angeles Harbor and is visible for miles around.

Title Guarantee Building   **7-C4**
Corner of Hill St & 5th St, LA. (John & Donald Parkinson) A zigzag-moderne office building, completed in 1931. Evidence of a gothic-revival influence is seen in the polished terra-cotta panels above the entry.

Union Station   **7-B5**
800 N. Alameda St, LA. (213) 683-6987. (John & Donald Parkinson) In 1939, Union Passenger Station opened to throngs of visitors and enjoyed good business until air travel took the bulk of the railroads' passenger trade. The building is mission style, with Moorish and moderne influences. A waiting room with 52-foot-high ceilings, marble floors, and grand seating conjures images of stylish travelers and excited immigrants. With the new high-speed trains, this beautiful station will bustle once again—this time with freeway-free commuters.

Venice Arcades   **4-F5**
Pacific & Windward Aves, Venice. A few archways still remain as a reminder of Abbott Kinney's Venice of 1904. (*See* Beach Cities.)

Westin Bonaventure Hotel   **7-C3**
404 S. Figueroa St, LA. (213) 624-1000. (John Portman) A huge, shiny, space-age structure of five glass cylinders, the much-photographed Bonaventure (completed in 1978) is one of LA's most impressive modern buildings. A circular theme is repeated throughout, from reflecting pools in the lobby area to a revolving lounge and a restaurant on the 34th and 35th floors.

Westside Pavilion   **4-A8**
10800 W. Pico Blvd, W. LA. (Jon Jerde) Some love it, some think it an eyesore. Resembling a postmodernist version of Milan's Galleria, this modern shopping mall jumps out from the suburban landscape. The suitably pastel-colored exterior is a mixture of large geometric blocks and archways. The airy interior has tiled walkways and organized rows of interesting shops.

Wiltern-Pellisier Building   **6-G7**
3790 Wilshire Blvd, LA. (G. Albert Lansburgh) The Wiltern is a perfect example of zigzag-moderne architecture, with a lavish art deco interior. Built in 1930, the ground-floor Wiltern cinema offered every comfort, including fine leather furniture in the lobby and even a luxurious nursery for patrons' children. Today, as part of the new Wiltern Center, the newly restored theater is used for concerts.

World Trade Center   **7-C4**
350 S. Figueroa St, LA. (213) 489-3330. This is LA's facility to serve the world trade community. Shops, foreign trade offices, restaurants, and travel services (including a passport agency) are contained in an impressive two-level mall completed in 1977. Inside, a hand-carved mural, 5,000 feet long, describes the history of free trade.

Wrigley House   **8-D2**
391 S. Orange Grove Blvd, Pasadena. (818) 449-4100. (G. Lawrence Stimson) Completed in 1914, the house was the home of Mr. and Mrs. William Wrigley, Jr., until 1958. It is a fine example of a grand Pasadena residence and was donated by the Wrigleys in 1959 to the Tournament of Roses Association. It is often called Tournament House. *OPEN Wed 2-4pm.*

Zane Grey Pueblo Hotel
199 Chimes Tower Rd, Avalon, Catalina Island. (310) 510-0966. A beautiful house (now converted to a hotel) overlooking Avalon Bay. Fashioned after the Hopi Indian homes Zane Grey so often wrote about. The famous author lived here for over 13 years until his death in 1939. Modern fittings have been installed to blend with the original simple furnishings, some of which have been in the house since its construction in 1924.

CHURCHES

Academy Cathedral   **1-D4**
3141 Manchester Blvd, Inglewood. (213) 751-5151. Once a silent-screen movie palace, now a place of lively worship with gospel music filling the aisles. Art deco enthusiasts will appreciate the design and remaining interior decorations.

Angelus Temple   **1-C5**
1100 Glendale Blvd, LA. (213) 484-1100. An impressive 1922 circular structure overlooking Echo Park. The church was the focus of religious attention when Aimee Semple McPherson preached her Foursquare Gospel there during the 1920s.

Crystal Cathedral   **1-C5**
12141 Lewis St, Garden Grove. (714) 971-4000. (Philip Johnson & John Burgee) An all-glass, star-shaped church, 128 feet high, seating over 3,000. With white steel trusses supporting tempered glass, the structure shimmers in sunlight. The church's head, Dr. Robert Schuller, opened the cathedral in 1980, 25 years after beginning his ministry with a drive-in church.

Masonic Temple   **7-D4**
416 N. Main St, LA. (213) 626-4933; (213) 232-9949. An Italianate temple built in 1858. It is now part of the Pueblo State Historic Park. It has been completely restored and fitted with furnishings that were shipped years ago from the Orient by

Crystal Cathedral

clipper. *OPEN Tues-Fri 10am-3pm; Sat & Sun 10am-4:30pm.* FREE.

Mission San Fernando Rey de Espana   1-A3
15151 San Fernando Mission Blvd, Mission Hills. (818) 361-0186. The mission was founded in 1797 by Father Fermin Lasuen and for many years had a larger population than the Pueblo of Los Angeles. Today's building, constructed in 1974, is an exact replica of the original, which suffered irreparable damage in two earthquakes, one in 1812 and more recently in the 1971 Sylmar earthquake. (*See also* SIGHTSEEING, Tours.)

Mission San Gabriel Archangel   1-C6
537 W. Mission Dr, San Gabriel. (818) 282-5191. Founded in 1771, this mission once controlled 1.5 million acres, from the mountains to the sea. Franciscan fathers converted the Gabrieleno Indians to Christianity and used them as farm laborers and in their soap and candle factories. The mission's winery (no longer in use) is the oldest in California. A museum contains ancient church artifacts, tools, and utensils and details the history of California's missions. *OPEN 7 days 9:30am-4pm.* Low admission charge. (*See also* Main Districts: San Gabriel Valley.)

Mission San Juan Capistrano
Camino Capistrano & Ortega Hwy, San Juan Capistrano. (714) 493-1111. The mission was founded in 1776 by Father Junipero Serra. It was extensively restored in the 1920s, having sustained damage from various earthquakes. The new stone church is a replica of the original 1806 structure, which was built by Indian laborers and destroyed in the 1812 earthquake. Each year on St. Joseph's Day (March 19) excitement mounts

as crowds look out for the first of the cliff swallows, which faithfully return on this very day to build their nests in the old church ruins. *OPEN 7 days 8:30am-5pm.* Low admission charge. (*See also* SIGHTSEEING, Tours: Gray Line Bus Tours.)

Mormon Temple   5-F5
10777 Santa Monica Blvd, W. LA. (310) 474-5569. (Edward Anderson) A 15-foot, gold-leaf statue of the Angel Moroni heralds the dawn from atop a 257-foot tower that rises above this huge white temple. A local landmark, the church (built in 1955) has a visitors information center and a major genealogical library that contains census and military records.

Plaza Church (Church of Our Lady Queen of Angels)   7-B5
100 W. Sunset Blvd, LA. (213) 629-3101. Built between 1818 and 1822, the Plaza Church is the oldest place for religious worship in Los Angeles. It is part of the Pueblo State Historic Park and was built by Indian converts and Franciscan priests, who relied solely on donations for funding. *OPEN 7 days 8am-8:30pm.*

St. Saviour's Chapel   9-G1
Harvard School, 3700 Coldwater Canyon, N. Hollywood. (818) 980-6692. The chapel pews face the center aisle, in a design copied from the chapel of Rugby School, England. Built in 1914,

Mission San Gabriel Archangel

Plaza Church

it was moved to its present location in 1937. Twelve impressive stained-glass windows were added in 1964.

St. Sophia Cathedral   **1-C4**
1324 S. Normandie Ave, LA. (213) 737-2424. Traditional Byzantine design with no exterior decoration but a lavish interior. Built 1948-52, it is a Greek Orthodox cathedral filled with icons, bronze figures, murals, and crystal chandeliers. Considered to be one of the most beautiful churches in the world.

St. Vibiana's Cathedral   **7-C4**
114 E. 2nd St, LA. (213) 624-3941. (Ezra Kysor) Completed in 1876, St. Vibiana's was the first cathedral church for the diocese of Los Angeles and Monterey. Built in Spanish baroque style, it was named after an early Christian martyr whose relics are preserved in the church.

St. Vincent de Paul Roman Catholic Church   **7-F2**
621 W. Adams Blvd, LA. (213) 749-8950. A Spanish baroque style known as Churriguesque was chosen by architect Albert C. Martin for this ornate and impressive church that was completed in 1925. Colorful tile work and decorative ceiling embellishments adorn the interior.

Veterans Center Chapel   **5-F3**
Wilshire and Sawtelle Blvds, LA. (J. Lee Burton) An attractive wooden chapel built in 1900, it represents the colonial gothic style of the original

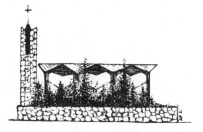

Wayfarer's Chapel

Veterans Center structures (most of which have been replaced by large modern buildings).

Wayfarer's Chapel   **1-G4**
5755 Palos Verdes Dr S., Rancho Palos Verdes. (310) 377-1650. A beautiful glass and redwood chapel that was designed by Lloyd Wright to harmonize perfectly with the natural surroundings of the peninsula. Completed in 1951, the chapel is a monument to Emmanuel Swedenborg, the 18th-century Swedish philosopher and religious reformer. NOTE: Lloyd Wright (Frank Lloyd Wright's son) was also responsible for the Hollywood Bowl.

SCHOOLS

Ambassador College   **8-C2**
300 W. Green St, Pasadena. (818) 304-6000. Four beautifully restored mansions, once part of "Millionaires' Row," form the heart of this liberal arts college. Scholastic emphasis is on theology.

Art Center College of Design   **1-B5**
1700 Lida St, Pasadena. (818) 584-5000. A space-age design by architect Craig Ellwood was completed in 1976 to rehouse this famous school, which has been influencing the art world since 1930. Specialized courses include illustration, industrial design, fine arts, and film.

California Institute of Technology (Cal-Tech)   **8-D5**
1201 E. California Blvd, Pasadena. (818) 356-6811. A private university founded in 1891, this superior school has one tutor for every four students. Containing two of the top scientific and engineering schools in the world, Cal-Tech is able to boast Albert Einstein as a former tutor. Extensive and historically important projects for NASA have been completed here, including the development of jet propulsion for missiles and control of the Viking Project to Mars. Buildings on the 90-acre site date back to 1910. Some medieval-inspired buildings designed by Bertram Goodhue were added in 1930.

Hollywood High School   **6-C5**
1521 N. Highland Ave, Hollywood. 461-3891. Trendy high school, noted more for its famous alumni than for it scholastic achievements. Hollywood High students have included Lana Turner, Carol Burnett, Rick Nelson, and Jason Robards. Today, 80 percent of Hollywood High's students are of foreign origin.

Loyola Marymount University   **3-A5**
7101 W. 80th St, LA. (310) 338-2700. Successor to the oldest college in Southern California (St. Vincent's, established in 1865), the present campus opened in 1929. Loyola is a private coed Catholic university with courses emphasizing the arts, business communications, and engineering. The library contains extensive information on early Los Angeles.

Misses Janes School   **6-C5**
6541 Hollywood Blvd, Hollywood. Mysterious old house owned by the Janes sisters, who taught children of movie celebrities here in the 1920s. (See also SIGHTSEEING, Walking Tours: Hollywood Boulevard.)

Pepperdine University   **1-D1**
24255 Pacific Coast Hwy, Malibu. (310) 456-4000. Spectacular location for a school of any kind. Pepperdine, designed by William Pereira, blends into the Malibu Hills impressively yet unobtrusively. Initially a liberal arts institution located in Downtown LA, it is affiliated with the Church of Christ and was founded in 1937. Pepperdine was named after its benefactor, a Los Angeles businessman with rather conservative views. The college moved to Malibu in 1973 and offers four-year courses specializing in business management.

UCLA—University of California, Los Angeles   **5-D5**
405 Hilgard Ave, Westwood. (310) 825-4321. UCLA is the southern branch of the University of California (which opened in Oakland in 1869, and moved to its present Berkeley location in 1873). Built on a bean field, the Westwood campus opened in 1929. The four original buildings make a quadrangle in the Romanesque style.
  Today the Westwood campus boasts close to 90 buildings and covers 410 acres. Diverse architectural styles blend comfortably in beautifully landscaped grounds. UCLA is noted for its library holdings (among the largest in the world); its Center for Health Sciences, which includes eight research institutes; a notable School of Business Administration; a College of Fine Arts; and national championship teams in major sports. (See also SIGHTSEEING, Tours.)

USC—University of Southern California 7-F1
University Park, LA. (213) 740-2311. A collection of 190 architecturally impressive buildings (dating from the founding of USC in 1880 to the present day) forms the 150-acre campus of this revered institution. USC is a private, non-denominational, coed university (the largest on the West Coast). The school is rich in resources, having been the fortunate recipient of valuable collections and bequests. It is conveniently located across from Exposition Park, which contains the museums of Science and Industry, Space, and Natural History. (See also SIGHTSEEING, Walking Tours: Exposition Park.)

OUTDOOR SCULPTURE

Atlantic Richfield Plaza (ARCO)   **7-C3**
515 S. Flower St, LA. Herbert Bayer's huge, red fountainpiece, Double Ascension, dominates the square and contrasts beautifully with the charcoal granite of ARCO's tower blocks. Two 20-foot-high, ornate bronze doors in the north tower were salvaged from the original art deco structure, built in 1928.

Beverly Hills Electric Fountain   **5-E7**
Wilshire Blvd at Santa Monica Blvd, Beverly Hills. Completed in 1931, the fountain depicts the history of California with a narrative frieze around the base and a central figure of a prospector. Water jets and lights produce 60 different color combinations.

B. Gerald Cantor Sculpture Garden   **6-G3**
Los Angeles County Museum of Art, 5905 Wilshire Blvd, LA. (213) 857-6111. An excellent collection of 39 casts of works by Auguste Rodin was donated to the museum by the B. Gerald Cantor Art Foundation. The larger works are displayed in a sculpture garden that borders three sides of the museum.

J. Paul Getty Museum   **1-C2**
17985 Pacific Coast Hwy, Malibu. (310) (458-2003. Bronze castings of Roman statues discovered at Pompeii, formerly placed in beautifully landscaped geometric gardens. The gardens form an important part of this amazing museum. (See also MUSEUMS & GALLERIES, Museums, General Art.)

Huntington Gardens   **8-E6**
1151 Oxford Rd, San Marino. (818) 405-2100. Fine 17th-century Italian sculpture completes the picture-perfect exterior of the renowned Huntington Library and Art Gallery. (See also MUSEUMS & GALLERIES, Museums, General Art.)

Malaga Cove Plaza   **1-F4**
200 Palos Verdes Dr, Palos Verdes. This attractive Spanish-style shopping plaza, built in 1924, has a central Fountain of Neptune that stood in a Venice (Italy) courtyard for 100 years before being shipped here in 1929. It is a copy of the famous bronze fountain in Bologna, Italy.

Monument to the Stars   **5-E8**
Beverly Dr & Olympic Blvd, Beverly Hills. In 1923 several famous residents of the independent community of Beverly Hills fought the city of Los Angeles to avoid annexation (which had been proposed because of water shortages). They won their fight, and this monument is a tribute to them. Beverly Hills remains unannexed today. Those famous residents included Mary Pickford, Douglas Fairbanks, Will Rogers, Rudolph Valentino, and Tom Mix.

Franklin D. Murphy Sculpture Garden   **5-D5**
UCLA, 405 Hilgard Ave, Westwood. (310) 825-4321. Adjacent to the Frederick S. Wight Gallery (see MUSEUMS & GALLERIES, Art Galleries, Westside & San Fernando Valley). An exceptional collection of 65 20th-century sculptures, including works of Henri Matisse, Henry Moore, Barbara Hepworth, and Auguste Rodin.

Music Center   **7-C4**
135 N. Grand Ave, LA. (213) 972-7211. Several artworks are placed around the central plaza. An imposing abstract sculpture, Peace on Earth, by Jacques Lipchitz, which looms over the reflect-

ing pool, and Robert Graham's *Dance Door* are the most impressive—especially at night.

Santa Monica Beach Sculptures **4-D3**
Santa Monica Beach south of the pier. Several outdoor sculptures include *Windharp Beach Chairs,* a cleverly constructed piece that chimes in response to the wind. *Santa Monica Art Tool* is a moving piece, resembling a giant steam roller; it moves slowly leaving a picture-image of the Santa Monica landscape.

Toppling Ladder **7-D2**
Loyola Law School, 1441 W. Olympic Blvd, LA. (Claes Oldenburg, 1986) A whimsical, 14-foot-high sculpture depicting a folding ladder balanced on one leg, with a spilling can of paint on top. Its placement here is quite appropriate; Oldenburg suggests the "balancing act of theory and practice."

The Triforium **7-C5**
Los Angeles Mall, Temple St at Main St, LA. Three 60-foot-high concrete and glass structures, interconnected and illuminated. Colored glass prisms reflect dancing lights in response to computer-controlled music. The Triforium was once ridiculed by LA art critics but has become a well-loved "ugly duckling" looming over the subterranean Los Angeles Mall. Free concerts are held here on Saturday evenings during summer.

Watts Towers **1-E5**
1765 E. 107th St, Watts. One man, Sabbatino (Simon) Rodia, spent 33 years creating these intriguing, majestic towers. He used scraps of glass, shells, and tiles, which he set into cement over frames of scrap steel. The central tower is 107 feet high and is surrounded by shorter towers and abstract structures that Rodia created as he went along. The towers were saved from demolition in 1957 (just three years after completion) when concerned citizens pulled to-

gether to save and renovate these fine examples of urban folk art.

BILLBOARDS & MURALS

Billboards entice travelers to visit, watch, listen, and buy. Messages are transmitted in a variety of ingenious ways as billboard art becomes increasingly creative.

For centuries people have expressed themselves through graffiti and wall paintings. In varied districts of Los Angeles there are murals reflecting local culture and community feeling. Some are filled with sunshine and contentment, others are fraught with suppression and protest. Each tells its own story.

Brandelli's Brig **4-E5**
W. Washington Blvd, Venice. Photo-likeness painting within a painting.

East Los Angeles Murals **1-D6**
Estrada Courts, Olympic Blvd and Grand Vista Ave, LA; Olympic Blvd & Lorena St, LA; Ramona Gardens, Alcazar St, LA. A number of vivid Chicano murals. Colorful portrayals of Hispanic culture and gang-related subjects. NOTE: This is a high-crime area. Caution should be exercised when entering any neighborhood where gangs are evident.

Farmer John Pig Murals **1-D6**
3049 E. Vernon Ave, Vernon. Pig fantasies on the walls of a meat-packing plant!

Glendale Boulevard **7-A3**
Across from Echo Park Lake. Well-designed abstract mural on a multilevel stairway that was previously covered with ugly graffiti.

The Isle of California **5-G4**
Butler Ave, W. LA (behind the Santa Monica Boulevard Post Office). Fantasy, post-earthquake scene, depicting a collapsed freeway overpass.

Watts Towers Entrance

quake scene, depicting a collapsed freeway overpass.

LA Federal Savings Mural   **9-B2**
12160 Victory Blvd, N. Hollywood. Huge, colorful, patriotic theme. Visible from the Hollywood Freeway.

LAX Billboards
Approach roads to Los Angeles International Airport are lined with oversized billboards, suggesting visits to Hawaii, Las Vegas, and other tempting flyaway places.

Ocean Park Murals   **4-D4**
Ocean Park Blvd between Main St & Lincoln Blvd, Santa Monica. Two murals by Jane Golden include her well-known 1920s-style beach/fairground scene. The best-loved mural is *Whales*, by Daniel Alonzo, which shows whales and dolphins in motion. Opposite is a fantasy mural showing carousel horses escaping to freedom along the beach.

Ed Ruscha Monument   **7-D3**
1031 S. Hill St, LA. A 70-foot effigy of artist Ed Ruscha by master muralist Kent Twitchell.

Spirit of Our Future   **1-C5**
Sunset Blvd & Hyperion Ave, Hollywood. Inspired by the Gay Street Fair, this expressive mural depicts friendship, within the community of Silverlake, between local businesspeople, the gay population, and local gangs—who work admirably to maintain peace among the diverse life-styles evident here.

St. Elmo Village   **1-C4**
4800 St. Elmo Dr, LA. An explosion of color, from abstract shapes on pathways to large family portraits on walls. Created by Rozzell and Roderick Sykes to brighten their part of the neighborhood.

Sunset Strip Billboards   **6-D1**
Sunset Blvd, Hollywood. Large and unique billboards line the Sunset Strip between Crescent Heights and Doheny Drive. Ingeniously creative and colorful art pieces advertise stars of the entertainment industry. Best viewed at night.

Trinity   **7-B2**
Otis Art Institute, 2401 Wilshire Blvd, LA. Famous personalities are substitutes for the Holy Trinity. Another excellent work by Kent Twitchell.

Tujunga Wash Mural   **9-C1**
LA County Flood Control Channel (parallel to Coldwater Canyon Blvd) between Burbank Blvd & Oxnard St. The longest mural in the world, it depicts the history of California. More scenes are added each year.

Venice Murals   **4-F5**
Market St & Windward Ave area, Venice. Skillful illusionary works include a strange desert scene facing Venice Beach.

MOTION PICTURE STUDIOS

Horray for Hollywood! Home of motion pictures, glitter, hoopla, and myth. During the golden years of moviemaking, when business magnates decided the fate of aspiring stars, fans swarmed around studio gates hoping to catch a glimpse of a young Gable, Bogart, or Garbo. Although much of that glamour has faded, there is still a haunting mystique—the allure of Scarlett O'Hara or Anna Karenina, the excitement of grand epics such as Ben Hur *or* King of Kings. *Most studios are still in use and two (Burbank and Universal) are open to the public. (See* SIGHTSEEING, Tours*.)*

**Burbank Studios (Warner Brothers &
Columbia)**   **9-F6**
4000 Warner Blvd, Burbank. (818) 954-6000. During the 1930s and 1940s Burbank was known as First National Studios. It is today the joint home of Columbia and Warner Brothers. The original location for Columbia Studios was 1483 N. Gower Street, Hollywood (**6-D6**). This part of Gower was a gathering place for movie extras during the 1920s, when unemployed cowhands traveled to Hollywood and waited hopefully for a chance to work in the first silent Westerns. The area soon became known as "Gower Gulch." The Gower Gulch Shopping Center at the corner of Gower Street and Sunset Boulevard (**6-C6**) was originally the site of the Century Studios, one of Hollywood's first movie lots.

The notorious head of Columbia in the early days was Harry Cohn. During his reign he produced *The Jolson Story, It Happened One Night,* and *Mr. Smith Goes to Washington.* Other great movies to come from Columbia include *The Wild Ones, From Here to Eternity, On the Waterfront, Porgy and Bess, Funny Girl,* and from the Burbank location *Towering Inferno* and *The Exorcist.*

The original Columbia lot has been renamed Sunset-Gower Studios and its five sound stages are used by ABC Television.

Culver Studios   **1-D4**
9336 W. Washington Blvd, Culver City. (310) 836-5537. Known more recently as Laird International Studios, this studio lot has quite a history. First to make motion pictures here was Thomas Ince in 1915. (Ince was a talented director who died suddenly, in 1924, aboard W. R. Hearst's yacht. The official verdict was thrombosis, but the scandal-hungry press of the day speculated that a jealous W.R. had Mr. Ince removed for another reason—a Miss Marion Davies.)

In 1925 the studios were taken over by Cecil B. DeMille; then, in 1927, it became Pathé Studios. By 1932, RKO-Pathé had formed, and by 1940 the studio's great white mansion (it still stands proudly on Washington Boulevard) was famous around the world, for this was the setting of David O. Selznick's epic *Gone with the Wind.* Two other great epics were filmed here, *King of Kings* in 1927 and *King Kong* in 1933. There is still plenty of activity at the Culver Studios. Television companies, independent filmmakers, and video production companies are busy creating tomorrow's success stories.

Hollywood Center Studios   **6-B5**
1040 Las Palmas Ave, Hollywood. (213) 469-
5000. Originally known as General Service Studios, then in 1927 as the Metropolitan Studios.
This is where Jean Harlow made her film debut
in Howard Hughes's production of *Hell's Angels*.
The first episodes of "I Love Lucy" were made
here in 1951.

Lorimar Telepictures   **1-D4**
3300 Riverside Dr, Suite 405, Burbank. (818)
954-5305. Until 1986, this was home to the legendary Metro-Goldwyn-Mayer studios (MGM).
Louis B. Mayer's kingdom dominated the movie
industry during the 1930s and 1940s. With "boy
genius" Irving Thalberg as production head and
a huge stable of stars—including the Marx Brothers, Spencer Tracy, Katharine Hepburn, Clark
Gable, Greta Garbo, and Lana Turner—MGM
made dozens of movie classics. The impressive
art deco architecture can be seen from the
street, but visitors are not allowed on the studio
backlot. MGM's corporate headquarters is now
located across the street in a huge new building
called "Filmland."

Paramount Pictures Corporation   **6-D6**
5555 Melrose Ave, Hollywood. (213) 956-5000.
Today Paramount devotes most of its studio
space to television productions ("Cheers" and
"Family Ties" have been produced here in recent years), but this famous studio can boast
dozens of award-winning films dating back to
the 1920s, including *The Sheik, Wings, Going
My Way, Greatest Show on Earth, The Godfa-
ther, Hud*, and *White Christmas*. Paramount's
stars included Marlene Dietrich, Bing Crosby,
Bob Hope, Charles Laughton, Betty Grable, and
Elvis Presley.

During the 1950s, Paramount purchased the
adjoining Desilu Production Studio, at 780
Gower Street (**6-D6**), from Lucille Ball and Desi
Arnaz. The couple had bought the studios from
their employers, RKO-Pathé (owned by Howard
Hughes, who had filmed *The Outlaw* there).
RKO-Pathé was previously known as RKO-Radio
Pictures, and they made great classics at their
Culver City Studios (*see above*). They were also
responsible for the wonderful Astaire-Rogers
movies *Top Hat, Follow the Fleet, Shall We
Dance*, and *Gay Divorcee*—films that thrilled the
world and epitomized the magic of Hollywood.
RKO artists included Barbara Stanwyck, George
Raft, Cary Grant, Danny Kaye, Robert Mitchum,
Gary Cooper, and Frank Sinatra.

Raleigh Studios   **6-E6**
650 N. Bronson Ave, Hollywood. (213) 466-
3111. America's sweetheart Mary Pickford and
her husband, Douglas Fairbanks, made all their
movies here during the 1920s and 1930s. They
went on to use this location to form United Artists. Famous films produced here include the
original *A Star Is Born, Guys and Dolls, The Mark
of Zorro, The Three Musketeers*, and *The Best
Years of Our Lives*.

20th Century-Fox Film Corporation   **5-F7**
10201 W. Pico Blvd, LA. (310) 277-2211. The

Paramount Studio Gate

Fox studio lot once covered hundreds of acres,
upon part of which Century City now stands.
They still produce first-rate films. Only visitors
with a pass are permitted through the gate, but
it is possible to glimpse movie sets of huge pro-
portion (such as New York's St. Patrick's Cathe-
dral and Public Library) from the approach road.
Nostalgia abounds here—studio stars included
Marilyn Monroe, Henry Fonda, Tyrone Power,
Ginger Rogers, and Shirley Temple. Movies
filmed here include *The Sound of Music, Butch
Cassidy and the Sundance Kid, The Grapes of
Wrath, Gentlemen Prefer Blondes*, and *The
Planet of the Apes*.

Universal Studios   **9-F5**
100 Universal City Plaza, Universal City. (818)
508-9600 or -4444. Absolutely the best place
for visitors to see Hollywood in action. This studio manages to cater to visitors, with well-
organized tours (*see* SIGHTSEEING, Tours),
while simultaneously producing fine movies
and television series. Well-informed guides en-
tertainingly explain every aspect of filmmaking,
both past and present. The studio was founded
in 1915 by Carl Laemmle. He built two stages
on this onetime chicken ranch to produce silent
films. People were charged 25 cents to watch
movies-in-the-making. Since then, Universal
has produced an average of 55 films a year,
including *Show Boat, The Glenn Miller Story,
The Sting, Earthquake, The Deer Hunter, The
Blues Brothers*, and *Jaws*, as well as movie se-
rials starring Abbott and Costello and the Dead
End Kids.

MCA Records is part of the Universal story
and has over 100 artists affiliated with the label,
including Tom Jones, the Who, and Olivia
Newton-John. The Universal Amphitheater (*see*
ENTERTAINMENT, Theater) features concerts
and shows by internationally famous artists from
Santana to Sinatra.

Walt Disney Studios   **9-E8**
500 S. Buena Vista St, Burbank. (818) 560-5151.
Although the Disney Studios are now located in
Burbank, the birthplace of Mickey Mouse (in
1925) was in the Disney Brothers Studio, which
was located at 4649 Kingswell Avenue, Hollywood (**1-C5**). This "studio" was actually a small,
empty, run-down store. Walt Disney's first workshop was in his uncle's garage, at 4406 Kingswell, where he worked after his arrival in
Hollywood in 1923. The rest is history and Mickey
is now in his 60s.

TELEVISION STUDIOS

*Hollywood is the television capital of the world
and dozens of popular shows are taped each
week before live audiences. Admission to tapings is always free and tickets can be obtained
from studio ticket offices. Since it is difficult to
obtain tickets for top-rated shows on short notice, applications should be made in writing
several months in advance. The following company will supply free tickets to numerous TV
tapings.*

Audiences Unlimited   **9-F5**
100 Universal City Plaza, Building 153, Universal
City, CA 91608. (818) 506-0043. Send a self-
addressed stamped envelope for up to six free
tickets or pick them up personally. Allow two to
three weeks for delivery by mail.

ABC Television Network   **1-C5**
4151 Prospect Ave, LA. (310) 557-7777. ABC
has several locations for taping shows. Perhaps
the most famous location is at Paramount TV Studios, 1438 N. Gower Street, Hollywood (**6-C6**)
(*see also* Motion Picture Studios: Paramount Pictures Corporation). People without tickets who
are willing to wait in line for an hour or two can
gain free admission to dress rehearsals. Call for
time schedules.

CBS Television Network   **6-E3**
7800 Beverly Blvd, LA. (213) 852-2345. The studios at Television City are leased to independents and other networks. A wide variety of
shows are taped here. For ticket information, call
(213) 852-2624.

Fox Television Center   **6-C7**
KTTV, 5746 Sunset Blvd, Hollywood. (213) 462-
7111. Home to many well-known shows, including (the late) "The Late Show" featuring Joan
Rivers. Free tickets through Audiences Unlimited (*see above*).

KTLA (Channel 5)   **6-C7**
5800 Sunset Blvd, Hollywood. (213) 460-5500.
Next door to Fox Television and once part of the
group of studios known as Metromedia Square.
"Jeopardy" and "Soul Train" are among the
many shows taped here.

NBC Television Network   **9-E7**
3000 W. Alameda Ave, Burbank. (818) 840-
4444. Famous for "The Tonight Show" starring

Johnny Carson and, more recently, Jay Leno.
Tickets for show tapings are all issued on a
standby basis, so even if you have a ticket be
sure to allow plenty of time to wait in line.

Universal Television   **9-F5**
100 Universal City Plaza, Universal City. (818)
777-1000. The huge Universal Studios complex
contains extensive television facilities. Shows
produced here have included "Magnum PI,"
"Miami Vice," and "Murder She Wrote." Lavish
motion pictures made especially for television
are also filmed here. Universal's TV shows do
not generally involve live audiences, but the studio's guided tour includes glimpses of many famous productions. (*See also* SIGHTSEEING,
Tours.)

STARS' HOMES

*For those wishing to view the homes of famous
personalities, a few words of advice may save
both time and energy. Maps to stars' homes may
sell by the thousands, but they are not a reliable
source of information. Understandably, celebrities, who have paid high prices for homes and
privacy, do not appreciate strangers gawking
over their garden fences. The best way to view
stars' homes (or, for the most part, just the entrances to them) is by an organized bus tour.
These are usually very entertaining and cover
areas of Hollywood and Beverly Hills. Tours last
from 2 to 6 hours, depending on the operator.
(See SIGHTSEEING, Tours: Gray Line and Starline tours.)*

CEMETERIES

Forest Lawn, Glendale   **1-B5**
1712 S. Glendale Ave, Glendale. (213) 254-
3131. Beautiful marble statues, a famous
stained-glass reproduction of da Vinci's *The Last
Supper,* huge religious paintings, and a museum
containing a gem collection and the Eaton Collection of every coin mentioned in the Bible can
be found here. Celebrities interred at this cemetery include Humphrey Bogart, Clark Gable,
Carole Lombard, Jean Harlow, Tom Mix, Clara
Bow, W. C. Fields, Errol Flynn, Spencer Tracy,
Nat King Cole, and Walt Disney.

Forest Lawn, Hollywood Hills   **9-F8**
6300 Forest Lawn Dr, LA. (818) 984-1711. Reproductions of objects saluting America's strug-
gle for independence are on display here. The
film *The Many Voices of Freedom* is shown each
afternoon in the Hall of Liberty. Celebrities interred here include Buster Keaton, Charles
Laughton, Stan Laurel, Freddie Prinz, and Ernie
Kovacs.

Hillside Memorial Park   **1-D4**
6001 Centinela Ave, LA. (213) 776-1931. Buried

here are Jack Benny, Eddie Cantor, Al Jolson, and Jeff Chandler.

Hollywood Memorial Park   **6-D6**
6000 Santa Monica Blvd, Hollywood. (213) 469-1181. Adjacent to Paramount Studios, this is the final resting place of over 73,000. The many stars buried here include Peter Finch, Peter Lorre, Rudolph Valentino, Tyrone Power, Paul Muni, Douglas Fairbanks, Sr., Marion Davies, Cecil B. DeMille, and silent star Norma Talmadge, who was the first to make footprints at the Chinese Theatre—when she accidentally stepped into wet cement.

Holy Cross Cemetery   **1-D4**
5835 W. Slauson Ave, Culver City. (310) 670-7697. Close to MGM studios, this cemetery is the final resting place of Bing Crosby, Jimmy Durante, Mario Lanza, Rosalind Russell, and Sharon Tate.

Westwood Memorial   **5-E3**
1218 Glendon Ave, Westwood. (310) 474-1579. Hollywood's most famous blond bombshell, Marilyn Monroe, is buried here. Former husband Joe DiMaggio made arrangements for fresh roses to be placed on her grave twice weekly, and for 20 years they were. Buried here more recently: Natalie Wood.

HAUNTED LA

The Barrymore House   **5-D7**
802 N. Roxbury Dr, Beverly Hills. Once the home of Lionel Barrymore, this house is reportedly haunted by several former tenants, including Mr. Barrymore and two of his family guard dogs.

Hollywood Roosevelt Hotel   **6-C4**
7000 Hollywood Blvd, Hollywood. Montgomery Clift stayed at the Roosevelt while filming *From Here to Eternity,* in which he played bugler Private Prewitt. Clift would often shatter the peace during the early morning hours to practice. Many claim to have heard his bugle music in the middle of the night.

Houdini's Mansion   **6-A2**
2380-98 Laurel Canyon Blvd, Hollywood. Famous magician Harry Houdini owned this eerie mansion, which is now in ruins. During the 1920s it was the site of many seances. The staircase that still stands is said to be haunted by Houdini and other restless spirits.

Leonis Adobe   **1-B1**
23537 Calabasas Rd, Calabasas. In 1878, Don Miguel Leonis moved into this 1844 adobe with his Indian bride, Espiritu. Present residents say the couple can be heard to slam upstairs doors and pound on the floor.

Park La Brea Towers   **6-F3**
The area to the rear of the ancient La Brea Tar Pits was once tribal Indian ground. Driven away by a rival tribe (who later suffered the same fate at the hands of the white man), the restless spirits of the original inhabitants play tricks on present-day tenants. Small items such as keys often disappear, but everything is eventually mysteriously returned.

Virginia Rappe's Grave   **6-D6**
Hollywood Memorial Park, 6000 Santa Monica Blvd, Hollywood. Virginia Rappe, a silent screen bit-actress, was brutally molested, allegedly by former child-star Fatty Arbuckle. She died of a ruptured bladder soon after the attack. Many have seen Virginia's silhouette standing near her grave site, still not able to rest.

George Reeves's House   **5-A5**
1579 Benedict Canyon Rd, Bel-Air. Since George Reeves shot himself to death in 1959, nine people have bought and sold this house. Their reason for leaving: the ghost of Superman! Reeves suffered intolerable depressions brought on by a loss of identity and fear of being typecast as a comic-book hero. His ghost is unfriendly, reportedly appearing with gun in hand.

Stage Coach Inn   **1-A1**
51 S. Ventu Park Rd, Newbury Park. (805) 498-9441. This reconstructed historic building (open to the public as a museum) is inhabited by the friendly ghost of a Basque sheepherder known as Pierre. Even though the building has been moved, harmed by fire, and expanded, Pierre refuses to leave. His footsteps have been heard, he is known to open and close doors, and he has placed his cold hands on visitors' backs.

Thelma Todd's House   **1-C2**
17531 Posetano Rd, Pacific Palisades. Known as the "Ice Cream Blonde," Thelma Todd was a top star in the 1920s and 1930s. Mystery surrounded her death—was it murder or suicide? She died of carbon monoxide poisoning in her open convertible, parked in the garage of her home. Psychics who visit the home today are often overcome by fumes and previous tenants have heard the car's motor running.

MUSEUMS & GALLERIES

Griffith Park Observatory

Los Angeles boasts an excellent selection of beautiful galleries and museums. Benevolent art lovers have endowed the city with a wealth of paintings and sculptures, and municipal galleries house art treasures dating from prehistoric times to the present day. In addition to traditional galleries, there are specialized collections, some linked to Hollywood's movie industry. The number of private galleries selling fine modern works increases annually and many are included in this selection. When in the West Hollywood area, art lovers may enjoy visiting La Brea Avenue, Melrose Avenue, and North La Cienega Boulevard, where numerous privately owned galleries are located. Opening hours and admission fees to galleries and museums vary according to the season and often change for new exhibitions. Whenever possible call in advance.

MUSEUMS

General Art

Fowler Foundation Museum   5-E8
9215 Wilshire Blvd, Beverly Hills. (310) 392-3313. European and Asian decorative arts. Fine silver collection; ivory, firearms, and model ships. *OPEN Mon-Sat 1-5pm. FREE*

J. Paul Getty Museum, Malibu   1-C1
17985 Pacific Coast Hwy, Malibu. (310) 458-2003. Re-creation of a palatial, 1st-century Roman villa. The product of one man's generosity, billionaire J. Paul Getty, the museum is now the most richly endowed in the world. Set in beautiful gardens, it houses impressive collections of antiques, paintings, sculpture, and decorative arts. (It is sad that Mr. Getty never lived to see this museum.) Tearoom, bookstore, library. *CLOSED Mon.* Call for parking reservations. FREE. *(See also* HISTORIC LA, Buildings & Landmarks.)

Grunwald Center for the Graphic Arts   5-D5
UCLA, 405 Hilgard Ave, Westwood. (310) 825-3783. Prized collection of drawings from the 15th century to the present day. Adjoining gallery acts as a showcase for the collection. Works include Tamarind lithographs, ornamental prints, and valuable pieces by Picasso and Matisse. *By appointment only. CLOSED weekends.*

Huntington Library, Art Gallery, and Botanical Gardens   8-E5

1151 Oxford Rd, San Marino. (818) 405-2275 or -2100. Perhaps the most gracious assemblage of beautiful artifacts in Southern California. Visitors can revel in railroad tycoon Henry E. Hunington's fabulous collections, which are housed in architecturally impressive buildings and surrounded by over 200 acres of splendid botanical gardens. The library, built in 1925, contains over half a million books and 5 million manuscripts—all in full use. Treasures include a first folio of Shakespeare's plays and a manuscript of Benjamin Franklin's autobiography. Rare books are always on display, together with an impressive collection of French decorative art. The art gallery, built in 1910, was originally Huntington's residence. It contains such famous paintings as Gainsborough's *Blue Boy* and Constable's *View on the Stour*. The botanical gardens contain a dozen specialized areas, including a palm garden, a Shakespeare garden, and an unparalleled cacti garden. The Herb Garden Room is open for lunch and afternoon tea. Tours, bookstore, refreshments. No picnics or pets. (*See also* PARKS & GARDENS, Botanical Gardens: Huntington Gardens.) *OPEN Tues-Fri 10:30-4:30pm. FREE.*

Long Beach Museum of Art   1-G5

2300 E. Ocean Blvd, Long Beach. (310) 439-2119. Beautifully situated in a 1912 mansion overlooking the Pacific, the museum specializes in 20th-century American art, primarily paintings and prints. Extensive collection of artists' videotapes. Sculpture garden, bookstore. *OPEN Wed-Sun noon-5pm.*

Los Angeles County Museum of Art   6-G3

5905 Wilshire Blvd, LA. (213) 857-6111. Four interconnecting buildings, linked by a central courtyard, house a large permanent collection and provide space for traveling exhibits. The new Robert O. Anderson Building (built at a cost of $35 million) houses the museum's impressive 20th-century collection with works from the European avant-garde as well as an extensive collection of works by California artists. Among the notable collections in the other three buildings are the prized Heeramaneck collection of Tibetan, Indian, and Nepalese works, and the Daumier print collection. Sculpture garden (*see also* HISTORIC LA, Outdoor Sculpture: B. Gerald Cantor Sculpture Garden), bookstore, cafe. *CLOSED Mon.* Reduced rates for seniors and children.

Mount St. Mary's College Fine Arts Gallery 5-E1
12001 Chalon Rd, LA. (310) 476-2237. Exhibits by Los Angeles-area artists, include printmaking, sculpture, photography, paintings, and performance art. Selected student works. *CLOSED July & Aug.* FREE.

Museum of Contemporary Art, Los Angeles (MOCA) 7-C4
250 S. Grand Ave, LA. (213) 621-2766. After years of planning, the long-awaited Museum of Contemporary Art opened in December 1986. The event was heralded around the world—at last Los Angeles would have a "real" art museum. Architect Arata Isozaki created a fittingly California-style building of monumental proportions. Seven galleries, some of which are lit by huge pyramid-shaped skylights, house lively

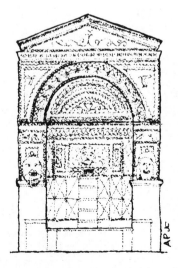

J. Paul Getty Museum, garden fountain

groupings of modern art. The well-endowed permanent collection features works by the world's most acclaimed modern artists. Gift shop, restaurant. *CLOSED Mon.* Free admission on Thursdays from 5 to 8pm. Rates include admission to Temporary Contemporary (*see below*). Reduced admission for seniors and students; children under age 12 free.

Newport Harbor Art Museum
850 San Clemente Dr, Newport Beach. (714) 759-1122. Good collection of 20th-century American art with emphasis on recent West Coast art. Sculpture garden, rental gallery, bookshop, cafe. *CLOSED Mon.*

Norton Simon Museum of Art 8-C2
Orange Grove Blvd at 411 W. Colorado St, Pasadena. (818) 449-3730. An impressive and expertly displayed treasure trove of valuable works. Excellent collection of Goya etchings. Fine selection of Impressionist paintings, early European works, Asian sculpture, and French tapestries. Beautiful sculpture garden with peaceful resting areas; bookstore. *OPEN Thurs-Sun noon-6pm.* Reduced rates for seniors and students.

Temporary Contemporary 7-C5
152 N. Central Ave, LA. (213) 626-6222. As a temporary space to exhibit works waiting for the completion of MOCA, the Temporary Contemporary proved to be such a popular gallery that it was decided to keep it as a permanent showcase. Local architect Frank Gehry transformed two huge warehouses into one of the lightest, largest, and most popular art spaces in the country. Changing exhibitions and spillovers from MOCA exhibitions are featured. Call for current schedule. (*See also* Museum of Contemporary Art *above*). *CLOSED Mon.* Reduced rates for seniors and students.

Science

Cabrillo Marine Museum 1-G5
3720 Stephen White Dr, San Pedro. (310) 548-7562. Marine plants, invertebrates, fish, birds, and nautical artifacts are displayed in a converted 1920 bathhouse. Smaller buildings house aquariums and laboratories. (*See also* PARKS & GARDENS, Zoos & Aquariums, *and* KIDS' LA, Children's Museums.) *CLOSED Mon.* FREE.

California State Museum of Science and Industry 7-G1
700 State Dr, LA. (213) 744-7400. Second largest museum of its kind in America. Enjoyable and educational. Lively exhibits with visitor participation encouraged. Auto, railroad, air, space, and telecommunications exhibits, a health museum and more, displayed in 20 different halls. (*See also* KIDS' LA, Children's Museums.) *OPEN 7 days 10am-5pm.* FREE.

Griffith Park Observatory & Planetarium 1-B4
Hall of Science, 2800 E. Observatory Rd, Griffith Park. (213) 664-1191. Impressive moderne-style planetarium with fantastic views of the city and the stars. Solar telescopes, space exhibits, seis-

mological instruments. Tours, bookshop. Laser light shows. (*See also* NIGHTLIFE, Rock: Laserium; KIDS' LA, Learning: Planetarium Show; *and* HISTORIC LA, Buildings & Landmarks.) *CLOSED Mon.*

Jet Propulsion Laboratory **1-A6**
4800 Oak Grove Dr, Pasadena. (818) 354-4321. See the famous spacecrafts Viking, Mariner, and Voyager.

Historic

American Military Museum/Heritage Park
1-D7
1918 N. Rosemead Blvd, El Monte. (818) 442-1776. Jeeps, trucks, tanks, and cannons from the U.S. and foreign countries. *OPEN Sat & Sun only, noon-4:30pm.* Low admission.

California History Gallery **7-G1**
Lando Hall, Los Angeles County Museum of Natural History, 900 Exposition Blvd, LA. (213) 744-3414. Impressive display chronicling California's history from 1540 to 1940. *CLOSED Mon.* Reduced rates for seniors and children.

El Monte Historical Museum **1-C7**
3150 N. Tyler Ave, El Monte. (818) 444-3813. Interesting artifacts tracing the region's history. Exhibits include pioneer diaries, maps, and photographs. *CLOSED Sat, Sun & Mon.* FREE.

Hebrew Union College Skirball Museum 7-F1
3077 University Ave, LA. (213) 749-8611. Jewish history from biblical times. Archaeological exhibits, fine arts, and ancient Israeli artifacts. Ceremonial art for children. *CLOSED Sat & Mon.* FREE.

Los Angeles County Museum of Natural History **7-G1**
900 Exposition Blvd, LA. (213) 744-3466. A monumental building, erected in 1913, is the centerpiece of this impressive museum—one of the best of its kind. Well organized, with 35 halls displaying everything from giant fossils to stuffed mammals, all presented in their native environment. Touring exhibits, often from the Smithsonian, are regularly featured. The museum is being expanded constantly—one exciting new addition is the Ralph Parsons Discovery Center, which consists of various walk-through habitats and allows visitors to experience noises, sights, and smells never encountered before. It's educational and entertaining. (*See also* KIDS' LA, Children's Museums.) *CLOSED Mon.* Reduced rates for seniors and children.

Malibu Lagoon Museum **1-D1**
23200 Pacific Coast Hwy, Malibu. (310) 456-1770. Located in the Moorish-style Adamson Beach House, designed by Stiles Clements in 1929, the museum is filled with period furniture; its exhibits include photo memorabilia of many of Malibu's famous residents, such as Clara Bow and Dolores del Rio. *By appointment only.* The surrounding park is a wildlife sanctuary and is open to the public year-round.

Maritime Museum **1-G5**
Berth 84 (foot of 6th St), San Pedro. (310) 548-7618. Nautical memorabilia, scale models (including a matchstick replica of the *Titanic*), hands-on exhibits, a full history of Los Angeles Harbor, and a promenade deck with good views of harbor operations. *CLOSED Mon.*

Martyrs Memorial and Museum of the Holocaust **6-G2**
Jewish Community Bldg, 6505 Wilshire Blvd, LA. (213) 852-1234, ext 3200. Photographs, documents, art, and artifacts relating to the Nazi period. *CLOSED Sat.* FREE.

Museum of Afro-American History and Culture **7-G1**
California State Museum of Science and Industry, 600 State Dr, LA. (213) 744-7432. Newest addition to Exposition Park's amazing collection of museums. Changing exhibits demonstrate the development of Afro-American culture. *OPEN 7 days.* FREE.

Museum of Cultural History **5-D5**
UCLA, 2 Haines Hall, 405 Hilgard Ave, Westwood. (310) 825-4659. Large collection of ethnic and folk art relating to modern, historic, and prehistoric cultures around the world. *By appointment only.* FREE.

Pacific Asia Museum **8-C3**
46 N. Los Robles Ave, Pasadena. (818) 449-2742. Housed in an ornate Chinese building decorated with dragons and surrounded by oriental gardens, this museum is the only institution in Southern California that deals exclusively with Pacific and Asian arts. *OPEN Wed-Sun noon-5pm.* Children under age 12 free.

George C. Page Museum and La Brea Tar Pits **6-G3**
5801 Wilshire Blvd, LA (213) 936-2230. The museum focuses on the 40,000-year-old La Brea Tar Pits and the fossils discovered there. Excellent displays in a well-planned space that is part of an earthen mound, designed specifically to house the huge reconstructed skeletons. An amazing collection of Ice Age fossils. Film shows, slide displays, murals, and scientific laboratory. Gift shop. *CLOSED Mon.* Reduced rates for seniors and children. The La Brea Tar Pits contain one of the world's largest deposits of Ice Age fossils.

Pasadena Historical Society Museum **8-C3**
470 W. Walnut St, Pasadena. (818) 577-1660. Antiques and local historical memorabilia displayed in a beautiful 18-room mansion built in 1905. Exquisite Finnish folk art exhibit. This was once the home of the Finnish consul who built Sauna House (a replica of a 16-century Finnish farmhouse) on the grounds. *OPEN Thurs-Sun.* Reduced rates for seniors and children.

Southwest Museum **1-C5**
234 Museum Dr, LA. (213) 221-2163. Devoted to recording the history of American Indian life. This exceptional museum houses an excellent collection of Western Indian artifacts, with impressive displays and dioramas portraying tribal scenes. Spanish colonial periods of California

La Brea Tar Pits

history are also illustrated. Library with good archaeological section. *CLOSED Mon.*

Transportation

Lomita Railroad Museum   1-F4
250th St and Woodward Ave, Lomita. (310) 326-6255. Interesting display of operational and stationary trains. (*See* KIDS' LA, Children's Museums.) *CLOSED Mon & Tues.*

The Museum of Flying   4-6C
2772 Donald Douglas Loop North, Santa Monica. (310) 392-8822. Working exhibits and displays of aerospace memorabilia. *CLOSED Mon & Tues.*

Planes of Fame Air Museum
Chino Airport, 7000 Merrill Ave, Chino. (714) 597-3722. Two large hangars plus an outdoor exhibit area of rare aircraft from the beginning of aviation to the space age. Old aircraft are restored, some completely rebuilt. *OPEN 7 days.* Low admission.

Travel Town   9-E8
Zoo Dr, Griffith Park, LA. (213) 662-5874. Open-air transportation museum. Trolley ride and climb-on exhibits for children. Interesting antique railroad cars. *OPEN 7 days.* FREE.

Entertainment Industry

Hollywood Studio Museum   6-F4
2100 N. Highland Ave, LA. (213) 874-2276. Housed in the original Cecil B. DeMille Barn where Lasky's Feature Play Company, with DeMille as director, made Hollywood's first feature-length movie *The Squaw Man*. Antique cameras, costumes (including some of Mary Pickford's), photographs, and a wealth of memorabilia. Screening room shows clips from early silent and sound movies. *OPEN 7 days. CLOSED Sun during winter.* Low admission; reduced rates for seniors and children

Hollywood Wax Museum   6-C5
6767 Hollywood Blvd, Hollywood. (213) 462-8860. Wax sculptures of over 170 famous people from show business and history. Also Chamber of Horrors, Oscar Movie Theater. *OPEN 7 days.* Reduced rates for seniors and children.

Movieland Wax Museum   1-F7
7711 Beach Blvd, Buena Park. (714) 522-1154 or -1155. A real tourist attraction. Over 200 wax effigies of famous movie personalities are presented in imaginative settings. A special "Black Box" exhibit contains full-size movie sets from recent horror and science fiction movies. The Palace of Living Art reproduces famous paintings with three-dimensional wax figures. Gift shops, photo gallery, portrait studio, restaurants. *OPEN 7 days.* Reduced rates for children.

Specialized

(*See also* KIDS' LA, Children's Museums.)
Angel's Attic   4-C3
516 Colorado Ave, Santa Monica. (310) 394-8331. Housed in a beautifully renovated Victorian house, this is the only museum of dollhouses, miniatures, and toys on the West Coast. Gift shop, refreshments. *CLOSED Mon-Wed.* Reduced rates for seniors and children.

Margaret Cavigga Quilt Collection   6-E1
8648 Melrose Ave, LA. (310) 659-3020. Early 1900s quilts, Victorian crocheted tablecloths, and lace christening gowns. Group lectures available by appointment. FREE.

Craft & Folk Art Museum   6-G3
6860 Wilshire Blvd, LA. (213) 937-5544. Ethnic exhibits from home and abroad dedicated to the preservation of folk artistry. Gift and book shops. *CLOSED Mon.* FREE.

Museum of Neon Art   7-D5
704 Traction Ave, LA. 617-1580. Unique—a space devoted to documenting, exhibiting, and preserving neon and electric art. Classes. *OPEN Tues-Sat 11am-5pm, Sun 1-5pm.*

ART GALLERIES

Central Los Angeles

Act   6-G3
5514 Wilshire Blvd, LA. (213) 935-4411. They claim to be the oldest contemporary gallery in California. Artists regularly represented are Frank Stella, Robert Rauschenberg, and Guy Dill. *CLOSED Mon.*

Asher/Faure Gallery   6-E1
612 N. Almont Dr, LA. (310) 271-3665. Established American and European artists, plus young painters and sculptors from California and the East Coast are represented. Exhibits are as-

sembled by major New York dealers. *CLOSED Sun & Mon.*

Barnsdall Municipal Art Gallery **6-C8**
4804 Hollywood Blvd, Hollywood. (213) 485-4581. Contemporary art by relatively unknown artists. Retrospectives, theme shows, involvement art. The gallery is located next to Frank Lloyd Wright's Hollyhock House (*see* HISTORIC LA, Buildings & Landmarks). *CLOSED Mon.*

Garth Clark Gallery **6-F4**
170 S. La Brea Ave, LA. (213) 939-2189. Functional, abstract ceramic works that resemble modern sculpture. Beatrice Wood and Akio Takamori are represented. *CLOSED Sun & Mon.*

James Corcoran Gallery **4-C3**
1327 5th St, Santa Monica. (213) 451-4666. Fine modern works by well-known artists such as James Rosenquist, Andy Warhol, Don Bachardy, Ed Ruscha, and Willem De Kooning. *CLOSED Sun & Mon.*

William & Victoria Daily **6-D2**
8216 Melrose Ave, LA. (213) 658-8515. A combination bookshop and gallery specializing in 19th-century French prints, works by Whistler, and Japanese prints. Rare books. *CLOSED Sun & Mon.*

George J. Doizaki Gallery **7-C5**
Japanese American Cultural and Community Center, 244 S. San Pedro St, Little Tokyo. (213) 628-2725. Excellent works by Japanese artisans and craftsmen. Changing exhibits. *CLOSED Mon.*

Gallery 170 **6-F4**
170 S. La Brea Ave, LA. (213) 936-7399. Unusual and renowned paintings from the 19th and 20th centuries provide a break from the modern trend along La Brea. American and European artists include Cecil Bell, Stephen Longstreet, and Michael Marsden. *CLOSED Sun & Mon.*

Gemini **6-D2**
8365 Melrose Ave, W. Hollywood. (213) 651-0513. American modern art—originals and lithographs. Noteworthy shows. *CLOSED Sat & Sun.*

L'Imagerie **6-D2**
8201 Melrose Ave, W. Hollywood. (213) 653-1676. Excellent decorative art featuring Icart etchings, Erte bronzes and graphics, original paintings, and a large selection of art deco and art nouveau posters. *CLOSED Sun.*

Margo Leavin Gallery **6-D1**
812 N. Robertson Blvd, LA. (310) 273-0604. High-quality works by well-known contemporary artists are displayed in several rooms. Drawings, paintings, sculpture, and graphics by such greats as Jim Dine, Claes Oldenburg, Tom Wudl, Frank Stella, George Segal, and David Hockney. *CLOSED Sun & Mon.*

Los Angeles Art Association **6-D1**
825 N. La Cienega Blvd, LA. 652-8272. Exhibition gallery for the Los Angeles Art Association (established 1925). Monthly exhibits, generally of mainstream and traditional works by association members. *CLOSED Sun & Mon.*

Louis Newman Galleries **5-E7**
322 N. Beverly Dr, Beverly Hills. (310) 278-6311. Well-respected gallery; only established artists who have been represented at several museums are shown. *OPEN 7 days.*

Otis Art Institute Gallery **7-B1**
2401 Wilshire Blvd, LA. (213) 251-0555. This major art school houses a good gallery featuring exhibitions of works by noted contemporary artists. *CLOSED Sun & Mon.*

Herbert Palmer Gallery **6-D1**
802 N. La Cienega Blvd, LA. 854-0096. Modern American and European masters from the 20th century are well represented—drawings, paintings, sculpture, and prints. *CLOSED Sun & Mon.*

Jack Rutberg Gallery **6-F4**
357 N. La Brea Ave, LA. (213) 938-5222. First-class paintings, drawings, and prints, often including works by Renoir, Degas, and Bonnard. *CLOSED Sun & Mon.*

Simard Gallery **6-E1**
665 N. La Cienega Blvd, W. Hollywood. (310) 652-0280. Well-established gallery concentrating on quality figurative American art. *OPEN Wed-Sat noon-5pm.*

Westside & San Fernando Valley

Angles **4-E4**
2230 Main St, Santa Monica. (310) 396-5019. Functional art and furniture from Europe and the U.S. Conceptual art and wall pieces are also displayed. *CLOSED Mon.*

Bl Gallery **4-E4**
2730 Main St, Santa Monica. (310) 392-9625. Graphics and multimedia pieces by contemporary American artists. *CLOSED Mon.*

Robert Berman Gallery **4-E4**
1044 Broadway, Santa Monica. (310) 453-9195. Contemporary paintings (many large works) and sculpture by New York and Los Angeles artists. New shows monthly. *CLOSED Sun & Mon.*

Hoffman-Borman Gallery **4-C3**
912 Colorado Ave, Santa Monica. (310) 394-4199. Contemporary American artists such as Richard Serra, John Miller, and John McCracken are well represented. *CLOSED Sun & Mon.*

LA Louver **4-F5**
55 N. Venice Blvd, Venice. (310) 822-4955. Lively exhibitions by renowned artists such as David Hockney, Ed Moses, and William Brice. A second gallery space nearby at 77 Market Street publishes compilations of artists' works. The gallery also keeps a large selection of graphics by internationally famous artists. *CLOSED Sun & Mon.*

Orlando Gallery **1-B3**
14553 Ventura Blvd, Sherman Oaks. (818) 789-6012. LA's oldest contemporary gallery. High-quality contemporary art with special interest in mixed-media works and assemblages. Theme exhibitions can include art deco or African art. New artists are featured. *CLOSED Sun & Mon.*

Palos Verdes Community Arts Association **1-G4**
5504 W. Crestridge Rd, Rancho Palos Verdes. (310) 541-2479. Excellent arts center. Monthly shows by local artists, plus ten major exhibitions annually by nationally known artists. Summer Artist in Residence program, museum tours series, active community program. *CLOSED Sun.*

Tortue Gallery **4-A5**
2917 Santa Monica Blvd, Santa Monica. (310) 828-8878. Varied international works, young California artists, plus high-quality drawings by Matisse, Degas, and Picasso. Small sculpture court, collection of artists' books. *CLOSED Sun & Mon.*

Frederick S. Wight Gallery **5-D5**
UCLA, Hilgard Ave, Westwood. (310) 825-9345. Student shows, visiting exhibitions, ethnic and craft art shows. Sculpture garden (*see* HISTORIC LA, Outdoor Sculpture: Franklin D. Murphy Sculpture Garden). *CLOSED Mon.*

Downtown & Eastern Area

Art Center College of Design **1-B6**
1700 Lida St, Pasadena. (818) 584-5000. Two galleries are housed in this nationally acclaimed design school. Student works are displayed in one gallery, and temporary exhibits relating to departmental programs are shown in the other. *CLOSED Sun.*

Biltmore Gallery **7-C4**
Biltmore Hotel, 515 S. Olive St, LA. (213) 624-6963. Established in 1924, this is the oldest gallery in Los Angeles. American expressionism and selections from the Taos School are included in a fine collection of Western art. *CLOSED Sat & Sun.*

California State University Fine Arts Gallery **1-C6**
Fine Arts Building, 5154 State University Dr, LA. (213) 343-3000 or -4023. Historic and contemporary exhibits range from oriental works to modern architectural drawings. A graduate show is presented each spring. *CLOSED Fri & Sat.*

Cirrus **7-D5**
542 S. Alameda St, LA. (213) 680-3473. Gallery and publishing house, producing graphic works and books. The gallery features unusual multimedia works such as Jay McCafferty's solar burns on graph paper and Eric Orr's environmental light works. Artists represented in print editions include Ed Ruscha, Ed Moses, and Joe Goode. *CLOSED Sun & Mon.*

Fisher Gallery **7-G1**
USC, Harris Hall, 823 Exposition Blvd, LA. (213) 740-4561. Exhibitions emphasize architecture and photography interrelated with contemporary art. Permanent collection of fine European paintings from 16th to 19th centuries. *CLOSED Sun & Mon.*

Los Angeles Contemporary Exhibitions (LACE) **7-E5**
1804 Industrial St, LA. (213) 624-5650. Nonprofit art center that encourages experimentation. Programs include performance art, video, audio work, music, and installation pieces. Twelve major exhibitions annually feature group exhibits and one-man shows. LACE forms a major part of the active Downtown art community. *OPEN Wed-Fri 11am-5pm; Sat & Sun noon-5pm.*

Oranges/Sardines **7-D5**
5400 E. Monte Vista St, LA. (213) 256-6172. *By appointment only.*

Neil G. Ovsey Gallery **7-D5**
170 S. La Brea Ave, LA. (213) 935-1883. Paintings, sculpture, and multiple images, plus limited-edition prints by David Hockney, Jasper Johns, and Roy Lichtenstein. Original etchings, silkscreens, and lithographs by major artists, including Robert Rauschenberg and Joe Goode. *CLOSED Sun & Mon.*

Oriental & African

Jan Baum Gallery **6-F4**
170 S. La Brea Ave, LA. (213) 932-9170. A friendly, unimposing gallery, showing primitive art from Africa, plus some contemporary pieces. *CLOSED Sun & Mon.*

Japanese-American Cultural & Community Center **7-C5**
244 S. San Pedro St, LA (213) 628-2725. Located on the first floor of a five-story cultural center devoted to Japanese cultural heritage, the gallery presents historic displays and fine-art exhibits. *CLOSED Mon.*

Museum of African American Art **1-D4**
4005 Crenshaw Blvd, 3rd floor, LA. (213) 294-7071. (Located in May Co.) Multimedia works by black artists from around the world. Continually changing shows. Gift shop. *CLOSED Mon & Tues.*

Photography & Posters

G. Ray Hawkins Gallery **4-D4**
908 Colorado Ave, Santa Monica. (310) 394-5558. Excellent display of vintage and contemporary photographs. Frequent exhibits by famous photographers including Ansel Adams and Max Yavno. *CLOSED Sun & Mon.*

Los Angeles Center for Photographic Studies (LACPS) **7-D4**
1048 W. 6th St, LA. (213) 482-3566. Emphasizing photography as a fine art. Exhibits, lectures, and publications. *CLOSED Sun, Mon & Tues.*

Art Rental

Richard Mann Gallery **6-E1**
671 N. La Cienega Blvd, LA. 659-3950. Paintings, limited edition prints, sculpture. Leasing and rental plans. *CLOSED Sun.*

PARKS & GARDENS

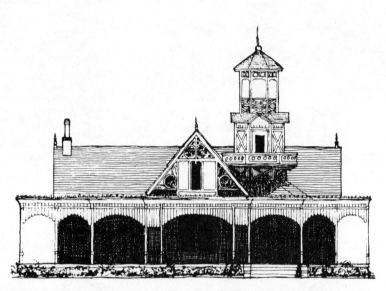

Queen Anne Cottage

PARKS

(*See also* SIGHTSEEING, Amusement Parks.)
   The rambling concrete and stucco metropolis of Los Angeles contains a surprising number of green and restful oases in the form of well-maintained parks and quiet gardens. Parklands cover over 13,600 acres and contain 80 miles of bridle trails, 90 miles of hiking trails, and 40 miles of bicycle trails. Some parks have historic themes, others focus on sporting activities. All are welcome retreats from the rush of city life.
   For general information on State Parks within Southern California, call (213) 620-3342. For parks in the Santa Monica Mountains, call (818) 706-1310.

Barnsdall Park   **1-C5**
4800 Hollywood Blvd, LA. Interesting park (containing Hollyhock House [*see* HISTORIC LA, Buildings & Landmarks], Municipal Art Gallery, and Junior Arts Center) set in 11 acres devoted mainly to cultural activities. Other facilities include basketball and volleyball courts and an outdoor gym. (*See also* KIDS' LA, Learning: Junior Arts Center.)

Brand Park   **1-B5**
1601 W. Mountain St, Glendale. The Moorish-style Brand Library and Art Center (*see* HISTORIC LA, Buildings & Landmarks) are located in this beautifully landscaped foothill park. Ideal for picnicking.

Brookside Park   **8-B1**
Arroyo Blvd, Pasadena. Attractive family park adjacent to the world-famous Rose Bowl. Recreational activities include golf, baseball, and swimming. There are also bicycle, hiking, and bridle trails. Picnic areas with barbecues.

Burton Chase Park   **4-G7**
Mindanao Way, Marina del Rey. Small, but good for viewing boating activities. Located in the center of Marina del Rey. Picnic facilities, watchtower.

Circle X Ranch   **1-C1**
12896 E. Yerba Buena Rd, Malibu. (310) 457-6408; (818) 597-9192. A former Boy Scouts of America camp, this 1,655-acre park has been preserved by the Santa Monica Mountains Conservancy. It has 22 miles of scenic hiking trails, an archery range, volleyball courts, a swimming pool (no lifeguard on duty), and 600 camping sites.

Echo Park   **7-A3**
1632 Bellevue Ave, LA. Fashioned after an English garden, the 26-acre park includes an attractive lake with paddle boats and a beautiful lotus pond. (Avoid after dusk.)

El Pueblo de Los Angeles   **7-C5**
622 N. Main St, LA. (213) 628-1274. This 44-acre state historic park is the birthplace of Los Angeles and the focus of the city's Mexican heritage. The Plaza and Kiosko are stages for year-round festivals. Attractions include Olvera Street, the

Plaza Church, Pico House, and the Avila Adobe. (*See also* SIGHTSEEING, Walking Tours: The Plaza & Chinatown; *and* Tours: Olvera Street Tour.)

Elysian Park   **1-C5**
929 Academy Rd, LA. (213) 485-5027; (213) 225-2044. A surprising discovery in the center of Downtown LA. Rare and exotic trees, a botanic garden, hiking trails, and large wilderness areas set in 600 acres. Contains Chavez Ravine Arboretum, the Police Academy, and Dodger Stadium.

Exposition Park   **7-G1**
Exposition Blvd between Vermont Ave & Figueroa St, LA. An awe-inspiring collection of cultural buildings and gardens, covering 114 acres in the heart of central Los Angeles. Until the turn of the century the space was used for agricultural fairs and horse racing. (It also contained several houses of ill repute.) Revitalization of the area began with the construction of the California State Museum of Science and Industry, completed in 1913. Today, Exposition Park also houses the Museums of Science and Industry, Natural History, and Afro-American History and Culture (*see* MUSEUMS & GALLERIES, Museums, Science *and* Historic), plus the Los Angeles Memorial Coliseum (site of two Olympic Games, 1932 and 1984), the Sports Arena, and the world's largest rose garden. A $12 million improvement plan provided for open-air exhibition space for arts and crafts, a decorative promenade to connect the major buildings and allow pleasant resting areas for visitors. Extensive parking facilities. (*See also* SIGHTSEEING, Walking Tours.)

Griffith Park   **1-B5**
Visitors Center, 4730 Crystal Springs Dr, LA. (213) 665-5188. Largest municipal park in the U.S. (4,063 acres). Griffith Park rises up from valley flatlands and extends over the southern end of the Santa Monica Mountains. Numerous facilities include Travel Town Transportation Museum (*see* MUSEUMS & GALLERIES, Museums: Transportation), LA Zoo (*see* Zoos & Aquariums), Griffith Park Observatory and Planetarium (*see* MUSEUMS & GALLERIES, Museums, Science), Greek Theatre (*see* ENTERTAINMENT, Theater), a 1926 merry-go-round, four riding stables, and an equestrian center (built for the 1984 Olympics). There are also extensive facilities for golf, tennis, cricket, swimming, baseball, soccer, and hiking and limited camping facilities for children (*see* SPORTS & RECREATION, Sporting Activities; *and* KIDS' LA, Sports). Mountain roads wind up through the park for scenic drives and picnicking. Park *OPEN 7 days 5:30am-10pm.*

Hancock Park   **6-G3**
5900 Wilshire Blvd, LA. Elegant mansions, the La Brea Tar Pits, and two fine museums—the George C. Page and the Los Angeles County Museum of Art (*see* MUSEUMS & GALLERIES, Museums, Historic *and* General Art)—provide an abundance of cultural pleasures.

William S. Hart Park
24151 San Fernando Rd, Newhall. (805) 259-0855. Bequeathed by the silent-film cowboy star, this wilderness preserve and animal compound includes a buffalo herd on its 253 acres. Picnic area. Hart's home is *OPEN Wed-Sun* and contains paintings and sculptures by Charles M. Russell.

LaFayette Park   **7-B1**
2800 Wilshire Blvd, LA. Multiuse park close to USC. Senior citizens' center, picnic area, scent garden for the blind, tennis courts, playground.

Lake Hollywood   **6-A5**
Weidlake Dr, Hollywood. A wonderful lake, surrounded by huge pine trees, just minutes from Hollywood Boulevard. Not exactly a park, more a rewarding retreat. *CLOSED Mon-Fri noon-2pm.*

Los Encinos State Historic Park   **10-E1**
16756 Moorpark St, Encino. (818) 784-4849. Attractive setting for the nine-room de la Osa Adobe, built in 1849. Once a stagecoach stop, now a pleasant 5-acre park with green lawns and duck ponds.

MacArthur Park   **7-B2**
2230 W. 6th St, LA. A Downtown garden of 32 acres. Originally (1890) named Westlake Park, it was renamed in 1942 to honor the famous general. Rare plants and trees, interesting environmental art pieces, children's playground, paddleboats, and a pavilion bandstand for summer concerts. (Not recommended after dark.)

Malibu Lagoon State Beach   **1-D1**
23200 Pacific Coast Hwy, Malibu. A beautiful oceanside nature preserve and wildlife sanctuary, surrounding the Malibu Lagoon Museum, which is located in the Adamson House, a ten-room beach house built in 1929. (*See also* MUSEUMS & GALLERIES, Museums, Historic: Malibu Lagoon Museum.)

Palisades Park   **1-D2**
Ocean Ave, Santa Monica. Beautifully maintained clifftop gardens with lofty palms and fantastic ocean views, Senior Citizens' Recreation Center, tourist information office, and picnic facilities.

Pan Pacific Park   **6-E3**
7600 Beverly Blvd, LA. Landscaped grounds surround the historic Pan Pacific Auditorium (*see* HISTORIC LA, Buildings & Landmarks). Park facilities include a par course, baseball diamond, picnic area, and jogging track.

Pio Pico State Park   **1-D7**
6003 Pioneer Blvd, Whittier. (310) 695-1217. The restored 1850 hacienda of former Governor Pio Pico is the main attraction at this small park.

Plummer Park   **6-D4**
7377 Santa Monica Blvd, Hollywood. (213) 876-1725. LA Audubon Society headquarters, once part of Rancho La Brea. Three acres with recreational facilities.

Point Fermin Park   **1-G5**
Gaffey St & Paseo del Mar, Palos Verdes. Landscaped park atop rugged cliffs. Lookout points with telescopes, a whale-watching station, and an 1874 lighthouse. (*See also* SIGHTSEEING,

Viewpoints & Drives, Scenic Drives: Palos Verdes Scenic Drive.)

Police Academy Rock Gardens   **1-C5**
1880 N. Academy Dr, LA. (213) 222-9136. The training center for the LAPD is here in Elysian Park. Beautiful rock gardens were built in 1937 to incorporate cascades and pools and provide a relaxing resting place. The rock gardens contain a small cafe, an amphitheater, and picnic facilities, all of which are open to the public.

Omelveny Park
Orozco St, LA. Little-known wilderness area in the San Fernando Valley. Over 400 acres with trees, meadows, and a running stream. Great for hikers.

Will Rogers State Historic Park   **1-C2**
14253 Sunset Blvd, Pacific Palisades. (310) 454-8212. Scenic 187-acre park, close to the beach. Hillside trails and picnic facilities. Visit Will Rogers's home and the interesting visitors center where a 10-minute film, narrated by his family and friends, details the famous cowboy/humorist's life. Weekend polo matches. *OPEN year-round 8am-7pm.*

Self-Realization Fellowship Lake Shrine 1-C2
17190 Sunset Blvd, Pacific Palisades. (310) 454-4114. A tranquil hideaway established in 1950 by Paramahansa Yogananada. Landscaped gardens with peaceful ponds, delicate waterfalls, a Dutch windmill, and gazebos. Some of the late Mahatma Gandhi's ashes are preserved here. The temple for all religions is often used for wedding ceremonies. *OPEN Tues-Sun 9am-4:45pm.*

Sepulveda Dam Recreational Area   **10-D4**
Burbank & Balboa, Encino. (818) 343-4143. A huge wasteland was transformed to provide tranquil gardens, three public golf courses, and multiple sporting facilities, including a 5-mile bike route, cricket field, archery range, and model-airplane flying field. Extensive picnicking facilities.

Whittier Narrows Recreation Area   **1-D7**
1000 N. Durfee Ave, S. El Monte. (818) 444-1872. Located along the San Gabriel River, these 277 acres offer a golf course, shooting range, bicycle path, campground, lake, bird sanctuary, and nature center.

Woodley Park
See Sepulveda Dam Recreational Area *above.*

BARBECUES

The following parks provide outdoor barbecue pits or stoves:

Brookside Park, Pasadena
Cheviot Hills Recreation Center, W. LA
Columbia Regional Park, Torrance
Culver West Park, Culver City
Del Rey Lagoon, Playa del Rey
Edison Community Park, Huntington Beach
Encino Park, Encino

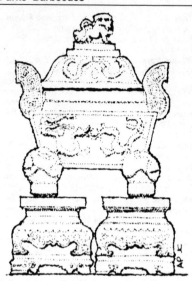

Self-Realization Fellowship Lake Shrine

Griffith Park, Los Angeles
La Cienega Park, Beverly Hills
Lincoln Park, Santa Monica
Palisades Park, Santa Monica
Palisades Recreation Center, Pacific Palisades
Palos Verdes Park, Rancho Palos Verdes
Point Fermin Park, San Pedro
Rustic Canyon Recreation Center, Pacific Palisades
Shadow Ranch, Canoga Park
Studio City Recreation Center, Studio City
Torrance Park, Torrance
Veterans Memorial Park, Culver City
Victor Park, Torrance
Westwood Park, Westwood
Woodley Park, Van Nuys

BOTANICAL GARDENS

Beverly Hills Cactus Garden   **5-D7**
Santa Monica Blvd, between Bedford Dr & Camden Dr, Beverly Hills. Interesting combination of cacti and succulents from around the world, set in a narrow park bordering the plush estates of Beverly Hills.

Descanso Gardens   **1-C5**
1416 Descanso Dr, La Canada. Over 600 varieties of plants and trees are displayed in 165 acres of natural beauty. Japanese teahouse, waterfalls, and streams. (*See also* SIGHTSEEING, Tours.)

Eaton Canyon Nature Center   **1-B6**
1750 N. Altadena Dr, Pasadena. (818) 794-1866. Native California plants are displayed through this 184-acre canyon park. Small museum with ecological displays. Self-guided tours.

Exposition Park Rose Garden   **7-G1**
701 State Dr, Exposition Park. (213) 749-5884; (213) 485-5515. Largest rose garden in the world, with 190 varieties and 16,000 bushes. Set in 7 acres of sunken gardens. (*See also* Parks: Exposition Park, *and* SIGHTSEEING, Walking Tours: Exposition Park Area.)

Huntington Gardens   **8-E6**
1151 Oxford Rd, San Marino. (818) 792-6141. Over 200 acres of beautiful botanical gardens with panoramic views. Specialized gardens merge harmoniously as they run down peaceful slopes toward lily ponds. Special features include a Shakespeare garden filled with plants mentioned in his work, a Japanese garden with an authentic 16th-century teahouse, a Zen rock garden, a bonsai court, a 12-acre desert garden containing the largest variety of cacti in any collection in the world, and a palm garden containing 200 mature specimens. The gardens surround the fabulous Huntington Library and Art Gallery. (*See also* MUSEUMS & GALLERIES, Museums, General Art.)

Los Angeles State & County Arboretum 1-B7
301 N. Baldwin Ave, Arcadia. (818) 821-3222. Exotic flower gardens cover 125 acres that contain a Santa Fe rail depot and the gingerbread-style Queen Anne Cottage (*see* HISTORIC LA, Buildings & Landmarks). A central lake is fed by natural spring waters and is surrounded by gardens representing each of the world's continents. The aboretum has been used in the making of over 100 motion pictures, including five Tarzan films and some of *The African Queen*, starring Humphrey Bogart and Katharine Hepburn. (*See also* SIGHTSEEING, Tours.)

South Coast Botanic Gardens   **1-F4**
26300 S. Crenshaw Blvd, Palos Verdes. (310) 421-9431. Built on 87 acres of reclaimed land and planted with trees and shrubs from around the world, the gardens were started in 1960 to cover a trash-dumping site. The results are quite remarkable. Gardening demonstrations, botanical displays, gift shop. (*See also* SIGHTSEEING, Tours.)

Donald Tillman Water Reclamation Plant
    10-D4
Woodley Ave, Van Nuys. Located in the Sepulveda Dam Recreational Area. Beautiful Japanese garden designed by Koichi Kawana, who describes it as a "wet garden with promenade." *OPEN Tues, Thurs & Sat only.* To arrange a free guided tour, call (818) 989-8166.

UCLA Botanical Garden   **5-E4**
Hilgard & Le Conte Aves, Westwood. (310) 825-3620. Exotic plants and cacti on 8 acres of carefully planned picturesque gardens.

UCLA Japanese Garden   **5-C4**
10619 Bellagio Rd, Bel-Air. (310) 825-4574. Zig-zag paths thread through this delightful, tradi-tional garden. Japanese trees and plants hang over fish ponds filled with koi. A teahouse, a shrine, and a hidden bathhouse add to the charm (reservations required). *OPEN Tues 10am-1pm; Wed noon-3pm.*

NATURE CENTERS & TRAILS

El Dorado Nature Center   **1-G5**
7550 E. Spring St, Long Beach. (310) 421-9431. Located at the east end of El Dorado Park recreational area. Eighty acres of trees and shrubs, carefully arranged in their natural settings, demonstrate how plants develop according to climate and environment. Ecological exhibits, nature trails, lectures, tours.

The Ferndell   **1-C5**
Ferndell Dr, Griffith Park. (213) 665-5188. A shady glen, cooled by a natural running stream, has been planted with a variety of interesting ferns. Pathways and benches encourage quiet meditation.

Malibu Creek State Park   **1-C1**
Las Virgines Rd & Mulholland Hwy, Malibu. (818) 706-8809. A Santa Monica Mountains park, full of wildlife. Fifteen miles of trails and a 2-acre lake set in 4,000 acres of woodland. This naturally rustic setting has been used for many Hollywood movies. (*See also* SIGHTSEEING, Viewpoints & Scenic Drives, Scenic Drives: Malibu/Mulholland Scenic Drive.)

Orcutt Ranch Horticultural Center   **1-A1**
23600 Roscoe Blvd, Canoga Park. (818) 883-6641. Large, landscaped gardens with hiking trails and picnic spots. The ranch house was built in 1920; tours are given the last Sunday of each month. Horticultural demonstrations.

Placerita Canyon Park
19152 Placerita Canyon Rd, Newhall. (805) 259-7721. Natural setting with live oaks and wildlife. The park is set in a canyon and covers 350 acres. A self-guided tour is designed to illustrate the relationships of native animals and plants. Nature center.

Point Mugu State Park
Pacific Coast Hwy, Leo Carrillo. (805) 499-2112. Idyllic inland canyons opposite Leo Carrillo State Beach. Huge sycamores, beautiful spring flowers, and an abundance of wildlife. Camping, hiking, scenic nature trails. (*See also* SIGHTSEEING, Viewpoints & Scenic Drives, Scenic Drives: Palisades/Coast Highway Scenic Drive.)

Topanga State Park   **1-C2**
20825 Entrada Rd, Topanga Canyon. (310) 455-2465. Nine thousand acres of undeveloped semiwilderness close to the city. Trails with panoramic views across the ocean and the San Fernando Valley. Picknicking, no camping, no dogs, no barbecues. NOTE: This area is noted for rattlesnakes; obey posted signs at all times.

The Wilderness Institute   **1-B1**
22900 Ventura Blvd, Woodland Hills. (818) 991-7327. This noteworthy organization arranges

field trips to wildflower areas such as Death Valley and the San Gabriel Mountains.

ZOOS & AQUARIUMS

Cabrillo Marine Museum   **1-G5**
3720 Stephen White Dr, San Pedro. (310) 548-7562. Saltwater marine life of every type displayed in small, specially designed buildings that create a playgroundlike environment. Excellent educational facility. (*See also* MUSEUMS & GALLERIES, Museums, Science.)

William S. Hart Park
24151 San Fernando Rd, Newhall. (805) 259-0855. A wilderness preserve covering 110 acres plus an animal compound (which includes a herd of rare buffalo and domestic beasts) that was left to the public by grateful cowboy star William Hart. (*See also* Parks.)

Los Angeles Zoo   **1-B5**
5333 Zoo Dr, Griffith Park, LA. (213) 666-4650. Every effort has been made to show the animals (over 2,000) in their natural surroundings without too many bars and cages. Beautiful garden setting in 75 acres of Griffith Park. Popular children's zoo with animal nursery. Picnic areas and snack bars. *OPEN 7 days 10am-5pm. CLOSED Christmas Day.*

BIRD SANCTUARIES

Griffith Park Bird Sanctuary   **1-B5**
Vermont Canyon Rd, Griffith Park. (213) 665-5188. Enjoy a guided walking tour through this attractive wooded glen where a variety of birds nest happily. Streams, ponds, picnic facilities. Call for tour schedule.

Marina del Rey Bird Sanctuary   **4-F6**
Between Washington St & Admiralty Way, Marina del Rey. Behind the trees lining Washington Street is a natural pond—home to the wild duck, once so abundant in this area. Duck marshes gave way to developers until all that remained was this small (but thriving) sanctuary. Visitors are not encouraged.

Whittier Narrows Nature Center   **1-D7**
1000 N. Durfee Ave, S. El Monte. (818) 444-1872. A 127-acre facility bordering the San Gabriel River. The sanctuary provides for a variety of plants and animals plus a huge variety of birds. There is also a small museum with aquatic exhibits. *OPEN 7 days 9am-5pm.*

BEACHES

Los Angeles County beaches are protected by lifeguards daily during summer, from 7am to 10pm. Busy beaches such as Santa Monica and Venice are patrolled year-round. All beaches have rules banning dogs, alcohol, and open fires (except where barbecue pits are provided). Surfers must use designated areas away from swimmers.

General Information

Lifeguard Emergency Services
   North beaches: (310) 457-2525
   Central beaches: (310) 394-3261
   South beaches: (310) 372-2162
Weather and Surfing Conditions
   North beaches: (310) 457-9891
   Central beaches: (310) 451-8761
   South beaches: (310) 379-8471
All beaches are accessible from Pacific Coast Highway. The following listing runs north-south. (See also HISTORIC LA, Main Districts: Beach Cities.)

Zuma
Long, breezy beach. Inexpensive parking for 2,500 cars and campers.

Leo Carrillo
Picturesque, popular with divers. (Named after the actor who played Pancho on TV's "Cisco Kid" and whose father was the first mayor of Santa Monica.) Good campground.

Point Dume
Craggy cliffs (beach can be hard to reach). Limited parking.

Malibu Surfrider   **1-D1**
Famous surfing beach. Waves are strongest during August and September. Arrive early to park—always.

Will Rogers   **1-D2**
Named after the famous cowboy/humorist. Popular with swimmers and surfers. Extensive facilities.

Santa Monica   **4-D3**
Busiest beach on the bay. Full facilities, food outlets, pier, rentals. The boardwalk starts here.

Venice   **4-F4**
Colorful hodgepodge of vendors and performers crowd the boardwalk. Popular with tourists; park early on weekends. Full facilities, ethnic foods, rental. Muscle Beach workout pit.

Dockweiler   **3-D2**
Below LAX. Wide sands, barbecue pits, ample parking, uncrowded.

Manhattan, Hermosa, Redondo, and Torrance   **2-E6**
Four lively communities whose beaches run into each other in a happy blend of fun and games. Predominantly young, good-looking beach set. Surfing and volleyball are major activities. Parking is a pain.

Royal Palms   **1-G3**
Pretty Palos Verdes coastline. Rugged cliffs, abundant marine life, limited facilities. Pleasant drive around the peninsula.

Cabrillo   **1-G5**
Good family beach. Calm waters, picnic tables, and barbecue pits. Nearby attractions.

Long Beach   **1-G6**
Huge expanse of white sand beaches. Calm waters. Boating, waterskiing, extensive facilities.

KIDS' LA

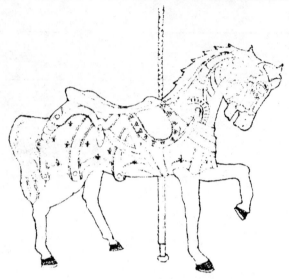

Griffith Park Merry-Go-Round

Southern California may be fairly described as a paradise for young people. Some attractions developed from the extravagant (and often eccentric) ideas rich Hollywood parents dreamed up to amuse their children; others are obvious examples of fantasies turned into reality. In addition to fun palaces and fantasy attractions, there are dozens of learning and sporting facilities designed specifically for children. Parades, festivals, and fiestas are detailed in ANNUAL EVENTS. *Amusement parks are covered separately in* SIGHTSEEING.

TOURS

Fire Department Open House
(213) 485-5971. Just one day a year (second Saturday in May) all Los Angeles fire stations are open to the public. Firemen give tours and demonstrate equipment. FREE.

Los Angeles Times   **7-C4**
1st & Spring Sts, LA. (213) 237-5000. See a newspaper in the making. Tours *Mon-Fri 3pm.* Meet in the 1st Street lobby. No reservations necessary. FREE.

Navy Open House   **1-G5**
Navy Public Information Office, (310) 547-6721. Tours aboard navy vessels docked at Long Beach shipyards are offered each weekend. Navy guides will explain procedures and answer questions. FREE.

Pacific Telephone Company
Call any central office of Pacific Telephone to arrange a tour of operations. Available Monday to Friday during regular office hours. FREE.

Pied Piper Tours
Expeditions and sightseeing tours for children age 5 and up. Two guides are provided for every ten children. For information, call (213) 466-5419.

Police Headquarters   **7-C5**
Parker Center, 150 N. Los Angeles St, LA. (213) 485-3281. Slide presentation and guided tours through LAPD HQ. See the crime lab and the jail. *Call for appointment.* FREE.

Queen Mary   **1-G6**
Pier J, Long Beach. (310) 435-4747. Board the famous ocean liner for an entertaining and educational tour through cabins, the wireless room, the bridge, and engine rooms. (*see* HISTORIC LA, Buildings & Landmarks). Tours daily throughout summer; weekends only in winter. Reduced rates for children age 5 to 11; children under age 5 free. (*See also* SIGHTSEEING, Tours.)

Racetrack Workouts   **1-D4**
Hollywood Park, 1050 Prairie Ave, Inglewood. (310) 419-1500. Watch thoroughbred racehorses in early morning workouts *Apr-July 7 days 7-10am.* FREE.

CHILDREN'S MUSEUMS

Angel's Attic   **4-C3**
516 Colorado Ave, Santa Monica. (310) 394-8331. Located in a renovated Victorian house.

The only museum of dollhouses, miniatures, and toys on the West Coast. Rare dollhouses, valued at up to $25,000, antique toy trains. Proceeds benefit autistic children. Gift shop, refreshments. OPEN Thurs-Sun 12:30-4:30pm. Reduced rates for children.

Cabrillo Marine Museum   **1-G5**
3720 Stephen White Dr, San Pedro. (310) 548-7562. Free classes for junior and senior high school students to study sea animals. Opportunities for graduates to help as tour guides. Over 3,500 sea creatures are displayed in 35 aquariums. A "hands-in" California tide pool contains sea anemones, starfish, and mollusks. Beach excursions. (See also PARKS & GARDENS, Zoos & Aquariums.) CLOSED Mon. FREE.

California State Museum of Science and Industry   **7-G1**
700 State Dr, LA. (213) 744-7400. Fun for all in a wonderland of learning. Twenty halls include exhibits dealing with transportation, computers, and communications. Children are encouraged to touch and operate the working displays. They can fire up a jet engine, move the planets into orbit, challenge an electric brain, learn about human reproduction and the workings of the body, and see live chicks hatch. The million-dollar Hall of Health exhibit includes a special section (with films and educational demonstrations) emphasizing the dangers of narcotics. The Space Museum (across the street from the main complex) contains scale models and actual rocket parts, plus a real Thor-Agena missile. Excellent summer science workshops (call for rates and schedules). OPEN 7 days 10am-5pm. FREE.

Craft and Folk Art Museum   **6-G3**
6860 Wilshire Blvd, LA. (213) 937-5544. Small museum with bright displays of ethnic art from around the world. CLOSED Mon. FREE.

Hobby City Doll and Toy Museum   **1-F8**
1238 S. Beach Blvd, Anaheim. (714) 527-2323. Lovely collection of over 3,000 antique dolls and toys, displayed in a half-scale replica of the 1917 White House. Puppet shows are held in the Puppet Center Theater. OPEN 7 days. Low admission.

Kidspace   **8-D3**
390 S. El Molina Ave, Pasadena. (818) 449-9143. Private, nonprofit museum designed to stimulate the imagination and encourage communication. Visit the "Grown-Up Tools" exhibit and dress up as a firefighter, jockey, astronaut, or racecar driver. Climb through a life-size anthill, or examine X-rays in the child-scale hospital. There is a child-size working TV station and a newsroom with video display terminals. Everything is there to be used, and Herman, the talking robot, assures children they can be whatever they want to be. Children must be accompanied by an adult. OPEN Wed 2-5pm; Sat & Sun 12:30-5pm. Low admission.

La Habra Children's Museum   **1-E8**
301 S. Euclid St, La Habra. (310) 694-1011. Excellent "hands-on" museum where children are free to touch exhibits. Located in an old railway depot that contains a model train village, nature walk exhibit, bee observatory, dollhouse, playhouse, stuffed animals, and a grandma's attic filled with old clothes to try on. CLOSED Sun. Low admission.

Lomita Railroad Museum   **1-F4**
37 250th St, Lomita. (310) 326-6255. Reproduction of a 19th-century train depot containing a 1902 Southern Pacific locomotive, a 1910 wooden caboose, a velocipede handcar, telegraph equipment, model trains, and railroad memorabilia. OPEN Wed-Sun 10am-5pm. Low admission.

Los Angeles Children's Museum   **7-B5**
310 N. Main St, LA. (213) 687-8800 or -8226. Dedicated to the inquisitive young mind, the museum is designed to teach through exploration; its "please touch" exhibits are an essential part of this function. Workshops and festivals are held throughout the year (call for schedules). Crawl through drains; sit on a police motorcycle in the "City Streets" exhibit; experience the feelings of the handicapped in the "How Would I Feel" exhibit; design buildings in the huge Lego room; operate TV cameras in the newsroom; visit the radio station, and much, much more. OPEN Wed & Thurs 2:30-5pm; Sat & Sun 10am-5pm. Extended hours during summer—call for hours. Low admission.

Los Angeles County Museum of Natural History   **7-G1**
900 Exposition Blvd, LA. (213) 744-3466. Impressive 1913 building housing 35 exhibition halls filled with fascinating collections. Fossils, insects, birds, marine life, gems, and huge stuffed mammals are among thousands of artifacts displayed in detailed, natural environments. Special displays include antique automobiles and a Western American Indian cultural exhibit. CLOSED Mon. Low admission; first Tuesday morning of each month free.

Maritime Museum   **1-G5**
Berth 84 (foot of 6th St), San Pedro. (310) 548-7618. Filled with nautical memorabilia that includes scale models of historic ships, such as the Titanic, early diving equipment, and navigation instruments. A promenade deck affords views of LA Harbor. CLOSED Mon. FREE.

The Museum of Flying   **4-C7**
2772 Donald Douglas Loop North, Santa Monica. (310) 392-8822. Interesting exhibits include a full-scale model of the Mercury space capsule and a piece of the Wright brothers' first plane. CLOSED Mon & Tues. FREE.

George C. Page Museum   **6-G3**
5801 Wilshire Blvd, LA. (310) 936-2230. Ancient fossils and huge prehistoric creatures are displayed in detail. The adjoining La Brea Tar Pits once trapped prehistoric animals in the sticky asphalt they mistook for water. Children can enjoy a special exhibit that allows them to play with the tar. (See also MUSEUMS & GALLERIES, Museums, Historic.) CLOSED Mon. Low admission; second Tuesday morning of each month free.

Pierce College   **1-B2**
6201 Winnetka Ave, Woodland Hills. (818) 347-0551. This agricultural college, containing a Life Science Museum and a Nature Center, offers an interesting tour of its own farm, which includes cattle, horses, sheep, and chickens. Book two weeks in advance. Low admission.

Travel Town   **1-B4**
Zoo Dr, Griffith Park. (213) 662-5874. The climb-aboard exhibits here include a Union Pacific steam engine, World War II fighter planes, and old wagons and buggies. Train rides are available (9am-4pm), and members of the LA Live Steamers Club demonstrate their own model trains nearby. *OPEN 7 days.* Low admission.

ZOOS & ANIMAL PRESERVES

Institute for Wild and Exotic Animal Studies
Moorpark College, Campus Rd, Moorpark. (805) 529-2324. The animal compound at this unusual institute contains a variety of exotic creatures trained by qualified students and lecturers. *OPEN Sun only.*

Kellog's Arabian Horse Farm
California State Polytechnic, 3801 W. Temple Ave, Pomona. (714) 869-2224. Purebred Arabian horses have been trained to perform amazing tricks. Shows given on the first Sunday of each month from October to June. Low admission.

Knott's Berry Farm
See SIGHTSEEING, Amusement Parks. Inside Camp Snoopy at Knott's, children will be delighted to find a petting zoo with over 150 animals—from miniature horses to a 450-pound tortoise.

Los Angeles Zoo   **1-B5**
5333 Zoo Dr, Griffith Park. (213) 666-4090. Over 2,000 animals, grouped by country of origin, are displayed in living areas designed to resemble their natural environment. Although this is a relatively small zoo, some unusual specimens may be seen. The Children's Zoo contains goats, sheep, geese, and ducks, and children are encouraged to examine and pet the friendlier animals. *OPEN 7 days 10am-5pm.* Low admission.

Santa Ana Zoo   **1-G8**
1700 E. 1st St, Santa Ana. (714) 835-7484. Fun zoo with a large selection of monkeys. Children's petting zoo, playground, and picnic facilities. *OPEN 7 days 10am-5pm.* Very low admission.

Six Flags Magic Mountain
See SIGHTSEEING, Amusement Parks. In addition to rides and amusements, Magic Mountain contains a delightful animal farm and petting zoo. "Animal Chatter" educational shows are held each afternoon.

Whittier Narrows Nature Center   **1-D7**
1000 N. Durfee Ave, S. El Monte. (818) 444-1872. This sanctuary for plants, animals, and birds contains a small museum with aquatic exhibits. The surrounding Whittier Narrows Dam Recreation Center includes children's play areas, picnic facilities, and a large lake for fishing and boating. *OPEN 7 days.* FREE.

BEACHES

Miles of protected beaches border LA County, from Zuma to Long Beach, providing a year-round playground. For details see PARKS & GARDENS, Beaches.

PARKS & PLAYGROUNDS

Chatsworth Park   **1-A2**
22360 Chatsworth St, Chatsworth. (818) 341-6595. Boulders to climb over, wagon ribs, a stockade, and log horses to play on.

Cheviot Hills Recreation Center   **5-G7**
2551 Motor Ave, W. LA. (310) 837-5186. A well-maintained city park in busy West Los Angeles. There are children's play areas, picnic facilities, and a swimming pool. Sporting facilities include five softball diamonds, an archery range, tennis courts, and outdoor and indoor basketball courts.

Harbor Regional Park   **1-F4**
25820 Vermont Ave, Harbor City. (310) 548-7515. Nautical-style play areas located in a 230-acre park. Large lake; fishing and sailing facilities.

Los Angeles Department of Recreation and Parks
Various activities, many specifically designed for young people, are managed by this large city department. The Camping Division ([213] 485-4853) sponsors camps in Griffith Park for boys age 8 to 12. Activities can include crafts, archery, hiking, and swimming. They also organize groups for the Decker Canyon Youth Camp in Malibu. The Department's Aquatic Division ([213] 485-2844) gives boating classes to children age 12 and up, plus swimming, scuba, and skin diving for children age 8 and up. For summer classes in golf, boxing, cooking, tennis, and many other subjects, call (213) 485-5515. A lifeguard program, including first aid, skin diving, surfing, and canoeing, is open to children age 10 to 17 ([213] 485-5520).

Reseda Park   **1-B2**
18411 Victory Blvd, Reseda. (818) 881-3882. Children's playground, picnic areas, and a lake full of ducks to feed.

Sand Dune Park   **2-A5**
33rd St at Bell Ave, Manhattan Beach. A huge, steep sand dune and safe sand pile are the main attractions here. Swings and climbing bars add to the fun. Toddler's play area; picnic facilities. *OPEN 7 days 5am-11pm.* FREE.

Seaside Lagoon 2-G7
200 Portofino Way, Redondo Beach. (310) 318-
0681 or -0680. Heated saltwater swimming lagoon within a recreational park. Playground,
picnic tables, and barbecues. *OPEN 7 days
June-Sept only, 10am-5:45pm.* Low admission.

Sepulveda Dam Recreation Area 10-B3
Victory Blvd & Woodley Ave, Encino. (818) 343-
4143. A vast oasis in the valley. Children's playgrounds, an 800-acre sportsground facility (with
space for every sport imaginable), and a 23-
acre picnic area.

CHILDREN'S SHOPPING

Clothing

Bear Threads 4-A3
1624 Montana Ave, Santa Monica. (310) 828-
6246. Expensive, quality clothing. Beautiful
hand-knit sweaters and imported dresses.
OPEN 7 days.

Splash 9-F2
12109 Ventura Blvd, Studio City. (818) 762-
6123. Their Backyard Boutique contains imported, avant-garde outfits plus a selection of
sunglasses, hats, and bags. The main store offers a selection of quality clothing at fair to high
prices. *CLOSED Sun.*

Bikes

Bikeology
Many locations (*see* local telephone directory).
America's number-one Nishiki dealer. All major
makes available. Repairs and accessories, mo-
torcross gear.

Pico Bicycle Center 1-C4
4573 W. Pico Blvd, LA. (213) 934-3882. Sales,
parts, and repairs on all makes. Quality bikes
(including Schwinn, Mongoose, and Nishiki) fully
assembled. Free 30-day check-up service on all
bikes purchased. *OPEN 7 days.*

Tom's Wheel Works 7-F1
3347 S. Hoover St, LA. (213) 747-2629. (In University Village Mall.) New and used bikes, parts,
accessories, and repairs. Peugeot, Raleigh,
Nishiki, Cycle-Pro, and Diamondback. *CLOSED
Sun.*

Books

(*See also* Learning: Beverly Hills Library Story
Hour *and* Los Angeles Central Library.)

The Comic Vendor 1-E4
17430-C Crenshaw Blvd, Torrance. (310) 515-
2676. Attracting adults and children alike, this
store is filled with comic book heroes, past and
present. *OPEN 7 days.*

Small World Books 4-F4
1407 Ocean Front Walk, Venice. (310) 399-
2360. Beachfront bookstore, with a children's
section covering literature, fine art, poetry, and
magazines. *OPEN 7 days.*

Toys & Hobbies

Allied Model Trains 4-A8
4411 S. Sepulveda Blvd, Culver City. (310) 313-
9353. One of the world's largest model train
shops. Huge selection of scale brass locomo-
tives. New and used trains of every make, all
gauges. *CLOSED Sun.*

Hobby and Model Center 7-C4
505 S. Flower St, LA. (213) 626-3339. Model airplanes, radio-controlled gliders, stamps, loco-
motives, model railroad equipment, plastic kits,
tools, and accessories. *CLOSED Sun.*

Hollywood Toys, Inc. 6-C5
6562 Hollywood Blvd, Hollywood. (213) 465-
3119. Extensive toy selection ranging from computer games to robots, props, costumes, boats,
motorized cars, and plain old-fashioned dolls.
They will ship anywhere. *OPEN 7 days.*

The Model Works 8-C5
1655 E. Colorado Blvd, Pasadena. (818) 793-
6061. Full range of scale miniatures including
military vehicles, railroads, and aircraft. Radio-
controlled models, reference books, paints,
tools, and building materials. No scale figures.
CLOSED Mon.

My New Friends 4-A3
1527 Wilshire Blvd, Santa Monica. (310) 395-
3905. Beautiful gifts and toys. Excellent selection of dolls and huggable soft toys. Monogram-
ming, shipping service, gift-wrapping. *CLOSED
Sun.*

Toyorama 5-G5
2018 Westwood Blvd, W. LA. (310) 474-7607.
Electronic toys and games. Dolls, crafts, party
favors, stuffed animals, cars, and skates. Free
gift-wrapping. *OPEN 7 days.*

Toys R Us
Dozens of locations (*see* local telephone directory). Reliable chain of successful stores, selling
a full range of good-quality toys.

CHILDREN'S ENTERTAINMENT

Amusement Parks
A first visit to Los Angeles should include that
world-famous park Disneyland. This landmark
institution, a world of happiness and perfection,
has thrilled millions for decades, but Southern
California has several more great amusement
parks. Since all were designed to entertain people of every age, they have been covered separately under SIGHTSEEING, Amusement Parks.

Bob Baker Marionette Theater 7-B3
1345 W. 1st St, LA. (213) 250-9995. Puppet
shows, parties, and theater tours each weekend.
Book in advance.

Camelot Waterslide 1-F8
3200 Carpenter Ave, Anaheim. (714) 630-3343.
A good way to cool off after a hot day at Disneyland. Slide down huge twisting tubes, over 400
feet in length, and splash into a swimming pool.

Century City Playhouse   **5-G6**
10508 W. Pico Blvd, Century City. (310) 478-0897. Audience participation is emphasized. One-hour plays may be followed by fun parties. Performances every Saturday (call for details).

Circus
The traveling circus still rolls into town (though not always with a canvas big top). Todays circus can usually be seen at the Sports Arena, Anaheim Convention Center, The Forum, or Long Beach Arena. Check the local press, or call the Visitors Bureau, (213) 624-7300, for summertime show dates.

Electronic Amusement Centers   **5-E4**
Villa Marina Shopping Center, Marina del Rey; (310) 823-1195. And 4989 Sepulveda Blvd, Sherman Oaks; (818) 990-8100. Also other locations citywide. Electronic game machines are now a fact of life. The habit can be addictive and expensive as manufacturers invent more challenging games. Opinions as to their merit vary, but one thing is certain: They're here to stay.

Golf 'n' Stuff   **1-E6**
10555 E. Firestone Blvd, Norwalk; (310) 863-8338. And 1656 S. Harbor Blvd, Anaheim; (714) 778-4100 (**1-F8**). Family fun centers with miniature golf and other amusements in fantasy surroundings.

Hayrides
The following establishments arrange hayrides, which may be accompanied by a barbecue and live Western music. Call in advance for rates and numbers required. Reservations are usually essential.

    Calamigos Ranch
    327 Latigo Canyon Rd, Malibu. (818) 889-9724.

    Hansen Dam Stables
    11127 Orcas Ave, Lake View Terrace. (818) 896-6514.

Kids in Costume   **6-D3**
7206½ Melrose Ave, LA. (213) 936-5437. A whole shop devoted to children's costumes. Dozens of off-the-rack items plus a custom-order service. A lot of the items (such as the fun sleepwear) make great gifts.

Let's Put on a Show   **6-D1**
Roxy Theatre, 9009 Sunset Blvd, Hollywood. (310) 276-2222. This fun review, featuring The Too Short for Prime Time Players, is staged every Sunday afternoon. Multitalented children, age 4 to 14, create and perform in their own shows. Dinner-theater seating allows for parties during the show.

Merry-Go-Round   **1-C4**
Griffith Park Dr, Griffith Park. (213) 665-5188. Beautiful antique carousel that will carry adults too. *OPEN year-round. CLOSED weekdays in winter.*

Santa Monica Pier   **4-D3**
Ocean Ave at Colorado Blvd, Santa Monica. This well-used pier has seen plenty of activity since it opened in 1875. In good pier tradition there are amusement arcades, a fortune teller, fishing and boating rentals, restaurants, snack bars, and, best of all, a wonderful 1922 carousel (housed in its original building and still gliding to the sounds of one of the oldest Wurlitzers in America).

Santa Monica Playhouse   **4-B3**
1211 4th St, Santa Monica. (310) 394-9779. Summer theater workshops plus weekend afternoon performances "recommended for ages 3 to 90."

Santa's Village
Off Highway 18, Sky Forest, San Bernardino Mountains. (714) 337-2481. A dream-come-true wonderland high in the pine woods where Santa greets his young visitors year-round. An amusement park has 12 mechanical rides, and there's a puppet show, a maze, gift shops, and a delightful zoo where you can meet Santa's reindeer. The Rainbow Man and Lollipop Lady entertain with songs and dance. *OPEN June-Dec 7 days, Jan-May Mon-Fri.* Call in advance during snow season—roads may be blocked.

Silent Movie Theater   **6-E3**
611 N. Fairfax Ave, LA. (213) 653-2389. Comedies, with old favorites from the 1920s, are shown every evening except Sunday. Children under age 13, accompanied by an adult, are admitted free. *Shows start at 7pm.*

Universal Studios   **9-F5**
100 Universal City Plaza, Universal City. (818) 508-9600. Everything here is designed to please. The Entertainment Center is a delight for children who love scary monsters, performing animals, and cowboy stunts. The studio tour (*see* SIGHTSEEING, Tours) has to be the best organized family tour available.

SPORTS

Bicycle Trails
For a variety of rides through scenic areas of Los Angeles, *see* SIGHTSEEING, Bicycle Trails.

Griffith Park   **1-B5**
Park HQ, 4730 Crystal Springs Dr, LA. (213) 665-5188. Rangers will give information on the varied sporting activities throughout the park. Free maps with trails. For pony rides, call (213) 664-3266; for train rides, call (213) 662-5874. Wagon and stagecoach rides are also available.

Ice Capades Chalet   **9-B2**
6100 Laurel Canyon Blvd, N. Hollywood; (818) 985-5555. And 550 Deep Valley Dr, Palos Verdes; (310) 541-6630 (**1-G4**). Skate rentals and instruction. Party facilities available; reserve two weeks in advance.

Kung Fu   **5-G5**
1730 Sepulveda Blvd, W. LA. (310) 478-9292.

Little League Baseball, Inc.
National organization for boys age 9 to 15. To start local league, apply by mail to P.O. Box 1127, Williamsport, PA 17701.

Los Angeles School of Gymnastics   **1-D4**
8675 Hayden Place, Culver City. (310) 204-1980. Nonprofit gymnastics center for children age 3 and up.

Malibu Grand Prix   1-D8
17871 Castleton St, City of Industry. (818) 964-
3071. Malibu Fun Centers are located throughout California and offer children the chance to
drive scaled-down models of formula race cars
around competition tracks. NOTE: Children must
be at least 4 feet 4 inches in height.

Pony Country and Rent-a-Pony   1-A2
8225½ Tampa Ave, Reseda. (818) 341-2770.
Farmyard fun and pony rides. (They will even
bring ponies to your house.) Two corrals (for
slow- and medium-paced pony rides) are located within a delightful farm that is full of chickens, turkeys, goats, pigs, and sheep.

Dave Rabb's Gym for Children   1-D3
10858 Washington Blvd, Culver City; (310) 559-
4110. And 5520 Crebs Ave, Tarzana; (818) 343-
1120 (**1-B2**). Exhilarating exercise classes for
children age 4 months to 8 years.

YMCA   7-C3
625 S. New Hampshire Ave, LA. (213) 380-6448.
Many activities are arranged for children age 3
and up. Gymnastics, martial arts, and aquatics
are often included. Call for location nearest you.

YWCA   7-C3
1125 W. 6th St, LA. (213) 482-3470. Arts and
crafts, entertainment, trips, tours, and many
other activities are organized in various locations.

LEARNING

Beachcombing   1-G5
Cabrillo Marine Museum, 3720 Stephen White
Dr, San Pedro. (310) 548-7562. Museum guides
conduct tidepool tours and encourage children
to explore and discover the varied marine life.
Educational as well as fun. CLOSED Mon.

Beverly Hills Library Story Hour   5-D8
444 N. Rexford Dr, Beverly Hills. (310) 288-2220.
Story, games, and a movie every Saturday morning at 10:30 (winter only) for children age 3 to 5.
Parents are excluded for the first half hour. FREE.

Hollywood Bowl Summer Open House 6-A5
2301 N. Highland Ave, Hollywood. (213) 850-
2000. Summer treats for children sponsored by
the Hollywood Bowl Volunteers. Puppets, magic,
dance, theater, and children's operetta.

Inner City Cultural Center   6-A8
1308 S. New Hampshire Ave, LA. (213) 387-
1161. Classes in various forms of dance, music,
drama, and art are available to children age 4 to
16. Fees vary and are charged monthly. This is a
professional, multiracial theater and dance company with an excellent Children's Ensemble
Workshop.

Junior Arts Center   6-C8
Barnsdall Park, 4800 Hollywood Blvd, LA. (213)
485-4474. Excellent classes for children age 4 to
18 include painting, drawing, sculpture, ceramics, video, photography, print making, and film.
Classes are limited to a maximum of 15 students.
Register in advance.

Junior Programs of California   5-E6
1230 Comstock Ave, LA. (213) 271-6402. And
six other LA-area locations. A nonprofit organization that arranges cultural events for children.
Call for brochure.

Los Angeles Central Library   7-C4
433 Spring St, LA. (213) 612-3200. Parents and
children are invited to the children's department
one night each month to enjoy live performances
in dance, theater, and magic. Facilities are provided for indoor picnic dinners. FREE.

Planetarium Show   6-A7
Griffith Observatory, 2800 E. Observatory Rd,
Griffith Park. (213) 664-1191. Explore the night
sky in an hour-long show created for children
under age 12. The show is both entertaining and
informative and may be followed by a tour of the
planetarium. CLOSED Mon. Low admission.

Red Cross Youth Program
Teenagers wishing to give their spare time to
worthy causes should call (818) 376-1700. Volunteers work in hospitals, camps, recreational
centers, etc.

Rustic Canyon Arts and Crafts Center 1-C2
601 Latimer Rd, Santa Monica. (310) 454-5734.
Beautiful setting opposite Will Rogers State Park.
Weekly classes and summer day camps for children age 6 to 12. Classes include music, dance,
drama, and art.

Summer Science Workshops   7-G1
California State Museum of Science and Industry
(see Children's Museums). A variety of workshops lasting one or two weeks for children up to
12th grade. Choose from 34 subjects including
photography, chemistry, aerospace, rocketry,
and radio technology.

WaldenKids   5-G6
Westside Pavilion, 10800 W. Pico Blvd, LA. (310)
474-2420. An international selection of toys,
games, books, and videos, all designed to challenge the imagination.

PARTIES

(See also Children's Entertainment.)

Animal Actors
864 W. Carlisle Rd, Thousand Oaks. (805) 495-
2122. A huge variety of expertly trained animals
are available for hire.

Chuck E. Cheese Pizza Time Theater 1-A2
8425 Reseda Blvd, Northridge. (818) 993-3446.
And several other locations. Rides, games, and
entertainment are all served up with the pizzas
and sandwiches. Staff, dressed in character
costumes, play and sing with Chuck E. and his
Pizza Time Players.

Western Costume Co.   6-D6
11041 Van Owen St, N. Hollywood. (213) 469-
1451. Famous costume rental company with
outfits to fit all ages. Props and accessories
available. CLOSED Sat & Sun.

FOR PARENTS

Alisal Guest Ranch
Solvang. (805) 688-6411. Summer family vacations. Counselors lead artistic and sporting activities for children age 5 and up. (*See also* SIGHTSEEING, Day Trips: Solvang.)

Baby-Sitters and Nanny Services

Baby Buddies   **5-E8**
144 S. Beverly Dr, Beverly Hills. (310) 273-2330. Nannies, baby nurses, governesses, cooks, and housekeepers.

Baby Sitters Guild   **6-C5**
6362 Hollywood Blvd, Hollywood. (213) 469-8246. Most sitters registered here are over 40 years of age. Service available 24 hours.

George's of Beverly Hills   **5-E8**
211 S. Beverly Dr, Beverly Hills. (310) 274-0711. European and American nannies from certified nanny schools. Housekeepers and baby-sitters.

Sandra Taylor Agency   **5-E8**
9437 Santa Monica Blvd, Beverly Hills. (213) 272-9748; (310) 278-7535. Nannies with NNEB degrees, governesses, and baby nurses. Full range of domestic help.

Tips on Trips and Camp, Inc.
(310) 452-4440. Advisory service providing information on camps, trips, and summer school programs. Call for appointment.

OUTDOORS

(*See also* Sports.)

Boy Scouts of America   **1-B3**
Great Western Council, Inc., Valley Service Center, 14955 Saticoy St, Van Nuys; (818) 784-4272. Los Angeles Area Council, 2333 Scout Way, LA; (213) 413-4400. Call for information on joining and for group nearest you.

Camp Fire Girls   **6-F8**
304 S. Kingsley Dr, LA. (213) 382-8321. These charitable young ladies help cheer up hospitalized armed service personnel, work voluntarily in local libraries, arrange camping trips, and organize various outdoor activities. Call for group nearest you.

Girl Scouts   **1-D4**
Los Angeles Girl Scout Council, 5057 W. Adams Blvd, LA. (213) 933-4700. Call for information on joining and for group nearest you.

Sierra Club   **7-A2**
3550 W. 6th St, LA. (213) 387-4287. A fine club for all ages sponsoring a multitude of outdoor activities, including backpacking and mountaineering. The club has its own Youth Chapter.

Woodcraft Rangers   **7-E2**
2111 Park Grove Ave, LA. (213) 749-3031. Recreational group focused on American Indian culture. Children age 7 to 16 can make camping trips and learn crafts. They are encouraged to organize their own activities. No uniforms required. Minimal membership fees.

SPORTS & RECREATION

LA Memorial Coliseum

Southern California's near-perfect climate encourages all kinds of sporting and recreational pastimes. The following activities (listed alphabetically) may be enjoyed in or around Los Angeles at almost any time of year. Equipment for many sports may be easily rented. For rental information, call the relevant organization or the nearest sporting goods store. For specialty sporting goods see SHOPPING & SERVICES, Specialty Shopping, Sporting Goods. Tickets for most events may be obtained through citywide ticket agencies (see ENTERTAINMENT, Tickets). See ANNUAL EVENTS for sporting events that occur annually.

INFORMATION

Amateur Athletic Foundation   1-C4
2141 W. Adams Blvd, LA. (213) 730-9600. Funding organization for amateur sports. Staff will help with information.

Athletic Foundation   3-C6
First Interstate Bank, 2141 W. Adams Blvd, LA. (213) 730-9600. A collection of sporting memorabilia and awards plus one of the world's finest sports libraries. *OPEN Mon-Fri 9am-5pm; Sat 9am-3pm.*

California State Parks System
Santa Monica Mountain District, 2860-A Camino Dos Rios, Newbury Park. (805) 620-3342. Information on California's 800,000 acres of parks, reserves, campgrounds, recreation areas, beaches, underwater parks, and historical sites. *OPEN Mon-Fri 8:30am-5pm.*

City of LA Department of Recreation and Parks   7-C5
200 N. Main St, LA. (213) 485-5515. Over 300 separate facilities including recreation centers, golf courses, swimming pools, bridle paths, hiking trails, tennis courts, archery ranges, parks, beaches, lakes, and historical sites. The recreation centers control leagues for various sports including archery, badminton, baseball, basketball, flag football, judo, skating, soccer, softball, surfing, and volleyball. For information, call the area office:
    Central LA: (213) 485-4876
    Southern LA: (213) 232-2696
    Eastern LA: (213) 485-5027
    Western LA: (310) 836-1040
    San Fernando Valley: (818) 989-8060

LA County Department of Recreation and Parks   4-E5
433 S. Vermont Ave, LA. (213) 738-2961. Responsibility for parks, playgrounds, golf courses, and swimming pools. Programs in basketball, soccer, softball, swimming, tennis, and underwater diving. Special programs for senior citizens and the physically handicapped.

Los Angeles YMCA   7-C3
625 S. New Hampshire Blvd, LA. (213) 380-6448.

Los Angeles YWCA   7-C3
1125 W. 6th St, LA. (213) 482-3470. Both YMCA and YWCA provide facilities for numerous indoor sports and organize swimming and fitness programs. Many locations. Call for information.

STADIUMS & ARENAS

Anaheim Stadium   1-F8
2000 State College Blvd, Anaheim. (714) 634-2000. This 67,000-seat stadium is the home of the Rams football team and the California Angels baseball team. Numerous events are held here, including summertime rock concerts.

Dodger Stadium   7-A5
100 Elysian Park Ave, LA. (213) 224-1500. Home of the Los Angeles Dodgers baseball team. 56,000 seats. (Note your parking area here—the huge parking lot can be confusing.)

The Forum   1-D4
Manchester Blvd & Prairie Ave, Inglewood. (310) 419-3100. An enclosed stadium that seats 19,000. The Forum is the home of the LA Lakers basketball team and the Los Angeles Kings ice hockey team. It is also used for numerous rock concerts, boxing events, tennis tournaments, circuses, and pantomime.

Hollywood Park   1-D4
1050 S. Prairie Ave, Inglewood. (310) 419-1500. A beautifully landscaped racecourse, featuring thoroughbred racing from April to July and from November to December. Harness racing is featured from August to October.

Los Alamitos Raceway   1-F7
4961 Katella Ave, Los Alamitos. (310) 431-1361. A beautiful racetrack near Anaheim that features

exciting harness racing from February to April, and quarter-horse racing from May to August.

Los Angeles Memorial Coliseum **7-G1**
3911 S. Figueroa St, LA. (213) 747-7111. Site of the 1932 and 1984 Olympics. The Coliseum was constructed in 1921 and enlarged in 1930 to seat 91,000 in time for the 1932 Olympics. Extensive remodeling was completed in 1982 to ensure first-rate facilities for the 1984 Olympic Games. This attractive stadium is home venue for the LA Raiders football team and the USC football team. Other sporting events and concerts are frequently staged here.

Los Angeles Sports Arena **7-G1**
3939 S. Figueroa St, LA. (213) 748-6136. Adjacent to the Coliseum, this multipurpose indoor stadium is used for a variety of sporting activities, concerts, shows, and conventions. It is also home of the USC basketball team.

The Rose Bowl **8-A1**
1001 Rose Bowl Dr, Pasadena. (818) 793-7193. Site of the famous Rose Bowl football game, played each New Year's Day between the winning teams of the Pacific Coast Conference and the Big Ten Conference. This huge stadium seats over 104,000 and stages various events, including concerts, a huge monthly flea market (*see* SHOPPING & SERVICES, Swap Meets & Flea Markets), and semiannual auto-swaps. The Rose Bowl is home to UCLA's football team, the Bruins.

Santa Anita Park **1-B7**
285 W. Huntington Dr, Arcadia. (818) 574-7223. Beautifully located in the foothills of the San Gabriel Mountains. An attractive 500-acre park, featuring thoroughbred racing from December to April and from September to November. Facilities include a children's playground, a golf course, and refreshment and restaurant areas. Free tram tours on weekends.

THE 1984 OLYMPIC GAMES

Olympic Sites
Los Angeles is proud that no public funds were used to provide facilities for the 1984 Olympic Games (the XXII Olympiad). Monies for extensive new facilities, and for the refurbishment of older facilities, were provided by private industry and sponsors. The 1984 Olympic Games were the first in modern history to make money. Peter Ueberroth, the successful president of the Los Angeles Olympic Organizing Committee, went on to become head of baseball's National Commission.

Opening and closing ceremonies were held at Los Angeles Memorial Coliseum. Other 1984 Olympic Games events were held at the following sites:

Archery	El Dorado Park, Long Beach
Athletics	Los Angeles Memorial Coliseum
Basketball	The Forum, Inglewood
Boxing	Los Angeles Sports Arena
Canoeing	Lake Casitas, Ventura County
Cycling	Cal State University, Dominguez Hills
Equestrian	Santa Anita Park, Arcadia
Fencing	Long Beach Convention Center
Gymnastics	UCLA, Pauley Pavilion
Handball	Cal State University, Fullerton
Hockey (Field)	East LA College, Monterey Park
Judo	Cal State University, Los Angeles
Modern Pentathlon	Coto de Caza, Trabuco Canyon
Rowing	Lake Casitas, Ventura County
Shooting	Coal Canyon, Orange County
Soccer	The Rose Bowl, Pasadena
Swimming & Diving	USC, Los Angeles
Volleyball	Long Beach Arena
Water Polo	Pepperdine University, Malibu
Weightlifting	Loyola Marymount University, LA
Wrestling	Anaheim Convention Center
Yachting	Long Beach Marina

SPORTING ACTIVITIES

Archery Ranges

Cheviot Hills Recreation Center **5-G7**
2551 Motor Ave, LA. (310) 837-5186.
El Dorado Park **1-F6**
7550 Spring St, Long Beach. (310) 425-8569.

Arm Wrestling

Southern California Arm Wrestling Association
For information on local competitions, call (714) 522-3316.

Backpacking

There are thousands of suitable hiking and backpacking trails throughout the surrounding moun-

tain ranges. Some are easy enough for young children, others should only be tackled by experts. The Sierra Club will provide information on trails suited to individual skills.

The Sierra Club   **6-G8**
3345 Wilshire Blvd, LA. (213) 387-4287. Wilderness outings include river tours, rock climbs, and local hikes.

Baseball

California Angels Baseball Club   **1-F8**
Anaheim Stadium, 2000 East Gene Autry Way, Anaheim. (714) 254-3100. Popular American League team.

Little League Baseball
6707 Little League Dr, San Bernardino. (714) 887-6444. Write or call for information on Little League (age 8 to 12), Senior League (age 13 to 15), and Big League (age 16 to 18).

Los Angeles Dodgers   **7-A5**
Dodger Stadium, 1000 Elysian Park Ave, LA. Ticket information (213) 224-1400; season tickets (213) 224-1471; publicity (213) 224-1301. The Dodgers moved from Brooklyn, New York, to LA in 1960 and have remained one of the top U.S. teams in the National League. The baseball season runs from April to September.

UCLA—University of California, Los Angeles
For information on Bruins games and tickets, call (310) 825-2106.

USC—University of Southern California
For information on Trojans games, call the ticket office, (213) 740-2311.

Basketball

Los Angeles Lakers   **1-D4**
The Forum, Manchester Blvd and Prairie Ave, Inglewood. (310) 419-3100. LA's popular, top professional team.

UCLA Basketball   **5-D4**
Pauley Pavilion, UCLA Campus, Westwood. (310) 825-2106.

USC Basketball   **7-G1**
Sports Arena, 3939 S. Figueroa St, LA. (213) 743-2620; (213) 748-6136.

Bicycling

(See also SIGHTSEEING, Bicycle Trails.)
Los Angeles Wheelmen Bicycling Club 2-C5
1010 Manhattan Ave, Manhattan Beach. (310) 533-1707. The club holds numerous rides and events throughout the year.

North Hollywood Wheelmen   **9-D2**
5346 Laurel Canyon Blvd, N. Hollywood. (818) 993-3929. Various organized rides, including a New Rider Development Ride every Saturday.

Olympic Velodrome   **1-F5**
Avalon Blvd and Victoria St, Cal State University, Dominguez Hills. (310) 516-4000. A world-class bike racing track measuring 333.3 meters with a capacity for 8,000 spectators.

—Tours

The following companies arrange bicycle tours:
Breaking Away Bicycle Tours
1142 Manhattan Ave, Manhattan Beach. (310) 545-5118.

—Training Rides

Weekend rides, for new enthusiasts, are organized in Griffith Park ([213] 993-3929) and Marina del Rey ([310] 392-3542).

Boardsurfing

See Windsurfing.

Boating

See Sailing & Boating.

Bodybuilding

See Weightlifting.

Bowling

Bowling lanes are located in most districts of Los Angeles. Check local Yellow Pages for detailed information. (See also NIGHTLIFE, After Hours, Bowling Alleys.) Some popular lanes:
Holiday Bowl   **1-D4**
3730 Crenshaw Blvd, LA. (213) 295-4325.

Hollywood Star Lanes   **6-D7**
5227 Santa Monica Blvd, Hollywood. (213) 665-4111.

Midtown Bowling Center   **1-C4**
4645 Venice Blvd, LA. (213) 933-7171.

Boxing

**Athletic Commission—Boxing and Wrestling
                                                 7-C4**
107 S. Broadway, LA. (213) 897-3224.

Canoeing

Southern California Canoe Association 7-G1
c/o Aquatics Section, LA City Department of Recreation and Parks, 3966 S. Menlo Ave, LA, CA 90037. (213) 485-2844.

Cricket

*Cricket matches are held regularly during summer at Woodley Park, 6350 Woodley Ave, Van Nuys **(10-C3)**. For information, call (818) 994-2420.*

Dancing Instruction

Cafe Danssa   **4-A7**
11533 W. Pico Blvd, W. LA. (310) 478-7866. Folk dancing.

Stanley Holden Dance Center   5-G6
10521 W. Pico Blvd, Westwood. (310) 475-1725.
Ballet, jazz.

Hollywood Dance Center   6-D5
817 N. Highland Ave, Hollywood. (213) 467-
0825.

Los Angeles Dance Center   7-B1
659 S. Westmoreland Ave, Hollywood. (213)
381-6003. Ballet, jazz, tap.

Lichine Riabouchinska Ballet Academy 5-B8
405 N. Foothill Rd, Beverly Hills. (310) 276-5202.
Ballet—all levels and ages.

Studio of the Performing Arts   6-E1
8558 W. 3rd St, W. Hollywood. (310) 275-4683.
Individual and group classes in aerobics, ballet,
jazz, Latin, modern, tap.

Darts

Southern California Darts Association   1-D4
11119 Washington Blvd, Culver City. (310) 839-
6972. Call for information on local league activities. Supplies.

Fishing

California Department of Fish & Game   1-G5
330 Golden Shore, Suite 50, Long Beach. (310)
590-5171. Information on clubs, prime fishing areas, and regional fishing conditions. Licenses
issued.

Castaic Lake
Large lake stocked with trout, bass, and catfish.
(See SIGHTSEEING, Day Trips.)

Green Valley Lake
San Bernardino, near Big Bear Lake (see SIGHT-
SEEING, Day Trips). Peaceful and uncrowded,
with a ban on powerboats. Rowboats and paddleboats for rent.

Kenneth Hahn State Recreation Area   1-D4
4100 S. La Cienega Blvd, LA. (213) 291-0199. A
stream-fed lake stocked with perch and carp.

Lake Cahuilla
South of Palm Springs, off California Hwy 111. A
65-acre reservoir in the desert stocked with catfish, bass, bluegill, carp, and crappie. Boats for
rent.

Lake Isabella
Sequoia National Forest, north of Mojave. Largest freshwater lake in Southern California (7
miles long, 4 miles wide) stocked with trout,
bass, bluegill, and crappie. Campgrounds,
lodging, and boating facilities available.

Ports O' Call Sports Fishing   1-B8
Berth 79, San Pedro. (310) 547-9916. Year-
round fishing; day excursions and charter boats.

Queen's Wharf Sport Fishing   1-G5
555 N. Pico Ave, Long Beach. (310) 432-8993.

Redondo Sport Fishing   2-F7
233 N. Harbor Dr, Redondo Beach. (310) 372-
2111. Deep-sea barge fishing, local boat fishing,
pier fishing, rentals, and bait.

Santa Monica Pier   4-D3
Santa Monica Pier. (310) 458-8694 or -8900. Call

for information on fishing excursions. Fishing
from the pier is free.

Troutdale
2468 Troutdale Rd, Agoura. (818) 889-9993.
South of Ventura Freeway at Kanan Road. Pond
fishing for trout. Bait and tackle supplied. Wed-
Sun & holidays 10am-5pm.

Ventura Sport Fishing Landing
1516 Anchors Way Dr, Ventura. (805) 644-7363.
Island excursions, all-day boat fishing. Tackle
shop.

Whittier Narrows Recreation Area   1-D7
1000 N. Durfee Ave, S. El Monte. (818) 444-
9305. Fishing in Lake Legg for trout during winter; crappie, bass, and catfish during summer.

Flying

*Many municipal and private airports have air-
plane rentals and instruction. (See TRANSPOR-
TATION & VACATION INFORMATION, Airport
Information.) Skydiving is covered separately
below.*

Peninsula Aviation   1-F4
2955 Airport Dr, Torrance. 326-5050. Lessons
(all ratings). Airframe, engine, and radio instruction. Charters, scenic, and photographic flights.

Football

King Football Conference
P.O. Box 271, Montebello, CA 90640. (213) 292-
7026. This particular football season runs from
August to Thanksgiving. There are five league
classifications: Mitey Mite (age 9 to 11, 55 to
80 pounds); Pee Wee (age 10 to 12, 70 to 95
pounds); Midget (age 11 to 13, 90 to 115
pounds); Junior Bantam (age 12 to 14, 105
to 135 pounds); and Bantam (age 13 to 15, over
135 pounds).

Los Angeles Raiders   7-G1
LA Coliseum, 3911 S. Figueroa St, LA. (213)
747-7111. Call for current schedule and ticket
information.

Los Angeles Rams   1-F8
Anaheim Stadium, 2000 East Gene Autry Way,
Anaheim. (714) 535-7267. Call for current
schedule and ticket information.

UCLA   8-A1
The Rose Bowl, 1001 Rose Bowl Dr, Pasadena.
(818) 793-7193. Call for information and schedule of UCLA's Bruins home games.

USC   7-G1
LA Coliseum, 3911 S. Figueroa St, LA. (213)
747-7111. For Trojan's schedule, call (213) 740-
2311.

Gambling

*Aside from the State Lottery, gambling is gener-
ally illegal throughout California. There are a few
exceptions, which may provide relief for the addict.*

—Horse Racing
*Betting on horse races is permitted only at the
track. See Horse Racing (below).*

—Poker

Individual cities in California can vote for (or against) allowing registered card rooms for public use. Two cities near Los Angeles with card rooms are Gardena and Lake Elsinore. Five-card draw, low or high, and panguingue (gin) are allowed, and the gambling is serious. Unlike Las Vegas, the house has nothing to do with the game.

Eldorado Club   1-E4
15411 S. Vermont Ave, Gardena. (310) 323-2800. Draw poker. *OPEN 24 hours.*

Golf

The City of Los Angeles Department of Recreation and Parks will provide information on local municipal golf courses (see Information). *For information relating to LA County golf courses, call (213) 744-4278. Any office of the Automobile Club of Southern California will provide booklets listing all courses in Los Angeles. (See local white pages for Automobile Club office nearest you.)*

Griffith Park   6-A8
Five golf courses within Griffith Park include two 18-hole courses. For information and starting times, call (213) 661-6777 or (213) 663-2555.

Industry Hills Sheraton Resort   1-D8
One Industry Hills Pkwy, City of Industry. (818) 965-0861. Two 18-hole world-class courses, including the tough Eisenhower course (home of LPGA's Olympic Gold Tournament).

Junior Golf Association of Southern California   1-D7
2323 W. Lincoln Ave, Suite 229, Anaheim. (714) 776-4653. Tournaments arranged for golfers age 7 to 17.

Miniature Golf
See Miniature Golf.

Rancho Park   5-G7
10460 W. Pico Blvd, LA. (310) 838-7373. Reputedly the world's busiest 18-hole course. Also a 9-hole course. Apply for reservation card in advance.

Sepulveda Courses   10-C2
16821 Burbank Blvd, Encino. (818) 995-1170. Two 18-hole courses and a driving range.

Southern California Golf Association   9-D5
3740 Cahuenga Blvd, N. Hollywood. (213) 877-0901; (818) 980-3630. This association represents most of Southern California's private golf clubs. They sponsor tournaments and keep handicap records. Women's Association: (714) 592-1281.

Westchester Country Club   3-B5
6900 W. Manchester Ave, LA. 670-5110. Driving ranges and a good 15-hole course. Close to LA International Airport.

Gymnastics

Gymnastics Olympica USA   1-B3
7735 Haskell Ave, Van Nuys. (818) 785-1537. Instruction.

Junior Gym   4-A6
2028 Stoner Ave, W. LA; (310) 479-2730. And Sherman Oaks; (213) 789-1293. Educational gymnastics.

Los Angeles School of Gymnastics   1-D4
3611 Hayden Ave, Culver City. (310) 204-1980. Instruction.

YMCA   1-B5
4160 Eagle Rock Blvd, LA. (213) 257-7516. Instruction, low rates.

Hang Gliding

The following location offers instruction and equipment sales and rentals. It will also suggest good places to practice this exciting sport.

U.S. Hang Gliding Association   1-D3
11421 Washington Blvd, Culver City. (310) 390-3065.

Hockey (Ice)

Los Angeles Kings   1-D4
The Forum, Manchester Blvd & Prairie Ave, Inglewood. (310) 419-3100.

Horseback Riding

Over 20 local riding establishments provide horses for rent, but not all are reputable. The following stables have well-treated horses, good equipment, and trained staff. All offer lessons and some will arrange night rides.

Palos Verdes Stables   6-A6
4057 Via Opata, Palos Verdes. (310) 375-9005.

Sunset Hollywood Stables   1-B5
3400 N. Beechwood Dr, Hollywood. (213) 469-5450.

Horse Racing

Hollywood Park   1-D4
1050 S. Prairie Ave, Inglewood. (310) 419-1500. Thoroughbred racing April to July and November to December. Harness racing August to October. (*See* SPORTS & RECREATION, Stadiums & Arenas.)

Los Alamitos   1-E7
4961 Katella Ave, Los Alamitos. (310) 431-1361. Harness and quarter-horse racing May to August.

Santa Anita   1-B7
285 W. Huntington Dr, Arcadia. (818) 574-7223. Thoroughbred racing December to April and October to November. (*See* SPORTS & RECREATION, Stadiums & Arenas.)

Hot-Air Ballooning

Adventure Flights
(714) 678-4334. Five regional locations. Champagne flights, balloon sales, and pilot training.

Piuma Aircraft Balloon Adventures
P.O. Box 1201, Malibu, CA 90265. (818) 888-0576; (800) THE RIDE. Weekend rides over Per-

ris Valley, Lancaster, and many other places. Takeoff at sunrise and sunset. Prices start at $100.

Jogging

See Running.

Judo & Karate

See Martial Arts.

Lacrosse

California Lacrosse Association   **3-B4**
7330 W. 88th St, LA. (310) 670-3355.

Martial Arts

Aikido Institute of America   **1-B4**
2235 Hyperion Blvd, LA. (213) 667-2428. Non-violent self-defense.
American Karate Academy   **1-D4**
9617 Venice Blvd, Culver City. (310) 837-6285. Training for all ages.
American Karate and Fitness Center   **5-G5**
1901 S. Pontius, LA. (213) 475-0011. Comprehensive martial arts programs. Lessons by world-class champion Greg Wilkinson.
Tai Chi Chuan Academy   **1-C5**
2741 Sunset Blvd, LA, and 1110 Bates Ave, LA. (213) 665-7773.

Miniature Golf

These specially built fantasy lands, containing miniature golf courses, provide fun for the whole family.
Arroyo Seco Golf Course   **8-F1**
1055 Lohman Lane, S. Pasadena. (213) 255-1506.
Castle Park   **1-F4**
4989 Sepulveda Blvd, Sherman Oaks; (818) 990-8100. And 12400 Van Owen St, N. Hollywood; (818) 765-4000.

Motor Racing

Long Beach Grand Prix   **1-G5**
Annual international formula-one race through the streets of Long Beach. World's top racing drivers compete. For information, call (310) 436-1251.
Malibu Grand Prix   **1-A2**
19550 Nordhoff Place, Northridge. (818) 886-3252. Scaled-down models of formula racing cars, available to anyone over 4 feet 4 inches. One-mile track with computerized timing system. *OPEN Mon-Thur 11am-11pm; Fri 11am-midnight; Sat 9am-midnight; Sun 9am-11pm.*

Mountaineering

The Sierra Club   **7-A2**
3550 W. 6th St, Suite 321, LA. (213) 387-4287.

Rock climbs and wilderness outings for all experience levels.

Polo

Equidome, LA Equestrian Center   **9-E8**
480 Riverside Dr, Burbank. (818) 895-1855. Covered, 4,000-seat equidome. Matches one evening a week, April to December. Call for ticket information.
Will Rogers State Park   **1-C2**
14253 Sunset Blvd, Pacific Palisades. (310) 454-8212. Matches each Saturday from 2 to 5pm and Sunday from 10am to 12:30 pm, weather permitting. FREE.

Racquetball

The Center Courts   **4-A6**
11866 La Grange Ave, W. LA. (310) 826-6648. Open to nonmembers. Eleven courts. Showers, saunas.
Holiday Harbor Racquetball   **4-G6**
14045 Panay Way, Marina del Rey. (310) 821-1662. Ten courts, equipment rental.
Santa Monica Spectrum   **4-A5**
1815 Centinela Ave, Santa Monica. (310) 829-6836. Membership only. Thirteen courts. Complete health club, Nautilus, aerobics classes.
Sports Connection Racquetball and Health Club   **10-D4**
5251 Sepulveda Blvd, Encino; (818) 788-1220. And 8612 Santa Monica Blvd, Beverly Hills; (310) 652-7440. Also West Los Angeles; (310) 450-4464 (mixed). Open to nonmembers for a guest fee. First-rate health club, sun decks, dance classes, nursery care.

Roller Skating

See Skating.

Rowing

Long Beach Rowing Association
P.O. Box 3879, Long Beach, CA 90803. (310) 433-9233. Club location: Marine Stadium, end of Marina Drive, Long Beach. The U.S. Olympic rowing trials were held here, and the club arranges regattas twice a year.

Running

(See also Track & Field.)
Running, for fitness and fun, has become an obsession with Angelinos. With miles of beaches and parklands, it is possible to run for a month and never retrace one's steps. Competitive events are held regularly. City Sports Monthly (see also Information) *lists forthcoming events in detail. The Amateur Athletic Foundation (see* Information) *will also help with information. A good publication, now available in bookstores, is the* LA Runner's Guides *by Lee Schear and Ed Reiners, published by Tarcher.*

Sailboarding

See Windsurfing.

Sailing & Boating

California Sailing Association and Academy
4-G6
14025 Panay Way, Marina del Rey. (310) 821-3433. Courses, cruises, racing, special presentations, rentals available to members.

Harbor Department
For information on local conditions, call (310) 477-1463.

Port Royal Marina　　**2-F7**
555 Harbor Dr, Redondo Beach. (310) 318-2772.

Rent-A-Sail Inc.　　**4-G7**
13179 Fiji Way, Marina del Rey. (310) 822-1868. Canoe, sailboat, and motorboat rentals. Lessons in basic skills.

Westwind Sailing Inc.　　**4-F7**
4223 Glencoe Ave, Marina del Rey. (310) 822-8022. Charters, rentals, and lessons.

Scuba/Skin Diving

Malibu Divers　　**1-D1**
21231 W. Pacific Coast Hwy, Malibu. (310) 456-2396. Scuba lessons, beginners to advanced. Spear fishing, underwater photography, boat trips.

Reef Seekers　　**6-F1**
8677 Wilshire Blvd, Beverly Hills. (310) 652-4990. Scuba lessons. Sales, rentals, repairs, photography equipment.

Scuba Haus　　**4-A4**
2501 Wilshire Blvd, Santa Monica. (310) 828-2916. Scuba lessons. Sales, rentals, custom wet suits, diving trips, photography equipment.

YMCA
625 S. New Hampshire St, LA. (213) 380-6448. Lessons in all aquatic sports. Call for location nearest you.

Shooting

Angeles Shooting Club　　**1-A5**
12651 N. Little Tujunga Canyon Rd, San Fernando. (818) 899-2255. Rifle, pistol, trap, combat. Picnic area.

California Rifle and Pistol Association　**1-G7**
12062 Valley View St, Suite 107, Garden Grove. (714) 892-9821.

Firing Line Indoor Shooting and Oak Tree Gun Club　　**1-A2**
23121 N. Coltrane Ave, Newhall. (805) 259-7441. Trap and skeet range.

South Bay Target Range　　**1-F4**
20441 Earl St. Torrance. (310) 371-9168. Any caliber handguns, rifles.

Skating

—Ice Skating

Culver Ice Rink　　**1-D4**
4545 Sepulveda Blvd, Culver City. (310) 398-5718. Daily public sessions. *Hours change daily—call.*

Ice Capades Chalets
6100 Laurel Canyon Blvd, N. Hollywood; (818) 985-5555. And 550 Deep Valley Dr, Rolling Hills Estate; (310) 541-6630.

Iceland　　**1-E6**
90723 Jackson St, Paramount. (310) 636-8066. Game and party rooms, group rates. *CLOSED Wed.*

Pickwick Ice Arena　　**9-E8**
1001 Riverside Dr, Burbank. (818) 846-0032. Daily public sessions, private and group instruction, sport shop.

—Roller Skating

Beach Skatepath
Santa Monica & Venice Beaches. Marked paths for roller skaters.

Skatepark Paramount　　**1-E6**
16000 Paramount Blvd, Paramount. (310) 630-4088.

Skiing

Before setting off for the local resorts, skiers should check road and weather conditions, equipment availability, and accommodations. Roads to resorts in and around Big Bear Lake and Wrightwood are generally accessible year-round, but in certain conditions chains may be required. The drive from central LA to these popular local resorts takes approximately 2 hours. For weather information, call (213) 554-1212. *For conditions at Big Bear, call* (714) 866-5652. (*See also* SIGHTSEEING, Day Trips.)

—Ski Reports

Southern California area: (310) 976-7873
Big Bear area: (714) 585-2519

—Ski Resorts

Bear Mountain
Big Bear Lake area. (714) 585-2517. Located between Big Bear Lake and Big Bear Lake Village. Five chair lifts, three tows; lessons, rentals (adult equipment only); restaurant, bar. Longest run 2.5 miles, vertical drop 1,500 feet. Tickets available through Teletron (*see* ENTERTAINMENT, Tickets, Ticket Agencies). Lodgings available, call (714) 866-5877 or -4601.

Mammoth Mountain
North of Bishop, via U.S. 395. (619) 934-2571, -6611, or -2505. Mammoth cannot be considered "local," but it's a worthwhile weekend trip. Accommodations available, call to book in advance. Definitely the best ski resort within driving distance of LA (approximately 5½ hours). Nineteen chair lifts, two T-bars, two gondolas, and two free poma lifts; lessons, rentals, ski shop; restaurant. Longest run 2.5 miles, vertical drop 3,100 feet. (*See also* SIGHTSEEING, Weekend Trips.)

Mountain High
Wrightwood. (714) 972-9242. Two ski areas, 42

runs, 11 lifts; night skiing, lessons, student discounts; four restaurants, four bars. Vertical drop 1,600 feet. Children under age 10 ski free with adult. Lodgings available, call (619) 249-5477. Weekends are busy, reserve lift tickets in advance.

Mount Baldy
San Bernardino. (714) 981-3344. Small facility, just 51 miles from LA. Four chair lifts.

Mount Waterman
La Canada. (818) 790-2002. Small resort, only 43 miles from LA. Three chair lifts, one rope tow; lessons, rentals; snack bar. Longest run ½ mile, vertical drop 1,100 feet.

Ski Sunrise
Wrightwood. (619) 249-6150. Small and picturesque. One quad, one rope, and three puma lifts; lessons; snack bar, cafeteria, barbecue; children's slope.

Snow Forest
Big Bear Lake area. (714) 866-8891. Specially designed for novice skiers and those who haven't seen the slopes in a while. Good mountaintop cross-country trails. Five lifts; learn-to-ski package; two restaurants. Lodgings available, call (714) 878-3000.

Snow Summit
Big Bear Lake area. (714) 866-5766. Large, busy resort. Eight chair lifts, six doubles, two quads, one triple lift; night skiing, lessons, rentals, ski shop; restaurant, snackbar, bar. Mountaintop restaurant with spacious decks. Longest run 1.25 miles, vertical drop 1,200 feet. Lodgings available, call (714) 878-3000.

Snow Valley
Big Bear Lake area. (714) 867-2751. Large, busy resort. Twelve chair lifts; night skiing, lessons, rentals, ski shop; restaurants, snackbar, cafeteria, bar. Separate area for advanced and advanced intermediates. Longest run 1.25 miles, vertical drop 1,100 feet. Lodgings available, call (714) 878-3000.

Skydiving

The following centers are all affiliated with the U.S. Parachuting Association, (703) 837-3495. Trainee skydivers must be 18 years of age or older (16 years with parental consent). Spectators may fly in observation planes for a minimal fee. Note: All locations are outside LA County.

California City Skydiving Center
California City Municipal Airport, California City. (619) 373-2733. Desert location for fun jumping. *OPEN 7 days.*

Perris Valley Skydiving
Perris Valley Airport. (714) 657-3904. All equipment provided. Jump on first day of training. *OPEN 7 days.*

Skydiving California
20701 Cereal Rd, Skylark Airport, Lake Elsinore. (714) 674-2141. Lessons offered daily. This school boasts over 270,000 jumps.

Soccer

Abraham Lincoln Soccer League   **1-C6**
1307 S. Atlantic Blvd, LA. (213) 267-1170.
American Youth Soccer Organization
(310) 454-5425.

Squash

Squash Club International   **1-F5**
19016 S. Vermont Ave, Torrance. (310) 532-4342. Tournaments, equipment, and supplies.

Surfing

(See also Windsurfing.*)*
*The following locations are favorites with local surfers and are well known in the surfing world. Huntington Beach, near the pier; Leo Carrillo State Beach, south end; Malibu Surfrider State Beach (**1-D1**); Redondo Beach, near the pier (**2-G7**); Santa Monica Beach, end of Ocean Park Blvd (**4-E3**); Venice Beach, end of Rose Ave (**4-E4**). (See also PARKS & GARDENS, Beaches.)*

Surfing Conditions, LA County Beaches
   Northern section: (310) 457-9701
   Central: (310) 451-8761
   South: (310) 379-8471

Natural Progression Surfboards   **1-D1**
22935½ W. Pacific Coast Hwy, Malibu; (310) 456-6302. And 1734 Colorado Blvd, Santa Monica; (310) 829-5952. Lessons, rentals, supplies, repairs. *OPEN 7 days.*

Swimming & Diving

Municipal pools throughout the city are well maintained and supervised. For information on locations and hours call the local office of the City of Los Angeles Department of Recreation and Parks (see Information). The following public pools are open year-round:
   Banning High School Pool, Wilmington:
      (310) 549-9017
   Rancho Cienega Pool, LA: (213) 294-6788
   Venice High School Pool, Venice: (310) 306-7997
   Franklin Roosevelt Park Pool, LA: (213) 587-6314
   Jesse Owens Park Pool, LA: (213) 756-0016
   E. G. Roberts Pool, LA: (213) 936-8483
   Echo Park Indoor Pool, LA: (213) 481-2640
   Hubert Humphrey Pool, Pacoima: (818) 896-0067

Beverlywood Swim School   **6-D2**
2612 S. Robertson Blvd, LA. (310) 838-4088. Certified instructors. Adults and children from 6 months.

LA County Department of Recreation and Parks
For information on nearest county swimming pool call the Aquatics Division, (213) 738-2961.

YMCA   **7-C3**
625 S. New Hampshire St, LA; (213) 380-6448.

And YWCA, 1125 W. 6th St, LA; (213) 482-3470. Swimming instruction at many locations city-wide.

Tennis

Recreation centers throughout greater LA provide extensive facilities for tennis. For information on locations and hours, contact the area office of the City of Los Angeles Department of Recreation and Parks (see Information). There are dozens of tennis clubs in Los Angeles, the majority of which require membership fees. The following listing is restricted to establishments open to the general public.

Anaheim Tennis Center   **1-F8**
975 S. State College Blvd, Anaheim. (714) 991-9090. Hourly fees; 12 lighted courts; lessons, locker rooms, showers.

Cheviot Hills Tennis Club   **5-G7**
Cheviot Hills Recreation Center, Pico Blvd at Motor Ave, W. LA. (213) 842-9702. City's busiest tennis facility: 14 lighted courts, warm-up backboard; racquet shop. (Local championship preliminaries are held here.)

Industry Hills Sheraton Resort   **7-D8**
One Industry Hills Pkwy, City of Industry. (818) 965-0861; (800) 325-3535. Over 650 acres of grounds include 17 lighted tennis courts plus first-class facilities for golfers and equestrians. The luxurious resort hotel has three health spas and a swim center.

Marina Tennis   **4-G7**
13199 Mindanao Way, Marina del Rey. (310) 822-2255. Good facilities with 11 lighted courts; lessons, locker rooms, showers; refreshment lounge.

Merchant of Tennis   **6-G1**
1118 S. La Cienega Blvd, LA. (310) 855-1946. Only two courts, but they're *OPEN 24 hours.*

The Racquet Center   **9-F4**
10933 Ventura Blvd, Studio City. (818) 760-2303. Twenty lighted tennis courts, racquetball, handball, and paddle-tennis. Videotaped instruction, pro shop, locker rooms, showers; lounge.

Southern California Tennis Association 5-D5
405 Hilgard Ave, Westwood. (310) 208-3838. Dozens of area clubs are affiliated with this association.

The Tennis Place   **6-F4**
5880 W. 3rd St, LA. (213) 931-1715. Fifteen lighted courts, practice lanes; lessons, locker rooms, showers; snack bar.

Track & Field

Amateur Athletic Union of the United States
437 Elm Ave, Burbank. (818) 955-7745.

California Special Olympics
(310) 453-7622.

Southern Pacific Association, AAU
See Amateur Athletic Union.

UCLA (University of California, Los Angeles)
(213) 825-4321.

Waterskiing

Ski Haus   **4-A5**
3101 Santa Monica Blvd, Santa Monica. (310) 828-3492. Lessons available during summer and fall. Full equipment rental and sales.

Weightlifting

For information on Olympic lifting, bodybuilding, power lifting, and junior Olympic competition, call the Weightlifting Committee of the AAU, (818) 955-7745.

Gold's Gym   **4-E4**
360 Hampton Dr, Venice. (310) 392-6004. Famous bodybuilders' gym. Devotees come here from around the world.

World Gym   **4-D3**
812 Main St, Venice. (310) 399-9888. Emphasis on bodybuilding.

Windsurfing

The following locations will provide information on windsurfing and other forms of board sailing. In addition to sales and rentals, all offer private and group lessons.

Long Beach Windsurfing Center   **1-G6**
3850 E. Ocean Blvd, Long Beach. (310) 433-1014.

Natural Progression   **1-D1**
22935 Pacific Coast Hwy, Malibu. (310) 456-6302.

South Bay Windsurfing   **1-G5**
2027 S. Pacific Ave, San Pedro. (310) 377-7775.

Wrestling

Athletic Commission—Wrestling and Boxing
                                             7-C4
107 S. Broadway, LA. (213) 897-3224.

Olympic Auditorium   **7-E3**
1801 S. Grand Ave, LA. 749-5171. Wrestling bouts every Thursday at 8pm.

Yoga

See SHOPPING & SERVICES, Self-Improvement, *and* ALTERNATIVES, Alternative Remedies.

ENTERTAINMENT

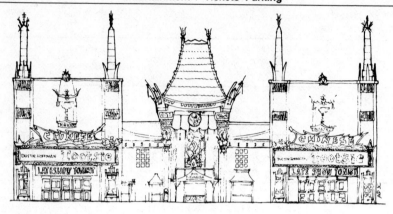

Mann's Chinese Theatre

TICKETS

Purchase tickets in advance whenever possible. Most theaters, arenas, and major clubs allot a portion of their tickets to citywide ticket agencies, who, in turn, add a small commission to the purchase price. Ticket brokers differ from agencies in that they vary their prices according to the popularity of the event. When buying through a broker, you should expect to pay at least twice the face value of a ticket, but the seats will usually be good—brokers tend to buy from press and music industry connections, or from season-ticket holders. Ticket scalping, although illegal, continues in LA, so those desperate to see a favorite performer can chance a last-minute purchase outside the venue.

Ticket Agencies

Charge Line   **7-D4**
900 Wilshire Blvd, LA. (213) 688-7380. Charge by phone with MasterCard or Visa. Tickets can be mailed to you, two weeks in advance, or collected at the theater box office at the time of the performance.
Teletron
(213) 480-3232. Division of Ticketron. Tickets by phone with major credit card. Service is limited to mid-size venues.
Ticketmaster/Chargit
Ticket centers are located in all Music Plus record stores (28 locations citywide), Federated Group stores (15 locations), and Sportmart stores. Instant tickets to concerts, theater, sporting events, and Catalina Island. Also charge by phone with American Express, Discover, MasterCard, or Visa—(213) 480-3232.

Ticket Brokers

Front Row Center Ticket Service   **5-F4**
1355 Westwood Blvd, W. LA. (310) 478-0848; (310) 879-6957. Mail and phone orders accepted; 24-hour information line. Cash, check, or major credit cards.
Ticket Time   **1-D4**
11625 Olympic Blvd, LA. (310) 473-1000. Deposits and phone orders accepted. Cash or major credit cards.
V.I.P. Tickets   **1-B3**
14515 Ventura Blvd, Sherman Oaks. (818) 907-1548. Deposits, mail, and phone orders accepted. Cash or major credit cards.

Ticket Clubs

Theater Club of California   **5-F7**
2049 Century Park East, Suite 825, LA, CA 90067. Mail-in ticket service. For $30 a year, members can order tickets for all major theater and concert locations. Hard-to-get tickets and discounts are often obtained.

Television Shows

For free tickets to tapings of TV shows, see HISTORIC LA, Television Studios.

PARKING

When attending performances at large theaters or arenas (such as the *Forum, Hollywood Bowl,* or *Anaheim Stadium*) allow an extra half hour to park and locate your seats. These huge auditoriums have equally huge parking lots. They are usually well supervised by attendants, but tempers can flare when 10,000 cars, filled with excited patrons, converge at once.

CAUTION

Most theaters and clubs will not allow flash-photography, or admit entrance to anyone with cans, bottles, alcoholic beverages, coolers, or drugs. Some amphitheaters (such as the Hollywood Bowl) do allow food and drink to be brought in, but it's always wise to call and check.

If you plan to attend an open-air evening performance, keep in mind that temperatures in LA can drop sharply at night. Some stadiums have bleacher seating, which can be very uncomfortable—take a small cushion!

THEATER

Live theater in Los Angeles is more popular today than ever before. The selection of theaters and the variety of entertainment is excellent. Productions range from experimental to traditional, and many shows get established here before moving to Broadway.

Theater tickets can be expensive, especially for the big houses, but Equity-Waiver houses (identified by EW in the following listing) are an excellent buy. These small theaters often stage productions with well-known actors who wish to maintain their ties with the stage and practice their craft in an intimate setting. Tickets are usually under $10.

No matter what the production, it is advisable to book seats in advance, either through the theater box office or at one of the citywide ticket agencies listed above. The best listing of theatrical events can be found in the LA Weekly or Reader (see BASIC INFORMATION, Newspapers & Magazines, Free Papers). Both publications list current performances for every theater in the Los Angeles area.

Ahmanson Theatre   **7-C4**
Music Center, 135 Grand Ave, LA. (213) 972-7211. Large capacity (2,100 seats). Summer season features touring Broadway musicals; winter season offers revivals, Broadway plays, and premieres. Beautiful setting, well-known performers.

Ambassador Auditorium   **8-C3**
300 W. Green St, Pasadena. (818) 304-6166. Plush theater with gorgeous decor inside and out. Winter season includes worldwide celebrities of dance and music.

Cast Theater   **6-D6**
804 N. El Centro Ave, LA. (213) 462-0265. A theater complex with two stages. Musicals and visiting shows are main features. EW.

Century City Playhouse   **5-G6**
10508 W. Pico Blvd, W. LA. (310) 839-3322. Famous for a long run of Bleacher Bums by the Burbage Theatre Ensemble. Well-directed, innovative productions. EW.

Dorothy Chandler Pavilion   **7-C4**
Music Center, 135 N. Grand Ave, LA. (213) 972-7211. Huge, luxurious auditorium that seats 3,250. Perfect acoustics. Established home of the LA Civic Light Opera Company, the LA Philharmonic Orchestra, and new home for the Joffrey Ballet. Setting for numerous star-studded events, including the Academy Awards presentations. The building is magnificent and has a stunning lobby with huge crystal chandeliers and marble walls.

Coronet Theatre (LA Public Theater)   **6-E1**
368 N. La Cienega Blvd, LA. (310) 652-9199. High-quality plays in a small theater setting. All seats are good.

James A. Doolittle Theatre   **6-C6**
1615 N. Vine St, Hollywood. (213) 462-6666. Built during the 1920s, this theater, previously the Huntington Hartford, was for years one of LA's largest. It was the location for Cecil B. DeMille's "Lux Radio Theater." Today, fine dramas, off-Broadway shows, and musicals are staged here. The atmosphere is civilized, and there is a comfortable bar upstairs.

Henry Fonda Theatre   **6-C6**
6126 Hollywood Blvd, Hollywood. (213) 480-3232; (213) 464-7521. A converted cinema that seats a comfortable 860. Theatrical dramas top the bill here.

Globe Playhouse   **6-D2**
1107 N. Kings Rd, W. Hollywood. (213) 654-5623. The interior is a half-scale reproduction of Shakespeare's Old Globe Theatre. Good Shakespearean productions. Rated among the nation's top three in its field. EW.

Greek Theatre   **6-A8**
2700 N. Vermont Ave, Hollywood. (213) 665-1927. Located in Griffith Park. The Greek is an outdoor amphitheater featuring all kinds of entertainment, from classical ballet to rock concerts. Seating capacity 4,000. *OPEN May-Oct.*

Hollywood Bowl   **6-A5**
2301 N. Highland Ave, Hollywood. (213) 850-2000. World-famous amphitheater built into a natural canyon in the Hollywood hills. Summer home of the LA Philharmonic Orchestra. The Bowl hosts many splendid events, from fireworks celebrations on the Fourth of July to cannon salutes during the "1812 Overture." Bring your own champagne supper and enjoy a concert under the stars. The dome, designed by Lloyd Wright, is acoustically perfect. Season tickets available. Seating capacity 17,000. (*See also* HISTORIC LA, Buildings & Landmarks.)

Irvine Meadows Amphitheater
8800 Irvine Center Dr, Laguna Hills. (714) 855-4515. Large, fan-shaped outdoor amphitheater south of LA. Festivals and rock concerts are popular here. There is reduced-rate meadow-seating to the rear of the regular seating complex.

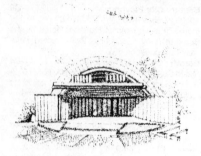

Hollywood Bowl

Japan America Theater　　　　**7-C5**
Japanese American Cultural and Community Center, Little Tokyo. (213) 680-3700. Beautifully designed, 800-seat theater that presents everything from Kabuki to chamber concerts.

Matrix Theater　　　　**6-D3**
7657 Melrose Ave, Hollywood. (213) 852-1445. Excellent small theater; original works by Actors for Themselves (a splendid group of well-known artists) and LA Theater Works. EW.

Melrose Theater　　　　**6-D5**
733 N. Seward St, Hollywood. (213) 465-1885. Small, attractive, art deco theater, one of the oldest in Hollywood. New plays and revivals. Professional workshop classes. EW.

MET Theatre　　　　**6-E4**
1089 N. Oxford, Hollywood. (213) 957-1741. A newer Equity-Waiver house producing original and established plays. Small—seats 90. EW.

The Music Center
See Ahmanson Theatre; Dorothy Chandler Pavilion; Mark Taper Forum.

Odyssey Theater　　　　**5-G2**
2055 S. Sepulveda Blvd, W. LA. (310) 477-2055. Three stages under one roof. Good-quality, avant-garde productions (including political themes). All shows are independently cast. EW.

Orange County Performing Arts Center
600 Town Center Dr, Costa Mesa. (714) 556-ARTS. One hour south of LA is Southern California's most extravagant center for the performing arts. An architecturally impressive auditorium that attracts top national and international performers, including the N.Y.C. Ballet and the Kirov.

Pacific Amphitheatre
100 Sair Dr, Costa Mesa. (714) 979-5944. Huge, outdoor amphitheater 40 miles south of LA with 8,000 fixed seats plus 10,000 lawn seats. Top international stars in all categories.

Pantages Theatre　　　　**6-C6**
6233 Hollywood Blvd, Hollywood. (310) 410-1062. A beautiful old movie palace, built in 1929 and decorated in elaborate art deco style. The Pantages hosted the Academy Awards for years. Changing to live drama in 1977, it now

stages touring Broadway musicals and comedies. (*See also* HISTORIC LA, Buildings & Landmarks.)

Pasadena Playhouse　　　　**1-C6**
39 S. El Molino Ave, Pasadena. (818) 356-PLAY. A beautifully restored, Spanish-style theater built in 1925. It has 700 seats.

Royce Hall　　　　**5-D4**
UCLA, Westwood. (310) 825-2953. Home of the California Chamber Symphony and scene of many forms of entertainment, from experimental plays to rock concerts. (*See also* HISTORIC LA, Buildings & Landmarks.)

Santa Monica Playhouse　　　　**4-C3**
1211 4th St, Santa Monica. (310) 394-9779. Lively productions performed by an energetic, enterprising group of actors. EW.

Shrine Auditorium　　　　**7-F1**
665 W. Jefferson Blvd, LA. (213) 749-5123; (213) 748-5116. Built in 1926 to seat 6,300, the Shrine has the largest stage in North America and hosts touring companies featuring ballet, theater, and musical concerts. (*See also* HISTORIC LA, Buildings & Landmarks.)

Shubert Theatre　　　　**5-F7**
2020 Avenue of the Stars, Century City. (800) 233-3123. Plush, glamorous, and large—it seats 1,832—the Shubert stages lavish Broadway productions, specializing in hit musicals.

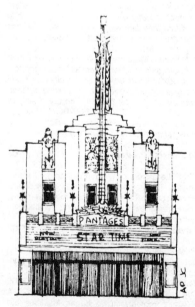

Pantages Theatre

South Bay Center for the Arts   **1-E4**
El Camino College, 16007 Crenshaw Blvd, Torrance. (310) 329-5345. The Marsee Auditorium is the setting for a variety of theatrical events including straight theater, musicals, ballet, classical and modern music.

Mark Taper Forum   **7-C4**
Music Center, 135 N. Grand Ave, LA. (213) 972-7211. Impressive, yet intimate, theater-in-the-round (¾ at least!) seating 750. Excellent new plays, classics, and experimental theater. Beautiful Music Center setting.

Universal Amphitheater   **9-G5**
Universal City Plaza, Universal City. (818) 777-3931. Attractive, covered amphitheater (on the Universal Studios lot) seating 6,200. Most seats are within 150 feet of the stage. Top entertainers (such as Frank Sinatra) are featured primarily but a full range of popular entertainment is presented year-round.

Variety Arts Theatre   **7-D3**
940 S. Figueroa St, LA. (213) 623-9100. LA's first "quake-safe" building (1924). Clark Gable made his LA debut here. The center houses the Variety Arts Theatre and the Little Theater, which stages old-style radio dramas. There is a library and collection of memorabilia from vaudeville days. The whole building has been beautifully restored to its original splendor. (*See also* RESTAURANTS, Downtown, Continental: Variety Arts Roof Garden.)

Wadsworth Theater   **5-E4**
UCLA, 650 Westwood Plaza, Westwood. (310) 825-2953. Contemporary dance, chamber music, jazz and folk ensembles.

Westwood Playhouse   **5-E4**
10886 Le Conte Ave, Westwood. (310) 208-5454. Attractive, intimate theater seating 500. Reliable productions, often avant-garde. Pleasant outdoor patio.

Wilshire Ebell Theatre   **6-G6**
4401 W. 8th St, LA. (213) 939-1128. Beautiful Spanish-style building. A variety of theatrical events are presented in a comfortable setting.

Concert Halls

The following venues feature a variety of changing programs, including orchestral concerts, operatic concerts, and ballet. Check newspapers for concert schedules and reservations.

Ambassador Auditorium   **8-C3**
300 W. Green St, Pasadena. (818) 304-6166. *See* Theater.

Anaheim Convention Center   **1-F8**
800 W. Katella Ave, Anaheim. (714) 999-8900.

Greek Theatre   **6-A8**
2700 N. Vermont Ave, Hollywood. (310) 410-1062. *See* Theater.

Hollywood Bowl   **6-A5**
2301 N. Highland Ave, Hollywood. (213) 850-2000. *See* Theater.

LA Convention Center   **7-D3**
1201 S. Figueroa St, LA. (213) 741-1151.

Long Beach Convention and Entertainment Center   **1-G6**
300 E. Ocean Blvd, Long Beach. (310) 436-3661.

Long Beach University Theatres   **1-G6**
6101 E. 7th St, Long Beach. (310) 985-5526.

Music Center—Dorothy Chandler Pavilion   **7-C4**
135 N. Grand Ave, LA. (213) 972-7211. Civic Light Opera Association, Los Angeles Philharmonic Orchestra, Joffrey Ballet. (*See also* HISTORIC LA, Buildings & Landmarks: Music Center.)

Schoenberg Institute   **7-F1**
USC, University Ave, LA. (213) 740-4090; (213) 743-5362.

Shrine Auditorium   **7-F1**
6555 W. Jefferson Blvd, LA. (213) 749-5123; (213) 748-5116. *See* Theater.

UCLA Center for the Performing Arts   **5-D5**
UCLA, 405 Hilgard Ave, Westwood. (310) 825-2953 or -4401. Schoenberg Hall, Royce Hall, and Pauley Pavilion. California Chamber Symphony. Season tickets available.

Wiltern Theatre   **6-G7**
3790 Wilshire Blvd, LA. (213) 380-5005.

CINEMA

Being the movie capital of the world, it is only fitting that Los Angeles can boast a fine selection of cinemas showing everything from first-run movies (screened here before general release) to old or rare films (shown nightly in the revival houses). The LA Weekly and Reader (see BASIC INFORMATION, Newspapers & Magazines, Free Papers) print lists of all current movies with up-to-date reviews.

Film "seasons" are featured year-round. The most notable is "Filmex." Screened for two weeks in the spring, Filmex specializes in international, contemporary cinema. (See ANNUAL EVENTS, April.)

Film events are well advertised in the local press, which also lists daily schedules for cinemas throughout the city. The following is a sampling of more interesting and unusual movie theaters in LA. Admission prices vary according to location and time of day. Many cinemas reduce their rates for the first screening of the day, and most offer reduced rates for seniors and students. Call for details.

Select Theaters

Cinerama Dome   **6-C5**
6360 Sunset Blvd, Hollywood. (213) 466-3401. This huge semisphere was the world's first cin-

erama theater. The vast, curved screen almost invites audience participation, and an excellent sound system defies reality!

Egyptian Theatre　　**6-C5**
6712 Hollywood Blvd, Hollywood. (213) 467-6167. Another Sid Grauman "epic" sits across from the Chinese, but this one is fashioned after a palace of ancient Thebes. During the great old days of Hollywood, extras, dressed as Egyptian guards, patrolled the theater and every usherette was a Cleopatra look-alike. Dozens of premieres have been screened at the Egyptian. The architecture remains impressive today. (*See also* SIGHTSEEING, Walking Tours: Hollywood Boulevard.)

Fairfax Cinemas　　**6-E3**
7907 Beverly Blvd, LA. (213) 653-3117. Three luxurious art nouveau and art deco theaters. Each auditorium has Dolby sound and a wide screen—and they put real butter on the popcorn.

Imax Theater　　**7-G1**
California State Museum of Science and Industry, 700 State Dr, LA. (213) 744-2014. Special features created especially for the Imax medium are screened daily from 10am. Incredible cinematography, projected onto a screen five stories high, allows the viewer the illusion of being part of the action. Call for schedule. No admission once show has started.

Mann's Chinese Theatre　　**6-C4**
6925 Hollywood Blvd, Hollywood. (213) 464-8111. A Hollywood landmark and tourist attraction. Originally Grauman's, this is probably the most famous cinema in America. Noted for its lavish premieres, Academy Awards presentations, and the more than 160 famous hand- and footprints in the paving outside. The decorative pagoda-style architecture is continued inside, with beautiful ceilings and rich wall coverings. (*See also* HISTORIC LA, Buildings & Landmarks.)

Revival and Art Houses

Perhaps the best value in cinema entertainment, theses houses usually present different films each night, ranging from old or rare classics to controversial and avant-garde productions. Film "festivals" are often held featuring a selection of one artist's films on consecutive nights. Rock music movies, cult classics, and stranger-than-fiction favorites are usually shown at midnight on weekends. Admission is generally lower than at regular cinemas.

Four Star Theater　　**6-G4**
5112 Wilshire Blvd, LA. (213) 936-3533. (70 mm and Dolby sound.)

New Beverly Cinema　　**6-E4**
7165 Beverly Blvd, LA. (213) 938-4038.

Nuart　　**5-G4**
11272 Santa Monica Blvd, W. LA. (310) 478-6379.

Rialto　　**8-A2**
1023 Fair Oaks Ave, Pasadena. (818) 799-9567.

Silent Movie　　**6-E3**
611 N. Fairfax Ave, Hollywood. (213) 653-2389.

Vagabond　　**7-B1**
2509 Wilshire Blvd, LA. (213) 387-2171.

Vista　　**1-C5**
4473 Sunset Dr, LA. (213) 660-6639.

Movie Theater Districts

Cineplex　　**6-E1**
Beverly Center (top floor), La Cienega Blvd, LA. (310) 652-7760. Largest cinema complex on the Westside with 14 theaters under one roof. First-run movies, obscure foreign films, and arts-related subjects. Sophisticated projection equipment.

Cineplex Odeon　　**9-G5**
Universal City Plaza, Universal City. There are 18 theaters under one roof showing first-run movies and arts-related films. Latest in projection and sound technology.

Hollywood Boulevard　　**6-C5**
Between Gower St and La Brea Ave are about 15 theaters, showing all types of films in all price ranges.

Westwood Village
A dozen or so theaters in Westwood show first-run movies and exclusive engagements (at higher-than-average prices). (*See also* HISTORIC LA, Main Districts: West Los Angeles & Westwood.)

Wilshire Boulevard　　**6-G3**
Between La Brea and Rodeo Dr are about 18 theaters screening first-run movies and popular revivals.

Cinema Centers

Cinema centers, with up to six movie theaters within one complex, are located throughout greater Los Angeles. Check local press for daily programs.

Drive-in Theaters

Drive-ins may be found in most areas of Los Angeles (though their popularity has faded over the years). Programming is good, and most show first-run movies plus popular revivals. With such a mild climate these theaters remain open year-round. Remember that performances cannot start until after dark! Some theaters charge per car, others per person. Always call ahead.

X-Rated Movies

Century Theater
See ALTERNATIVES, Gays, Cinemas.

Pussycat Theaters　　**6-C5**
1442 2nd St, Santa Monica. (213) 394-9515. Continual screenings of sexually explicit movies.

FREE ENTERTAINMENT

Festivals, parades, and tours are always fun and very often free. (See SIGHTSEEING, Tours, and ANNUAL EVENTS. *The following less-likely sources of free fun should also prove entertaining.*

The Hollywood Bowl   6-A5
2301 N. Highland Ave, Hollywood. (213) 850-2000. LA Philharmonic rehearsals, weekday mornings in summer.

Concerts in the Sky   7-C4
ARCO Plaza, 400 S. Flower St, LA. (213) 972-7480. Lunchtime musical presentations atop an impressive shopping plaza and arts center. Concerts three times weekly during summer.

Concerts in the Park   2-B5
Polliwog Park, 1600 Manhattan Beach Blvd, Manhattan Beach. (310) 545-5621. Free concerts start at 5:30pm on Sundays during the summer. Music can be jazz, bluegrass, orchestral, or brass band. Great place for an after-the-beach picnic.

"Live at Noon"   5-F7
ABC Entertainment Center, 2020 Avenue of the Stars, Century City. (310) 557-6491. Every Monday, Wednesday, and Friday throughout the summer there is a free "festival of the performing arts." Hour-long presentations begin at midday on the plaza level outdoor stage. Jazz, classical, and popular music are presented, along with a variety of performing arts, including mime.

Sundays at Four   7-G1
LA County Museum of Art, 5905 Wilshire Blvd, LA. (213) 485-2433. Chamber music series in the Bing Theater, sponsored by the museum in cooperation with the city of Los Angeles Cultural Affairs Dept. Free and also broadcast on KUSC-FM (91.5).

Chamber Concerts   1-C5
Barnsdall Park, 4800 Hollywood Blvd, LA. (213) 485-2437. Free chamber concerts in the park's Gallery Theatre most Sundays at 2pm.

Saturday Nights at the Triforium   7-C5
Triforium, Temple St at Main St, LA. (213) 485-2437. Impressive location for outdoor concerts (*see* HISTORIC LA, Outdoor Sculpture). Saturday concerts, held during summer, begin at 8pm. Each week has a different theme—it could be swing, salsa, folk music, strings, or country. Call for schedule.

Happy Hour Hors d'Oeuvres
Between the hours of 5 and 7pm, when business can be slow, cocktail prices are normally reduced, and many bars and restaurants offer free food to encourage patrons to linger. Tidbits at the following locations are definitely superior.

Arriba!, W. LA
Bel-Air Sands Hotel, Brentwood
Carlos 'n Charlies, Hollywood
Crystal Seahorse, Marina del Rey Hotel
Crystie's Bar & Grill, Beverly Hills
Cyrano, Marina del Rey
Famous Enterprise Fish Co., Santa Monica
Fiasco, Marina del Rey
Jumping Frog Saloon, Brentwood
Merlin McFly, Santa Monica
Monty's, Westwood
Red Onion, Beverly Hills
Simply Blues, Hollywood
O'Shaughnessy's, Downtown
Sportsmen's Lodge, Studio City
Vine St. Bar and Grill, Hollywood

Bio-Medic   6-C5
6433 Sunset Blvd, Hollywood. (213) 463-2182. "Free" but not exactly fun. Be a plasma donor and earn $8 per donation.

Beach Entertainment
On any fine weekend a variety of talented entertainers perform along LA's beaches. Musicians, comedians, jugglers, improvisational groups, clowns, mime artists, acrobats, magicians, and "soapbox stars" delight beachgoers with spontaneous performances. The best viewpoints are at Venice Beach, near the pavilion (**4-G5**), and Redondo Beach, near the pier (**2-G7**).

Films
Regular screenings of great classics, travel films, and documentaries can be enjoyed at the following locations (call for schedules):

Santa Monica Library: (310) 458-8600
Hearst Theater, Museum of Science & Industry: (213) 774-7400

Television Shows
Free tickets to tapings of popular television shows can be obtained from studio ticket offices and from Audiences Unlimited, (818) 506-0043.

Polo
Will Rogers State Historic Park. (*See* PARKS & GARDENS, Parks.) Polo matches weekend afternoons during summer. Spectators admitted $5 per vehicle.

Wine Tasting   7-B6
San Antonio Winery, 737 Lamar St, LA. (213) 223-1401. Informative tours and free tastings are available Monday to Saturday from 8am to 7pm and Sunday from 10am to 6pm. (*See* SIGHTSEEING Tours: San Antonio Winery.)

TV & RADIO

TV Stations

Los Angeles is the television center of America. Most shows originate in Hollywood, and many are taped (recorded) before live audiences. For free tickets phone the TV station (or contact Audiences Unlimited, 100 Universal City Plaza, Bldg. 153, Universal City, CA 91608; (818) 506-0043). Apply well in advance for the more popular shows. Several studios offer organized tours (see also HISTORIC LA, Television Studios). Children under age 12 are not usually admitted. Weekly TV program guides are free with Sunday newspapers.

—VHF Stations

Channel 2 KCBS
CBS. Tickets. (213) 460-3000.
Channel 4 KNBC
NBC. Tickets, tours. (818) 840-4444.
Channel 5 KTLA
Independent. Tickets. (213) 460-5500.

Channel 7 KABC
ABC. Tickets. (310) 557-7777.
Channel 9 KCAL
Independent. (213) 467-5459.
Channel 11 KTTV
Fox Television. Tickets. (213) 462-7111.
Channel 13 KCOP
Independent. Tickets. 851-1000.

—UHF (Local) Stations

Channel 18 KSCI
"Developing higher states of consciousness."
Foreign-language programs. (310) 479-8081.
Channel 22 KWHY
Financial. (213) 466-5441.
Channel 28 KCET
PBS. Noncommercial, community supported.
(213) 666-6500.
Channel 30 KHOF
Religion. (213) 245-7575.
Channel 34 KMEX
Spanish-language station. Mexican topics.
(213) 466-3434.
Channel 50 KOCE
PBS. Educational. (714) 895-5623.
Channel 58 KLCS
PBS. Educational. (213) 625-6958.

Subscription Television

Television sets can be converted to receive special programs transmitted by signal or cable. Programming usually includes recent movies (uncut), news features, concerts, pop music videos, and live sporting events with no commercial interruption. (Some hotels have this service installed.)
Century Cable Television
(213) 258-8500. Arts & Entertainment, CNN, Disney, MTV, and more.
Home Box Office (HBO)
(310) 201-9200
Showtime/Movie Channel
(310) 208-2340
USA Network
(310) 277-0199

Radio Stations

—AM

KABC: 790.
Talk shows, sports. (310) 557-7777
KALI: 1430.
Spanish language and music. (213) 466-6161
KBLA: 1580.
Korean language. (310) 788-1580
KEZY: 1190.
Album rock. (213) 260-7407
KFI: 640.
Top 40. (213) 385-0101
KFRN: 1280.
Christian. (310) 435-0103
KFWB: 980.
All news. (213) 462-5392

KGER: 1390.
Religion. (213) 636-4774
KGFJ: 1230.
Black urban. (213) 462-3007
KGIL: 1260.
News, talk. (213) 877-3466
KGRB: 900.
Big bands. (213) 686-0300
KIEV: 870.
Talk shows, sports. (213) 245-2388
KMPC: 710.
All sports. (213) 460-5672
KNSE: 1510.
Spanish music. (714) 981-8893
KNX: 1070.
All news. (213) 460-3000
KRLA: 1100.
1950s, 1960s, 1970s hits. (213) 383-4222
KTNQ: 1020.
Spanish hit music. (213) 465-3171
KTYM: 1460.
Religion, foreign language. (213) 678-3731
KWIZ: 1480.
Spanish adult contemporary. (714) 554-5000
KWKW: 1330.
Spanish language. (213) 466-8111

—FM

KBIG: 104.3.
Adult contemporary. (213) 874-7700
KBOB: 98.3.
Big band. (213) 686-0300
KCRW: 89.9.
Jazz, pop, reggae. (310) 450-5183
KCSN: 88.5.
Variety, drama, classical. (818) 885-3089
KDUO: 97.5.
Oldies. (714) 825-5555
KEZY: 95.9.
Top 40. (213) 625-7018
KFSG: 96.3.
Religion. (213) 484-1100.
KGIL: 94.3.
Adult contemporary. (213) 877-3466
KHTZ: 97.1.
Adult contemporary. (800) 540-9797
KIIS: 102.7.
Top 40. (213) 466-8381
KJLH: 102.3.
Soul, R&B. (213) 299-5960
KKBT: 92.3.
Urban contemporary. 466-9566
KKGO: 105.1.
Classical. (310) 478-5540
KKLA: 99.5.
Christian. (818) 762-5552
KLIT: 101.9.
Soft rock. (213) 464-5483
KLOS: 95.5.
Rock albums and hits. (310) 840-4861
KLVE: 107.5.
Spanish music. (213) 465-3171
KMAX: 107.1.
Gospel. (213) 681-2486

KOCM: 103.1.
Easy listening. (714) 644-2727
KROQ: 106.7.
Alternative rock. (818) 567-1067
KRTH: 101.1.
Adult contemporary. (213) 937-5230
KUSC: 91.5.
Classical. (213) 743-5872

KXEZ: 98.7.
Easy listening. (213) 469-9968
KYMS: 106.3.
Christian. (714) 835-1063
KZLA: 93.9.
Country. (213) 466-0004
MARS FM: 103.1.
Alternative music. (310) 393-9681

NIGHTLIFE

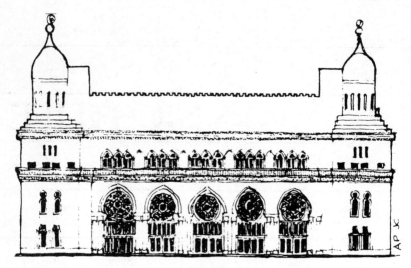

Shrine Auditorium

Los Angeles has an enormous variety of nightlife accommodating all tastes and age groups. Nightclubs that serve alcohol require photo-identification to prove patrons are over the age of 21.

CODE

Over 18s	persons aged 18 to 21 may be admitted, but served no alcohol
No age limit	minors admitted (usually over 16)
Low admission	under $5 cover charge
Full bar	cocktails (hard liquor), beer, and wine

Dress codes vary but are notably more casual here than in other major cities.

Venues can close without warning and new ones appear overnight. Styles and tastes change faster than the Top 20. Always call ahead or check local publications. (See also BASIC INFORMATION, Newspapers & Magazines.) For ticket information, see ENTERTAINMENT, Tickets.

BIG-BAND SOUNDS

Beverly Hillcrest Hotel   **5-G8**
1224 S. Beverly Blvd, LA. (310) 277-3800. *OPEN Tues-Sat 8:30pm-1am.*

The Hollywood Palladium   **6-C6**
6215 Sunset Blvd, Hollywood. (213) 962-7600. Glenn Miller and the Dorsey Brothers played here to capacity crowds in the 1940s. Big bands are still featured occasionally, but the theme is more often set to a Latin beat.

Kelbo's   **4-A7**
11434 W. Pico Blvd, W. LA. (310) 473-3050. Big-band records from the 1930s, 1940s, and 1950s. Dinner and dancing.

Myron's Ballroom   **7-D3**
1024 S. Grand Ave, LA. (213) 748-3054. Downtown's most lavishly remodeled ballroom. It boasts an upscale gourmet restaurant and four full bars. A ten-piece orchestra belts out big-band oldies on Sundays from 5pm to 11pm. Latin music is played on Wednesdays from 7pm to 2am. Dance classes. Low admission. Friday and Saturday nights are reserved for Vertigo (*see Discos & Dance Clubs, below*).

Stardust Ballroom   **6-C7**
5612 Sunset Blvd, Hollywood. (213) 462-2712. Last of the swing-era dance halls in Hollywood. Still alive (though showing signs of wear) with a full orchestra, reminiscent of Glenn Miller days. Great nostalgia. Full bar.

CABARET

Most large hotels in LA provide a variety of cabaret entertainment. Numerous restaurants feature entertainers (look for the music note symbol in RESTAURANTS). The following clubs are noteworthy and do not fall into the typical hotel or restaurant categories.

Backlot at Studio One **6-E1**
657 N. Robertson Blvd, W. Hollywood. (310) 659-0472. Somehow detached from the famous Studio One disco (*see also* Discos & Dance Clubs), the Backlot offers a variety of interesting entertainers. Occasional celebrity acts. Two-drink minimum. Talent showcase every Monday.

The Body Shop **6-C2**
8250 Sunset Blvd, W. Hollywood. (213) 656-1401. Nonmembership club featuring topless burlesque and magicians. Full bar, dinner. *OPEN nightly till 2am.* Over 18s.

Carlos 'n Charlie's **6-C2**
8240 Sunset Blvd, Hollywood. (213) 656-8830. Lounge entertainment nightly: comedians, magicians, improvisation groups, and musical acts. Two-drink minimum plus cover charge.

Cinegrill **6-C4**
Hollywood Roosevelt Hotel, 7000 Hollywood Blvd, Hollywood. (213) 466-7000. Intimate cabaret showcase with a cozy bar. Name acts featured each week. Good location—in the lobby of the gorgeous Roosevelt. Full bar.

El Cid **1-C5**
4212 Sunset Blvd, Hollywood. (213) 668-0318. Replica of a 16th-century Spanish tavern. Beautiful garden patio with fountains. The finest in authentic flamenco music and dancing. Shows Thursday to Sunday at 8pm. Full dinners from 6:30pm, cocktails. Two-drink minimum.

Gio's **6-C3**
7574 Sunset Blvd, Hollywood. (213) 876-1120. Beautiful gourmet restaurant with fine continental cuisine. A variety of entertainment, from big-band jazz to celebrity cabaret and comedy. Full bar, dancing.

L.A. Cabaret **10-E1**
17271 Ventura Blvd, Encino. (818) 501-3737. Plush art deco lounge and showroom for a variety of entertainment (mostly comedy). Full bar. *OPEN nightly.*

La Cage Aux Folies **6-E1**
643 N. La Cienega Blvd, W. Hollywood. (310) 657-1091. Almost as outrageous as the movie! First-rate female impersonators bring you Dolly Parton, Ann-Margret, Bette Midler, and more. Full bar, piano bar, continental cuisine. *CLOSED Sun.*

Mayfair Theatre **4-C3**
214 Santa Monica Blvd, Santa Monica. (310) 451-4684. One of California's oldest theaters has been lovingly restored to its Edwardian splendor. Variety, comedy, and revues. Full bar, dinner. *CLOSED Mon.*

Natural Fudge Co. **6-C7**
5224 Fountain Ave, Hollywood. (213) 669-8003.

Vegetarian restaurant featuring musical and comedy acts. Entertainment (evenings only) Monday to Saturday.

The Queen Mary **9-F2**
12449 Ventura Blvd, Studio City. (818) 506-5619. You'd never know the barmaid was a man. Excellent female impersonators attract a mixed crowd. Good fun for all.

Rose Garden Performance Centre **6-E1**
665 N. Robertson Blvd, W. Hollywood. (310) 854-4455. Three separate rooms, each with a stage. Available in the various rooms are dinner and a show, a club cabaret for drinks and appetizers, and a New York–style cabaret; also, a piano bar.

Swedish Inn **1-B2**
19817 Ventura Blvd, Woodland Hills. (818) 884-7461. The Showboat Dinner Theatre features full stage productions every Friday, Saturday, and Sunday. Dinner is served 2 hours before curtain.

Tibbies Music Hall
16360 Pacific Coast Highway, Huntington Beach. (310) 592-4072. Now a comedy club with local and big-name talent and a variety of different acts, including a hypnotist and magician. Shows Friday and Saturday at 8:30pm and 10:30pm. Two-drink minimum plus a cover charge.

The Tropical Club **1-D4**
8641 Washington Blvd, Culver City. (310) 559-1127. Latino salsa club, featuring live bands. Full bar, food, dancing.

COMEDY & MAGIC

Comedy and Magic Club **2-E6**
1018 Hermosa Ave, Hermosa Beach. (310) 372-1193. Name comics. Shows every night of the week, and two on Friday and Saturday. Two-drink minimum and a cover charge

The Comedy Store **6-C2**
8433 W. Sunset Blvd, Hollywood. (213) 656-6225. Formerly Ciro's (one of Hollywood's most glamorous nightclubs, where stars samba'd to Xavier Cugat's Latin band), now LA's most famous laugh-house. Top comedians start out here and often return to perform. Three separate rooms offer frivolity nightly from 8pm. Improvisational groups, in the Mainroom, on Mondays. The Best of the Comedy Store on Thursday, Friday, and Saturday. Full cocktail service. Two-drink minimum. Admission varies. Over 21 only.

Bud Friedman's Improvisation
See The Improvisation (*below*).

Groundlings Theater **6-D4**
7307 Melrose Ave, Hollywood. (213) 934-9700. These talented comedy players offer a variety of satire and improvisation plus excellent rehearsed skits. Shows Friday and Saturday at 8pm and 10pm. Admission moderate.

The Ice House Comedy Showroom **8-C4**
24 N. Mentor Ave, Pasadena. (818) 577-1894. A well-known launching pad for comedians. Six

nights of comedy and magic weekly from
8:30pm. Full bar. Low admission.

The Improvisation   **6-D2**
8162 Melrose Ave, Hollywood. 651-2583. This
West Coast version of the famous New York club,
known affectionately as The Improv, offers a variety of comedy acts. Celebrity comedians who
started here often make surprise appearances.
Full bar, Italian menu. Monday-night jazz. Two-
drink minimum Thursday to Saturday. Admission
varies. *OPEN nightly.*

LA Connection
13442 Ventura Blvd, Sherman Oaks. (818) 784-
1868. Casual club features comedy improv
based on audience suggestions. Friday 7:30pm,
for groups and private parties only. Saturday
shows at 7:30pm & 10:30pm; Sunday at 7pm
and 8:30pm. All ages welcome. No drinks minimum.

L.A. Cabaret   **10-E1**
17271 Ventura Blvd, Encino. (818) 501-3737.
Excellent comedy club featuring top professional-
als. Plus decor. Full bar, piano lounge, food. Admission varies. *OPEN nightly.* Over 18s.

The Laugh Factory   **6-C2**
8001 Sunset Blvd, LA. (213) 656-8860. Wide variety of comedy acts nightly. Refreshments, two-
drink minimum. Low admission.

Merlin McFly   **4-D4**
2702 Main St, Santa Monica. (310) 392-8468.
"Magical bar and grill." Lavish decor. Magic acts
most nights from 8pm. Live band Saturday evenings. Ghostly mirrors in the bathrooms. Full bar,
food. *OPEN 7 days, Mon-Fri 5pm-2am; Sat &
Sun 11am-2am.*

COUNTRY, FOLK, R&B

The Forge   **1-B5**
617 S. Brand Blvd, Glendale. (818) 246-1717. A
country music institution. Long established and
ever-thriving, The Forge offers country sounds
and dance lessons.

Ice House Cabaret   **8-C4**
24 N. Mentor Ave, Pasadena. (818) 577-1894.
Concert-style seating. Excellent sound system.
Separate bar where roving magicians perform
Friday and Saturday. Variety of blues, folk, and
rock bands. Full bar, light food. Admission varies. Shows nightly from 8pm.

McCabe's   **4-B6**
3101 Pico Blvd, Santa Monica. (310) 828-4497.
A well-respected club (set in a guitar shop) famous for authentic folk music. Relaxed atmosphere. Tea and cookies fare. Featured artists
Friday to Sunday.

The Palomino   **9-A3**
6907 Lankershim Blvd, N. Hollywood. (818)
764-4010. LA's premier country music showcase. Top-name acts from across the nation.
Occasional R&B and rock bands. Thursday is
talent night. Steak and seafood. Admission varies.

DISCOS & DANCE CLUBS

Cassidy's West Coast Exchange   **2-C7**
500 Sepulveda Blvd, Manhattan Beach. (310)
372-7666. The title continues "Pub Extraordi-
naire." Comfortable lounge, decorative outdoor
patio with stained glass and ocean views. Disco
dancing to a wide variety of popular music. Casual beach crowd. *OPEN nightly from 5pm.*

Chippendale's   **1-D3**
3739 Overland Ave, W. LA. (310) 396-4045. A
swanky setting for striptease-with-a-difference.
Male strippers perform for women only, Wednesday to Sunday. Men are admitted after 10:15pm
to enjoy the frivolous atmosphere. Good Tuesday night dance party with excellent rock videos
shown on screens around the dance floor. New
Wave and import sounds Tuesday. Pop and rock
Wednesday to Sunday. Full bar, dancing, back-
gammon. *OPEN Fri & Sat until 4am. CLOSED
Mon.*

Circus Disco   **6-D5**
6655 Santa Monica Blvd. (213) 462-1291. Appropriately named—a big-top fun house theme
and carnival atmosphere. Jammed on weekends. Lively, mixed crowd dressed in "anything
goes" clothes. Two bars, good quadraphonic
sounds, floating dance floor, shops. Low admission.

Club Lingerie   **6-C5**
6507 Sunset Blvd, Hollywood. (213) 466-8557.
Large and comfortable with a long bar, sunken
dance floor, upstairs lounge with couches. Live
bands, usually progressive and avant-garde
acts, are featured most nights. Admission varies.
CLOSED Sun. 21 and over.

Coconut Teaser   **6-C2**
8117 Sunset Blvd, Hollywood. (213) 654-4773.
Liveliest place on the strip these days. Dancing
nightly to latest new music. Two dance floors.
Late dancing Friday and Saturday. Busy bars
filled with Hollywood trendies, food. Outdoor patio. Over 18s allowed after 1:30am (when the
booze is cut off).

Maxfield's   **4-F7**
Marriott Hotel, 13480 Maxella Ave, Marina del
Rey. (310) 822-8555. Musically varied (four
nights Top 40 hits, two nights jazz, one night
big-band sounds). Casual dress. *OPEN nightly.*

The Oar House   **4-E4**
2941 Main St, Santa Monica. (310) 396-4725.
Main Street's original fun house and "den of in-
iquity." Sawdust floor, full bar, loud music, popcorn. An amazing collection of stuffed creatures, antiques, and junk is strewn across walls
and ceiling. Dance anywhere there's space,
and wear your old jeans! Strong-arm bouncers.
Good hamburgers next door, at Buffalo Chips.
When in Hollywood, try their smaller cousin: J.
Sloan's, 8623 Melrose Avenue; (213) 659-0250
(**6-E1**).

Peanuts   **6-D3**
7969 Santa Monica Blvd, Hollywood. (213) 654-
0280. Mirrored walls, murals, and blue lights.

Dancing nightly. Dance contests. Pool table. Low admission.

The Rainbow   **6-D1**
9015 Sunset Blvd, Hollywood. (310) 278-4232. A Sunset Strip landmark now showing signs of wear and tear (even the groupies look a little weary!). Dancing nightly upstairs. The downstairs bar and grill is still popular with musicians. Bar *OPEN from 6pm.* Disco *OPEN from 9pm.*

The Red Onion   **5-D8**
4215 Admiralty Way, Marina del Rey. (310) 821-2291. Formerly a pseudo-1920s tavern and restaurant, now incorporating a disco and serving Mexican food. Comfortable booths. Elegant location means you can dress up. Other locations: Woodland Hills, (818) 340-5653; Redondo Beach, (310) 376-8813. *OPEN 7 days.*

Studio One   **6-E1**
652 N. La Peer St, W. Hollywood. (213) 659-0471. Famed for its fabulous decor and silly dress code (shoes must be totally closed, heel and toe). This fun palace is West Hollywood personified. Dance amid swirling lights and neon decor. Predominantly gay males but comfortable for all persuasions. "Backlot" cabaret (*see also* Cabarets). Low admission. Club *OPEN nightly 9pm-2am.*

Sunspot Music Box   **1-C2**
15145 Pacific Coast Hwy, Pacific Palisades. (310) 459-3409. Small, oceanside motel with a lively night scene. Attractive setting. Outdoor dancing on warm evenings. Loud music—latest rock mixed with oldies. Lower bar prices before 10pm. Interesting crowd. No T-shirts. Arrogant bouncers. Low admission. Free Thursday. *CLOSED Mon.*

Tango   **7-C3**
333 S. Figueroa St, LA. (213) 617-1133. In the glamorous Sheraton Grande Hotel. Lavish decor, romantic lighting. Dancing Monday through Saturday to everything from jazz to tango. A great excuse to dress up and trip the light fandango.

Tropicana   **6-D7**
1250 N. Western Ave, Hollywood. (213) 464-1653. Older Hollywood fun spot reviving itself with dance parties every Friday and Saturday until 4am. New Wave Tuesday. Female mud wrestling and boxing. Male exotic shows. Disco and live bands. Full bar. Admission varies.

Underground
Underground clubs, which have continually changing venues, have been operating in Los Angeles for the last five years. These popular, avant-garde dance clubs are usually open just one or two days a week. Although it is difficult to keep track of them, it is safe to say that they usually operate between Thursday and Saturday nights and the following locations are used on a regular basis:

Myron's Ballroom   **7-D3**
1024 S. Grand Ave, LA. (213) 748-3054.

Stardust Ballroom   **6-C7**
5612 Sunset Blvd, Hollywood. (213) 462-2712.

Vertigo   **7-D3**
Myron's Ballroom, 1024 S. Grand Ave, LA. (213) 747-4849; (213) 748-3054. Simply the place to pose. A glam-rock palace catering to Hollywood-ites (known and unknown) plus a collection of trendsetters from around the world. Gorgeous girls come here to cruise, stars table-hop. Everyone seems to have fun—and money. Enormous dance floor, four bars, patio and gourmet restaurant. Dress code—"must be fashionably attired" is strictly enforced (unless, of course, you happen to be famous). Frantic dancing. *OPEN Fri & Sat 10pm-4:30am.*

Womp's Restaurant, Bar and Grill   **9-G5**
Universal City Plaza, Universal City. (818) 777-3939. This daytime restaurant turns into a wild party dance place at night. Special nights feature lip sync and air guitar contests. Lots of prizes and merriment always. Conveniently located next to the Universal Amphitheater and Studios.

JAZZ

Numerous clubs and restaurants in LA offer jazz entertainment that ranges from solo musicians to 20-piece bands. Some locations feature jazz nightly, others just occasionally.

Alleycat Bistro   **1-D4**
3865 Overland Ave, Culver City. (310) 204-3660. Good showcase for jazz and blues. Variety nights, name acts. Full bar, dinner. *CLOSED Sun.*

At My Place   **4-B3**
1026 Wilshire Blvd, Santa Monica. (310) 451-8597. Relaxed atmosphere. Full bar (huge selection of beers), dinner, snacks. Admission varies. *OPEN nightly.* No age limit.

The Baked Potato   **9-G5**
3787 Cahuenga Blvd, N. Hollywood. (818) 980-1615. Intimate dining room serving up jazz on a nightly basis. Resident band plus guest artists. Huge selection of delicious baked potatoes. Full bar. Admission varies. No age limit.

Hop Singh's   **4-F7**
4110 Lincoln Blvd, Marina del Rey. (310) 822-4008. A variety of new and name acts perform Wednesday to Sunday in this Chinese club-cum-restaurant. Excellent sound system. *CLOSED Mon & Tues.* No age limit.

Jax   **1-B5**
339 N. Brand Blvd, Glendale. (818) 500-1604. Popular restaurant open for lunch and dinner. Live jazz nightly. Name acts are featured weekends. Full bar. No age limit.

Le Cafe   **1-B3**
14633 Ventura Blvd, Sherman Oaks. (818) 986-2662. Selected jazz acts in "The Room Upstairs." Restaurant downstairs. Jazz Thursday to Saturday. Admission varies.

The Lighthouse   **2-E6**
30 Pier Ave, Hermosa Beach. (310) 372-6911. Reputedly the world's oldest jazz club. Recently

renovated (to the dismay of some old-timers) to include real tables and chairs! (Many will remember the old bare benches.) Top performers are always featured in addition to new and unusual jazz and blues acts. Full bar, lunch and dinner. Music nightly. Admission varies.

Manhattan Jazz Club   **2-B6**
304 12th St, Manhattan Beach. (310) 546-4777. Cozy beach restaurant and lounge. Full bar, dinner. Two-drink minimum. No age limit in restaurant, over 21 in lounge.

Money Tree   **9-E6**
10149 Riverside Dr, Toluca Lake. (818) 769-8800. Jazz six nights. Established musicians and fine vocalists. Full bar, lunch and dinner daily.

ROCK

Including New Wave and reggae.
Anti-Club   **6-D8**
At Helen's Place, 4658 Melrose Ave, Hollywood. (213) 661-3913; (213) 667-9762. Strange setting for progressive rock and performance art—in a former country and western club. Beer and wine only, food. Schedule varies. No age limit.

The Beverly Theatre   **5-E8**
9404 Wilshire Blvd, Beverly Hills. (310) 274-7106. Gorgeous art deco theater with great acoustics and a good view from every seat. Top-name bands from rock to blues to jazz. Admission varies. Full bar.

Bogart's   **1-G6**
6288 Pacific Coast Hwy, Long Beach. (310) 594-8976. Good local showcase for established rock bands. Full bar.

The Central   **6-D1**
8852 Sunset Blvd, Hollywood. (213) 855-9183. On the Strip. (*See also below and* After-Hours: F.M. Station). Changing program now features the latest local sounds in soul, rock, and reggae. Full bar. Fun dancing. Low admission. *OPEN nightly 8:30pm-2am.*

Club Lingerie   **6-C5**
6507 Sunset Blvd, Hollywood. (213) 466-8557. Large, airy, and comfortable. Sunken dance floor; upstairs lounge. Rock bands often featured on a varied bill, call for schedule. Full bar. *CLOSED Sun.*

The Country Club   **1-B2**
18415 Sherman Way, Reseda. (818) 881-5601. Plush club setting on three levels. Spacious seating plan and the best sound equipment around. Excellent showcase venue featuring top-name acts. Huge video screen. Dinner and cocktails (overpriced). Overenthusiastic security check at door (the bouncers here really muscle in). Admission varies. No age limit.

Florentine Gardens   **6-C6**
5951 Hollywood Blvd, Hollywood. (213) 464-0706. Huge, bare basics club-cum-concert-hall—2,000 capacity—with a changing format of live bands and New Wave dance parties. Full bar. *OPEN Wed-Sun.* Over 18s.

F.M. Station   **9-B3**
11700 Victory Blvd, N. Hollywood. (818) 769-2220. F.M. stands for Filthy McNasty. He once ran a notorious nightclub on the Sunset Strip and now owns this equally dingy (though interesting) club. It's always filled with interesting characters out to have a good time. Live bands perform nightly—often into the early hours. Female mud wrestlers are often featured. Call for schedule.

The Forum   **1-D4**
Manchester Blvd & Prairie Ave, Inglewood. (310) 673-1300. This is where big-name acts play to capacity audiences of 19,000. Take binoculars if your seats are in the colonnade area (or beyond). Acoustics vary with band. Large, organized, impersonal. Security check at door. No age limit.

Frogs   **1-E4**
16714 Hawthorne Blvd, Lawndale. (310) 371-2257. Well-known local bands play nightly. Video screens, two bars. Attractive cafe-style decor. Fun dancing. Full bar. Low admission.

Gazzari's   **6-D1**
9039 Sunset Blvd, Hollywood. (310) 273-6606. A landmark for teens on the Sunset Strip for over 20 years. Two stages and two dance floors. Young dancing crowd, fun atmosphere. Good showcase for new bands. Full bar. Low admission. *OPEN Thurs-Sun.*

Grandia Room   **6-D6**
5657 Melrose Ave, Hollywood. (213) 462-8628. Formerly a Latino nightclub (note the decor). New booking policy provides for rock 'n' roll, reggae, and New Wave bands and records. Full bar. Dance floor. Low admission.

Greek Theatre   **6-A8**
Large, outdoor amphitheater in Griffith Park, used extensively for rock concerts during summer. Internationally famous artists are often featured. (*See* ENTERTAINMENT, Theater.)

Hollywood Bowl   **6-A5**
Occasionally used for rock concerts during summer. (*See* ENTERTAINMENT, Theater.)

The Hollywood Palladium   **6-C6**
6215 Sunset Blvd, Hollywood. (213) 962-7600. Famous for big bands in the 1940s. Rock concerts, featuring well-known artists, are often held here. Thorough security check at door.

Hop Singh's   **4-F7**
4110 Lincoln Blvd, Marina del Rey. (310) 822-4008. Varied lineup of rock and jazz acts. Some has-beens, some will-bes, all presented in a Chinese club atmosphere. Excellent sound system. Full bar, dinner. Admission varies. *CLOSED Mon & Tues.* No age limit.

Kingston XII   **4-C3**
814 Broadway, Santa Monica. (310) 451-4423. Live music nightly, featuring LA bands. Rockabilly, New Wave, rock, and reggae. Beer and wine only. Low admission.

Laserium   **6-A8**
Griffith Park Observatory, 2800 E. Observatory Rd, Griffith Park. (213) 664-1191. Amazing laser-light shows performed to rock music within a "starlit" dome high above the city in the plane-

tarium. New formats added regularly. The visual experience defies description. No refreshments, no age limit. Tickets available through Teletron (*see* ENTERTAINMENT, Tickets, Ticket Agencies). Low admission. *CLOSED Mon.*

Long Beach Arena   **1-G6**
300 E. Ocean Blvd, Long Beach. (310) 436-3661. Large, enclosed arena that seats 14,300. Big name rock bands are featured regularly. Admission varies. No age limit.

Madame Wong's   **4-A5**
2900 Wilshire Blvd, Santa Monica. (310) 828-5656. Established westside showcase for local and new bands. Two floors of fun—both featuring live bands and dance floors. Video games. Two cocktail bars (drinks can be expensive), Chinese restaurant. Age limit and admission prices vary. *OPEN nightly.*

The Music Machine   **4-B6**
12220 W. Pico Blvd, W. LA. (310) 820-5150. Mid-size venue (500 capacity) with above-average sound system and excellent lighting system. Full bar, food, and considerate service. Dancing. Big-name rock bands of yesterday and today plus local favorites. Call for schedule. *OPEN 7 days at 4pm for happy hour and jukebox music.* Admission varies. 21 and over.

The Palace   **6-C6**
1735 N. Vine St, Hollywood. (213) 462-3000. A cool $7 million was spent on refurbishing the old El Capitan Theater (built in 1927) to create this truly palatial nightclub. Laser lights flash on the sculpted ceiling, sophisticated lounge lizards frequent the art deco bar, and lovely young couples fill the huge dance floor. An upstairs balcony has theater seating and affords a good view of the stage. Name bands are featured weekends. There is an adjoining restaurant with an outdoor patio and a private club with a piano bar. Full bar. Admission varies. *CLOSED Tues & Wed.* Over 18s.

Pier 52   **2-E6**
52 Pier Ave, Hermosa Beach. (310) 376-1629. Right on the beach. Attractive decor, skylights, carpeting. Good lighting and sound systems. Full bar. Low admission. Live bands every night.

The Roxy   **6-D1**
9009 Sunset Blvd, Hollywood. (310) 276-2222. Great showcase for established, celebrity acts. One of LA's best venues. Good acoustics. Perfect cabaret-size but cramped when they have

to pack 'em in! (The bouncers here are a little overzealous at times.) Full bar, food available. Age limit and admission prices vary. Call for schedule.

Santa Monica Civic Auditorium   **4-D3**
1855 Main St, Santa Monica. (310) 393-9961. Popular venue for rock concerts featuring top-name acts. Acoustics depend on sound engineer's capability and quality of band's equipment. (Take your chances.) Good seating/dancing arrangement. Full bar for most events. Friendly security check at door. No age limit.

Stage West   **1-A2**
17044 Chatsworth St, Granada Hills. (818) 360-3310. A huge "Dance Fever"-style dance floor attracts the Valley's best movers. Live bands nightly, satellite TV sports. Two full bars. No cover charge.

Troubadour   **6-E1**
9081 Santa Monica Blvd, W. Hollywood. (310) 276-6168. Legendary Hollywood venue (still ruled by Doug Weston) that has changed little over the years. Live bands nightly. Good seating arrangement; everyone can see! High stage. Full bar and menu. Separate bar with street access. Low admission. No age limit.

Universal Amphitheater   **9-G5**
Large, covered amphitheater used extensively for rock concerts featuring internationally known stars. (*See* ENTERTAINMENT, Theater.)

Whiskey A Go Go   **6-D1**
8901 Sunset Blvd, Hollywood. (310) 652-4202. For years the premier showcase club in LA for rock bands. Almost every famous rock group in the world has played here. Completely remodeled in 1983 (to the disappointment of old fans). Latest rock sounds. Parking is a problem—avoid frustration and pay to park next door. Full bar. Admission low to medium. Call for schedule. No age limit.

Wiltern Theatre   **6-G7**
3790 Wilshire Blvd, LA. (213) 380-5005. A truly gorgeous old theater (lovingly restored to its former glory) in the impressive zigzag-moderne Wiltern building. A real treat to see class rock acts in such a sumptuous showcase. Full bar. Call for schedule. Admission varies. No age limit.

SINGLES' BARS

The hottest bar in town tonight could be cold and empty by next week. These well-known watering holes should stand the test of time. NOTE: *Most bars are open from 11am to 2am, some open evenings only. Schedules can change seasonally.*

Barney's Beanery   **6-D1**
8447 Santa Monica Blvd, Hollywood. (213) 654-2287. A longtime favorite. Strangely decorated with old auto license plates. Casual and social. Huge selection of imported beers, food. Pool, video games. For some unknown reason the service can be a little snooty.

Roxy

Tom Bergin's   **6-D3**
840 Fairfax Ave, LA. (213) 936-7151. Very lively Irish pub and restaurant. Good Irish coffee.

Brennan's   **4-F7**
4089 Lincoln Blvd, Marina del Rey; (310) 821-6622. And 3600 Highland Ave, Manhattan Beach; (310) 545-4446 (**2-A5**). Neighborhood establishments, these lively Irish bars attract a young, friendly crowd. Occasional live rock bands, ferns, brass, and photographs. Small dance floor (both locations). Turtle races are featured in the parking lot every Thursday night at the Marina location. Crab races are featured at the Manhattan Beach bar.

Cafe del Rey   **4-F6**
4451 Admiralty Way, Marina del Rey. (310) 823-6395. The bar at this restaurant (formerly Fiasco) is a great gathering place, attracting a casual Marina crowd. Romantic quayside setting. Good happy hour.

Casey's Bar   **7-C4**
613 N. Grand Ave, Downtown. (213) 629-2353. Favorite after-work retreat for Downtown office workers. Best on weekdays. Lunch and dinner available. Strong drinks, lively music, and friendly faces. Typically Irish. *CLOSED Sun.*

Carlos 'n Charlie's   **6-C2**
8240 Sunset Blvd, Hollywood. (213) 656-8830. Popular Hollywood restaurant, attracting a trendy, flashy set. Busy bar. Upstairs disco.

Chez Jay   **4-C3**
1657 Ocean Ave, Santa Monica. (310) 395-1741. Small surprise package of fun people. Good drinks and gourmet food. Dim lights, jukebox, sawdust.

Crystal Palace Saloon   **5-E4**
945 Broxton Ave, Westwood. (310) 208-1888. In the heart of Westwood, with a view of the village. Lively atmosphere, light food, and generous libations.

Denim and Diamonds   **4-C6**
3200 Ocean Park Blvd, Santa Monica. (310) 452-3446. Located in a business park. Large, multilevel gathering place for local yuppy COWBOYS!

The Ginger Man   **5-E7**
369 N. Bedford Dr, Beverly Hills. (310) 273-7585. A lively, affluent set gathers in the bar of this well-known restaurant. Best just after office hours. Excellent service.

Harry's Bar   **5-F7**
2020 Avenue of the Stars, Century City. (310) 277-2333. Replica of its namesake in Italy, which Hemingway made famous. Chic clientele, unusual cocktails. (*See also* RESTAURANTS, Beverly Hills & Century City, Italian.)

Hennessey's   **1-F4**
1712 Catalina Ave, Redondo Beach; (310) 540-8443. And 8 Pier Ave, Hermosa Beach; (310) 372-5759 (**2-E6**). Casual, fun atmosphere in two beach locations. Irish pub theme with live music on weekends.

King's Head   **4-C3**
116 Santa Monica Blvd, Santa Monica. (310) 394-9458. Home-away-from-home for local British population. Imported beers, darts, fish 'n' chips (the best in town), jukebox. Lively, often rowdy, smoky. Adjoining restaurant serves typically English fare. Popular with Anglophiles and in-town musicians from Britain.

Merlin McFly   **4-D4**
2702 Main St, Santa Monica. (310) 392-8468. They spared no expense with the lavish decor here. Attractive clientele, good food, magic acts. Excellent happy hour. Can get crowded. Live music Monday and Friday nights.

Mom's Saloon   **5-F2**
11777 San Vicente Blvd, Brentwood. (310) 820-1516. Close enough to UCLA campus to attract a classy collegiate crowd.

Monahan's   **8-B4**
110 S. Lake Ave, Pasadena. (818) 449-4151. Lovely Irish pub. Good drinks at fair prices. Friendly service. Very popular gathering place. Young and lively.

Moonshadows   **1-D2**
20356 W. Pacific Coast Hwy, Malibu. (310) 456-3010. Beautiful, romantic location on the beach. Great for lovers. Cocktails and dinner.

Polo Lounge   **5-C7**
Beverly Hills Hotel, 9641 Sunset Blvd, Beverly Hills. (310) 276-2251. Famous haunt of chic jet-setters. The Polo Lounge is really a restaurant, but you can sit at the bar and people-watch (with discretion, please). Go just once—even if you're not rich. Strict dress code. (*See also* SIGHTSEEING, Walking Tours: Beverly Hills.)

San Francisco Saloon Co.   **4-A7**
11501 W. Pico Blvd, W. LA. (310) 478-0152. Ferns, couches, stained glass, good cocktails, professional service. Casual, friendly crowd. Long bar—good for bar-sitting.

J. Sloans/The Oar House
Both locations (*see* Discos & Dance Clubs: The Oar House) attract a similar crowd. Noisy and lively.

Teasers   **4-C3**
1351 3rd St, Santa Monica. (310) 394-8728. Located in the outdoor mall. A fresh and friendly upscale bar with a restaurant that serves healthy gourmet delights at below-average prices. Drink and dine inside or out and admire the local color. Special "Yuppie Night"—everything is a dollar more!

T. G. I. Friday's   **4-F7**
13470 Maxella Ave, Marina del Rey. (310) 822-9052. Guaranteed gathering of attractive Marina singles around the bar. Good food served at the upper-tier tables (great for talent spotting).

AFTER-HOURS

A variety of activities.

Beverly Hills Massage and Spa   **6-D1**
8574 Santa Monica Blvd, W. Hollywood. (310) 657-2134. Legitimate massage. *OPEN 24 hours.*

Bowling Alleys

Of the numerous lanes open 24 hours, these are a reliable selection:

Bahama Lanes   **1-B7**
3545 E. Foothill Blvd, Pasadena. (818) 351-8858.

Cal Bowl   **1-F6**
2400 E. Carson St, Lakewood. (310) 421-8448.

Holiday Bowl   **1-D4**
3730 S. Crenshaw Blvd, LA. (213) 295-4325.

Hollywood Star Lanes   **6-D8**
5227 Santa Monica Blvd, Hollywood. (213) 665-4111.

Mar Vista Bowl   **4-D8**
12125 Venice Blvd, LA. (310) 391-5288.

Chippendale's   **1-D3**
Notorious disco, open Friday and Saturday until 4am. (*See* Discos & Dance Clubs.)

F.M. Station   **9-B3**
11700 Victory Blvd, N. Hollywood. (818) 769-2220. Formerly Filthy McNasty's, Filthy (and his Foxy Filthettes Band) often performs in a shabby lounge that gets filled to capacity. Local rock bands and name acts are also featured. Bawdy atmosphere. *OPEN Fri & Sat till 4am.*

Television
Several TV stations transmit programs around the clock. A variety of movies are screened between midnight and 7am.

Tropicana
(*See* Discos & Dance Clubs.) Weekend rock music. Dance parties every Friday and Saturday till 4am.

Western Union Wake-Up Service
(800) 325-6000. They'll phone at any time you request and get you up in time for more fun! (The charge is added to your phone bill.)

THE GAY SCENE

Good clubs and bars catering to LA's large gay population (both male and female) are plentiful. For specialized information see ALTERNATIVES, Gays, Bars, and Clubs.

LATE-NIGHT EATERIES

There are dozens of "after-hours" eateries in Los Angeles. The following are a little unusual and generally worth experiencing.

Barry's Donut Shop   **5-G2**
12100 Santa Monica Blvd, W. LA. (310) 826-8489. Established in 1948 and still serving the best doughnuts in town. Over 50 varieties are baked on the premises. Fresh from the ovens from 1am on through the night. Sandwiches, burgers, and hotdogs too. *OPEN 24 hours.*

Canter's   **6-E3**
419 N. Fairfax Ave, LA. (213) 651-2030. Famous, popular Jewish deli-restaurant in the heart of LA's best-known Jewish community. Hearty food. Deli, bakery, calories! *OPEN 24 hours.*

The Original Fatburger   **6-F1**
450 S. La Cienega Blvd, W. Hollywood. (310) 652-8489. Good at 3am, when a greasy burger will calm an aching stomach. Lively atmosphere, jukebox. *OPEN 24 hours.*

Original Pantry Cafe   **7-D3**
877 S. Figueroa St, LA. (213) 972-9279. Open since 1924—an institution. Good old-fashioned service, with steaks and chops cooked simply but very well. Huge breakfasts served from 4am. Excellent all-around value. *OPEN 24 hours.*

Pink's   **6-D4**
709 N. La Brea Ave, Hollywood. (213) 931-4223. Hollywood's most famous chili dogs are served from this tiny shack that's been frequented by rich and famous, poor and obscure since 1939. *OPEN till 2:30am.*

Tommy's Hamburgers   **7-A2**
2575 Beverly Blvd, LA. 389-9060. Accept no substitute—this is the original. Probably the best chili burgers in the world! A drive-in, reminiscent of a 1950s teen scene. *OPEN 24 hours.*

Vickman's Restaurant & Bakery   **7-E5**
1228 E. 8th St, LA. (213) 622-3852. Established in 1930 and still much the same. Great menu, from omelettes to poached salmon—and everything is fresh. Also houses Downtown's largest bakery, producing fresh breads and pastries every night. In the center of the busy market district. *OPEN Mon-Fri 3am-3pm; Sat 3am-1pm.*

Zucky's
431 Wilshire Blvd, Santa Monica. (310) 393-0551. Popular deli-restaurant. *OPEN 24 hours.* (*See also* RESTAURANTS, Santa Monica, Venice & Marina del Rey, Specialized.)

RESTAURANTS

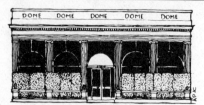

Le Dome

There are several thousand restaurants in Los Angeles. A selection for each major area of the city is listed below. They were chosen for good food and service, and to suit a variety of tastes.

In addition to hundreds of ethnic and theme restaurants, Los Angeles has thousands of inexpensive fast-food outlets, such as the large McDonald's and Kentucky Fried Chicken chains. Many stay open for long hours and prove invaluable to travelers. (Most will prepare food "to go.") See also NIGHTLIFE, Late-Night Eateries.

Numerous restaurants have outdoor patio dining. LA's favorable climate makes eating out of doors a pleasure, day or night.

When tipping, give 10% of the total bill for average service, 15-20% for good to excellent service. (Remember, the waiter personally tips the busperson, and often the bar and kitchen staff.) European visitors should note that a 6.5% sales tax is added to the bill. This should not be confused with service charge or gratuity.

Opening hours can vary according to season and location. Normal hours are 8 to 11:30 am for breakfast, 11:30am to 2:30pm for lunch, and 6 to 10:00pm for dinner. Sunday brunch normally runs from 11am to 3pm. Unless otherwise indicated, all restaurants are open 7 days.

Restaurant selections are listed by area and type of food.

SMOKING IN RESTAURANTS

Numerous Los Angeles restaurants have non-smoking areas for people who object to tobacco smoke, and some restaurants do not allow the smoking of cigars or pipes in their dining rooms. A 1987 law banned smoking in the dining sections of restaurants within the city of Beverly Hills (with the exception of restaurants located in hotels). However, smoking is permitted in the bar areas of all restaurants in Beverly Hills.

ABBREVIATIONS

Average price for dinner for one person without wine.

$	Under $12
$$	$12–$25
$$$	Over $25
B	Breakfast
L	Lunch
D	Dinner
♀	Wine & beer
♈	Cocktails
↙	Reservations accepted
✳	Outdoor patio
♪	Entertainment

CREDIT CARDS

AE	American Express
CB	Carte Blanche
D	Discover
DC	Diners' Club
MC	MasterCard
V	Visa

A NOTE ON CALIFORNIA WINES

California has dozens of wineries producing excellent wines, and many have won gold medals in European competition. Retail prices for local wines are low compared with imported wines. In restaurants expect to pay a few dollars above retail per bottle. Since overseas visitors may be unfamiliar with California varietals, this comparison chart should assist in selection.

California	European
Cabernet Sauvignon	Bordeaux, Claret
Chardonnay	Chablis, White Burgundy
Chenin Blanc	Vouvray
Gamay	Beaujolais
Gewurtztraminer	Alsatian
Gray Riesling	Light Riesling
Johannesburg Riesling	Rhine
Pinot Blanc	White Burgundy
Pinot Noir	Full-bodied Burgundy
Sauvignon Blanc	Aromatic Sauterne
Semillon	Fruity Sauterne
Zinfandel	Fruity Red

BEACH CITIES

(Santa Monica, Venice & Marina del Rey are listed separately.)

American

The Chart House   **1-C2**
18412 Pacific Coast Hwy, Malibu. (310) 454-9321. One of several locations, all serving good-quality food with special attention to detail. Attractive beachside setting. Specialties include steak and fresh seafood.
          $$ D ♀ ♈ ↙ ✳   AE CB D DC MC V

Kings Hawaiian Bakery & Restaurant   **2-A7**
2808 W. Sepulveda Blvd, Torrance. (310) 530-0050. Focusing on Hawaiian and tropical cuisine, this is casual dining with a family atmosphere. Open for breakfast, lunch, and dinner, they have authentic Hawaiian-style cuisine as well as an on-premises bakery with over 500 different items for sale.

$$ B L D ♀ MC, V

Moonshadows   **1-D2**
20356 W. Pacific Coast Hwy, Malibu. (310) 456-3010. Beautiful oceanside location with a view from every table. Steak and lobster are house specialties. Salad bar with fresh vegetables. Heated outdoor patio for romantic summer evenings.

$$ D ♀ Y ✳ AE D DC MC V

T. J. Peppercorn's   **3-D6**
6225 W. Century Blvd, LA. (310) 670-9000. In the Hyatt Hotel at Los Angeles International Airport. Comfortable dining. Menu includes five-star duckling, prepared on a whirling rotisserie, salad bar, and dessert bar. Rooftop lounge.

$$ L D ♀ Y AE CB D DC MC V

Continental

Chez Melange   **2-G8**
1716 Pacific Coast Hwy, Redondo Beach. (310) 540-1222. Dedicated to the utmost enjoyment of fine food and first-rate wines. Here's a mixture of tastes and textures for every palate. Breakfast, from 7am, includes kippers, calf's liver, scrambled eggs and oysters. Daily specials are offered at lunch and dinner. Smoked duck salad, fresh pastas, mixed grills, rabbit, lamb, and chicken—all served in a variety of ways. Lively sushi bar. Good food, good service, fair prices. Refreshing! Reservations essential on weekends.

$$ B L D ♀ Y ✔ AE MC V

Delius   **1-G6**
3550 Long Beach Blvd, Long Beach. (310) 426-0694. A husband and wife team own and operate this special little place. Five nights a week (and only five nights) they offer prix-fixe feasts fit for kings. Dinner can include freshly made quiche, soup, filet mignon, chicken, or other meats—prepared with delectable sauces. Fresh vegetables, fruits, sorbets, pastries, chocolate gateaux. Good champagne, cognac, and exceptional wines are included. Reservations essential. *CLOSED Sun & Mon.*

$$$ D ♀ ✔ MC

555 East   **1-G6**
555 E. Ocean Blvd, Long Beach. (310) 437-0626. Sumptuously sophisticated and exceedingly popular. This is the place to dine in Long Beach. Everything from the lavish bar to the velvet-boothed dining room is drenched in elegance. No expense has been spared. Eating here is a special treat. Tuxedoed waiters will surprise you with their personal knowledge of food and wine—take their recommendations seriously! Exquisite entrees include rack of lamb

with Dijon mustard, veal liver with pippin apples, poached salmon, and marinated chicken. Reservations essential. *No lunch Sat.*

$$ L D ♀ Y ✔ AE CB DC MC V

Geoffrey's   **1-D1**
27400 Pacific Coast Hwy, Malibu. (310) 457-1519. Long-established clifftop restaurant, formerly the Holiday House, a favorite place for romantics during the 1950s. A gorgeous, flower-filled outdoor terrace is the ideal lunchtime setting for sampling healthful "Malibu Fare." The indoor "greenhouse" is best for glamorous dinners of rack of lamb or filet mignon with three sauces. Clientele often includes local celebrities. Good service.

$$$ L D ♀ Y ✔ ✳ AE D MC V

Saddle Peak Lodge   **1-B1**
419 Cold Canyon Rd, Calabasas. (310) 456-PEAK; (818) 222-3888. A 50-year-old building, lovingly transformed into a tall hunting lodge reminiscent of Roosevelt's days. Rustic furniture, Victorian prints, taxidermy, antiques, old books, beams, trophies, log fires, and cozy nooks. You could be high in the Austrian Alps but for a meandering garden where the balmy air reminds you that this is Malibu. Real game is always on the menu. Buffalo steaks, salmon cured in vodka, Long Island duckling with wild mountain honey, venison with burgundy sauce, and a superb New York steak stuffed with oysters. Service is formal though somewhat unprofessional. Reserve ahead for Sunday brunch. *CLOSED Mon & Tues.*

$$$ L ♀ Y ✔ ✳ AE MC V

The Sandcastle   **1-D1**
28128 Pacific Coast Hwy, Malibu. (310) 457-2503. Popular and respected Malibu landmark. The Sandcastle sits on a private beach with romantic views across the Pacific. Nautical decor completes the setting. Extensive menu, ranging from beef Wellington and baked trout to excellent cheesecakes topped with fresh fruit. Daily champagne brunch includes eggs Benedict and crab Mornay. Children's menu available. *OPEN 7 days at 6am!*

$$ B L D ♀ Y ✔ AE CB DC MC V

Cuban

El Rincon Criollo   **1-D3**
4361 Sepulveda Blvd, Culver City. (310) 397-9295. Authentic Cuban dishes at modest prices. Black beans, rice, chicken, and squid—all cooked to perfection. Unusual breads and vegetables. Children's menu.

$ L D ♀ Y ✔ ♪ MC V

French

Chalet de France   **1-F4**
23254 Robert Rd, Torrance. (310) 540-4646. Complete French country dishes served in the atmosphere of an old inn. Beamed ceilings, formal service. Chateaubriand bouquetiere, lobster thermidor, or roasted quail with Madeira will

merely whet the appetite for their crepe suzette or baked Alaska. Worth seeking out.

$$$ L D ♀ Ⓨ ⚲ ✳ AE CB D DC MC V

La Rive Gauche   **1-F4**
320 Tejon Pl, Palos Verdes. (310) 378-0267. Hidden away on the peninsula but worth finding—if just to sample their well-prepared seafood dishes or try one of the 1,200 wines. *No lunch Mon.*

$$ L D ♀ Ⓨ ⚲ ♪ AE CB DC MC V

Saint Estephe   **2-B7**
2640 N. Sepulveda Blvd, Manhattan Beach. (310) 545-1334. Original Warhols, fresh white linen, potted plants, bright young attendants, and every dish a work of art. Each entree is well thought out and beautifully presented. Specialties include saddle of lamb, veal chop, and enchiladas of shrimp. *No dinner Mon; no lunch Sat. CLOSED Sun.*

$$ L D ♀ ⚲ ✳ AE MC V

Greek

Papadakis Taverna   **1-G5**
301 W. 6th St, San Pedro. (310) 548-1186. Bright, happy atmosphere. Authentic Greek dishes, using old family recipes and only the best ingredients. Moussaka, souvlaki, and baklava are excellent. Menu also includes roast lamb, octopus, and spiced fish. *CLOSED Mon.*

$$ D ♀ ⚲ ♪ AE MC V

Mexican

Mi Ranchito   **1-D4**
8694 W. Washington Blvd, Culver City. (310) 837–1461. A warm welcome awaits you at this unassuming West Side Mexican storefront. Authentic tasty fare includes garlic shrimp, the not-to-be-missed chili rellenos, and white red snapper Vera Cruz.

$ B L D ♀ ⚲ MC V

Pancho's   **2-A5**
3615 Highland Ave, Manhattan Beach. (310) 545-6670. Two-story hacienda with a plant-filled courtyard and cozy (often lively) bar. Gourmet Mexican specials include camarones à la Vallarta and enchiladas de Cagrejo.

$ L D ♀ Ⓨ ⚲ ♪ AE CB D DC MC V

The Red Onion   **2-F7**
655 N. Harbor Dr, Redondo Beach; (310) 376-8813. And 4215 Admiralty Way, Marina del Rey (**4-F6**); (310) 821-2291. A bright mixture of Mexican food and disco dancing. Specialties include a variety of Sonora-style dishes.

$ L D ♀ Ⓨ ⚲ ♪ AE MC V

Seafood

Charlie Brown's   **1-C1**
21150 Pacific Coast Hwy, Malibu. (310) 456-2810. Gigantic eatery (formerly Malibu Sea Lion) owned and operated by the successful Bob Morris of Gladstone's—a few blocks south. Morris's

ability to create a dining experience attracts crowds daily. His supermarket-size salad bar, called the Green Grocery, has the freshest of everything. Clay-baked potatoes come with every garnish you can dream of. Best of all: Every seat has an ocean view.

$$ B L D ♀ Ⓨ ⚲ ♪ AE CB DC MC V

Monroes   **1-C1**
6800 Westward Beach Rd, Malibu. (310) 457-5521. Hard to find but worth the effort (turn off Pacific Coast Highway at Zuma Beach). A ground-floor bar offers cocktails until your table is ready—when a small elevator takes you to the upper dining areas. Decor is crisply upscale, and remarkable modern art is everywhere. The menu is small but entirely dependable, as is the service. Broiled fish-of-the-day is a must. Clams and oysters are shucked to order and there is a superb linguine with chopped clams prepared tableside. Meat dishes are available and include leg of duck and an interesting chicken curry. *CLOSED Mon.*

$$ D ♀ Ⓨ ⚲ AE CB D DC MC V

Orville & Wilbur's   **2-A5**
401 Rosecrans Ave, Manhattan Beach. (310) 545-6639. Theme restaurant honoring the Wright Brothers. Pretty waitresses, ocean views, entertainment. Fresh fish daily, salad bar, steaks, and veal. *No lunch Sat & Sun*

$ L D ♀ Ⓨ ♪ AE DC MC V

Tony's Fish Market   **2-G7**
112 Fisherman's Wharf, Redondo Beach. (310) 376-6223. On the pier with great ocean views. Italian-influenced dishes include cioppino, lobster, veal marsala, and veal parmigiana.

$$$ L D ♀ Ⓨ ♪ AE MC V

Tony's on the Pier   **2-G7**
210 Fisherman's Wharf, Redondo Beach. (310) 374-9246. Ocean views and good fresh seafood. Specials include shrimp stuffed with crabmeat and filet of sole with lobster stuffing. *No lunch Mon.*

$$$ L D ♀ Ⓨ ♪ AE MC V

Specialized

Inn of the Seventh Ray   **1-C2**
128 Old Topanga Canyon Rd, Topanga. (310) 455-1311. Beautiful garden setting next to a running stream and away from the city bustle. Pure, organic food. Fresh fish, egg dishes, and hormone-free chicken. Fresh bread baked on premises.

$$ L D ♀ ⚲ ✳ MC V

The Princess/Mardi Gras Cruise   **1-G5**
Ports O' Call Village, San Pedro. (310) 547-2833. A 145-passenger Mississippi-style paddlewheeler. Patrons take 2½-hour dinner cruise through LA harbor (Friday, Saturday, or Sunday evening). Huge buffet dinner. Dixieland jazz band and dancing. Bars. Fixed price (under $30) includes dinner without drinks. Special rates for children.

$$$ D ♀ Ⓨ ⚲ ✳ ♪ No cards

The Terrace, Ritz-Carlton Hotel
33533 Ritz-Carlton Dr, Laguna Niguel. (714) 240-2000. Although the hotel is 50 miles from central LA, its culinary delights are too exceptional to be missed. The double-tiered stone-landscaped dining room offers the most sumptuous Sunday brunch in California—the variety of gourmet delights is dazzling. An enormous buffet is resplendent with smoked fish (salmon, gravlax, eel, and trout); red, black, and golden caviar; various pâtés-en-croute; cold cuts; hot entrees (including rack of lamb and filet of beef) carved to your liking. Eggs Benedict served on artichoke bottoms, mushrooms with cheese sauce, three kinds of potatoes. Make as many trips as you like, but save room for dessert! There are perfect eclairs, Napoleons, chocolate-dipped strawberries, and assorted truffles. At under $30 per person this is a truly memorable feast. Reserve well ahead. (*See also* SIGHTSEEING, Day Trips: Laguna.) *Sun brunch 11am-3pm.*

$$$ B L D ♀ ⍑ ⋁ ✳ AE CB DC MC V

BEVERLY HILLS & CENTURY CITY

American

The Cheesecake Factory　　5-E8
364 N. Beverly Dr, Beverly Hills; (310) 278-7270. And 4142 Via Marina, Marina del Rey (**4-G6**); (310) 306-3344. What a gorgeous place to stuff yourself! Everyone else will be doing the same, so don't feel guilty. Enormous menu includes ribs, scallops, chopped steaks, and chili (no beans). However, most people come for the namesake cheesecakes: 43 wicked flavors include raspberry chocolate truffle, Kahlúa and cappuccino. Always crowded—expect to wait.
$ L D ♀ ⍑ AE MC V

Chrystie's Bar and Grill　　6-F1
8442 Wilshire Blvd, Beverly Hills. (213) 655-8113. A convivial little meeting place, warm and welcoming. Good food, well prepared (mostly grilled) and served with care. Salmon, steaks, veal, chicken, salads, and desserts. Next door to the Wilshire Theatre (same art deco influence). Amusing "attitude improvement hour" weekdays 4:30pm–6pm. Late suppers till 1am. *No lunch Sat. CLOSED Sun.*
$ L D ♀ ⍑ ⋁ AE D MC V

The Grill　　5-E8
9560 Dayton Way, Beverly Hills. (310) 276-0615. An elegant hideaway tucked in the alley behind Giorgio's. Take a seat at the rich mahogany bar and imagine you're having cocktails with Cary Grant. This comforting abode is a welcome relief from the glut of "nouvelle" establishments hereabouts. Good honest steaks, veal stew, lamb shanks. Juicy beefsteak tomatoes, apple pie, real rice pudding. *CLOSED Sun.*
$$ L D ♀ ⍑ ⋁ AE CB DC MC V

Hard Rock Cafe　　6-E1
8600 Beverly Blvd, Beverly Hills. (310) 276-7605. Another hit for Peter Morton (owner of Morton's and the original Hard Rock Cafe in London). More a gathering place for young pacesetters than a formal restaurant. Rock music is pumped from huge speakers and crowds gather around the focal point of the room—a circular bar. The ceiling has angled skylights through which one sees a vintage Cadillac plunging toward earth. Food is simple and good. Excellent hamburgers, honest ribs. Chicken, chili, and fish. Attentive down-to-earth service.
$ L D ♀ ⍑ AE MC V

Hy's　　5-F7
10131 Constellation Blvd, Century City. (310) 553-6000. If it's meat and potatoes you crave, Hy's has 'em. Gargantuan portions of meat are served with garlic toast and baked potatoes or spaghetti marinara (who knows why?). New York steak is recommended. Chicken, duck, and fish are also available, but perhaps the best item on this menu is the fresh eastern oysters. Decor is elegant with rose-colored linen and pale wood paneling. *No lunch Sat. CLOSED Sun.*
$$$ L D ♀ ⍑ ⋁ AE CB DC MC V

Lawry's the Prime Rib　　6-E1
55 N. La Cienega Blvd, Beverly Hills. (310) 652-2827. Unequaled for their prime rib specialty. This famous, stylish restaurant resembles an English manor house with paneled walls and hardwood floors. Impressive dining room, excellent service.
$$ D ♀ ⍑ ⋁ AE D MC V

Mr. H, Beverly Hilton Hotel　　5-E7
9876 Wilshire Blvd, Beverly Hills. (310) 274-7777. Buffet-style cuisine with a wide range of salads, cold cuts, and hot daily specials. Fresh-baked pastries, pies, and cakes. Champagne Sunday brunch.
$$ B L D ♀ ⍑ AE CB D DC MC V

Muse　　6-E4
7360 Beverly Blvd, LA. (213) 934-4400. Hard to spot but a worthy find. Interior walls are clear-white and hung with bright paintings by local artists. Natural wood rafters have been exposed; skylights add natural light. The menu changes daily, the artwork every few months. Experimentation is important and refreshing. Pretty pink (from beet juice) pasta, pecan smoked crisp duckling with plum wine and ginger. Excellent staff throughout.
$$ D ♀ ⍑ ⋁ AE MC V

Nate 'n Al's　　5-D8
414 N. Beverly Dr, Beverly Hills. (310) 274-0101. A haven for New Yorkers. A popular deli-restaurant serving the best in combination sandwiches, cheese, blintzes, salamis, and chicken favorites. Huge menu, high quality. (Jewish holidays observed.)
$ B L D ♀ AE CB DC MC

Carroll O'Connor's Place　　5-E7
369 N. Bedford Dr, Beverly Hills. (310) 273-7585. Owned by a famous personality, Carroll O'Connor, who has created a warm, friendly

gathering place that offers fine food and cocktails. Specialties include seafood.

$$ L D ♀ 𝕐 ↙ ♪ AE MC V

RJ's, The Rib Joint   **5-E8**
252 N. Beverly Dr, Beverly Hills. (310) 274-3474. A bright and colorful greengrocery forms the extensive salad bar at RJ's, accompanied by hickory-smoked meats—there's no better value in Beverly Hills. Impressive bar, stained glass, and natural wood surroundings.

$ L D ♀ 𝕐 ↙ AE CB DC MC V

Sports Deli   **5-E7**
2040 Avenue of the Stars, Century City. (310) 553-5800. Sports fans and TV addicts can enjoy a tuned-in meal at a reasonable price. Banquet, salad bar, and Mexican food. TV-set decor.

$$ B L D ♀ 𝕐 ↙ AE DC MC V

The Terrace   **5-F6**
Century Plaza Hotel Tower, 2025 Avenue of the Stars, LA. (310) 277-2000. Romantic garden setting; plush banquettes, candlelight, white linen, discreet service. Perfect pretheater location—across from the Schubert. Prix-fixe dinner is a bargain with the choice of over a dozen entrees. *No dinner Mon & Tues.*

$$ B L D ♀ 𝕐 ↙ AE CB D DC MC V

Tony Roma's   **5-D8**
319 Santa Monica Blvd, Santa Monica. (310) 393-0139. A sophisticated rib joint. Specialties include pork and veal. The ribs are excellent—of course. *OPEN till 11pm.*

$$ L D ♀ 𝕐 AE CB D DC MC V

Chinese

Jade West   **5-E7**
2040 Avenue of the Stars, Century City. (310) 556-3388. Probably the most expensively decorated restaurant in the area. Gorgeous antiques, silk-veiled lighting, fabulous handcrafted Chinese works of art, and plush carpets. Tuxedoed waiters serve onto hand-painted china dishes. Bird's-nest soup, sesame chicken, and Jade West beef are favorites. Desserts are not excellent. Convenient for Shubert Theatre. *No lunch Sat & Sun.*

$$ L D ♀ 𝕐 ↙ AE CB DC MC V

Mandarin   **5-D7**
430 N. Camden Dr, Beverly Hills. (213) 272-0267. Informal elegance. The Peking duck is perfect. Guests may grill their own food at a Mongolian fire pit. Spacious and luxurious dining rooms are filled with antiques and greenery. Floors shine with jade green tiles. *No lunch Sat & Sun.*

$$ L D ♀ 𝕐 ↙ AE CB DC MC V

Mandarin Wok   **5-D8**
424 N. Beverly Dr, Beverly Hills. (213) 276-1034. Mandarin, Szechuan, and Cantonese specialties served in comfortable surroundings. Mongolian beef, shrimp in lobster sauce, and Peking duck are highlights here.

$$ L D ♀ 𝕐 ↙ MC V

Mr. Chow LA   **5-E8**
344 N. Camden Dr, Beverly Hills. (310) 278-

9911. Western-style Chinese cuisine that doesn't quite come off. The surroundings are stylish, however, and the location attracts a dressy clientele. Dramatic black-and-white modernism, silver, crystal, and formal service. Good for Peking chicken. *No lunch Sat & Sun.*

$$$ B L D ♀ 𝕐 ↙ AE CB DC MC V

Continental

Bel-Air Hotel   **1-C3**
701 Stone Canyon Rd, Bel-Air. (310) 472-1211. Aristocratic elegance. Fantasy dining in fantasyland. Trailing purple blossoms run down to streams with pretty bridges and gliding swans. An indoor dining room provides luxurious intimacy for dinner, but a patio lunch, bathed in sunlight, cannot be matched. Best on the menu are the fish and veal dishes.

$$$ B L D ♀ 𝕐 ↙ ♪ AE CB D DC MC V

The Bistro   **5-E8**
246 N. Canon Dr, Beverly Hills. (310) 273-5633. To be seen here is more important (and more rewarding) than to eat here. Service depends on who you are, but the food is good. Veal is excellent and all seafood dishes can be recommended. Tables are cramped (you may be rubbing elbows, rather than shoulders, with the jet set). *CLOSED Sun.*

$$$ D ♀ 𝕐 ↙ ♪ AE CB DC MC V

Bistro Garden   **5-E8**
172 N. Canon Dr, Beverly Hills. (310) 550-3900. Be prepared to pay a high price for snobbish informality. Same crowd as at The Bistro, but relaxed here, in a beautiful garden setting. Excellent souffles. *CLOSED Sun.*

$$$ L D ♀ 𝕐 ↙ ✳ ♪ AE CB DC MC V

Cafe D'Etoile   **6-E1**
8941½ Santa Monica Blvd, W. Hollywood. (310) 278-1011. Warm, cozy, and welcoming. This unpretentious little dinner-house has won the hearts of the rich and famous who come for food and fulfillment. The owner personally welcomes all who enter, confident that his superb cuisine will satisfy. The most extraordinary desserts in town. *CLOSED Sun.*

$$ L D ♀ 𝕐 ↙ AE CB DC MC V

Cafe Rodeo   **5-D8**
360 N. Rodeo Dr, Beverly Hills. (310) 273-0300. Perfect location for people-watching on this formidable shopping street. An elegant yet intimate open-fronted restaurant. Lunchtime favorite of the "beautiful people." The menu is above average with filet of sole bonne femme and calf's liver Belle Helene coming out ahead.

$$ B L D ♀ 𝕐 ↙ ✳ AE CB DC MC V

Chasen's   **6-E1**
9039 Beverly Blvd, Beverly Hills. (310) 271-2168. Well-established, warm ambience. Old stomping ground of Howard Hughes, W. C. Fields, John Barrymore, et al. Still a favorite with Hollywood's elite (and that includes the Reagans when they're in town). Rather arrogant service and outrageous prices causes Chasen's to lose customers daily, but the food is good and the

rich regulars love the whole idea. Best items are hobo steak, spinach salad, and, for nostalgia's sake, Chasen's unique chili. *CLOSED Mon.*

$$ L D ♀ Y ✔ AE D MC V
Polo Lounge   **5-C7**
Beverly Hills Hotel, 9641 Sunset Blvd, Beverly Hills. (310) 276-2251. Here it is, Hollywood in action —negotiating between bites or socializing on the patio. Beautiful ladies, manicured men, discreet staff. Luncheon is a selection of good salads (the Beverly Hills is recommended) and amazing sandwiches. Delightful garden patio.

$$$ B L D ♀ Y ✔ ✳ ♪ AE MC V

French

Bruno's Chartreuse   **5-G7**
1909 Wilshire Blvd, Santa Monica. (310) 552-2521. Small, delightful with good food and ambience. A converted firehouse that warms the spirit inside and out. Lamb chops baked in pâté, toasted Camembert in a green salad, duckling garnished with gooseberries. Affordable wines. *No lunch Sat. CLOSED Sun.*

$$ L D ♀ Y AE CB DC MC V
Chez Helene   **5-E8**
267 S. Beverly Dr, Beverly Hills. (310) 276-1558. Reminiscent of a French country house. There are two dining rooms (one has a fireplace) furnished with comfortable old tables, and a delightful garden patio. Delicious smells drift from the busy kitchen, where great food is prepared with pride. Specials change daily—the chicken and lamb dishes are always good. Reservations suggested. *No lunch Sun.*

$$ L D ♀ ✔ ✳ AE CB D DC MC V
Colette   **5-E8**
Beverly Pavilion Hotel, 9360 Wilshire Blvd, Beverly Hills. (310) 273-1151. They opened in 1985 and sensational reviews continue to flood in. Chef Christopher Blobaum has proven that superior food can be offered at reasonable prices—even in a plush Beverly Hills hotel. His dishes arouse all the senses. Every plate, without exception, is presented as a work of art.

$$ B L D ♀ Y ✔ AE CB DC MC V
Jimmy's   **5-E7**
201 Moreno Dr, Beverly Hills. (213) 879-2394. Comfortable and refined; upper-class dining in a serene atmosphere. Perfect setting for the city's beautiful people. Meats and seafoods well cooked and attractively presented. *No Lunch Sat. CLOSED Sun.*

$$ L D ♀ Y ✔ ♪ AE CB DC MC V
L'Ermitage   **6-E1**
730 N. La Cienega Blvd, LA. (310) 652-5840. Rated among the nation's top ten restaurants. A beautiful dining experience here is no longer marred by arrogant service, although the high prices can still add a sour note. Pale wood, pastels, and bright flowers have replaced the more somber decor of yesteryear, but the food remains classically artistic. Superb quality throughout. Try poached scallops with saffron, smoked salmon, or breast of duckling. Follow

with chilled souffle (finished with Grand Marnier and raspberries). *CLOSED Sun.*

$$$ D ♀ Y ✔ AE CB DC MC V
L'Escoffier   **5-E7**
Beverly Hilton Hotel, 9876 Wilshire Blvd, Beverly Hills. (310) 274-7777. An institution perched atop the Hilton with a view of Beverly Hills and Century City. Feast on sumptuous French food and dance until midnight. The setting is luxurious; the food, perfection. Choose from an extensive menu and wine list. Everything here can be recommended and is consistently good. Reservations essential. *CLOSED Sun & Mon.*

$$$ D ♀ Y ✔ ♪ AE CB DC MC V
L'Orangerie   **6-D1**
903 N. La Cienega Blvd, LA. (310) 652-9770. A celebration, direct from Paris. Special delights for special occasions. High ceilings, waterfalls, greenery, pale colors, and a garden. Expensive furniture and silverware. Richness perfectly blended. Duckling and rack of lamb are certain to please. Fresh fish is imported daily from France and topping the dessert list are sumptuous fresh-fruit tarts with whipped cream.

$$$ D ♀ Y ✔ ✳ AE CB D DC MC V
Michel Richard   **6-G1**
310 S. Robertson Blvd, LA. (310) 275-5707. The most delectable French pastries in the world. Brioches, croissants, and chocolate cakes. Crepes, omelettes, salads, and quiche too. Simple decor.

$$ B L D ♀ AE MC V

Indian

Bombay Palace   **6-E1**
8690 Wilshire Blvd, Beverly Hills. (310) 659-9944. Phone your favorite rajah and head down to the palace. This lofty, marbled dining room, swathed in pastels and palms, is a fittingly regal setting for superior Indian food. Begin by ordering one of the tandoori breads (palace nan is stuffed with chicken and almonds), then sample the samosa. Spices are blended skillfully to produce dozens of exotic sauces for the well-cooked meat dishes and there are wonderful vegetarian combinations. Avoid dessert—at all costs! *No lunch Sat & Sun.*

$$ L D ♀ Y ✔ AE DC MC V
Rangoon Racquet Club   **5-D8**
9474 Little Santa Monica Blvd, Beverly Hills. (310) 274-8926. Imagine the days of Victoria's Empire—colonial mansions in the Punjab, rattan furniture, officers sipping pink gins beneath brass ceiling fans, palms, and impeccably dressed Indian servants. The menu is varied here and curries represent just a fraction of it. Excellent salads, boiled beef, chicken, and good lamb dishes. *No lunch Sat. CLOSED Sun.*

$$$ L D ♀ Y ✔ AE CB DC MC V

Italian

Adriano's   **1-B3**
2930 Beverly Glen Circle, Bel-Air. (310) 475-

9807. Gentility, serenity, and elegance. A beautifully decorated restaurant in the grand style, perched on a hilltop. Lovely patio bordered by trimmed hedges. High-quality food, intelligent service. Lobster with linguine, crab with oranges, trout with pine nuts and grapes. Homemade pastas and desserts. Excellent wines. *CLOSED Mon.*

$$$ L   D   ⚲   ⅋   ✳   AE D MC V

Andre's of Beverly Hills   **6-F1**
8635 Wilshire Blvd, Beverly Hills. (310) 657-2446. Best value in Beverly Hills. Andre's embraces several European countries but emphasizes the cuisine of Northern Italy. Huge portions at reasonable prices make this a popular choice for lunch (although often too crowded for comfort). Excellent antipasto. Some good Italian wines. *No lunch Sat & Sun.*

$$ L   D   ⚲   ⅋   AE CB D DC MC V

Celestino   **5-E8**
236 S. Beverly Dr, Beverly Hills. (310) 859-8601. If you like Andre's you'll love Celestino. Here's a true taste of Italy. Simple clean lines, good honest food, terrific wines, charming service. Zupetta di cozze (mussels in a delicate tomato broth), warm seafood salad, spinach fettuccine with pepper sauce, black linguini, roast chicken with roast potatoes, perfect veal chops. No heavy sauces to keep you awake but the irresistible Il Fornaio bread could do it! *No lunch Sat. CLOSED Sun.*

$$$ L   D   ⚲   ⅋   AE CB DC MC V

Da Vinci   **5-E7**
9737 Little Santa Monica Blvd, Beverly Hills. (310) 273-0960. An impressive newcomer to Beverly Hills. Elegant and expensive. Well-mannered, formal service. The menu is large but several dishes stand out. Try the vermicelli puttanesca, poached salmon, whitefish, or roasted peppers with anchovies. Their best dessert is the flambeéd crepe (which should be ordered at the start of dinner). Good vintage wines. *No lunch Sat & Sun.*

$$$ L   D   ⚲   ⅋   AE CB DC MC V

Harry's Bar and American Grill   **5-E7**
2020 Avenue of the Stars, Century City. (310) 277-2333. Luxurious reproduction of that establishment in Florence, Italy, made famous by Hemingway. Close proximity to the Shubert Theatre guarantees a steady clientele, but food quality is not always steady. (Take a chance, it can be superb.) Try the carpaccio (sliced raw beef with mustard sauce) or a pasta dish with their award-winning pesto sauce. Service is erratic. Interesting. *No lunch Sat & Sun.*

$$ L   D   ⚲   ⅋   AE MC V

Il Giardino   **5-E8**
9235 W. 3rd St, Beverly Hills. (310) 275-5444. A romantic, flower-filled restaurant—the perfect setting for truly Italian fare. Artichokes alla Romana, risotto, gnocchi with Gorgonzola, lobster, and marinated steak. Celebrity clientele. *No lunch Sun.*

$$ L   D   ⚲   ⅋   AE CB D DC MC V

Jacopo's Pizzeria   **5-D8**
490 N. Beverly Dr, Beverly Hills. (310) 858-6446. Busy, family pizza house. Menu extends to great pastas, chicken, and Italian ice cream with real fruit. Dine in or takeout. Delivery and catering service.

$ L   D   ⚲   AE MC V

La Dolce Vita   **5-E7**
9785 Little Santa Monica Blvd, Beverly Hills. (310) 278-1845. Busy and attractive, warm brick walls and woodwork. Wealthy clientele who know good Italian food when they taste it. Only the finest ingredients are used and no expense is spared. Try the calamari salad, lasagna verdi Bolognese, or their special veal steak. Extensive wine list. Small bar. *CLOSED Sun.*

$$$ D   ⚲   ⅋   AE CB DC MC V

La Famiglia   **5-D8**
453 N. Canon Dr, Beverly Hills. (310) 276-6208. Country prints, flowers, and candles. A smart, intimate, neighborhood restaurant attracting a celebrity clientele. New dishes appear regularly to delight the rich regulars. Homemade pasta served al dente. Good selection of antipastos, unusual treatment of veal, excellent poached fish, and steamed eggplant. Fine wines. *No lunch Sat. CLOSED Sun.*

$$$ D   ⚲   ⅋   AE CB DC MC V

La Scala   **5-D8**
410 N. Canon Dr, Beverly Hills. (310) 275-0579. Classic perfection. Could this be the best Italian restaurant ever? Knowledge, care, and quality are obvious. Owner Jean Leon's professionalism has earned him admiration from the highest ranks. Everything is excellent, but fettuccine Leon and chicken galleto are especially so. There is an amazing wine list with some rare selections from Mr. Leon's own vineyard in Spain. Celebrity clientele every night. *CLOSED Sun.*

$$ L   D   ⚲   ⅋   AE D MC V

Prego   **5-E7**
362 N. Camden Dr, Beverly Hills. (310) 277-7346. Nouvelle Roma? Perhaps. Truly scrumptuous Italian fare—freshly made in the open kitchen and presented with pride and perfection. Try tagliolini del lago—freshwater scampi, pimiento, and snails in a cream sauce poured over delicate noodles. Lamb with sage and rosemary, chicken marinated in lime, veal, steaks, fish. Decor is simple, people simply beautiful. *No lunch Sun.*

$$ L   D   ⚲   ⅋   AE CB DC MC V

Japanese

Benihana of Tokyo   **6-E1**
38 N. La Cienega Blvd, Beverly Hills. (310) 659-1511. One of six locations. (*See* Santa Monica, Venice & Marina del Rey: Japanese.)

Polynesian

Trader Vic's   **5-E7**
9876 Wilshire Blvd, Beverly Hills. (310) 276-

6345. Adventurous Victor Bergeron has achieved the impossible in creating a large chain of top-quality restaurants with superb food and service to match. From 40 years' experience he has developed a huge menu. Now-famous items include his Indonesian rack of lamb (baked in Chinese clay ovens) and bongo bongo, a lovely oyster and spinach soup. The best rum drinks in the world are to be found here. Try missionary's downfall or tiki puka puka. Decor is Captain Cook nautical. Great food for great occasions.

$$$ D ♀ ▼ ✔ AE CB D DC MC V

Specialized

The Beverly Center **6-E1**
La Cienega Blvd at Beverly Blvd, LA. The eighth floor of this most chic of shopping malls is devoted entirely to restaurants, plus a 14-theater cinema complex. With 16 restaurants from which to choose (serving everything from Cantonese crab to Russian blintzes) no one need go hungry!

Kaktus **5-E8**
400 N. Canon Dr, Beverly Hills. (310) 271-1856. Well-regarded spot for creative gourmet Mexican fare. Fine variety of seafood dishes, including swordfish tacos. Fun enticing desserts. *No lunch Sun.*

$$ L D ♀ ▼ ✔ AE DC MC V

Larry Parker's Beverly Hills Diner **5-E8**
206 S. Beverly Dr, Beverly Hills. (310) 274-5655. Quite a change for formal Beverly Hills: a 24-hour "dining experience" where you can zip in for lunch and get on with business via the telephone in your booth. Fast-food fare includes steaks, ribs, chicken, salads, and fish.

$ B L D ♀ ✔ MC V

Stellini's **5-F8**
9184 W. Pico Blvd, Beverly Hills. (310) 274-7225. Imagine New York-noisy with oriental undertones! Ferns, fans, and wood paneling surround a celebrity clientele who enjoy this bustling atmosphere. Excellent ribs and steaks (served simply, without sauces). Chinese chicken salad and French lamb chops. Good bar. *CLOSED Sun.*

$$$ D ♀ ▼ ✔ AE MC V

DOWNTOWN

American

Casey's Bar **7-C4**
613 S. Grand Ave, LA. (213) 629-2353. A bustling Irish/American pub. Plenty of atmosphere and lively piano entertainment. Steaks, corned beef and cabbage, fresh fish. Popular with Downtown office workers. *CLOSED Sat & Sun.*

$$ L D ♀ ▼ ♪ AE MC V

Clifton's Cafeteria **7-D4**
648 S. Broadway, LA. (213) 627-1673. Old-fashioned cafeteria serving short-order meals in traditional American style. Unusual forest decor with a waterfall and a running stream. Food quality is good, fruit pies are great. *Closes at 7pm.*

$ B L D No cards

Gazebo **7-C3**
LA Hilton, 930 Wilshire Blvd, LA. (213) 629-4321. Beautiful dining room. Decorative gazebos are used to present extravagant salads and the grand California buffet, a nightly feast of appetizers, vegetables, hot and cold entrees, and desserts.

$$ B L D ♀ ▼ ✔ AE CB DC MC V

Lawry's California Center **1-C5**
570 W. Avenue 26, LA. (213) 224-6850. A true California dining experience located in 15 land-scaped acres near Dodger Stadium. Mexican-American influences are evident in the attractive mission-style architecture—a garden oasis where edible delights are laid before you. Twinkling lights flicker in foliage, fountains splash, and mariachi bands serenade on balmy nights. Fabulous steaks, hickory-smoked chicken, fresh seafood. All dining is outdoors. Lunch served daily, dinner from May to October only. (*See also* SIGHTSEEING, Tours.)

$$ L D ♀ ▼ ✔ ✳ ♪ AE MC V

Little J's **7-D3**
1119 S. Olive St, LA. (213) 748-3646. Downtown gem-of-a-restaurant serving wholesome fare at great prices. Nightly specials are a must; try their seafood gumbo, chicken tarragon, or house chili. *CLOSED Sun.*

$ L D ♀ ▼ ✔ ♪ MC V

The Original Pantry **7-D3**
877 S. Figueroa St, LA. (213) 972-9279. More than an institution, the Pantry remains remarkable after almost 70 years in business. Wholesome, reliable food at amazingly low prices. Waiters in long aprons still bring fresh sourdough bread to the tables 24 hours a day, 7 days a week. Specially cured bacon, fresh eggs, beef stew, pot roasts, superb steaks, hash browns, and the best pancakes around spill out of an untiring kitchen. Breakfast is the meal of the day.

$ B L D No cards

Pacific Dining Car **7-C3**
1310 W. 6th St, LA. (213) 483-6000. As the name suggests, you are about to dine in an authentic railroad car. Plush rooms have been added to create a cozy, homey atmosphere. This highly respected eatery offers some of the best beef in town. Aged on the premises and carefully cooked over charcoal, it's every bit as delicious as it promises to be. Fresh seafood dishes are excellent, homemade cheesecake (a sin). Service is formal, prices are high. First-class wine list. *OPEN (surprisingly) 7 days, 24 hours.*

$$$ B L D ♀ ▼ ✔ AE MC V

Stepps **7-C4**
Crocker Center, 2nd level, 350 Hope St, LA. (213) 626-0900. Not exactly pure American but a very American idea—an eclectic menu with dishes borrowed from China, Italy, Hawaii, and Korea joining specialties from around the USA.

Spicy Cajun meat loaf, Quilcene Bay oysters, al dente vegetables, good onion soup. Anyone familiar with Cutters in Santa Monica (same owners) will recognize this enormous, continually changing menu—with dozens of little hearts next to the low-fat, low-sodium items. The bar menu is equally enormous—22 kinds of Scotch, 21 beers. A "yuppie" atmosphere, but it suits.

$ L D ♀ ▼ ✔ AE CB DC MC V

Top of Five **7-C3**
Westin Bonaventure Hotel, 404 S. Figueroa St, LA. (213) 624-1000. On the 35th floor of a space-age hotel, the Top of Five (five glass towers) offers a 360° view of Los Angeles. Prime steaks and seafood are specialties. Service needs improvement.

$$$ L D ♀ ▼ ✔ AE CB D DC MC V

Velvet Turtle **7-B5**
708 N. Hill St, LA. (213) 489-2555. One of several successful locations serving reliable fare in comfortable surroundings at reasonable prices. Generous portions, high-quality food, and caring service. Excellent prime rib, dependable seafood, roast potatoes, light desserts. *No lunch Sat & Sun.*

$$ L D ♀ ▼ ✔ AE CB D DC MC V

Vickman's **7-E5**
1228 E. 8th St, LA. (213) 622-3852. Another Downtown old-timer still as busy as ever. Cafeteria-style setup, serving hearty fare from 3am to 3pm. Strange hours, but consider the location—in the heart of the produce mart. Hard-working deliverymen line up for roast beef, stuffed chops, hot soups, and freshly baked breads, pies, and pastries. Plain and simple—and good. *CLOSED Sun.*

$ B L ♀ No cards

British

Tam O'Shanter **1-B5**
2890 Los Feliz Blvd, LA. (213) 664-0228. A Scottish-style pub serving English fare. Huge hunks of prime rib with light Yorkshire pudding, reminiscent of Lawry's. Comfortable and welcoming, with beamed ceilings and an open fire. *No lunch Sat.*

$$ L D ♀ ▼ ✔ ♪ AE CB D DC MC V

Burgers Etcetera

The Bucket **1-B5**
4541 Eagle Rock Blvd, LA. (213) 255-8501. Some of the best burgers in LA come across the counter at this no-frills, honest-to-goodness hamburger joint. Triple-burgers, over 6 inches thick, are accompanied by fries and a secret sauce.

$ L ♀ No cards

Marty's Patio **7-C2**
1936 E. 7th St, LA. (213) 623-4028. The small garden patio makes a change from usual Downtown dining. Burgers are the best items on a menu that includes steaks and grills. *CLOSED Sat & Sun.*

$ L ♀ ▼ ✳ MC V

Phillippe's Original **7-F5**
1001 N. Alameda St, LA. (213) 628-3781. Open over 70 years. Long wooden tables for busy, communal dining; simple fare, honestly prepared, and devoured with relish. World-famous French-dip sandwiches made with freshly sliced beef, pork, or ham. Thick stew, chili, and beans, and the lowest-priced coffee in town. *OPEN 7 days from 6am.*

$ B L D ♀ No cards

The Substation **7-E2**
2212 S. Figueroa St, LA. (213) 749-0844. Huge portions of various meats, piled high and garnished with suitable accompaniments to make great submarine sandwiches.

$ L D ♀ ✳ No cards

Chinese

Chinese Friends **7-B5**
984 N. Broadway, LA. (213) 626-1837. A tiny, bare room where unusual Hunan dishes delight the devoted regulars—shrimp in hot pepper sauce, terrific noodles, sea cucumbers, unique sauces. Friendly service.

$ L D MC V

Chiu Chow **7-B5**
925 Sun Mun Way, Chinatown. (213) 628-0097. Authentic fare served with pride in humble surroundings. Beef and seaweed soup, pork with asparagus, and clams in black bean sauce are all excellent.

$$ L D ♀ ✔ MC V

Grand Star **7-B5**
943 Sun Mun Way, Chinatown. (213) 626-2285. Superior Cantonese cuisine. Everything is carefully prepared with knowledge and expertise. Dignified and comfortable. Exquisite combinations, such as clams steamed in rum, then flamed in cognac. Mongolian beef marinated in wine, whole cod, winter melon soup, and Peking duck (order ahead). Piano bar.

$ L D ♀ ▼ ✔ ♪ AE CB D DC MC V

Green Jade **7-B5**
Chunsan Plaza, 750 N. Hill St, Chinatown. (213) 680-1528. Authentic Hunan and Mandarin dishes (notice the clientele is mostly Oriental). Eggplant with brown sauce and mushrooms, pan-fried shrimp, spicy abalone, and hot shredded pork are rewarding choices from an extensive menu.

$ L D ♀ ✔ MC V

Mon Kee's Live Seafood Restaurant **7-B5**
679 N. Spring St, LA. (213) 628-6717. Bare-basics decor (and service), but the prices are right and the menu superb. Each seafood has its own category on the menu. Everything is clearly explained—in English!

$$ L D ♀ AE CB DC MC V

Yang Chow **7-B5**
819 N. Broadway, LA. (213) 625-0811. Superior Mandarin food served by knowledgeable staff. Huge menu containing an array of subtly spiced dishes—drunken chicken, beef and scallops in

oyster sauce, sautéed live crab, and the best sautéed shrimp in Chinatown.

$$ L D ♀ ✔ AE CB DC MC V

Continental

Grand Avenue Bar   **7-C4**
Biltmore Hotel, 510 Grand Ave, LA. (213) 624-1011. Italian marble tables; plum velvet chairs; original artwork by Jim Dine, Michael Graves, and the like; tropical plants; and vintage wines, by the glass. Their cold buffet luncheon is superb (for full dinners, *see* French: Bernard's). Stylish and fun. *CLOSED Sun.*

$$ L ♀ Y ✔ ♪ AE CB DC MC V

Marquis   **6-G7**
3701 Wilshire Blvd, LA. (213) 385-8191. Decorated in the grand style: marble pillars, fountains, heavy brass chandeliers looming overhead, red velvet. Food is finished with flair and can be very memorable. Good steaks and crepes. Continental menu for lunch. Sushi bar. *CLOSED Sat & Sun.*

$$ L ♀ Y ✔ AE CB DC MC V

Pavilion   **7-C4**
135 N. Grand Ave, LA. (213) 972-7333. Above the Dorothy Chandler Pavilion at the Music Center. Haute cuisine in a luxurious setting: crystal chandeliers, elegant theatergoers dressed in their finery. Formal service. Elaborate appetizer buffet (with fresh oysters); entrees include rack of lamb. Good buffet lunches (except for dinner on performance days).

$$$ L D ♀ Y ✔ ♪ AE CB D DC MC V

Scarlatti   **7-C3**
Sheraton Grande Hotel, 333 S. Figueroa St, LA. (213) 617-1133. A gorgeous dining room with etched-glass screens providing subtle privacy. Colors are softly sensuous. The food is arousing. Appetizers make conversation pieces in themselves. Distinguished food for discerning palates.

$$$ D ♀ Y ✔ AE CB D DC MC V

French

Bernard's   **7-C4**
Biltmore Hotel, 506 S. Grand St, LA. (213) 612-1580. Superb nouvelle cuisine in sumptuous surroundings. This is one of LA's best restaurants, located in one of her best hotels: the beautiful old Biltmore, lovingly restored and full of stylish elegance. Bernard's is a pleasure with its hand-decorated beamed ceiling, oak-paneled walls, and Mies van der Rohe furniture. Tables are dressed with old silver. Courses come presented as sculpted masterpieces. Indescribable desserts, superior wines. *No lunch Sat. CLOSED Sun.*

$$$ L D ♀ Y ✔ AE CB DC MC V

7th Street Bistro   **7-C3**
815 W. 7th St, LA. (213) 627-1242. Dare we say this is the best French restaurant in Downtown LA? Rave on! The building itself (1920s art nouveau) is a feast for the eyes. Inside, behind a splash of neon window art, hang modern works

by popular artists. Tables are not crammed in this airy space and patrons exude that new elegance. Food is sublime and not as expensive as it could be given the enormous effort required to provide perfection at every table. Sample their homemade pâté with warm brioche, salmon tartare, goat cheese salad, scallops with ginger, fresh squab with shallots, loin of pork in puff pastry. For those who like to graze, half portions are available—at almost half prices. *No lunch Sat. CLOSED Sun.*

$$$ L D ♀ Y ✔ AE DC MC V

The Tower   **7-D3**
1150 S. Olive St, LA. (213) 746-1554. High atop the Transamerica Center (Occidental Building) with tall ceilings and stunning panoramic views through tinted glass. Expensive and once again a respected dining venue.

$$$$ L D ♀ Y ✔ AE CB DC MC V

Italian

Little Joe's   **7-B5**
900 N. Broadway, LA. (213) 489-4900. A meandering assortment of busy rooms. Little Joe's opened in 1910 as a food store. (The owners would serve spaghetti to the construction workers then building City Hall.) Today it's a neighborhood institution that feeds 1,500 daily. Homemade ravioli, spaghetti with ladles of rich sauce, and plenty of fresh bread. Their huge menu includes Italian meat loaf and an excellent seafood salad. *CLOSED Sun.*

$$ L D ♀ Y AE CB D DC MC V

Rex Ristorante   **7-D4**
617 S. Olive St, LA. (213) 627-2300. Located in the Oviatt building, a breathtaking example of art deco style. This place must have cost a small fortune to furnish: Lalique crystal, frosted glass in subtle tones, Italian marble, pastel fabrics, magnificent oak columns, brass fittings, curves, space, and high chandeliers. Tuxedoed waiters in wing-collared shirts bring Italian specialties, skillfully presented (by the best Italian chefs in LA) and beautifully presented. Everything on this menu can be recommended. A wide staircase curves up to an impressive lounge; dance on black marble floors to music played at the grand piano. *No lunch Sat. CLOSED Sun.*

$$$ L D ♀ Y ✔ ♪ AE CB DC MC V

Japanese

Hama Sushi   **7-C5**
347 E. 2nd St, LA. (213) 680-3454. Experts in the sushi business, offering hamachi (yellowtail), uni (sea urchin), and maguro (tuna) sushi around an 18-seat bar. Pale walls, lacquer bowls, precise attention to detail. *No lunch Sat.*

$$ L D ♀ ✔ MC V

Horikawa   **7-C5**
111 S. San Pedro St, LA. (213) 680-9355. Part of a major chain of respected restaurants in Japan. Authenticity is guaranteed; the chefs are trained in Tokyo—as their dazzling performances of

food preparation with razor-sharp knives attest. A great place to entertain friends, especially if they're from Europe. Longest sushi bar outside Japan.

$$ L D ♀ ❡ ↙ AE CB DC MC V

Inagiku 7-C3

Westin Bonaventure Hotel, 404 S. Figueroa St, LA. (213) 614-0820. A real Japanese village. There are six dining areas of which the tempura bar stands out as excellent. (A special imported flour is used to make a light batter, which shrouds the freshest of ingredients before they are quickly deep-fried in pure sesame oil.) A vast array of condiments is on hand. Shrimp, squid, crab, peppers, and mushrooms are all delicately stuffed with exotic combinations, providing a myriad of new tastes. *No lunch Sat. CLOSED Sun.*

$$$ L D ♀ ❡ ↙ AE CB DC MC V

Katsu 1-C5

1972 N. Hillhurst Ave, LA. (213) 665-1891. Lovely dining room tastefully decorated in black and white. Simple elegance. Clean lines, high tech yet inviting. Excellent sushi—freshwater eel, salmon roe, and sea urchin are all presented as works of art. Fresh fish, teriyaki steaks, and chicken also. *No lunch Sat. CLOSED Sun.*

$$ L D ♀ ↙ AE CB DC MC V

A Thousand Cranes 7-C5

New Otani Hotel, 120 S. Los Angeles St, LA. (213) 629-1200. A calming atmosphere. Lovely garden setting with rocks, a pond, and a fountain to soothe the spirit. Great views across Little Tokyo. Classic Japanese cuisine tailored to suit Western tastes. The tempura bar is excellent and includes lobster, crab legs, and scallops. *No breakfast Sat & Sun.*

$$ B L D ♀ ❡ ↙ ♪ AE CB D DC MC V

Tokyo Kaikan 7-C5

225 S. San Pedro St, LA. (213) 489-1333. Five separate bars serve sushi, shabu shabu, and cocktails! For more formal service there is a dining room, but the bars are fun (and much better). *No lunch Sat. CLOSED Sun.*

$$ L D ♀ ❡ ↙ AE CB DC MC V

Mexican

El Cholo 1-C4

1121 S. Western Ave, LA. (213) 734-2773. This is the original (there are now three locations), which opened in 1931, and it continues to serve hearty, authentic Mexican dishes in colorful surroundings. It's the best value in Mexican food in the city. Make sure you fast for a day before entering—the portions are enormous. Great margaritas.

$ L D ♀ ❡ ↙ AE MC V

El Paseo 7-C5

11 E. Olvera St, LA. (213) 626-1361. In the center of El Pueblo de Los Angeles State Historic Park, Olvera Street is stocked with market stalls and Mexican food outlets that cater to a busy tourist trade. El Paseo stands out for authentic Sonora-style cooking.

$$ L D ♀ ❡ ↙ ♪ AE CB D DC MC V

Nicaraguan

Managua 7-C2

1007 N. Alvarado St, LA. (213) 413-9622. Bright, clean, friendly, and unusual. Family run with a pride that comes through in good, hearty fare. Sweet yucca and sautéed plantains are offered as appetizers. Soups are so bountiful they should be shared. The house specialty is fish in garlic sauce. There are good beef and chicken dishes, and wonderful homemade desserts. Jukebox entertainment. *OPEN till 11pm Fri & Sat.*

$ L D ↙ ♪ AE CB DC MC V

HOLLYWOOD & WILSHIRE DISTRICT

American

Tom Bergin's 6-G3

840 S. Fairfax Ave, LA. (213) 936-7151. This landmark Irish pub contains a cozy dining room to the rear of the lively bar. Staples on the menu are prime rib, Long Island duckling, chops, and traditional corned beef and cabbage. *(See also NIGHTLIFE, Singles' Bars.) No lunch Sat.*

$$ L D ♀ ❡ ↙ AE MC

Duke's 6-D1

8909 Sunset Blvd, W. Hollywood. (310) 652-3100. Sometimes snappy service (always with a smile), and menus that state "Your mother wants you to eat your breakfast." Well, you will—it's terrific. With 26 variations on eggs plus 35 different omelettes, blintzes, hotcakes, hash browns, and ham, how could you resist? Everything is freshly made to order, even the orange juice is freshly squeezed. Check out the customers; you may see your favorite movie personality. *Closes 9pm; Sat & Sun 4pm.*

$ B L D No cards

The Ivy 6-E1

113 N. Robertson Blvd, W. Hollywood. (310) 274-8303. The Ivy's two cozy dining rooms seem more French country provincial than New American. The food is as comforting as the ambience. Refreshingly attentive service has drawn an impressive clientele. Superb grilled dishes include fresh fish, chicken, steaks, and chops. Their popular Santa Fe chili comes with blue corn tortillas; the freshly made desserts are the best in the area. Attractive patio. *CLOSED Sun.*

$$$ L D ♀ ❡ ↙ ✳ AE CB DC MC V

The Palm 6-E1

9001 Santa Monica Blvd, LA. (310) 550-8811. Sawdust on the carpet, cartoons on the walls, what's all the fuss about? Look around, you'll see celebrities every night of the week. This famous New York steak house is now an institution in LA. Steak and lobster are superlative. Portions are enormous (anything on this menu will serve two people) and quality is first class. Their (unexceptional) cheesecake is flown in from the Bronx. *No lunch Sat & Sun.*

$$$ L D ♀ ❡ ↙ AE CB DC MC V

Starky's Deli   **6-E1**
Beverly Center, 8522 Beverly Blvd, LA. (310) 659-1010. Possibly the best New York-style deli (and pizzeria) in LA County. The menu is enormous and includes chicken soup (rated #1 in Los Angeles), "sky-high" sandwiches, and great cheesecake. Rooms are appropriately noisy—TV monitors show satellite stations continuously. *OPEN 7 days 9am–11pm.*
$ B L D ♀ ♈ ✔ AE CB DC MC V

Taylor's Prime Steaks   **6-G8**
3361 W. 8th St, LA. (310) 382-8449. Sirloins, pot roasts, simple sauces, one fish special daily, and a very special clam chowder. Taylor's is a gregarious place, comfortable, and popular with local legal buffs. *No lunch Sat & Sun.*
$$ L D ♀ ♈ ✔ AE CB DC MC V

Burgers Etcetera

Cassell's Hamburgers   **6-G8**
3266 W. 6th St, LA. (213) 480-8668. Plain and simple. No-nonsense burgers baked (in a special oven) to order, baked ham, and a variety of sandwiches. Colorado prime beef is freshly ground each morning; the blue cheese dressing contains real Roquefort; the mayonnaise, potato salad, and lemonade are all homemade. *CLOSED Sun.*
$ L   No cards

Fatburger   **6-F1**
450 S. La Cienega Blvd, LA. (213) 652-8489. One other location. This neighborhood institution claims to be "the last great hamburger stand." Order your burger in varying degrees of greasiness and let the sauce run down your face! *OPEN 24 hours.*
$ B L D   No cards

Hampton's Kitchen   **6-C5**
1342 N. Highland Ave, Hollywood; (213) 469-1090 or -3038. And 4301 Riverside Dr, Burbank; (818) 845-3009. The humble hamburger is elevated to haute cuisine. Imagine ordering a "medium-well burger with caviar." Here, you may. Lovely decor, garden patio, excellent wines.
$ L D ♀ ✔ ✱ AE MC V

Nucleus Nuance   **6-D3**
7627 Melrose Ave, Hollywood. (213) 939-8666. *(See* Continental.)

Old World   **6-D1**
8782 Sunset Blvd, Hollywood. (310) 208-4033. Great location on the busy part of Sunset Strip. Sit outside and people-watch, or dine inside in calm comfort. The food is wholesome and wholly good! Finest natural ingredients are used (as their menu reminds you). Burgers, home-fried potatoes, salad bar, fresh fish, and terrific Belgian waffles.
$ B L D ♀ ♈ ✔ ✱ AE MC V

Pink's   **6-D4**
711 N. La Brea Ave, LA. (213) 931-4223. A roadside shack famous for gooey chili dogs. Comforting on a bleak winter evening. *(See also* NIGHTLIFE, Late-Night Eateries.)
$ B L D   No cards

Tommy's   **7-A2**
2575 W. Beverly Blvd, LA. 389-9060. An odd collection of locals are usually standing in line—there must be some ingredient that makes these burgers addictive. *OPEN 24 hours. (See also* NIGHTLIFE, Late-Night Eateries.)
$ B L D   No cards

Upstage Cafe   **6-G7**
Wiltern Building, 3750 Wilshire Blvd, LA. 739-9913. A turquoise, pink, and gray art deco eatery located in the gorgeous, art moderne Wiltern-Pellisier building. Good hamburgers, sandwiches, and salads plus some Greek specialties. Ideal for a quick pretheater bite.
$ B L D ♀ ✱ AE MC V

Caribbean

Cha Cha Cha   **6-D8**
656 N. Virgil (at Melrose), LA. (213) 664-7723. Grab your maracas, wear your wildest outfit, and swing down to the "other" end of Melrose. This Carmen Miranda–bright, wacky, wonderful place puts the flash back in the pan. Everything is a delight—from the zany service to the tropical-pop decor. Best treat of all is the food. Starters include tiny tortillas with sautéed chicken and pretty Latin pizzas. All the entrees are memorable—Cha Cha chicken is marinated in lime and comes covered in an orange sauce. They have yucca fries and platanos (fried plantains—delicious). Clientele is too hip to mention.
$$ B L D ♀ ✱ AE CB DC MC V

Chinese

Chinese Expression   **6-G4**
706 S. Detroit St, LA. (213) 932-0518. Modern, untraditional decor—gray linen, black chairs, opera masks—is suited to an unusual menu. Everything is cooked without MSG and follows the guidelines of the American Heart Association. Salt is present only in 10 percent of the items. Shrimp with orange peel and Hunan chicken (with a spicy black bean sauce that brings tears to your eyes) are recommended. *No lunch Sun.*
$ L D ♀ ✔ AE CB DC MC V

Fortune Fountain   **6-F2**
8408 W. 3rd St, LA. (213) 655-3917. Small, attractive, and knowledgeable. A good blend of textures, tastes, and degrees of hotness. Intricate dishes in the Szechuan style. *CLOSED Tues.*
$$ L D ♀ ✔ MC V

Mandarette   **6-E1**
8386 Beverly Blvd, W. Hollywood. (213) 655-6115. Excellent Chinese food, attentive service, reasonable prices. Simplistic decor (with some good pieces of art) allows the food to take center stage. Shiao-tsu (fingerfood) is popular—try their steamed dumplings filled with pork. A huge bowl of Szechuan noodles is enough for two, as is an order of minipancakes made with onions.

Exotic seafood entrees are available for under $10. *Dinner till 1am Fri & Sat.*

$$ L D ♀ ↙ MC V

Lew Mitchell's Orient Express   6-G4
5400 Wilshire Blvd, LA. (213) 935-6000. A beautiful restaurant: copper pots, cane chairs, potted palms, low lights, and gentle piano music. Mandarin and Szechuan specialties are made with care and experience. Beggar's chicken, oyster sauce beef, mu shu pork. Western entrees are also available (solving many a dilemma with awkward relatives). Good wine list. *No lunch Sat. CLOSED Sun.*

$$ L D ♀ ✝ ↙ ♪ AE MC V

Shanghai Winter Garden   6-G4
5651 Wilshire Blvd, LA. (213) 934-0505. An experienced owner/chef presides over this traditional Chinese restaurant. He trained in China and in Paris and knows how to please. Peking, Hunan, and Szechuan are all represented. Imperial shrimp with red sauce and eight-precious duck are both highly recommended. *No lunch Sun.*

$$ L D ♀ ✝ ↙ AE CB DC MC V

The Twin Dragon   1-C4
8597 W. Pico Blvd, LA; (213) 655-9805. And 2046 Ventura Blvd, Woodland Hills **(1-B2)**; (818) 887-4505. Seafood and soups from the coastal regions of China. Spiced delicacies from Peking and Shanghai. Authentic and rewarding. Try their shrimp toast, three-flavor sizzling rice soup, and Szechuan duck.

$ L D ♀ ✝ ↙ AE D DC MC V

Continental

City Restaurant   6-E4
180 S. La Brea Ave, LA. (213) 938-2155. Susan Feniger and Mary Sue Milliken, who also own and operate the Border Grill (*see* Mexican *below*), have trekked the world's kitchens to glean experience. Their passion has reaped just rewards. This exciting restaurant defies real definition, but it's more intercontinental than European. A tandoor oven bakes wonderful poultry and skirt steak; they offer roast beef sandwiches, Italian rigatoni, Portuguese fish stew, beef Stroganoff, baby back ribs, turkey, and roast leg of lamb with garlic. Milliken's desserts are beyond compare. Go, before they embark on a new adventure.

$$$ L D ♀ ✝ ↙ AE MC V

Hugo's   6-D2
8401 Santa Monica Blvd, W. Hollywood. (213) 654-3993. The owner, Terry Kaplan, is not quite sure how to describe this amazing place. "A specialty grocer, a takeout, a deli, a restaurant." The restaurant is rewarding. *Closes 9pm; Sun 7pm.*

$$ B L D ♀ ↙ AE MC V

Los Feliz Inn   1-C5
2138 Hillhurst Ave, LA. (213) 663-8001. Small, cozy, and comfortable; open fireplace. Warm service, talented chef. Excellent fresh fish, veal, and chicken. Good wine list.

$$$ L D ♀ ✝ ↙ ♪ AE CB DC MC V

Musso & Frank's Grill   6-C5
6667 Hollywood Blvd, Hollywood. (213) 467-7788. This old faithful has managed to ignore the adverse changes of the neighborhood. They opened in 1919 and have wined, dined, and entertained as many famous personalities as there are stars embedded in Hollywood Boulevard. Well worn and comfortable, with the same old menu that offers chicken pot pie, baked ham, and flannel cakes. A sentimental journey. *CLOSED Sun.*

$$ L D ♀ ✝ ↙ AE CB DC MC V

Nicky Blair's   6-C3
8730 Sunset Blvd, Hollywood. (310) 659-0929. Nicky Blair has made upwards to 75 movies, but the general public does not seem to recognize him. Nicky could care less—his devoted followers hail from another galaxy. On any given night countless members of Hollywood's movie establishment jam the bar and hop tables in this clubby eatery right next door to Le Dome. The food, although good, is not celestial. Try filet of beef with green peppercorns or broiled veal chop. All pasta dishes are reliable and are made with fresh herbs and vegetables. Nice service.

$$$ D ♀ ✝ ↙ AE CB DC MC V

Nucleus Nuance   6-D3
7267 Melrose Ave, Hollywood. (213) 939-8666. Pleasing art deco lines, cinnamon walls, black booths, white linen, a trelliswork patio, original art by famous entertainers. The food is nouvelle and good. Steaks, scampi, duckling, and linguini. Excellent wine list. A wine boutique, vintage wines by the glass, and wine tastings encourage the timid to experiment with great California wines. *No lunch Sat. CLOSED Sun.*

$$ D ♀ ✝ ↙ AE DC MC V

Ports   6-D4
7205 Santa Monica Blvd, W. Hollywood. (213) 874-6294. Warm and inviting. Country dishes from Europe include boeuf bourguignon, eggplant parmigiana, and an unsurpassed Greek pie made with goat cheese.

$$ D ♀ ✝ ↙ AE MC V

Trumps   6-E1
8764 Melrose Ave, W. Hollywood. (310) 855-1480. A large airy space, dotted with trees. Young, noisy, friendly. Bare tiled floor, concrete tables, angular rattan chairs, abstract art, and a new statement from the kitchen. This sensational restaurant has perked up the taste buds of many a connoisseur and shown LA what nouvelle really means. Afternoon tea is sociable and civilized. *Dinner served until midnight. CLOSED Sun.*

$$ L D ♀ ✝ ↙ ✳ AE MC V

English

The Cat and Fiddle   6-C5
6530 Sunset Blvd, Hollywood. (213) 468-3800. At what seems an unlikely location for an English pub-cum-restaurant, Anglophiles, transplants, and music industry types gather to make this a popular watering hole and a place to eat some

traditional English food. Fish 'n' chips, roasts, pies, sausages, and steaks are available. Service is surly. The pub sits behind a shady garden patio, which can be pleasant on a warm Hollywood night. Expensive British beers. Sunday jazz.

$ L D ♀ Ⴔ 🖑 ✳ AE MC V

Filipino

Bayanihan　　　　　　　　　　**7-A2**
2300 Beverly Blvd, LA. (213) 383-8357. Impressive supper club, restaurant, and food mart. Filipino dishes include cured pork entrees such as tocino (slices of side meat cured in strong sherry). Traditional noodles and stewed vegetables are unusual. Native San Miguel beer is served over ice. American entrees also available. CLOSED Tues.

$ L D ♀ Ⴔ 🖑 ♪ MC V

French

Citrus　　　　　　　　　　**6-D4**
6703 Melrose Ave, LA. (213) 857-0034. The latest (and best) of Melrose's scene-stealing eateries. This is the long-awaited child of LA's celebrated pastry chef Michel Richard. As its name implies, Citrus is bright, clean, and zesty. White walls, lemon linens, fresh flowers, sparkling service. A spacious outdoor patio extends from the open kitchen, creating a very Californian setting for essentially French food. Incredible desserts. Reservations suggested. CLOSED Sun.

$$ L D ♀ Ⴔ 🖑 ✳ AE DC MC V

Diaghilev　　　　　　　　　　**6-D1**
Le Bel Age Hotel, 1020 N. San Vicente Blvd, W. Hollywood. (310) 854-1111. A Franco-Russian restaurant styled in the grand manner—fit for a czar. Plush banquettes, rose-colored lighting, original paintings by Dufy and Kisling. There is live, classical Russian music tranquil enough to soothe the soul. A prix-fixe dinner will allow you to sample both Russian and nouvelle cuisine of the highest order. There are numerous caviars and flavored vodkas. Oysters Muscovite are marinated in lemon vodka. Entrees include quail stuffed with foie gras, truffles, and mushrooms; broiled lobster with sautéed chanterelle mushrooms in a smooth seafood sauce. Finish with Russian tea, which is served with marinated chestnuts and cherries. CLOSED Sun & Mon.

$$$ L D ♀ Ⴔ 🖑 ♪ AE CB D DC MC V

La Toque　　　　　　　　　　**6-C2**
8171 Sunset Blvd, Hollywood. (213) 656-7515. The dining room is country comfortable and the food comes from California's bounteous basket of fruits, vegetables, seafood, premium meats, and game. Everything can be recommended. CLOSED Sun.

$$ L D ♀ Ⴔ 🖑 AE CB D DC MC V

Le Chardonnay　　　　　　　　　　**6-D2**
8284 Melrose Ave, LA. 665-8880. The main dining room is a gorgeous tribute to art nouveau—

fabulous woodwork, brass, mirrors, tiles, heavy linen, expensive china. The skylit Garden Room is pale pastels—perfect for lunch. The food is sumptuous: smoked salmon with sauerkraut, calf's liver with shallots, roast duck, chicken with Dijon. The large wine list includes three dozen chardonnays! No lunch Sat. CLOSED Sun.

$$$ L D ♀ Ⴔ 🖑 AE CB DC MC V

Le Dome　　　　　　　　　　**6-D1**
8720 Sunset Blvd, Hollywood. (310) 659-6919. A beautiful restaurant from the refined exterior to the dark green and maroons of the chrome-tinged interior. Their extensive menu contains surprises, such as hot oysters wrapped in lettuce with shredded vegetables and caviar, grilled Dover sole with wild rice, endive salad with walnuts. Service is splendid. Celebrity clientele. Dinner served till midnight. No lunch Sat. CLOSED Sun.

$$$ L D ♀ Ⴔ 🖑 AE CB DC MC V

Moustache Cafe　　　　　　　　　　**6-D2**
8155 Melrose Ave, W. Hollywood. (213) 651-2111. Also in Westwood. A reasonably priced gathering place for the young and lighthearted. Food is not haute but does not claim to be. Soups, omelettes, salads, and seafood—all fresh and vigorous. It's good to sit outside beneath an umbrella.

$ L D ♀ Ⴔ 🖑 ✳ AE MC V

German

Lowenbrau Keller　　　　　　　　　　**7-A1**
3211 Beverly Blvd, LA. (213) 382-5723. The decor is overwhelming—carvings, stuffed animals, and huge wooden horses pulling a beer wagon. Huge portions are served by friendly frauleins. Veal loaf, sauerbraten, and smoked pork chops. Strong German beer. No lunch Sat. CLOSED Sun.

$ L D ♀ Ⴔ MC V

Indian

Paru's　　　　　　　　　　**6-C8**
5140 Sunset Blvd, Hollywood. (213) 661-7600. Ring the bell and enter through their sunny patio. Paru's menu comes from the region of southern Madras, where emphasis is placed on vegetables. Not the steamed kind, but vegetables cooked with pungent spices. Masala dosa, described as a "superpancake," is really a giant crepe filled with an intriguing potato curry. Their homemade yogurt drink, lassi (unfortunate name), is pure nectar. CLOSED Mon.

$$ L D ♀ 🖑 ✳ MC V

Italian

Alberto's　　　　　　　　　　**6-E1**
8826 Melrose Ave, W. Hollywood. (310) 278-2770. Alberto rebuilt his restaurant after a disastrous fire and came back with something even better. The new wood paneling is expertly soundproofed, so the piano music no longer

bounces around the walls. There's comfort now, and the same capable hands are in the kitchen. Choose from homemade or imported pasta, veal, and chicken dishes from Northern Italy, and steaks that include one Steak Sinatra. *Dinner served till midnight.*

$$ D ♀ ❢ ⋫ AE CB D DC MC V

Chianti   **6-D4**
7383 Melrose Ave, LA. (213) 653-8333. Possibly the finest Italian restaurant in Los Angeles. Soon to celebrate 50 successful years in business. Located in a gorgeous art nouveau building, the room is small, subtly lit, and glows with satisfaction. The food is nothing short of magnificent, true *alta cucina*. Reserve well in advance.

$$ D ♀ ❢ ⋫ AE CB DC MC V

Ciatto   **1-B5**
3000 Los Feliz Blvd, Los Feliz. (213) 664-2955. A happy Italian experience. Northern Italian cuisine, large menu with reasonable prices. Dishes such as chicken cacciatore and veal presidente are served with gusto (and pesto!) *CLOSED Mon.*

$$ D ♀ ❢ ⋫ ♪ AE CB D DC MC V

Dan Tana's   **6-E1**
9071 Santa Monica Blvd, W. Hollywood. (310) 275-9444. Just a few strides from the Troubadour, Dan Tana's has always been popular with celebrities. (Don't be intimidated, they're not snooty here.) Chianti bottles hang from the ceiling; tables are covered with checkered cloths. The cuisine must be described as *alta*. Scaloppine with peppers, chicken Florentine baked in cream, perfect minestrone, and heavenly parfait. *Dinner served Mon-Sat till 1am, Sun till midnight.*

$$ D ♀ ❢ ⋫ AE D MC V

Emilio's   **6-D5**
6602 Melrose Ave, Hollywood. (213) 935-4922; (213) 937-9422. Another award-winning Italian restaurant in Hollywood. How can they stand it! Emilio's is a grand affair with a central fountain and balconies. There are over 120 pastas—of which spaghettini alla chitarra should not be missed.

$$ L D ♀ ❢ ⋫ ♪ AE CB DC MC V

Giuseppe!   **6-E2**
8256 Beverly Blvd, LA. (213) 653-8025. Giuseppe Bellisario (what a great name) opened his own lovely restaurant after years as the maître d' at Scandia. The setting is sumptuous: carved chairs, silver, crystal, skylights, and plants that never droop. Fettuccini Rosina, boccanini di aragosta (lobster with a sour cream and caviar sauce). Wide selection of wines. *No lunch Sat. CLOSED Sun.*

$$$ L D ♀ ❢ ⋫ AE CB DC MC V

Pane Caldo   **6-E1**
8840 Beverly Blvd, LA. (310) 274-0916. An unpretentious treat. Located on the second floor of the Antiquarius building, not far from the flashy Beverly Center. It's small, a little cramped, but oh what a bistro! The menu, which is brought to your table with a complimentary appetizer, contains dozens of items—all dependably good and reasonably priced.

$$ L D ♀ ⋫ ❋ AE CB D DC MC V

Rondo   **6-D3**
7966 Melrose Ave, LA. (213) 655-8158. As noisy and as crowded as ever, but worth the wait. Italian country cooking at its best. Zuppa di pesce (fish soup) is packed with mussels, shrimp, squid, and whitefish. Risottos are good; the smoked salmon crepes are better. Meat dishes include veal with lemon sauce. Specials change daily. *CLOSED Sun.*

$$ L D ♀ ❢ ⋫ AE MC V

Spago   **6-D1**
8795 Sunset Blvd, Hollywood. (310) 652-4025. The (still) young and famous Wolfgang Puck (ex-Ma Maison) remains happy in his own little place. Spago opened in 1982, immediately shot to the top, and remains firmly there. Mr. Puck shrugged off "la nouvelle" for his own clean-cut style. Wild mushrooms from California woods, hormone-free meats and chicken treated simply, fresh fish, fresh herbs, lightness, little meddling. Perfect pizzas made with goat cheese and fresh tomatoes, angel hair pasta, sublime desserts. The dining room buzzes with celebrities and excitement. There's a lovely patio. Book well in advance.

$$$ D ♀ ❢ ⋫ ❋ AE CB D DC MC V

Virgilio's   **1-D4**
2611 S. La Cienega Ave, LA. (310) 559-8532. Down at the "other" end of La Cienega is a meandering stucco bungalow with a garden patio and a menu that's been a well-kept secret for too long. Virgilio Del Mare worked long and hard on his dream and his sincerity comes through in food that rises to a new high. *No lunch Sat & Sun.*

$$ L D ♀ ❢ ⋫ ♪ AE MC V

Japanese

Amagi   **6-C6**
6114 Sunset Blvd, Hollywood. (213) 464-7497. An angular restaurant where everything is set with orderly precision. There's a small sushi bar. Authentic Japanese food is served at tables. Complimentary hors d'oeuvres. Ginger crab and teriyaki eel are worth trying. *Dinner served till midnight Fri and Sat.*

$$ L D ♀ ❢ ⋫ AE CB D DC MC V

Japon   **6-E2**
8412 W. 3rd St, LA. (213) 852-1223. Superb Japanese sushi bar and restaurant. The amazing sushi chef performs to the sound of 50s rock 'n' roll, and doesn't miss a beat. From the restaurant, the sukiyaki is recommended. *No lunch Sat & Sun.*

$$ L D ♀ ⋫ AE MC V

Tenmasa   **7-C5**
9016 Sunset Blvd, Hollywood. (310) 275-7808. Amid the hustle and bustle of the Sunset Strip, Tenmasa stands out for good tempura shrimp—that's all, but it is good. *CLOSED Sun.*

$ L D ♀ ⋫ AE MC V

Yamashiro   **6-B4**
1999 N. Sycamore Ave, Hollywood. (213) 466-5125. Perched high on the hillside above the

Magic Castle is a hidden oriental oasis with breathtaking views of the city. The impressive pagoda that houses Yamashiro sits in 12 acres of gardens, perfected as only the Japanese know how. New staff in the kitchen have transformed a once mundane menu into an inspirational one to complete a spectacular dining experience. There is a choice of Japanese and American food. Aim for a seat on the terrace.

$$ D ♀ Y ✔ ✳ AE CB D DC MC V

Mexican

Antonio's 6-D3
7472 Melrose Ave, W. Hollywood. (213) 655-0480. Rousing mariachi bands perform with pride, and the owner, Antonio Gutierrez, is resplendent in his traditional costume. His award-winning Mexico City–style restaurant has surprises on the menu. A jicama (pronounced "hicama") salad with fresh fruit, peppers stuffed with beef and apples. Desserts include flan in three flavors. CLOSED Mon.

$$ L D ♀ Y ✔ ♪ AE MC V

Border Grill 6-D4
7407½ Melrose Ave, LA. (213) 658-7495. Montmartre it's not and neither is it Venice, but a gathering of artists, writers, and assorted Hollywoodites have made the Border Grill their home-away-from-home. The owner makes the best chili rellenos this side of Guadalajara. There are soft crab tacos, huaraches, and surprisingly good Mexican desserts.

$ L D ♀ ✔ AE MC V

Carlos 'n Charlie's 6-C2
8240 Sunset Blvd, Hollywood. (213) 656-8830. Always happy, always crowded, surprisingly successful. It's run by a Jewish grandmother from the Bronx who likes to see her patrons fulfilled. (Her menu tells you to "yell for more.") There are traditional Mexican dishes, but the menu leans toward continental (with the addition of New York cheesecake, of course). No lunch Sat & Sun.

$$ L D ♀ Y ✔ ✳ AE CB DC MC V

El Cid 1-C5
4212 Sunset Blvd, Hollywood. (213) 668-0338. An authentic replica of a 16th-century Spanish tavern, with a multilevel garden patio that glitters with fountains and candlelight. Dancers, singers, and musicians perform fabulous flamenco shows each evening. Full Spanish dinners include chicken, paella, shrimp, and beef entrees. Sunday brunch is served on the patio. CLOSED Mon & Tues.

$$ D ♀ Y ✔ ✳ ♪ AE CB DC MC V

The Gardens of Taxco 6-D2
1113 N. Harper Ave, W. Hollywood. (213) 654-1746. Big booths, all bulky and comfortable, bright tablecloths, archways. Here you are greeted with the good news that this is the "real" food of Mexico (not your average taco and burrito fare). Everything is made from scratch; dedication comes through. Drinks are also unusual. Their "Margarite" is a special house drink, made from wines blended with fresh guava. CLOSED Mon.

$ D ♀ ✔ ♪ AE MC V

La Fonda 7-B1
2501 W. Wilshire Blvd, LA. (213) 380-5055. "The world's greatest mariachi band," Los Camperos, entertains here. (They have performed in such venues as Carnegie Hall and the Hollywood Bowl.) They are in fact a splendid orchestra and La Fonda sets an inspiring stage with its grand dining room and huge, impressive balcony. Menu selections include some excellent chicken dishes. Four musical performances nightly.

$$ L D ♀ Y ✔ ♪ AE CB DC MC V

Villa Sombrero 1-C5
6101 York Blvd, LA. (213) 256-9784. Gaudy, almost garish, Tijuana tinsel. Never mind the decor, you're here to eat. The food is more than authentic, it's great. Tender chunks of barbecued pork, scallops ranchero, carne asada (they use filet mignon here), whole lobster (split, and finished on the grill). No lunch Sat & Sun.

$ L D ♀ Y ✔ AE CB DC MC V

Moroccan

Dar Maghreb 6-C3
7651 Sunset Blvd, Hollywood. (213) 876-7651. The blank stucco exterior with two large brass doors is intriguing. Inside, a fountained courtyard leads to dimly lit rooms filled with Eastern promise. Floor cushions are stacked around low, carved tables; costumed waiters bring bowls for hand washing; and dinner begins with hot pita bread and a huge bowl of salad. All seven courses are eaten with fingers and everything is shared. Entrees include pigeon, rabbit, lamb, and chicken. The atmosphere is so authentic you almost expect Peter Lorre to emerge from the shadows.

$$ D ♀ Y ✔ ♪ CB DC MC V

Moun of Tunis 6-C3
7445½ Sunset Blvd, W. Hollywood. (213) 874-3333. Traditional Moroccan and Tunisian foods are served in the traditional manner (and eaten with the fingers). Couscous and bistilla are excellent. Low stools and brightly striped cushions are scattered around brass tables for communal eating. Belly dancers perform. Dinner served till midnight.

$$ D ♀ ✔ AE D DC MC V

Spanish

La Masia 6-E1
9077 Santa Monica Blvd, W. Hollywood. (310) 273-7066. Energetic, busy, talkative, ready to awaken taste buds with new ideas. Roast lamb (in the Basque style) with fresh mint leaves, beef Andaluza (filet mignon stuffed with ham and mushrooms), and paella, that glorious concoction of tossed rice, chicken, seafood, and vegetables. CLOSED Mon.

$$ D ♀ Y ✔ ♪ AE CB DC MC V

Specialized

**The Assistance League of Southern
California**   **6-C7**
1370 N. St. Andrews Pl, Hollywood. (213) 469-
1973. Walk through their delightful gift shop to a
beautiful foyer (furnished with Chippendale and
Queen Anne chairs), then on to the grand oval
dining room. Everything is quietly civilized (including the low prices). Luncheon (not tea) is
served. Sit inside or out (there's a lovely foun-
tained patio). Try the Nordic salad with salmon
and shrimp or one of their excellent omelettes.
The League has close ties with the entertainment
industry—you may see a famous face or two.
CLOSED Sat & Sun.
                    $ L ♀ ✳ AE CB DC MC V

Canter's   **6-E3**
419 N. Fairfax Ave, LA. (213) 651-2030. Although Canter's is a shadow of its former self, it
lives on, still loved by the faithful regulars. A Jewish deli where chicken soup, blintzes, and
corned beef are churned out 24 hours a day.
Well-rounded, well-meaning waitresses remind
you to finish your food (if it doesn't finish you
first). It's fun and the customers are a picture.
Good bakery.
                    $ B L D ♀ ♈ ♪ MC V

Carl's   **1-C4**
5953 W. Pico Blvd, LA. (213) 934-0637. This barbecue stand produces some of the most succu-
lent barbecued beef in the world. Ribs, hot links,
and Carl's dirty rice (a New Orleans specialty)
are guaranteed to bring solace to a starved
stomach. Caution: The hot sauce is *hot.*
                              $ L D No cards

Farmer's Market   **6-F3**
W. 3rd St at Fairfax Ave, LA. (213) 933-9211. An
international marketplace where you can sample
foods from many lands. The cluttered eating
area, filled with bare tables and metal chairs, is
surrounded by stalls that offer all kinds of culinary experiences. (*See also* SHOPPING & SER-
VICES, Shopping Centers.)
                                $ B L No cards

Golden Temple   **6-E3**
7910 W. 3rd St, LA. (310) 652-2440. An acclaimed vegetarian restaurant that brings to
mind the peace and love generation of the 60s.
Good-for-you bean soups, hearty cornbread, oriental salads, Punjabi vegetable curry, freshly
squeezed juices, lemonade spiked with raspberries, and many other earthly delights. *CLOSED
Sun.*
                                  $ L D MC V

Greenblatt's   **6-C2**
8017 Sunset Blvd, Hollywood. (213) 656-0606.
Hollywood's favorite deli. They opened down the
street 30 years ago. Success has allowed ex-
pansion, and they no longer exhibit bounced
checks in the display case (an amusing practice
that left many a star abashed). Still friendly, busy
with chatter of recording and filming, still serving
delicious smoked ribs, hams, and huge sand-

wiches. Vast selection of wines "to go" (no alcohol is served on the premises).
                    $ B L D ♀ ♈ AE MC V

Maurice's Snack 'n Chat   **1-C4**
5553 W. Pico Blvd, LA. (213) 931-3877.
Southern-style home cookin' at its best. Short
ribs, pork chops, liver and onions, and all the
unusual trimmings. *No lunch Sat & Sun.*
                        $ L D ✔ No cards

Nowhere Cafe   **6-E3**
8009 Beverly Blvd, LA. (213) 655-8895. Organically grown natural foods that surprise the taste
buds. Discover an array of flavorful dishes designed for the health-conscious gourmet. Tuna
sashimi, Cajun shrimp, pasta primavera, turkey
in marsala sauce, and swordfish with Dijon mustard.
                    $ L D ♀ ✔ AE CB DC MC V

Rosalind's   **1-D4**
1044 S. Fairfax Ave, LA. (213) 936-2486. Exotic
dishes from West Africa guarantee an unusual
dining experience. Yam balls, shrimp with pilli
pilli sauce, and fish imojo are just a few of the
tribal delights you can experience at this award-
winning restaurant. *No lunch Sun.*
                $ L D ♀ ♈ ✔ AE CB DC MC V

**Roscoe's House of Chicken and
Waffles**   **6-C6**
1514 N. Gower St, Hollywood. 466-7453. Satis-
fying soul food. Their chicken livers can't be
beat. Grits, biscuits, and juicy chicken portions—all covered in a rich, lip-smacking sauce.
The waffles are made from a secret recipe.
                    $ B L D ♀ AE CB DC MC V

The Source   **6-C2**
8301 Sunset Blvd, Hollywood. (213) 656-6388.
A vegetarian restaurant that exudes an almost
spiritual mood. (Don't panic, it's organic, should
be their motto.) Salads, soups, sandwiches, and
just-squeezed juices—everything to make you
feel smugly healthy. No smoking, but you can
get your carcinogens by sitting on their patio—
right on busy Sunset Strip!
                        $ B L D ✳ AE MC V

Thai

Siamese Princess   **6-F3**
8048 W. 3rd St, LA. (213) 653-2643. A beautiful
1940s building that has been modified to include
skylights. Beige walls are hung with framed pictures of lovely princesses, tables are lit with candles, gold Buddhas emit well-being, and a gracious staff (are there any more gracious than the
people from Thailand?) quietly attend to your every need. The food is ethereal. Sautéed stuffed
squid, quenelle of sea bass and mussels, fish
with ginger sauce, pork with garlic, spicy
chicken in a variety of ways. The menu is extensive. *No lunch Sat & Sun.*
                    $ L D ♀ ✔ AE CB D DC MC V

Tepparod Thai   **1-C5**
4649 Melbourne Ave, LA. (213) 669-9117. One
of LA's original Thai restaurants. Courteous and
inexpensive. Spicy hot Thai dishes calmed with

fresh herbs and vegetables. The noodles here are great. There's a good pork soup, and some shrimp dishes that are hard to beat. *CLOSED Mon.*

Tommy Tang's   **6-D3**
$ L D ♀ No cards

7473 Melrose Ave, W. Hollywood. (213) 651-1810. Bright, stylish, and full of chatter. Squid is served with mint leaves and chili peppers; there's good barbecued chicken; and crab can be ordered with a special curry sauce.
$ L D ♀ ✔ ✳ AE CB DC MC V

Yugoslavian

Nickodell   **6-D6**
5511 Melrose Ave, LA. (213) 469-2181. They've been serving the people from Paramount since 1928, and those in the know still sneak in through the back door. Nick Slavich died in 1980 but four of his former employees bought the restaurant and continue to serve such dependables as goulash, stuffed cabbage, seafood, and prime rib. *No lunch Sat. CLOSED Sun.*
$ L D ♀ Υ ✔ AE MC V

PASADENA & SAN GABRIEL VALLEY

American

Beadle's Cafeteria   **8-C4**
825 E. Green St, Pasadena. (818) 796-3618. Popular and dependably good. Above-average food for this kind of establishment. Everything is homemade, including their hearty soups and traditional desserts. Meat dishes are good, especially the (very affordable) prime rib. *CLOSES at 7:45pm.*
$ L D No cards

Parkway Grill   **8-D3**
510 S. Arroyo Pkwy, Pasadena. (818) 795-1001. Pasadena-trendy. Large and stylish, with an open kitchen where talented young chefs prepare baby vegetables, angel hair pasta, and mesquite grilled chicken with flair and confidence. The individual pizzas are almost as good as Spago's! A comfortable adjoining bar features live music from a grand piano. *No lunch Sat.*
$$$ L D ♀ Υ ✔ ♪ AE CB DC MC V

Talk of the Town   **1-B6**
3730 E. Foothill Blvd, Pasadena. (818) 793-6929. Near Santa Anita Raceway, this truly horsey establishment, founded by famous jockey Ralph Neves, is very popular during the racing season. Colorful racing memorabilia are displayed around a lively bar. The dining room is warm with wood paneling, fireplaces, and friendly waitresses ready to make you feel at home. Prime rib, lobster, and scampi are accompanied by baked potatoes, unusual salads, and homemade desserts.
$$ L D ♀ Υ ✔ ♪ AE MC V

Chinese

Panda Inn   **8-D8**
3472 E. Foothill Blvd, Pasadena. (213) 681-2700. Choose from Mandarin and Szechuan specialties in varying degrees of spiciness. Caring staff and a kitchen prepared to accommodate all tastes.
$$ L D ♀ Υ ✔ D MC V

3-6-9   **1-C6**
1277 E. Valley Blvd, Alhambra. (818) 281-9261. Anyone familiar with Shanghai will recognize the cold-plate specialties at 3-6-9. Beef with anise, chili-sauce cucumber, and wine chicken are as popular as the restaurant's amazing dim sum. Excellent value.
$ L D No cards

Wonder Seafood Restaurant   **1-C6**
2505 W. Valley Blvd, Alhambra. (818) 282-9688. The San Gabriel Valley is home to dozens of authentic Chinese restaurants, and Wonder stands out as one of the best. Friendly waiters are happy to explain the daily specials, which are written (in Chinese) on festive banners strung across the room. On the menu is snake soup—made from cobra and dried scallops. There is a stew that contains turtle and conch, and you can choose your own lobster or fish from one of the restaurant's tanks. This is not food for the fainthearted, but as a dining adventure it's hard to beat.
$ L D ♀ MC V

Continental

The Chronicle   **8-D4**
897 Granite Dr, Pasadena. (818) 792-1179. Comfortable old-world elegance. Antiques, formal service, fine wines. Main courses are creative yet simple. Seafood is a specialty. Steaks, veal, and lamb are all good. A huge wine list carries over 800 labels. *No lunch Sun.*
$$ L D ♀ Υ ✔ AE CB DC MC V

Maldonaldo's   **8-C4**
1202 E. Green St, Pasadena. (818) 796-1126; (213) 681-9462. Opera and musical comedy are the order of the evening while at lunch the sounds of a grand piano fill the room. High-quality entertainment is accompanied by equally fine food. Great margaritas, unusual coffees, and good wines; fairly priced. Two dinner seatings: 6 and 9pm. Reservations essential.
$$$ L D ♀ Υ ✔ ♪ AE MC

The Raymond   **8-E2**
1250 S. Fair Oaks, Pasadena. (818) 441-3136. This was once the caretaker's cottage to the old Raymond Hotel, a 1930s wood-crafted bungalow with three lovely garden patios filled with flowers. Four small dining rooms offer intimate dining. Cozy and caring. Their award-winning menu includes classic continental dishes. Occasional classical guitar music. *CLOSED Mon.*
$$$ L D ♀ Υ ✔ ✳ ♪ AE CB DC MC V

English

Beckham Place   **8-C2**
77 W. Walnut St, Pasadena. (818) 796-3399.
Professionally put together to please the most
discriminating of English tastes. A lovely restaurant, cozy bar, caring attendants, and attractive
"serving maids" (who really know their stuff). The
food outclasses most pub fare to be found here
or there: stuffed salmon, roast beef with Yorkshire pudding, braised veal joint, prime rib. Desserts are overly sweet. Good wine list features
low-priced "wine of the month" (great value).
Imported beers. Sandwich fare in the bar.
                $$ L D ♀ Ⴤ ⊯ AE MC V

French

Bistro 45   **8-C4**
45 S. Mentor Ave, Pasadena. (818) 792-2535.
Stylish dining room near the Pasadena Play-
house. Caring, attentive service, superb French/
California cuisine, and an excellent wine list
make this a first-class choice. Lunch Tues-Fri.
CLOSED Mon.
         $$ L D ♀ Ⴤ ⊯ AE CB D DC MC V
Chez Vous   **8-C3**
713 E. Green St, Pasadena. (818) 792-4340.
Beamed ceiling, cane chairs, linen, and fresh
flowers. Friendly and enthusiastic. CLOSED
Mon.
                $$ L D ♀ ⊯ AE MC V

Italian

Dino's   **8-C6**
2055 E. Colorado Blvd, Pasadena. (818) 449-
8823. An honest and friendly young restaurant—
even after 33 years in business! Authentic Italian
dishes, all personally tested by Dino himself. Try
manicotti, cannelloni, or mostaccioli Sorrento.
Special children's menu. OPEN 7 days.
                 $ D ♀ AE CB D DC MC V
Domenico's   **8-A6**
2411 E. Washington Blvd, Pasadena. (818) 797-
6459. The pizza here is considered by many to be
the best in Los Angeles—quite a statement considering the field. Excellent pizza combinations
include ingredients you've never dreamed of.
                     $ D ♀ AE MC V
Italian Fisherman   **8-E2**
35 S. Raymond Ave, Pasadena. (818) 792-2236.
A large, beautifully furnished room with exposed
brick and soft pastels. Fish specialties are the
highlight of an extensive menu that includes pastas, veal, and beef dishes. No lunch Sat & Sun.
          $$ L D ♀ Ⴤ ⊯ ♪ AE CB DC MC V
Rosa's   **1-C7**
3077 Baldwin Park Blvd, Baldwin Park. (818)
960-2788. Rosa's multitalented family created
this beautiful restaurant, making everything from
the chandeliers to the handmade chairs. The
food is alta cucina (cuisine of Northern Italy) at
its best. Rosa's celebrated fish stew tops a superb menu that includes veal, seafood, Italian

sausage specialties. No lunch Sat. CLOSED
Sun.
             $$ L D ♀ Ⴤ ⊯ AE CB DC MC V

Japanese

Kabuki   **8-C8**
3539 E. Foothill Blvd, Pasadena. (818) 351-
8963. Every dish is presented as a work of art—
the chef here is a real master. Emphasis is on
high-quality full dinners rather than the usual
mixture of incompatible "sides" we all tend to
pick from oriental menus. Experience exciting
new tastes with beef shabu-shabu or isobeoge.
No lunch Sat & Sun.
         $ L D ♀ Ⴤ ⊯ AE CB D DC MC V
Miyako   **8-C3**
139 S. Los Robles, Pasadena. (818) 795-7005.
Attractive decor, reminiscent of ancient times.
Charming waitresses, skilled in the preparation
of sukiyaki (at your table). Tempura and sashimi
are also good, but the teriyaki reigns supreme.
No lunch Sat & Sun.
                $$ L D ♀ Ⴤ ⊯ AE MC V
Shogun   **8-C8**
470 N. Halstead St, Pasadena. (818) 351-8945.
Beautiful decor, hard-working staff, and a well-
intentioned menu. Their sushi is superior—a delight in the outer regions of Pasadena. No lunch
Sat & Sun.
          $$ L D ♀ Ⴤ ⊯ AE CB D DC MC V

SAN FERNANDO VALLEY

American

Adam's   **10-E1**
17500 Ventura Blvd, Encino. (818) 990-7427.
Great name for a rib joint, but Adam's is much
more than that. Prime rib, steaks, buckets of
clams, fresh seafood, and a 50-foot-long salad
bar stocked with crisp fresh vegetables. The saloon bar offers 50 different beers and 200 brands
of liquor. There's an in-house bakery where foot-
high chocolate cakes are created. Adam's is
large, lively, and sure to please. No lunch Sun.
          $$ L D ♀ Ⴤ ⊯ ♪ AE CB D DC MC V
Amber's Chicken Kitchens   **1-B3**
13701 Ventura Blvd, Sherman Oaks; (818) 788-
0881. And 16900 Burbank Blvd, Encino (**10-D1**);
(818) 995-3200. Home of the "broasted"
chicken—a process that results in oil-free
chicken while retaining the juices. There are ribs,
scallops, and jumbo shrimp too. Everything is
cooked to order.
                      $ L D No cards
Dr. Hoggly Woggly's Texas Bar-B-Que   **1-A3**
8136 Sepulveda Blvd, Van Nuys. (818) 780-
6701. Gigantic portions of beef, pork, ribs, ham,
and chicken, all smoked in a special hickory,
black oak, and ash wood pit. Still made in the
same way the owner's grandfather created back
in 1926. All meals are served with a doggie bag

(only one man has ever finished their four-way combination plate). Desserts include a spicy sweet potato pie.

$ L   D   No cards

Burgers Etcetera

Hampton's Kitchen   **9-E6**
4301 Riverside Dr, Burbank. (818) 845-3009. *(See* Hollywood & Wilshire District, Burgers Etcetera.)

$ L   D   ♀   ✔   ✱   MC V

Law Dogs   **10-A4**
14114 Sherman Way, Van Nuys. (818) 989-2220. Opened by an attorney who gives free legal advice on Wednesday evenings. The hot dogs, despite names like Plaintiff (plain), Police (sauerkraut), and Jury (mustard and onions), are quite good.

$ L   D   No cards

Chinese

Bao Wow   **10-E1**
17209 Ventura Blvd, Encino. (818) 789-9010. A hip, dim sum restaurant owned by rock 'n' rollers. Ads invite you to "tai won on" and the variety of dim sum (little dumplings stuffed with a variety of sweet or savory fillings) is impressive. Other menu items include exceptional pastas, sizzling platters, and imperial shrimp.

$ L   D   ♀   MC V

Fung Lum   **9-G5**
222 Universal Terrace Pkwy, Universal City. (818) 763-7888. A fabulous pagoda lights up the night sky on Universal's hillside. The breathtaking interior is resplendent with carvings, wall hangings, gorgeous oriental antiques, waterfalls, screens, and murals—a $5 million spectacle. Hong Kong specialties and traditional Chinese dishes include lemon chicken, Peking duck, and salt-baked prawns.

$$ L   D   ♀   ⊤   ✔   ✱   AE CB DC MC V

Mandarin House   **1-A3**
13864½ Chase St, Panorama City. (818) 894-0332. One of those little gems, hidden in a nondescript shopping center in an uninspiring section of the city. For those who adore Szechuan food this is heaven (and well worth the trip). Fish in a special brown bean sauce, barbecued pork, a special (never-to-be-forgotten) chicken-albalone soup. Extensive menu, enthusiastic service.

$ L   D   ✔   MC V

Continental

Epicure Inn   **1-B2**
7625 Topanga Canyon Blvd, Canoga Park. (818) 888-3300. Several countries come to mind—Scotland, Germany, France, and old England. The decor is country comfortable and the food is consistently good. Beef or chicken Wellington, roulade of beef, authentic Wiener schnitzel and sauerbraten. Lively entertainment in the

lounge on weekends. *No lunch Sat. CLOSED Sun.*

$$ L   D   ♀   ⊤   ✔   ♪   AE CB D DC MC V

94th Aero Squadron   **1-A3**
16320 Raymer St, Van Nuys. (818) 994-7437. At the edge of an industrial estate, next to the Van Nuys airport, sits an unlikely building. Bolstered by sandbags and guarded by World War I machine guns, this delightful re-creation of an old French farmhouse holds innumerable surprises. There are replicas of airplanes on the lawn, goats and ducks live happily in the garden, waiters and waitresses come dressed in uniforms of the Great War, and the menu is as interesting as the ambience. Superior omelettes, rich desserts, cappuccino. Sunday brunch is a genuine feast.

$$ L   D   ♀   ⊤   ✔   AE CB D DC MC V

Shain's   **1-B3**
14016 Ventura Blvd, Sherman Oaks. (818) 986-5510. An old country inn set back from the hurry of Ventura Boulevard. It resembles a Tudor cottage—cozy with wood, stained glass, lace curtains, and French windows that open out to a garden patio. Veal piccata is served with capers and fried zucchini, salmon is prepared in a puff pastry case; there are thoughtful vegetarian entrees and a selection of ripe cheeses.

$$ L   D   ♀   ⊤   ✔   ✱   AE CB DC MC V

Sportsmen's Lounge   **9-F1**
12833 Ventura Blvd, Studio City. (818) 984-0202. Gone are the days when guests could fish from the stream for their own trout and 40 was capacity seating. Today, up to 1,000 guests pack the Lodge on weekends, but the swans still glide, rustic bridges span the stream, and the food is undoubtedly good. Seafood and shellfish specialties stand out. In-house bakery, good wine list. Popular Sunday brunch.

$$ D   ♀   ⊤   ✔   ♪   AE CB DC MC V

English

The London Bus Depot   **1-B4**
281 E. Palm Ave, Burbank. (818) 843-1424. More a pub, where copper, brass, polished woods, and pewter surround a convivial gathering of beer drinkers. Pub grub (served from the deli) is backed up with a selection of prime beef dishes and chunky pork chops. Adjoining butcher shop. *No lunch Sat; no dinner Mon & Tues. CLOSED Sun.*

$ L   D   ♀   ⊤   AE MC V

French

Camille's   **1-B3**
13573 Ventura Blvd, Sherman Oaks. (818) 995-1660. Decidedly pretty. Lattice booths, plants, gilt mirrors, old photos, soft classical music. Beef with port wine; a pairing of smoked salmon and filet of sole served with a cream and wine sauce to which mussels and shrimp are added. Outrageous! *No lunch Sat. CLOSED Sun & Mon.*

$$ L   D   ♀   ✔   ♪   AE CB D DC MC V

La Frite **1-B3**
15013 Ventura Blvd, Sherman Oaks; (818) 990-1791. And 22616 Ventura Blvd, Woodland Hills (**1-B2**); (213) 225-1331. Tastes of Paris, crowded and fun. A jumble of checkered tablecloths, fresh flowers, framed cartoons. Crepes, fresh fish, hamburgers served on French bread, ratatouille, fruit tarts, and espresso. *OPEN Fri & Sat till 2am. CLOSED Sun.*
$ L D ♀ Y ✔ MC V

La Serre **9-F1**
12969 Ventura Blvd, Studio City. (818) 990-0500. Brick floors, trelliswork, a profusion of potted plants and flowers (*la serre* means "the greenhouse"). The food, prepared by revered chef Jean-Pierre Peiny, can be somewhat pretentious. Pâté de fois gras is wrapped in cabbage leaves and simmered in butter; chicken is sautéed in vinegar then glazed with honey and finished under the broiler. For dessert, fresh berry tarts are surpassed only by a miraculous chocolate souffle. *No lunch Sat. CLOSED Sun.*
$$$ L D ♀ Y ✔ AE MC V

Le Cafe **1-B3**
14633 Ventura Blvd, Sherman Oaks. (818) 986-2662. High-tech French; metal slats, angles, informality, young people gathering. Stuffed mushrooms. A market section offers tasty morsels for gourmets-on-the-go. The Room Upstairs is a popular nightspot for jazz connoisseurs.
$$ B L D ♀ Y ✔ ✳ ♪ AE MC V

Le Papillon **1-B2**
22723 Ventura Blvd, Woodland Hills. (818) 347-2900. A tiny treasure. Lights are softened by burlap-covered walls, candles flicker on tables, lovers linger over memorable dinners. The blackboard menu changes according to what's fresh. Seafood is special, and there are freshly baked fruit tarts to finish. *No lunch Sat & Sun; no dinner Mon.*
$$ L D ♀ ✔ AE MC V

Le Petit Chateau **9-E4**
4615 N. Lankershim Blvd, N. Hollywood. (818) 769-1812. A lofty room with a comforting fireplace surrounded by family antiques and leather banquettes. They've served gastronomic delights here for over 20 years, and today's menu is better than ever. Bouillabaisse, broiled shrimp, rack of lamb, stuffed trout, sweetbreads with béarnaise sauce. Good wines at fair prices.
$$ L D ♀ Y ✔ AE CB DC MC V

Le Sanglier **1-B2**
5522 Crebs Ave, Tarzana. (818) 345-0470. In the style of a French country inn, Le Sanglier ("the boar") specializes in wild game. According to the season, there may be stuffed partridge, salmon moutarde, duck served several ways, and, yes, wild boar. *CLOSED Mon.*
$$$ D ♀ Y ✔ AE CB D DC MC V

L'Express **1-B3**
14910 Ventura Blvd, Sherman Oaks. (818) 990-8683. Fashionably casual and unpretentious. A typical California bistro serving French food to the strains of New Wave music. A large-screen TV dominates the bar. Sit on the patio and watch

Ventura Boulevard race away to both ends of the Valley. Casual does not extend to the kitchen, from which comes perfectly grilled seafood, steaks, souffles, and homemade desserts. *OPEN till 1am.*
$$ B L D ♀ Y ✔ AE MC V

Mon Grenier **1-B2**
18040 Ventura Blvd, Encino. (818) 344-8060. Literally "my attic." The theme is contrived, a little forced—the food is anything but. Escargot in Roquefort butter served en croute, duck with wild cherry sauce, côte de veau with chanterelle mushrooms, fresh kiwi fruit tarts, and homemade cheesecake. *CLOSED Sun & the month of Sept.*
$$$ D ♀ Y ✔ AE MC V

Wine Bistro **9-F2**
11915 Ventura Blvd, Studio City. (818) 766-6233. Unpretentious and inviting; a real brasserie, one that is making a statement and following through with fine food to complement fine wines. High chairs line a solid bar that is enhanced by a huge brass espresso machine. Small tables dressed with flowers. Baskets of fresh bread, salmon with a light mustard sauce, sole Veronique. The smell of fresh coffee. *No lunch Sat. CLOSED Sun.*
$$ L D ♀ ✔ AE CB DC MC V

Indian

Salomi **9-D4**
5225 Lankershim Blvd, N. Hollywood. (818) 506-0130. Dim lights and plastic-flower decor. Authentic foods from India and Bangladesh come in varying degrees of hotness. (You'll need practice to take the heat of their vindaloo dishes.) Over 100 different spices are used in preparation and there are over 70 curries on the menu. Tandoori chicken is a specialty. Order a side of raita (cucumber in yogurt) to cool the palate. *No lunch Sun.*
$ L D ♀ ✔ AE DC MC V

Italian

Fresco **1-B5**
514 S. Brand Blvd, Glendale. (818) 247-5541. A noble Roman restaurant resplendent with white columns, shuttered windows, fine art, and music from a rippling harp. Specialties are endless. Vegetables are served al dente, pasta is made on the premises, and their homemade ice cream is made with fresh fruit and natural ingredients (a good excuse to order dessert).
$$ D ♀ Y ✔ ♪ AE MC V

Gennaro's **1-B5**
1109 N. Brand Blvd, Glendale. (818) 243-6231. Gennaro's exudes elegance. The softly lit dining room, with its expensive furnishings, compliments the delicate cuisine of Northern Italy. Pasta dishes include a creamy fettuccine prepared with cognac and angel hair pasta with scallops, calamari, and crabmeat. Fish and meat entrees are never less than perfect—each dish

receiving the chef's personal attention. *No lunch Sat. CLOSED Sun.*

$$$ L D ♀ ϒ ⊮ AE MC V

Japanese

Aoba **1-B5**
201 W. Harvard St, Glendale. (818) 247-9789. Faintly quaint, sporting an odd assortment of furniture and strange booths. The food is superb and rivals the best Japanese food to be found anywhere in LA. Sukiyaki, sashimi, and teriyaki dishes are gratifying to the knowledgeable, exciting to the uninitiated.

$$ L D ♀ ⊮ MC V

Sushi House Okubo **1-B2**
21630 Ventura Blvd, Woodland Hills. (818) 247-9789. The Valley's first sushi bar. A popular gathering place for the raw fish aficionados of Woodland Hills. *No lunch Sat & Sun. CLOSED Tues.*

$$ L D ♀ AE MC V

Teru Sushi **9-F2**
11940 Ventura Blvd, Studio City. (818) 763-6201. This well-known sushi bar is usually packed to capacity (deservedly so) with Angelinos happily hooked on tiger's eye and sea blossoms. Chefs, dressed in samurai costumes, are skillful, vociferous, and entertaining. Dining here is so enjoyable you can easily spend a small fortune on those bite-size morsels of fish and rice. *No lunch Sat & Sun.*

$$ L D ♀ ⊮ ✳ AE CB DC MC V

Mexican

Mucho Mas II **9-E3**
11669 Sherman Way, N. Hollywood. (818) 982-1336. A good, honest family restaurant serving unpretentious, hearty fare. All the dependable Mexican staples are available. Homemade salsa, ample margaritas.

$ L D ♀ ϒ AE MC V

Sagebrush Cantina **1-B1**
23527 Calabasas Rd, Calabasas. (818) 888-6062. Margaritas on the sunny patio on a Sunday afternoon—a pure delight. There's a rambling, casual atmosphere, the food is exceptionally good, and service comes with a smile. There can be a wait on weekends but live music soothes the spirit.

$ L D ♀ ϒ ✳ ♪ AE DC MC V

Moroccan

Marrakesh **9-F1**
13003 Ventura Blvd, Studio City. (818) 788-6354. The traditions of Morocco call for participation and respect, so guests here are treated like nobility. At Marrakesh you will experience the royal treat of an Arabian night in splendid surroundings. There are tables inlaid with mother-of-pearl, hand-painted tiles, fountains, and costumed waiters who kneel at the table. Gentle music completes the mood. Food is eaten with the fingers and serving boys bring hot towels between each course. The complex menu is explained in detail and measures up to the grandeur of the ambience. Quite a treat.

$$ D ♀ ϒ ⊮ AE CB DC MC V

Seafood

The Sea Shell **1-B2**
19723 Ventura Blvd, Woodland Hills. (818) 884-6500. Wood paneling, lovely padded couches, plants, and prints. Seafood with more than a hint of Marseilles. Fresh mussels, salmon chowder, clams with escargot butter, scallops au gratin, and a rich saffron-flavored bouillabaisse. The owners are ever present to assure satisfaction. Excellent wine list, some unusual labels.

$$ L D ♀ ϒ ⊮ ♪ AE CB DC MC V

Specialized

Art's **9-F2**
12224 Ventura Blvd, Studio City. (818) 762-1221. Strange and lovely, as only a deli can be. Art works behind the counter, larger than life, slicing (and sampling) the lean meats that go into his triple-decker combinations. Colossal sandwiches are devoured by the regulars (some of portly proportions), who start streaming in at 7:30am.

$ B L D ♀ No cards

Swiss

St. Moritz **9-G3**
11720 Ventura Blvd, Studio City. (818) 980-1122. A flourishing garden suggests something wholesome, and that's just what Swiss food is all about. Crusty schnitzels, chicken tarragon, brisket of beef, and cannelloni with cheese and spinach. *No lunch Sat & Sun. CLOSED Mon.*

$$ L D ♀ ϒ ⊮ ✳ AE CB DC MC V

Thai

Anajuh Thai **1-B3**
14704 Ventura Blvd, Sherman Oaks. (818) 501-4201. Attractively decorated with cane chairs and trelliswork. Thai specialties include summer palace beef, chicken curry, and imperial shrimp delight. *No lunch Sat & Sun.*

$$ L D ♀ ⊮ AE MC V

Bangkok West **1-B3**
13539 Ventura Blvd, Sherman Oaks. (818) 990-7384. Considered by some to be the best Thai restaurant in Los Angeles. That's debatable, but the food is skillfully prepared and undoubtedly good. Satay and meekrob, sake and imported beers. *No lunch Sun.*

$ L D ♀ ⊮ AE MC V

Lannathai **1-B3**
4457 Van Nuys Blvd, Sherman Oaks. (818) 995-0808. These premises once belonged to a swimming pool company. Present owners filled the demo pool with koi fish, added a pretty pagoda,

and created a captivating dining environment. Lannathai honey duck is their specialty, noodles are excellent. *No lunch Sat & Sun.*

$ L D ♀ Ⴤ ✔ AE CB DC MC V

Thai Gourmet   **1-A2**
8650 Reseda Blvd, Northridge. (818) 701-5712. One of those hard-to-find ordinary little places that serves superb food at incredibly reasonable prices. Specialties from Northeastern Thailand can range from "not hot" to "very"! There are intricate curries, rice noodles, chicken or beef satay marinated in coconut milk, homemade ice cream. A myriad of tastes. *CLOSED Sun.*

$ L D ♀ ✔ MC V

SANTA MONICA, VENICE & MARINA DEL REY

American

Black Whale   **4-F7**
3016 Washington Blvd, Marina del Rey. (310) 823-9898. Comfortable old-world atmosphere. Prime rib, steaks, Alaskan king crab, steamed clams, shrimp, and lobster. Cozy upstairs oyster bar serves dinner from 5pm to midnight. *Breakfast Sat & Sun only.*

$$$ B L D ♀ Ⴤ AE MC V

Bob Burns   **4-C2**
202 Wilshire Blvd, Santa Monica. (310) 393-6777. One of several locations. Scottish setting with plaid walls, soft lighting, and comfortable seating. Piano bar. Specialties include Scottish plaice, Long Island duckling, steaks, and veal.

$$ L D ♀ Ⴤ ✔ ♪ AE CB DC MC V

Camelions   **4-A4**
246 26th St, Santa Monica. (310) 395-0746. Located in an adobe-style house designed by John Bryers and now a historic landmark. The restaurant wanders from a front-yard patio into a cozy parlor and on to a formal dining room. Service is quiet, voices are hushed, the food is savored. Scallops, squab, chicken, and veal are allowed their own identity—flavors remain clear (though portions are small). Fresh ingredients are purchased daily, and the menu changes with the seasons. Reservations essential. *CLOSED Mon.*

$$ L D ♀ Ⴤ ✔ ✸ AE MC V

Cutters   **4-B4**
2425 Colorado Ave, Santa Monica. (310) 453-3588. The airy, open structure of this expansive restaurant gives it the feeling of a noisy cafeteria. Fortunately that impression is softened by the high quality of the food. There are over 75 items on an eclectic menu, from which you are encouraged to choose anything at any time. Wonderful Italian-style pan bread accompanies all meals and mesquite wood is used for charbroiling chicken, fish, and ribs. The large sunken bar (usually packed with upwardly mobile singles) stocks more than 20 varieties of Scotch and as many brands of beer. The wine list is extensive.

$$ L D ♀ Ⴤ ✔ AE CB DC MC V

The Golden Bull   **4-B1**
170 W. Channel Rd, Santa Monica Canyon. (310) 454-2078. Close to Pacific Coast Highway. Best value in town for prime rib and steaks. Weekday specials are excellent value. Chicken, lobster, and fish dishes also. Dark, semiprivate booths; questionable decor; adjoining bar caters to a predominantly gay clientele. *Dinner from 4:30pm.*

$ D ♀ Ⴤ ✔ ✸ MC V

Maxfield's   **4-F7**
Marina Marriott Hotel, 13480 Maxella Ave, Marina del Rey. (310) 822-8555, ext 6039. Lovely outdoor patio, lively indoor bar. Omelettes, steaks, burgers, and full dinners. Champagne Sunday brunch. Popular dance music nightly.

$$ L D ♀ Ⴤ ✔ ✸ ♪ AE CB DC MC V

72 Market Street   **4-F5**
72 Market St, Venice. (310) 392-8720. The Westside's wittiest redhead, Julie Stone, co-owns and runs this gem of a restaurant. Housed in an authentic Venice arcade, the elegant dining room displays good art (often by the local art elite) and is illuminated by skylights and candlelight. Attention to detail prevails. New American cuisine at its best. Service is impeccable. Excellent oyster bar. Live piano music nightly.

$$$ L D ♀ Ⴤ ✔ ♪ AE MC V

Wildflour Boston Pizza   **4-E4**
2807 Main St, Santa Monica. (310) 392-3300. Award-winning, thin-crust Boston pizza. All the usual toppings plus a choice of whole wheat or white crust. Other (lesser) offerings include antipasto, spaghetti, salads, and sandwiches. Casual, sawdust floor, bench seating, small outdoor patio.

$ L D ♀ ✸ No cards

Burgers Etcetera

Hamburger Henry's—Apples   **4-A4**
3001 Wilshire Blvd, Santa Monica. (310) 828-3000. Attractive restaurant and bar. Dozens of burger variations presented in home-baked (award-winning) buns. Salads, soups, chicken, seafood, and omelettes make this more than just a burger lover's paradise.

$ B L D ♀ Ⴤ ✸ AE CB D DC MC V

Patrick's Roadhouse   **4-B1**
106 Entrada Dr, Santa Monica. (310) 459-4544. Opposite Santa Monica beach. A real rough-and-tumble place where you'll sit next to an assortment of regulars and travelers. Ignore the verbal assaults coming out of the kitchen, but don't ignore the great burgers (and other fast-food delights) prepared here. The decor is vintage thrift shop.

$ B L No cards

Chinese

Chiné West   **4-F7**
4130 Lincoln Blvd, Marina del Rey. (310) 827-1414. Good place to visit when funds are low. Mandarin and Szechuan dishes, often overladen

with MSG but great value for the money. Dimly lit; pleasant service.

$ L D ♀ AE MC V

Chinois on Main　　　　　　　　**4-D4**
2709 Main St, Santa Monica. (310) 392-9025. Not satisfied with one smashing success (Spago in Hollywood), Mr. Wolfgang Puck does it again—in Santa Monica. This time he perfects French-Chinese cuisine starring sizzling catfish, Peking duck, and Mongolian lamb. The small but lavish setting is a strange collage of trendy art and the noise level is high. Service is impeccable. *Lunch Wed–Fri only.*

$$$ L D ♀ ¥ ✔ AE CB D DC MC V

Madame Wu's Garden　　　　　　**4-A4**
2201 Wilshire Blvd, Santa Monica. (310) 828-5656. The decor is beautiful and the service enchanting. Expensively decorated banquet rooms for dining in the grand manner, or intimate booths for a happy luncheon. The gracious Sylvia Wu is always available to help with the menu (over 200 choices). Cantonese, Mandarin, and Szechuan specialties include Wu's Beef, sizzling go-ba, and shredded chicken. *No lunch Sat & Sun.*

$$ L D ♀ ¥ ✔ AE CB DC MC V

Continental

Back on Broadway　　　　　　　　**4-C3**
2024 Broadway, Santa Monica. (310) 453-8919. A New York–style eating house. Menu veers toward Italian with dishes like linguine royale and scallops Rosanna. There are also steaks and chicken dishes, super-fresh vegetables, and sumptuous desserts.

$ B L ♀ ✔ ✱ AE CB D DC MC V

Gilliland's　　　　　　　　　　　**4-D4**
2424 Main St, Santa Monica. (310) 392-3901. Gerri Gilliland, an Irish native who once taught cooking in LA, enlisted the help of a Cordon Bleu chef to create her small, yet varied, menu. Pasta and seafood dishes are always present, as are superior desserts. The cozy dining room has tables brightened with fresh flowers and crayons for doodling. Service is friendly and attentive.

$$ L D ♀ ¥ ✔ ✱ AE MC V

Monica's on Main　　　　　　　　**4-D4**
2640 Main St, Santa Monica. (310) 392-4956. This is the oldest house in Santa Monica and was moved four blocks (from 4th Street) to accommodate an elegant restaurant. Charming rooms remain intact and antique furniture is authentic. Old-fashioned, formal service. Menu features veal, steaks, and seafood and stresses quality with simplicity. Superb wine list with some very rare bottles.

$$ L D ♀ ¥ ✔ AE CB D MC V

Rockenwagner　　　　　　　　　　**4-E5**
2435 Main St, Santa Monica. (310) 399-6504. Pleasant service and an informal atmosphere set a soothing background for exceptional food. Everything is expertly prepared and presented.

$$$ B L D ♀ ✔ AE MC V

The Warehouse　　　　　　　　　　**4-F6**
4499 Admiralty Way, Marina del Rey. (310) 823-5451. Lovely setting; deck-style patio on the water's edge and a large indoor dining room built from wooden crates once used to import liquor. There are sacks and swag lamps, posts and palms. A wooden bridge leads over a carp pond to the entrance. Good buffet, and a menu that includes continental and Polynesian specialties. Try Tahitian chicken or steak teriyaki. A special appetizer bar serves escargot, clams, and a few Mexican tidbits. Great cocktail concoctions.

$$ L D ♀ ¥ ✱ ♪ AE CB DC MC V

Crepes and Omelettes

The Omelette Parlor　　　　　　　**4-D4**
2732 Main St, Santa Monica; (310) 399-7892. And 22969 Pacific Coast Hwy, Malibu (**1-D1**); (310) 456-6106. Some say these are the best omelettes on the Westside—and the wait on weekends seems to verify that. Interesting decor, using old dressers, bench seats (fine for small people), cane chairs, and blown-up photos of Victorian beach scenes. Charming back patio.

$ B L ♀ AE MC V

Sidewalk Cafe　　　　　　　　　　**4-F5**
1401 Ocean Front Walk, Venice. (310) 399-5547. On the boardwalk in the heart of Venice, near the pavilion. Best place for omelettes-by-the-beach. Sit outdoors and watch a cavalcade of roller skaters, musicians, and street vendors do their thing. Salads and fresh seafood daily, entertainment nightly. Crowded early evening and weekends.

$ B L D ♀ ¥ ✱ ♪ AE DC MC V

English

Ye Old King's Head　　　　　　　**4-C3**
116 Santa Monica Blvd, Santa Monica. (310) 394-9458. Favorite hangout for local and visiting British. The busy pub was here first (*see* NIGHTLIFE, Singles' Bars: King's Head). When word got around about their fish 'n' chips (better than any to be found in England), a restaurant was added, then another room, and another. A variety of typically English dishes are served for lunch and dinner.

$ L D ♀ ¥ No cards

French

Cafe Parisien　　　　　　　　　　**4-F7**
3100 Washington Blvd, Marina del Rey. (310) 822-2020. A true French cafe, in the best tradition. Comfortable, with soft lighting and attention to detail. Lovely garden patio, wrought iron, and flowers. The carefully planned menu includes rack of lamb, beef Wellington, and a bouillabaisse with huge Alaskan king crab legs. Specials change twice daily. *No lunch Sat, Sun & Mon.*

$$ L D ♀ ¥ ✔ ✱ AE CB DC MC V

Drago   **4-A4**
2628 Wilshire Blvd, Santa Monica. 310) 828-1585. Chef Celestino Drago's wonderful Sicilian restaurant specializing in herb-infused seafood pastas; also interesting dishes such as rabbit with black olive sauce. Extensive wine list. *No lunch Sat & Sun.*
    $$ D ♀ ♥ ⚋ AE CB DC MC V

Venice Bistro   **4-E4**
323 Ocean Front Walk, Venice. (310) 392-3997. On the boardwalk with a patio facing the beach. Pleasing, red-brick building, rejuvenated and brightened. Lively Sunday brunch.
    $ L D ♀ ✳ MC V

Les Pyrenees   **4-A4**
2445 Santa Monica Blvd, Santa Monica. (310) 828-7503. A small, quiet restaurant owned by three French brothers. Warm atmosphere, polite service—perfect for that discreet, romantic rendezvous. Daily specials. Duck pâté is superior. Also recommended: fresh quail and all the veal dishes. *CLOSED Mon.*
    $$ D ♀ ♥ ⚋ AE CB DC MC V

Michael's   **4-C2**
1147 3rd St, Santa Monica. (310) 451-0843. An almost streamline-moderne look brings immediate attention to this converted house. Gorgeous decor enhanced by Hockney originals, a sunken garden patio, spiffy staff. Michael McCarty is an amiably pretentious young American who learned his craft at the Cordon Bleu. His young kitchen staff have been trained in the strictest of French traditions. A combination of great talents and an insistence for perfection will be appreciated by the connoisseur. La nouvelle cuisine exemplified. Originality, simplicity, professionalism. Portions are small—taste buds are teased, hunger is not satisfied. But then, who ever goes to Michael's when they're hungry? Very expensive.
    $$$ L D ♀ ♥ ⚋ ✳ AE CB D DC MC V

German

Knoll's Black Forest Inn   **4-A4**
2454 Wilshire Blvd, Santa Monica. (310) 395-2212. Authentic German food served with enthusiasm in a friendly family restaurant. Charming garden patio, perfect for sipping German beer on summer evenings. Sauerbraten, veal, roast goose. *Dinner from 5:30pm. CLOSED Mon.*
    $$ D ♀ ♥ ⚋ AE MC V

Indian

Akbar   **4-F6**
590 Washington St, Marina del Rey. (310) 822-4116. Hiding between Venice and Marina del Rey is a quality Indian restaurant. Courteous service and excellent Eastern Indian food. Unusual appetizers and breads. For a main course try shrimp marsala, rara meat, or lamb vindaloo (hot). In-house tandoori oven. *No lunch Sun.*
    $$ L D ♀ ♥ ⚋ AE CB DC MC V

British Raaj   **4-C3**
502 Santa Monica Blvd, Santa Monica. (310) 393-9472. An expensively decorated two-tier eating house. Brass chandeliers, pink table linen, napkins decorating wineglasses, sitar music. Quiet and formal. Attractive tables and well-mannered service by costumed waiters. Calmer tastes with foods from Northern India. Authentic noncurried tandoori dishes, or hot, spicy vindaloos. *No lunch Sat & Sun.*
    $$ L D ♀ ⚋ AE CB DC MC V

Dhaba   **4-D3**
2104 Main St, Santa Monica. (310) 399-9452. A cozy indoor dining room plus a pretty garden patio provide an intimate setting for exotic Eastern tastes. They specialize in tandoori chicken, fish curries, and lamb dishes. Complete vegetarian meals are available. *CLOSED Mon.*
    $ D ♀ ✳ MC V

Italian

Anna Maria's Ristorante Italiano   **4-C3**
418 Wilshire Blvd, Santa Monica. (310) 395-9285. Friendly, bustling atmosphere; simple decor; efficient service. Anna Maria is always there (she's the one who greets you as if you were a long-lost cousin; she's also the one who sings). Good Neapolitan cooking. Chicken cacciatore, veal dishes, and lasagna are reliable. Daily specials. *CLOSED Mon.*
    $ L D ♀ ♥ AE MC V

Casa Monica   **4-A3**
1110 Montana Ave, Santa Monica. (310) 394-2070. Small and intimate (only 12 tables). Try the house specialty, fettuccini Casa Monica, or their homemade lasagna. Also recommended are the cannelloni and milk-fed veal. Fresh fish daily.
    $$ D ♀ AE MC V

The Marquis West   **4-A5**
3110 Santa Monica Blvd, Santa Monica. (310) 828-4567. Established, reliable, and warmly welcoming. Elegant surroundings, formal service, Northern Italian cuisine. Excellent fish soup. Calamari, veal piccata, and crema fritta stand out from an extensive menu. *No lunch Sat & Sun.*
    $$ L D ♀ ♥ ⚋ AE CB DC MC V

Papa Louie   **4-E4**
2911 Main St, Santa Monica. (310) 392-4664. Charming and comforting. Eat indoors in their cozy dining room or outside on the long patio, where water runs over a curved glass roof into a walled garden. Regional Italian dishes make up a small, carefully thought-out menu. The surprising house specialty is Buffalo chicken wings. Eggplant and lasagna are particularly recommended. All dishes are prepared and presented with pride—and *con amore.*
    $$ L D ♀ ✳ AE MC V

Valentino   **4-B6**
3115 Pico Blvd, Santa Monica. (310) 829-4313. Owner Piero is always on hand to ensure perfection at every table. The imposing dining room is supervised by a professional staff. Food is pre-

pared with pride. Unusual pastas, fresh seafood, veal, lamb, and chicken. Huge wine list (includes 170 Cabernet Sauvignons). *Lunch Fri only.* *CLOSED Sun.*

$$$ D ♀ ❢ ↙ AE CB DC MC V

Verdi, Ristorante de Musica   **4-B3**
1519 Wilshire Blvd, Santa Monica. (310) 393-0706. Beautiful, spacious, and musical. Scenes from Verdi's operas line the walls; the Verdi Overture is a special cocktail. Agnolotti Verdi is stuffed veal roll. A 20-member repertory company performs (usually in groups of four or five) selections from Verdi's operas during dinner. The menu is excellent and consists of light, Tuscan dishes. *CLOSED Mon.*

$$$ D ♀ ❢ ↙ ♪ AE MC V

Vito's   **4-C6**
2807 Ocean Park Blvd, Santa Monica. (310) 450-4999. For those who love fresh garlic, anchovies, and rich pastas, this is the place. It's comfortable, enthusiastic, and friendly. The fish soup is crammed with mussels, shrimp, crab, and lobster—a meal in itself. There is also a special no-fat, no-salt menu inspired by Pritikin. *No lunch Sat. CLOSED Sun.*

$$ L D ♀ ❢ ↙ AE CB D DC MC V

Japanese

Benihana of Tokyo   **4-G6**
14160 Panay Way, Marina del Rey. (310) 821-0888. (*See also* Beverly Hills & Century City, Japanese.) One of several locations. Not strictly Japanese, but highly recommended if just for entertainment value. Fish, chicken, and steaks are prepared and cooked at the table by chefs who perform wonders with razor-sharp knives. Unusual cocktails. *No lunch Sat & Sun.*

$$ L D ♀ ❢ ↙ AE CB DC MC V

Hakata   **4-A4**
2830 Wilshire Blvd, Santa Monica. (310) 828-8404. High-quality Japanese food. Their chicken teriyaki is superb. *No lunch Sat & Sun.*

$$ L D ♀ ❢ AE MC V

Hama Sushi   **4-F5**
213 Windward Ave, Venice. (310) 396-8783. Close to the Venice art scene, Hama attracts an interesting avant-garde crowd. Small, clean lines; simple. Excellent sushi, tempura, and teriyaki.

$ L D ♀ ↙ ✳ MC V

Mexican

Baja Cantina   **4-G5**
311 Washington St, Marina del Rey. (310) 821-2252. A well-kept secret. What appears to be a tumbledown adobe is really a charming restaurant (accompanied by a lively bar) producing great American-Mexican food. Huge portions, friendly service, very fresh ingredients, moderate prices. Sometimes a wait, but there's always the bar!

$ L D ♀ ❢ ✳ MC V

Guadalajara   **4-C3**
205 Broadway, Santa Monica. (310) 395-5171. Bright, friendly, and reliable. Quality Mexican food. Special oven burritos.

$ L D ♀ MC V

La Cabana   **4-E5**
783 Rose Ave, Venice. (310) 399-9841. Authentic Mexican food carefully prepared and available until 3am (although better at 9pm!). Tortillas are handmade and cooked on a special open fire in the dining area. Worth seeking out.

$ L D ♀ ❢ Cash only

Marix Tex Mex   **1-C2**
118 Entrada Dr, Santa Monica Canyon. (310) 459-8596. Large, bustling, and very trendy; Tex-Mex food—the latest extension of great Mexican-American fare to sweep LA is brought sizzling to your table. Fajitas are the best item on the menu and come with very fresh tortillas. The "kick-ass" margaritas are easy to swig (they're served by the pitcher) but pack a punch.

$ L D ♀ ❢ ↙ MC V

Rebecca's   **4-F5**
2025 Pacific Ave, Venice. (310) 306-6266. Positively the place to see (and be seen in) on this side of town. A gourmet Mexican restaurant with gourmet prices and clientele to match. (Someone has to pay for that artwork.) This is delightful LA decadence. The food needs improving and portions are spartan. Carnitas, charred lobster, seafood, enchiladas, and seared steaks. Reservations advised.

$$$ D ♀ ❢ ↙ AE CB DC MC V

Tampico Tilly's   **4-B3**
1025 Wilshire Blvd, Santa Monica. (310) 451-1769. Built to resemble a hacienda, it's much larger than most Mexican restaurants. There is a huge bar with entertainment and a dance floor. The menu is extensive and includes steak piccata, carnitas, Mexican pizza, and their special Tampico Tillie Plate.

$ L D ♀ ❢ ✳ ♪ AE MC V

Polish

Warszawa   **4-C3**
1414 Lincoln Blvd, Santa Monica. (310) 393-8831. An unusual dining experience. Taste unique Polish dishes, such as pierogi (pasta stuffed with meat sauce and mushrooms) or traditional hunter's stew. Everything is homemade by the owner. Located in a lovely old building.

$$ D ♀ ❢ ↙ AE CB D DC MC V

Seafood

The Famous Enterprise Fish Co.   **4-E4**
174 Kinney St, Santa Monica. (310) 392-8366. An airy dining room located in a converted redbrick warehouse just off busy Main Street. Mesquite char-broiled fish, steamed clams, and an oyster bar. Good happy hour. Perfect for an after-beach dinner.

$$ L D ♀ ❢ AE MC V

Fish Kitchen   4-A4
2002 Wilshire Blvd, Santa Monica. (310) 828-4425. Fresh seafood at reasonable prices. Cioppino and Alaskan crab legs are recommended. Salad bar. *No lunch Sat & Sun. Dinner Mon–Fri 3:30pm; Sat & Sun 4:30pm.*
                                $ L D ♀ MC V

The Galley   4-D4
2442 Main St, Santa Monica. (310) 452-1934. Worth finding if only for the clams. Absolutely no frills (especially where service is concerned), no soups or desserts either. But the food is good and worth that wait at the bar. Excellent steaks too; they age and cut their own beef.
                        $ D ♀ ¥ ✔ AE CB DC MC V

Gladstones 4 Fish   1-C2
17300 Pacific Coast Hwy, Pacific Palisades. (310) 454-3474. Attractive beachside location; extremely popular and always busy. Huge portions of the freshest fish to be found. Special all-you-can-eat nights. In-house bakery. The day starts early with a great fisherman's breakfast, served from 7am.
                        $$ B L D ♀ ¥ ✔ ✳ AE MC V

Specialized

Cafe Casino   4-C2
1299 Ocean Ave, Santa Monica. (310) 394-3717. Bustling, French-style buffet or better-class cafeteria? Choose from a huge selection ranging from quiches through a dozen salads to baked fish and grilled chicken. Expensive decor, comfortable seating. Interesting outdoor patio (pretty at night) with ocean views. Good value for the money.
                                $ B L D ♀ ✳ MC V

Early World   4-C3
401 Santa Monica Blvd, Santa Monica. (310) 395-7391. One of several locations providing low-cost, quality food. Fresh vegetables, soups, and salads always available. Organic entrees include chicken, seafood, and meat dishes. Package dinners.
                                $ B L D ♀ MC V

Le Marmiton   4-A3
1327 Montana Ave, Santa Monica. (310) 393-7716. What a good idea—takeout gourmet food. The menu offers 20 entrees including beef bourguignon and filet of sole. Quiches, pâtés, and pastries also. *CLOSES at 6pm.*
                                $ L D ♀ No cards

Maxwell's   4-E7
13329 Washington Blvd, Venice. (310) 306-7829. Best breakfasts on the Westside. Wholesome, healthy food, served with pride. Everything is consistently good. Home-baked ham, creamy omelettes, crispy home fries. Six breads to choose from, fresh juices, and fruit. There are great New York steaks and chunky pork chops too. Specials change daily.
                                $ B L No cards

Pioneer Boulangerie   4-D3
2012 Main St, Santa Monica. (310) 399-7771. Cafe-cum-cafeteria plus deli and bakery all under one roof. Strong French influence. Hearty soups, salads, quiches, and full Basque dinners. Excellent in-house bakery (that supplies numerous restaurants and supermarkets). Pastries, pâtés, ground coffee, imported cheeses, wine shop, gift shop. Outdoor patio with open fire. Very busy on weekends.
                        $ L D ♀ ¥ ✔ ✳ AE MC V

The Rose Cafe and Market   4-E4
220 Rose Ave, Venice. (310) 399-0711. A casual and friendly gathering place. Indoor/outdoor restaurant, specializing in continental cuisine plus a walk-up counter for lighter fare (choose from a variety of sandwiches, salads, and desserts, or just drop in for coffee and croissants). The market section is filled with kitchenwares, imported teas, coffees, fresh flowers, pâtés, pastries, and desserts. A bright new concept for the gourmet. *No dinner Sun.*
                        $$ B L D ♀ ✳ MC V

Zucky's   4-C3
431 Wilshire Blvd, Santa Monica. (310) 393-0551. The area's most famous deli-restaurant. Try the corned beef hash, stuffed cabbage, smoked fish or the soup du jour. Good bakery. *OPEN 6am–2am; weekend 24 hours.*
                        $ B L D ♀ ✔ AE CB DC MC V

WEST LOS ANGELES & WESTWOOD

American

Alice's   5-E4
1043 Westwood Blvd, Westwood. (310) 208-3171. A place that came through the flower-power era to prove that healthy food and happy service make an attractive couple. Huge salads full of goodness, omelettes stuffed with interesting vegetables, steaks, chicken, and terrific desserts.
                        $$ L D ♀ ¥ ✔ AE CB DC MC V

Monty's   5-E4
1100 Glendon Ave, Westwood. (310) 208-8787. Perched atop a high rise with great views of the Westside (including the billion-dollar condo corridor), Monty's large menu has all the usual steaks, salads, and ribs—but here everything is given special treatment and the food almost rivals the view. Best time of day is happy hour. Relax after work, enjoy the sunset, and ignore the traffic jams in the streets below. *No lunch Sat & Sun.*
                    $$ L D ♀ ¥ ✔ ♪ AE CB DC MC V

Burgers Etcetera

The Apple Pan   5-G6
10801 W. Pico Blvd, W. LA. (310) 475-3585. A favorite for over 45 years. Sit at the busy counter and enjoy some of the best burgers in West Los Angeles. Sandwiches, desserts, and plenty of pies too. *CLOSED Mon.*
                                $ L D No cards

Hamburger Hamlet 5-F3
11648 San Vicente Blvd, W. LA. (310) 826-3558. Best of three Westside locations. The Hamlet was one of the first restaurants to elevate the humble hamburger to haute status. Comfortable decor, a lively bar, and quality on the menu.
$ L D ♀ Y AE CB D DC MC V

Mom's Saloon 5-F2
11777 San Vicente Blvd, W. LA. (310) 820-1516. Billed as "a notorious meeting place," Mom's certainly attracts some of the best-looking singles in town. Sandwiches (hot or cold), burgers, and salads from a serve-yourself bar.
$ L D ♀ Y AE MC V

Orleans 4-C8
11705 National Blvd, W. LA. (310) 479-4187. A Cajun-Creole restaurant. Here's your chance to try alligator. For the faint of heart there are such staples as blackened prime rib, gumbo, and crayfish. Breads and desserts are truly down-home and worth coming back for. *No lunch Sat & Sun.*
$$$ L D ♀ Y ✔ ♪ AE DC MC V

Chinese

Chin Chin 5-F2
11740 San Vicente Blvd, Brentwood; (310) 826-2525. And 8616 Sunset Blvd, LA; (310) 652-1818. Always busy, always interesting, and always easy on the pocketbook. A good variety of dim sum, plus Hunan chicken, Cantonese beef, and salads with names like Jade (spinach, shrimp, pine nuts, and mushrooms). Everything is prepared without MSG.
$ L D AE MC V

Chung King 4-A7
11538 W. Pico Blvd, W. LA. (310) 477-4917. An old dependable for those who know good Szechuan. Big, circular tables are perfect for groups of five or six. A variety of dishes, ranging from spicy to peanuty, can be passed around for sampling. There are Mandarin selections plus enough rice and noodles to soothe a spiced throat. Beer only. *No lunch Sat & Sun.*
$ L D No cards

Lotus West 5-F2
11930 San Vicente Blvd, Brentwood; (310) 826-5535. And 10974 W. Pico Blvd, W. LA; (310) 475-9597. Teakwood panels, wood carvings, and the lotus flower (a symbol of purity). Hunan, Szechuan, and Mandarin are all represented on a first-rate menu. Sizzling beef with fresh scallops, three-flavor chicken, Hunan shrimp, plus more unusual specialties for the adventurous (try carp's head for a change!). *No lunch Sun.*
$$ L D ♀ Y ✔ AE MC

French

Bicycle Shop Cafe 5-G2
12217 Wilshire Blvd, W. LA. (310) 826-7831. Bright and breezy brasserie serving light French food. Bicycles of all shapes and sizes hang from the walls and ceiling. Wide selection of hors d'oeuvres, salads, homemade soups, excellent omelettes, a variety of crepes, plus meat and fish specials daily. Expect a wait at lunchtime on weekdays.
$ L D ♀ D DC MC V

La Fondue Bourguignonne 5-D4
1085 Gayley Ave, Westwood. (310) 208-8542. Need a lesson in creative dining? Every table has its own fondue pot and you are presented with the raw ingredients (filet mignon, scallops, chicken, shrimp) to cook to your liking. Added attractions include escargots, quiches, and some interesting desserts. Dinners are prix fixe. Lunch available for private parties. *CLOSED Sun.*
$$$ D ♀ ✔ AE CB DC MC V

La Grange 5-G5
2005 Westwood Blvd, LA. (310) 279-1060. Suitably named "the barn," but only for the decor: pine walls, overhead beams, a collection of antique farming equipment, copper pots, plants, and old lamps. Quails are served (boneless) en croute (how do they do it?), mussels Normande, stuffed eggplant, and cassoulet to warm you in winter. Good French wines. *No lunch Sat. CLOSED Sun.*
$$ L D ♀ Y ✔ AE CB DC MC V

Italian

Bruno's Ristorante 4-A5
3838 Centinela Ave, Mar Vista. (310) 397-3777. Lofty columns, archways, and baroque decor. Entrees hail from Northern Italy and are prepared in the traditional manner. The wine selection is outstanding—in addition to gaining an education from detailed explanations, there are over 250 wines to choose from, all at retail prices!
$$ L D ♀ Y ✔ AE MC V

Damiano's 5-G6
412 N. Fairfax Blvd, W. LA. (310) 475-6751. Anyone looking for New York Italian (as opposed to Chicago Italian or even Italian Italian) will find solace here. Three styles of pizza come in 16 ways, pastas and soups are homemade, and house specialties include shrimp marinara, eggplant parmigiana, white veal, and fresh fish.
$$ L D ♀ Y ✔ AE D MC V

Guido's 5-G3
11980 Santa Monica Blvd, W. LA. (310) 820-6649. Carved dark woods, red booths, beamed ceilings, and low lights. There's a lovely brick patio in front (sit and watch the celebrities arrive). Lengthy selection of appetizers (hot and cold), homemade pastas, and, best of all, bocconcini alla romana (filet mignon stuffed with prosciutto, cheese, and mushrooms). *No lunch Sat & Sun.*
$$ L D ♀ Y ✔ ✱ AE CB DC MC V

Mario's 5-E4
1001 Broxton Ave, Westwood. (310) 208-7077. Mario's opened here 25 years ago and chef Giovanni has been performing small wonders for the past 18 of them. Specials change daily and are always good. Pizza is pizza-perfect and the blue

cheese dressing (made with oil and vinegar) should be marketed.

$$ L D ♀ ✔ AE CB DC MC V

Matteo's   **5-G5**
2321 Westwood Blvd, Westwood. (310) 475-4521. It's pretty and stylish and popular with stars (both fading and blooming). A little smug, but the food merits that. *Alta cucina* for *alta* dollars. *CLOSED Mon.*

$$$ D ♀ ▼ ✔ AE CB DC MC V

Primi   **5-G6**
10543 W. Pico Blvd, W. LA. (310) 475-9235. The sharp black-and-gray room, with its metal ceiling and cane chairs, could be 80s Milan.

$$$ L D ♀ ▼ ✔ ✳ AE CB DC MC V

Japanese

Asuka   **5-F4**
1266 Westwood Blvd, Westwood. (310) 474-7412. Sensational selection of sushi (new combinations are added each day, according to what's fresh). Full Japanese menu. *No lunch Sat & Sun.*

$$ L D ♀ ✔ AE DC MC V

Mexican

Gilbert's El Indio   **4-A8**
2526 Pico Blvd, W. LA. (310) 450-8057. A humble roadside eatery with just a few tables (all sparkly clean), a real Latino jukebox, friendly service, and terrific food in the Sonora style. Fresh avocado goes into burritos, the chili verde is mild and zesty.

$ B L D No cards

La Salsa   **5-E4**
11075 Pico Blvd, W. LA. (310) 479-0910. Part of a small chain of Mexican fast-food outlets producing truly authentic tacos, quesadillas, and tortas. The salsa bar offers six sauces ranging from salsa gringo to salsa fuego (translation unnecessary).

$ B L D No cards

Moroccan

Koutoubia   **5-G5**
2116 Westwood Blvd, Westwood. (310) 475-0729. Intimate and very romantic. Sink into large lounging cushions and enjoy a Moroccan feast fit for a king. There are multicourse wedding feasts and a selection of à la carte dishes (all eaten with the fingers of course) brought to your table by diligent servers wearing native costume. *CLOSED Mon.*

$$ D ♀ ▼ ✔ AE MC V

Specialized

Dem Bones BBQ   **5-G3**
11619 Santa Monica Blvd, W. LA. (310) 475-0288. Attention to decor sets this rib joint apart.

There's also a small salad bar and a choice of beans, black-eyed peas, collard greens, or potato with those smoky ribs. Big Daddy's Texas chili comes without beans, just as it should. Sweet potato pie and peach cobbler are tempting desserts. *OPEN Mon–Sat 11am–11pm; Sun 10am–10pm.*

$ L D ♀ No cards

The Good Earth   **5-E4**
10700 Pico Blvd, LA. (310) 475-7557. Downstairs from Hunter's Books. Possibly the busiest in a successful chain of amazing health food restaurants. White sugar, preservatives, and chemicals have been banished to the fiery depths and replaced with honey, whole grains, and everything that's fresh and healthy. Lasagna made with spinach noodles and covered in a marinara sauce, Malaysian cashew chicken, omelettes for breakfast, and a selection of sandwiches for lunch, all made with ten-grain bread.

$ B L D ♀ AE D MC V

Junior's   **5-G5**
2379 Westwood Blvd, Westwood. (310) 475-5771. Wander in and out of the rooms at Junior's and you'll see how they really do serve over 100,000 blintzes each year. A popular, neighborhood deli-restaurant-bakery known for huge sandwiches (named after classic cars—significance unknown) that are presented with little potato pancakes. Cold fish platters are served with home-baked bagels, and house specialties include roast brisket of beef, fried matzos, and corned beef and cabbage. *OPEN 7 days from 7am.*

$ B L D ♀ AE MC V

Nick's   **1-D3**
10893 National Blvd, Westwood. (310) 470-2661. Natural wood covers the walls and hanging plants add greenery. The food is au naturel. No additives are allowed in the kitchen; it's strictly fresh fish, hormone-free meats, vegetarian dishes, and a profusion of salads. Nick's own pumpkin-walnut muffins are a sin.

$$ L D ♀ ✔ AE CB DC MC V

Thai

Siam Hut   **4-A7**
11500 W. Pico Blvd, W. LA. (310) 477-5118. A charming young couple from Thailand runs the little-known Siam Hut. Dedicated to making their guests as content as possible, their simple little restaurant succeeds where others fail. Everything is specially prepared and nothing is too much trouble. Their menu is extensive. Mint, cilantro, garlic, and curry are all happily present.

$ L D ♀ MC V

SHOPPING & SERVICES

F.M.

Farmer's Market

In Los Angeles it is possible to buy or rent almost anything imaginable. Quality department stores are located throughout the city and major drugstore chains have outlets in most areas. The following guide to shopping districts, individual stores, consumer services, and body and health-care facilities places an emphasis on quality and good value, and lists some of the more unusual services that are perhaps peculiar to LA.

Store hours vary, but most retail outlets are OPEN Mon-Sat 10am-6pm. Shopping malls stay open later (usually until 9pm) and most are open on Sundays.

SHOPPING MALLS

These are specially designed enclosed complexes for convenience shopping. Most have one or two large department stores and up to 200 smaller retail stores. The stores are arranged on several levels facing a central plaza. Newer centers are architecturally interesting and often feature indoor gardens, artwork, and fountains. Rest areas, restaurants, and carefully planned parking facilities add merit to this form of trouble-free shopping.

Mall stores generally include men's and women's fashions, shoes, sporting goods, gifts, records, crafts, souvenirs, housewares, toys, and refreshments. Of the 70 or so malls around the city, these are some of the most impressive.

Atlantic Richfield Shopping Plaza (ARCO)
                                              7-C3
505 S. Flower St, LA. (213) 625-2132

Beverly Center   **6-E1**
8500 Beverly Blvd, W. Hollywood. (310) 854-0070.

Broadway Plaza   **7-C3**
700 S. Flower St, LA. (213) 624-2891.

Century City Shopping Center   **5-E6**
10250 Santa Monica Blvd, Century City. (310) 553-5300.

Del Amo Fashion Center   **1-F4**
Hawthorne Blvd at Carson St, Torrance. (310) 542-8525.

Fashion Island
Pacific Coast Hwy and MacArthur Blvd, Newport Beach. (714) 721-2000.

Fox Hills   **1-D4**
Intersection of San Diego & Marina Freeways, Culver City. (310) 390-7833.

Galleria at South Bay   **1-E4**
1815 Hawthorne Blvd, Redondo Beach. (310) 371-7546.

Glendale Galleria   **1-B5**
Brand Blvd at Broadway, Glendale. (818) 240-9481.

Hawthorne Plaza   **1-E4**
Hawthorne Blvd at El Segundo Blvd, Hawthorne. (310) 675-4427.

Los Cerritos Center   **1-E7**
239 Los Cerritos Center, Cerritos. (310) 860-0341.

Promenade Mall   **1-B2**
6100 Topanga Canyon Blvd at Oxnard St, Woodland Hills. (818) 884-7090.

Puente Hills Mall   **1-D8**
449 Puente Hills Mall, City of Industry. (818) 965-5875.

Santa Anita Fashion Park   **1-B7**
400 S. Baldwin Ave, Arcadia. (818) 445-3116.

Santa Monica Place   **4-C3**
Between 2nd and 4th Sts at Colorado Ave, Santa Monica. (310) 394-5451.

7th Market Place   **7-C3**
735 S. Figueroa St, LA. (213) 955-7150.

Sherman Oaks Galleria   **1-B3**
15301 Ventura Blvd, Sherman Oaks. (818) 783-7100.

South Coast Plaza
3333 Bristol St, Costa Mesa. (714) 241-1700.

Westside Pavilion   **5-G6**
Pico Blvd at Westwood Blvd, W. LA. (310) 474-6255.

SHOPPING CENTERS

Abbott Kinney Blvd.   **4-E5**
Between Main St & Venice Blvd, Venice. Most shops here are in semirefurbished premises in an interesting section of old Venice. Several good restaurants are intermingled with 50 businesses, which include fashion boutiques, shoe shops, antique merchants, and art studios.

Alpine Village   **1-F4**
833 W. Torrance Blvd, Torrance. (310) 323-6520; (310) 327-4384. Replica of a Bavarian vil-

Size Comparison Chart for Clothing

Ladies' dresses, coats & skirts										
American -	3	5	7	9	11	12	13	14	15	16	18
Continental -	36	38	38	40	40	42	42	44	44	46	48
British -	8	10	11	12	13	14	15	16	17	18	20
Ladies' blouses & sweaters										
American -						10	12	14	16	18	20
Continental -						38	40	42	44	46	48
British -						32	34	36	38	40	42
Ladies' stockings										
American -						8	8½	9	9½	10	10½
Continental -						1	2	3	4	5	6
British -						8	8½	9	9½	10	10½
Ladies' shoes										
American -						5	6	7	8	9	10
Continental -						36	37	38	39	40	41
British -						3½	4½	5½	6½	7½	8½
Children's clothing										
American -							3	4	5	6	6X
Continental -							98	104	110	116	122
British -							18	20	22	24	26
Children's shoes										
American -			8	9	10	11	12	13	1	2	3
Continental -			24	25	27	28	29	30	32	33	34
British -			7	8	9	10	11	12	13	1	2
Men's suits										
American -				34	36	38	40	42	44	46	48
Continental -				44	46	48	50	52	54	56	58
British -				34	36	38	40	42	44	46	48
Men's shirts										
American -				14	15	15½	16	16½	17	17½	18
Continental -				37	38	39	41	42	43	44	45
British -				14	15	15½	16	16½	17	17½	18
Men's shoes										
American -					7	8	9	10	11	12	13
Continental -					39½	41	42	43	44½	46	47
British -					6	7	8	9	10	11	12
Men's hats										
American -						6⅞	7⅛	7¼	7⅜	7½	7⅝
Continental -						55	56	58	59	60	61
British -						6¾	6⅞	7⅛	7¼	7⅜	7½

lage with 28 old-world shops, a farmer's market, old-country delicatessen, German beer garden, restaurants, chapel, a small farm, and entertainment. *OPEN 7 days 11am-9pm.*

Chinatown   **7-B5**
Between Broadway & Hill, College & Bernard Sts, LA. Authentic Chinese architecture, quaint shops, and numerous Cantonese restaurants. Fascinating for shoppers and sightseers alike. (*See also* SIGHTSEEING, Walking Tours: The Plaza & Chinatown.)

El Mercado   **1-C6**
3425 E. 1st St, LA. (213) 268-3451. A lively Mexican marketplace filled with music and color.

Shops, restaurants, and open stalls offer a variety of Mexican products and produce. Bargains galore. Shops *OPEN 7 days 10am-8pm*. Restaurants *OPEN 7 days noon-midnight*.

Farmers Market   **6-F3**
3rd St & Fairfax Ave, LA. (213) 933-9211. This famous shopping complex has over 160 individual businesses. Excellent fresh produce and imported delicacies are offered in the market section, and foods from around the world are available at a variety of international food outlets. Specialty shops sell everything from Scandinavian glass to Indian moccasins to gift-wrapped peanuts. *OPEN Mon-Sat 9am-6:30pm; Sun 11am-5pm*.

Fisherman's Village   **4-G7**
13755 Fiji Way, Marina del Rey. (310) 823-5411. Variety of gift and souvenir shops and restaurants, set in a replica of a New England fishing village. Promenade with views across Marina del Rey. Boat trips. *OPEN Sun-Thur 10am-9pm; Fri & Sat 10am-10pm*.

Grand Central Public Market   **7-C4**
317 S. Broadway, LA. (213) 624-2378. This huge bustling indoor market, with its million-dollar facelift, is a favorite with Downtown's new residential community. (The neighborhood Mexican Americans have known about it for the past 70 years!) Dozens of produce stalls are packed with fresh fruits, unusual vegetables, pastries, fish, kosher meats, chorizos, cold cuts, cheeses, and oriental delicacies. Free parking is available at the Hill Street entrance. *OPEN Mon-Sat 9am-6pm; Sun 10am-5pm*.

Little Tokyo   **7-C5**
1st & 2nd Sts, between San Pedro St & Central Ave, LA. A unique collection of authentic restaurants and shops. Craft centers here specialize in oriental merchandise. (*See also* HISTORIC LA, Main Districts.)

Main Street, Santa Monica   **4-D4**
Between Pier Ave & Pico Blvd, Santa Monica. A number of refurbished Victorian buildings housing antique shops, chic restaurants, bars, boutiques, and galleries (some of the property is owned by celebrities). Lively, with lots of stained glass, flags, ferns, and frivolity. A free park-'n'-shuttle trolley service is provided from the beach parking lots from August to December, Tuesday to Sunday.

Melrose Avenue   **6-D3**
Hollywood. LA's avant-garde shopping street. Interior design studios, fine antique stores, fashion boutiques, vintage clothing stores, and restaurants line Melrose, between Doheny Boulevard and Highland Avenue. The Pacific Design Center is located at its westerly end. Both European and local designers have outlets. (*See also* Women's Clothing, Boutiques, *and* Men's Clothing, Boutiques.)

Montana Avenue   **4-B3**
Santa Monica. Dozens of charming boutiques and fashionable eateries are nestled along Montana between 7th and 20th streets. This is a lovely place to stroll—especially during the hol-

iday season when the shop windows are beautifully decorated and the avenue's trees are trimmed with ribbons and lights.

Olvera Street   **7-C5**
El Pueblo de Los Angeles State Historic Park, LA. Over 80 shops and stalls specialize in Mexican jewelry, pottery, leather, and glass goods. Several restaurants and fast-food outlets. Great for those who can't make it to Tijuana! (*See also* SIGHTSEEING, Viewpoints *and* Walking Tours: The Plaza & Chinatown.)

Ports O' Call Village   **1-G5**
Berth 77, San Pedro. (310) 831-0287. Recreation of a 19-century New England whaling port. Seventy-five specialty shops sell souvenirs and gifts, including fine china wares and Indian artifacts. Cobblestone walkways, good restaurants, and theme bars, with views of harbor operations. Boat excursions, sky tower. *OPEN 7 days 11am-9pm*.

Rodeo Drive   **5-D7**
Beverly Hills. Reputedly the most expensive shopping street in the world, this is a great place to window-shop and star-gaze. Mercedes and Rolls-Royce limousines glide up to such famous stores as Gucci, Giorgio, or Hermes of Paris to drop off pampered ladies of wealth. A fascinating street filled with gorgeous shops and beautiful people. (*See also* Women's Clothes, Boutiques, *and* Men's Clothes, Boutiques, *and* SIGHTSEEING, Walking Tours: Beverly Hills.)

Santa Monica Boulevard   **6-D1**
W. Hollywood. The section of Santa Monica Boulevard east of Doheny Drive is stocked with interesting boutiques full of bright new fashions, homewares, and gifts. Several high-fashion shops cater to the local gay community. New Orleans Square, in the 8500 block, contains an interesting variety of unique shops.

Sawtelle Boulevard   **4-A7**
A small Japanese section of West Los Angeles (between National and Santa Monica boulevards). Interesting shops offer a variety of inexpensive Japanese imports. Nurseries sell beautiful bonsai trees and unusual plants. Peaceful browsing.

Solvang
Although some distance from LA, Solvang is a popular jaunt for Angelinos and well worth a visit. This is Denmark re-created. Windmills house gift shops and restaurants; there are wonderful bakeries, jewelers, clog shops, and an abundance of china and crystal from Copenhagen. (*See also* SIGHTSEEING, Day Trips *and* Weekend Trips.)

Sunset Boulevard   **6-C2**
At the center of Sunset Strip is the Sunset Plaza. Beautiful Georgian buildings contain the finest in designer clothes. There are silversmiths, art galleries, and beauty salons catering to Hollywood stars. (*See also* SIGHTSEEING, Walking Tours: Sunset Strip.)

   Additional noteworthy shops are located farther east along Sunset Boulevard, in Silverlake (**1-C5**).

Third Street   6-F3
Between La Brea Ave & La Cienega Blvd, LA (close to Beverly Hills and W. Hollywood). Third Street is full of unusual, inexpensive boutiques interspersed with galleries, bakeries, and restaurants.

Westwood Village   5-E4
Close to UCLA. Expensive stores specializing in high-quality collectibles, plus a huge variety of stylish fashion boutiques (some moderately priced), several record stores, shoe shops, beauty salons, bookstores, and interesting restaurants and bars. The abundance of movie theaters in the area makes late afternoon and evening parking a problem. (*See also* HISTORIC LA, Main Districts: West Los Angeles & Westwood.)

SUPERMARKETS & LIQUOR STORES

LA has several huge supermarket chains. (Major ones are listed below.) All carry a vast selection of fresh, frozen, and canned food; liquor, beer, and wine; and many nonfood items such as toiletries, cleaning materials, and magazines. Most are OPEN 7 days 9am-9pm, some stay OPEN 24 hours. Liquor stores (smaller convenience stores) often stay open until midnight. They cater to local communities, providing liquor, beer, wine, and a limited supply of groceries, newspapers, magazines, cigarettes, etc.

Major Supermarkets

Alpha Beta, Boys, Gelsons, Hughes, Lucky, Market Basket, Ralphs, Safeway, Smith's Food King, Thriftimart, Vons, Youngs. For specialized produce, *see* Food.

DISCOUNT SHOPPING

Everyone loves a bargain, and there are plenty to be found in all areas of Los Angeles. A wide range of top-quality merchandise is offered at discount prices. With a huge garment industry, fashion bargains are common, and prices are often below wholesale. (See also Women's Clothes, Discount, and Men's Clothes, Discount.) Bargains in merchandise other than clothes can be found at the following stores.

A.B.C. Premiums   6-D4
7266 Beverly Blvd, LA. (213) 938-2724. Photographic and hi-fi equipment and appliances. *CLOSED Sun.*

Cost Plus Imports   1-B2
21825 Erwin St, Woodland Hills. (818) 999-3501. Also in several other locations. Discount department stores with goods from around the world.

The Martinel Company   6-E2
8151 Beverly Blvd, LA. (213) 651-2800. Large and small appliances. *CLOSED Sun.*

Optic City   6-G1
8920 W. Pico Blvd, LA. (310) 276-6511. Prescription and other eyeglasses. *CLOSED Sun.*

Perfumes for Less   5-G5
2099 Westwood Blvd, Westwood. (310) 470-8556. Ladies' and men's designer perfumes. Not fakes—the real thing.

Pic 'n' Save   4-B8
11341 National Blvd, W. LA. (310) 473-7844. Several other locations. Discount department store.

Sid's Baby Furniture   3-B4
8338 Lincoln Blvd, LA. (310) 397-3903. Baby furniture, clothing, layettes, etc. *CLOSED Sun.*

Toyorama   5-G5
2018 Westwood Blvd, Westwood. (310) 474-7607. Brand-name toys.

Video & Audio Center   4-B3
619 Wilshire Blvd, Santa Monica. (310) 458-3172. Also in Palos Verdes and Torrance. Brand-name video and stereo equipment at up to 70% below retail.

World of Plants & Gifts   1-D4
2485 Lincoln Blvd, LA. (310) 823-3883. Plants, art deco gifts.

THRIFT & SURPLUS OUTLETS

Angelinos tend to discard the most wonderful reusable items, from couturier clothes to nearly new furniture. Amazing bargains can be found at thrift shops, vintage clothing stores, and surplus outlets. Those listed below are worth seeking out and fun to visit.

Aardvark's Odd Ark   6-D3
7579 Melrose Ave, Hollywood; 655-6769. And 85 Market St, Venice (**4-F5**); (310) 655-6769. Recycled clothing. Huge selection for men and women. Jackets, dresses, shirts, denim.

Bell Sales Co.   1-D4
910 W. King Blvd, LA. (213) 234-7883. Jeans, shoes, oversize clothing, hardware, electrical goods.

California Surplus Mart   6-D6
6263 Santa Monica Blvd, Hollywood. (213) 465-1002. Clothing, camping, army surplus, binoculars.

Goodwill Industries of Southern California   5-G4
1608 Sawtelle Blvd, W. LA. (310) 473-9844. Huge variety of merchandise. Low prices.

National Council of Jewish Women Thrift Shops   6-E3
429 N. Fairfax Ave, LA. (213) 651-2080. Several other locations. You never know what you'll find! *CLOSED Sat.*

Salvation Army Thrift Stores   4-C4
1658 11th St, Santa Monica. (310) 450-7235. Many other locations. Clothing, furniture, appliances, etc. *CLOSED Sun.*

Supply Sergeant   6-C5
6664 Hollywood Blvd, LA. (213) 463-4730. Camping, army and navy surplus, jeans.

Surplus Value Center   **1-C5**
3828 Sunset Blvd, LA. (213) 662-8132. New and
used Levi's, camping goods, and supplies.
Victory Salvage Company   **1-D5**
8211 S. Alameda St, LA. (213) 581-7272. Industrial surplus, forklifts, generators, hoists, etc.
CLOSED Sat & Sun.

SWAP MEETS & FLEA MARKETS

*Los Angeles does not have street markets in the
European sense, but it does offer lively alternatives. Swap meets and flea markets are organized open marketplaces with hundreds of independent merchants (who set up stands to sell
individual wares). Held in many areas of the city,
usually on weekends, they are especially popular during summer and holiday seasons. Prices
are much lower than in retail stores and the bustling fairground atmosphere is quite enjoyable.
Bargains can be found in antiques, collectibles,
clothing, and homewares. These are some of the
larger swap meets held regularly around Los Angeles:*
Indian Hill Indoor Swap Meet
1600 E. Holt Blvd, Pomona. (714) 620-4792.
Over 600 vendors offer all-new merchandise at
up to 80% below retail and antiques at bargain
prices. *OPEN Fri, Sat & Sun 10am-6pm.*
Marina del Rey Indoor Swap Meet   **4-E7**
Washington Blvd at Lincoln Blvd, Venice. 306-
~094. Large indoor marketplace offering a wide
variety of new goods: clothing, jewelry, plants,
household appliances, records, etc. *OPEN Sat &
Sun 10am-6pm.*
Pasadena Rose Bowl Flea Market   **8-B1**
991 Rosemont Blvd, Pasadena. Flea market information (213) 588-4411. At the world-famous
Rose Bowl. The organizers claim this is the
world's largest flea market. Hundreds of merchants sell everything imaginable, from World
War memorabilia to handmade Christmas decorations. *OPEN second Sun of the month, 9am-
3pm.*
Pomona Swap Meet
LA County Fairgrounds, 1101 W. McKinley Ave,
Pomona. (714) 623-3111. A huge variety of automobiles. Held every six weeks (except during
LA County Fair).
Roadium Swap Meets   **1-E4**
2500 W. Redondo Beach Blvd, Torrance. (213)
321-3920. Held in a drive-in movie theater; over
450 merchants show a huge variety of goods.
OPEN 7 days 7am-4pm.

GARAGE SALES

The garage sale is a custom that should be prac-
ticed worldwide. Throughout the city handmade
signs adorn telephone poles and fences an-
nouncing garage or yard sales. (To the foreign
visitor this is quite confusing—who would try to
sell their yard?) With an accumulation of items
no longer needed, such as clothing, furniture, or
kitchen equipment, families and neighbors often
get together, post sale signs around the neighborhood, and set up displays in front of their
homes. Prices run from a few cents to a few
dollars. Listings of garage sales can be found in
newspapers such as the *Recycler* (*see also* BA-
SIC INFORMATION, Newspapers & Magazines:
Newspapers). It can be fun to visit several on a
sunny afternoon.

COMPLAINTS & CONSUMER SERVICES

Better Business Bureau
Complaints: (213) 382-0917. Inquiries: (213)
383-0992.
Business Hotline   **7-C4**
Los Angeles City Hall. (213) 485-2000. Advice
and referrals for small and new businesses.
Civil Liberties Union
Free assistance providing your cause preserves
the Constitution of the U.S. (213) 977-9500.
Consumer Affairs
Los Angeles County Department of Consumer
Affairs. (213) 974-1452. Assistance in directing
complaints to the appropriate party.
Consumer Product Safety Commission 7-C4
Los Angeles City Hall, Room 1700. (213) 485-
4515. Product complaints and referrals.
Credit Ratings
TRW Credit Data, Box 5450, Orange, CA. (714)
991-5100. Recorded message advises how to
obtain a credit report.
**Department of Fair Employment and
Housing**   **7-C4**
322 W. 1st St, Room 2126, LA. (213) 897-1997.
State of California fair housing, job discrimina-
tion, and human relations departments.
Federal Communications Commission
18000 Studebaker Ave, Room 660, Cerritos.
(310) 809-2096. Complaints relating to TV or ra-
dio reception.
Forgery & Fraud (LAPD)   **7-C5**
LAPD, 150 N. Los Angeles St, Room 302, LA. For
complaints concerning forgery: (213) 485-4131.
For fraud (bunco): (213) 485-3795.
General Crime (F.B.I.)   **5-F4**
11000 Wilshire Blvd, W. LA. (310) 477-6565. This
24-hour number can be used to report a crime or
for information about a crime across state lines.
Los Angeles City Attorney   **7-C4**
Los Angeles City Hall East, Room 1700, LA.
(213) 485-4515. Written complaints relating to
consumer fraud.
LA County Department of Consumer Affairs
                                                     7-B4
500 W. Temple St, LA. (213) 975-1452. Con-
sumer affairs, information, and complaints.

Los Angeles Police Department (LAPD) 7-C5
Parker Center, 150 N. Los Angeles St, LA. (213)
485-3795. Complaints of consumer fraud.

Medical Association of Los Angeles   7-C2
1925 Wilshire Blvd, LA. (213) 483-1581. Complaints pertaining to medical practices.

Office of Environment Quality   7-C4
LA City Hall, Room 517, LA. (213) 237-2771.
Complaints or concern about quality of environment.

Rent Control
City of Los Angeles. (213) 624-7368. Information on rent control.

Wild Animals
Animal Airlift, Department of Animal Regulation.
(818) 882-8800. Wild animals are lifted by helicopter and returned to their natural habitat.

ADVICE TO DUTY-FREE SHOPPERS

Shopping for items such as perfume, liquor, jewelry, cigars, and cigarettes should not be left until the last minute. Several stores in the Los Angeles area sell these items at prices well below the "duty-free" prices offered at airports or by airline companies. Make comparisons. Large supermarket chains sell liquor and cigarettes at reduced prices. Discount drugstores, such as Thrifty, sell good perfumes, jewelry, watches, and other luxury items at below duty-free prices.

BEAUTY

Los Angeles is full of beautiful people, many of whom spend small fortunes ensuring they stay that way. There are specialists (for both men and women) experienced in everything from skin peeling to body alignment. The following is a selection of reliable and interesting salons. Most are unisex.

Hair Care

Allen Edwards   5-D8
345 N. Camden Dr, Beverly Hills. (310) 274-8575. Innovative styling. Beauty treatments and cellulite wraps. Celebrity clientele.

Barron   9-F2
11908 Ventura Blvd, Studio City. (818) 763-4337. Avant-garde, imposing. Coloring, braiding.

Bruno & Soon-He   5-D8
404 N. Canon Dr, Beverly Hills. (310) 275-8152.
Quality cuts. Excellent air-oxidized perms. Natural treatments.

Dusty Flemming   5-E8
275 N. Canon Dr, Beverly Hills. (310) 273-5313.
Shaping and perms. Consultant to film studios.

Hair Club for Men   6-G3
5757 Wilshire Blvd, Suite 347, Beverly Hills.
(213) 938-6268. Reversible, nonsurgical hair replacement.

Herb Yerman Esquire   6-F2
8112 W. 3rd St, LA. (310) 659-4940. Twenty years' experience in men's hair replacement.

Joe Oliveri Hair Design Salon   1-F4
1401 S. Pacific Coast Hwy, Redondo Beach.
(310) 540-5454. Full service. Fifteen years as beauty consultants.

Main Street Salon   4-E4
3110 Main St, Santa Monica. (310) 392-3951.
Total beauty care. Full-service hair salon, manicures, pedicures, facials, and aromatherapy.

Menage à Trois   6-F1
8822 Burton Way, Beverly Hills. (310) 278-4430.
Full service. Celebrity clientele.

Norm Tuch Company   6-F2
8210 W. 3rd St, LA. (213) 655-0046. Full service, outdoor patio. Fun.

Roni Michel's Salon   4-A4
1914 Wilshire Blvd, Santa Monica. (310) 453-5497. Consistently good. Considerate cuts, kind perms, personal attention.

Sally Russells   4-F5
2730 Neilson Way, Santa Monica. (310) 392-7888. Evening appointments.

Vidal Sassoon   5-D8
405 N. Rodeo Dr, Beverly Hills. (310) 274- 8791.
Distinctive look. Price varies according to who cuts your hair.

Scissors   4-D4
2303 Main St, Santa Monica. (310) 396-6477.
Friendly atmosphere. Facials, manicures.

Strugar Hair Company   6-E1
466 N. Doheny Dr, Beverly Hills. (310) 273-1672.
Custom cuts, image consulting.

Villella   6-C2
8616-A Sunset Blvd, Hollywood. (310) 657-4756 or -4757. One step ahead. Superb hair cutting.
Celebrity clientele.

Wave   6-D2
8062 Melrose Ave, W. Hollywood. (213) 653-7841. Trendy cuts, colors, perms.

Nail Care

Most hair salons have full-time manicurists. The following establishments specialize primarily in nail care.

Dushon   1-D6
7817 E. Florence Ave, Downey. (310) 927-3431.

Love Those Nails   4-G8
12740 Culver Blvd, Marina del Rey. (310) 306-2966. Liquid Juliettes for men and women, sculptured nails, facials, waxing.

The Nail Garden   5-F4
1410 Westwood Blvd, W. LA. (310) 475-0500.
Manicures, pedicures, full leg waxing, acrylics, facials.

Yuki   6-C1
8640 Sunset Blvd, W. Hollywood. (310) 652-7474. Excellent Japanese pedicures. Full hair care.

Skin Care & Cosmetics

Aida Grey   **5-E8**
9549 Wilshire Blvd, Beverly Hills; (310) 276-3276. And 255 Main St, Santa Monica; (310) 394-7068. High-quality cosmetics. Facials, acupressure.

Aida Thibiant's Skin and Body Care Center
                                                 5-D8
449 N. Canon Dr, Beverly Hills. (310) 278-7565. French body facials and massages.

The Beehive   **5-E7**
9615 Brighton Way, Suite 219, Beverly Hills. (213) 278-7374. Natural, painless hair removal. Complete skin care.

Bella Bellissimo Waxing and Skin Care 6-G2
6363 Wilshire Blvd, Room 305, LA. (213) 658-8396. Full waxing, for men and women. Acne treatment.

Columbia Stage and Screen Cosmetics 6-C7
1440 N. Gower St, Hollywood. (213) 464-7555. Inexpensive theatrical makeup.

The Face Place   **6-D2**
8460½ Melrose Pl, W. Hollywood. (213) 855-1150. Electrical impulses for face-firming. Vacuum therapy, deep-pore cleansing.

Imre Gordon   **6-C3**
7080 Hollywood Blvd, Suite 920, LA. (213) 465-4111. Electrolysis.

Merle Norman Cosmetics
2,200 studios throughout the U.S. (800) 421-2060. Free skin care and makeup lessons by appointment only. Call for salon nearest you.

New Beginning Salon   **8-C4**
138 N. Lake Ave, Pasadena. (818) 449-1231. Twenty-one different skin care services. Makeup lessons.

Ole Henriksen of Denmark   **6-C1**
8601 Sunset Blvd, Hollywood. (310) 854-7700. Individual treatments using machines. Nutritional products.

Shaw Health Center   **6-C7**
5336 Fountain Ave, LA. (213) 467-6278. Chiropractic treatments.

Susan Tarjan Skin Care   **6-G1**
458 S. Robertson Blvd, LA. (310) 278-2274. Free expert advice by telephone.

Christine Valmy   **4-F7**
4770 Admiralty Way, Marina del Rey. (310) 821-8892. All natural Christine Valmy products. Full service, including massage.

Vanity Inc.   **6-D1**
704 N. La Cienega Blvd, Beverly Hills. (310) 659-7011. Full range of men's and women's cosmetics. Consultations.

HEALTH CLUBS & SPAS

Most clubs offer free introductory visits for potential members. Some are affiliated to clubs worldwide. (Visitors may find they are able to use local clubs at no charge.) Clubs listed as having full or extensive facilities will have a gym, *sauna, steam room, Jacuzzi or whirlpool, and will offer exercise classes. (See also SPORTS & RECREATION, Sporting Activities, Racquetball.)*

The Ashram   **1-B1**
2025 McKain Rd, Calabasas. (818) 888-0232. Very serious business here. Strict, strenuous, one-week programs for the dedicated.

Biltmore Health Club   **7-C4**
Biltmore Hotel, 506 S. Grand Ave, LA. (213) 612-1567. Full facilities; swimming pool, pro shop. Juice bar. Yearly memberships only. Luxurious location.

Century West Health Club   **5-F7**
2040 Avenue of the Stars, Century City. (310) 556-3312. Full facilities; racquetball, running track, yoga, health food restaurant.

Family Fitness Center   **5-F7**
9911 W. Pico Blvd, LA. (310) 553-7600. Full facilities; racquetball.

Fox Fitness   **1-D4**
6237 Bristol Pkwy, Culver City. (310) 670-1380. Gym, spa, yoga, water-exercise classes, belly dancing.

Great Shape, A Women's Health Club   5-F2
11980 San Vicente Blvd, Brentwood. (310) 820-6602. Full facilities; individual evaluation, dance aerobics, massage. Juice bar. Ladies only.

Holiday Harbor Racquetball   **4-G6**
14045 Panay Way, Marina del Rey. (310) 821-1662. Nonmembership, racquetball for fitness.

Holiday Spa Health Clubs
Several Southern California locations. Call (310) 820-7571 for club nearest you. Full facilities; Nautilus equipment and massage.

Jack LaLanne's European Health Spas
Twenty-seven Southern California locations. Call (213) 938-3851 for spa nearest you. Full facilities. Juice bars, makeup products, and free demonstrations.

Manhattan Health Club for Women   2-B7
1829 Sepulveda Blvd, Manhattan Beach. 545-6641. Extensive facilities, including weight training. Nutrition bar.

Marina Athletic Club   **1-D4**
12980 Culver Blvd, Marina del Rey. (310) 301-2582. Indoor/outdoor aerobics classes, sauna, Jacuzzi, pool, tanning salon, jogging track, volleyball.

Nautilus Fitness & Training Centers
Several locations. Call (310) 204-2030 or (213) 488-0095 for center nearest you. Revolutionary equipment (now installed in all good health clubs). "It's torture but it works" is their motto. Nautilus centers offer a variety of membership plans and all facilities are coed.

Paradise Dance & Aerobics   **10-E3**
16571 Ventura Blvd, Encino. (818) 986-1624. Aerobics for physical fitness, plus a variety of modern dance.

Pasadena Athletic Club   **8-C2**
25 W. Walnut Ave, Pasadena. (818) 793-8161. Full facilities; racquetball, tennis, jogging track, and supervised workouts. Family memberships available.

Santa Monica Spectrum 4-A6
1815 Centinela Ave, Santa Monica. (310) 829-6836. Full facilities; racquetball, handball, Nautilus, massage. Private coed club.

Sanwa Health Spa 7-C5
New Otani Hotel, 120 S. Los Angeles St, Little Tokyo. (213) 687-4597, ext 120. Excellent shiatsu massage in a luxurious spa facility.

The Sports Club/LA 5-G5
1835 Sepulveda Blvd, W. LA. (310) 473-1447. Huge, luxurious health and fitness complex. Large coed gym, private women's gym, cardiovascular conditioning center, aerobics, lap pool, yoga, basketball, volleyball, racquetball, fully-equipped spas, fitness evaluation, on-staff physicians and nutritionists, sun deck. Juice bar, deli, grill, sports/TV/seafood bar. Tanning salon, sleep rooms, pro shop, hair salon, nursery, car detailing, and valet parking! Private, limited membership.

The Sports Connection 4-B7
2929 31st St, Santa Monica. (310) 450-4464. Coed. Coed club in Encino. Extensive facilities; strenuous exercise classes, weight training, full Nautilus equipment and racquetball. Nutrition bar.

Voight Fitness & Dance Center 6-D1
980 N. La Cienega Blvd, LA. (310) 854-0741. Emphasis on cardiovascular fitness and muscle tone. The 2-hour advanced aerobics is the hardest in town. Classes for all levels. Low impact and trampoline classes also. Nonmembership (pay per class). Locker rooms, showers.

Women Only 9-D2
4070 Laurel Canyon Blvd, Studio City. (818) 766-5657. Also in Palos Verdes and Woodland Hills. Aerobics, jazz, prenatal and post-injury programs. Steam, whirlpool, sauna, massage, yoga, beauty salon. Private health clubs for women.

SELF-IMPROVEMENT

(See also ALTERNATIVES, Alternative Remedies.)

The Athletic Club 6-D1
8560 Santa Monica Blvd, W. Hollywood. (310) 659-6630. Formerly Jim Morris's Gym. Weight training for men.

Beverly Hills Cosmetic Surgery Medical Group 5-D7
465 N. Roxbury Dr, Beverly Hills. (310) 858-1505. If you really must be improved by this method, these Board Certified surgeons will give free consultations.

Body Builder's Gym 1-C5
2516 Hyperion Ave, LA. (213) 668-0802. Men-only gym for dedicated weight trainers. Several membership plans available.

Body 2200 4-G7
4820 Lincoln Blvd, Marina del Rey. (310) 821-0029. Passive exercise generated by electrical impulses to tone muscles, firm up after weight loss, or accelerate healing. Certified staff.

Carreiro Physical Fitness Studio 6-D1
722 N. La Cienega Blvd, W. Hollywood. (310) 652-3060. Gymnastics designed to build strength and endurance, and to increase flexibility. All ages, all levels.

The Fit Dimension 4-B3
1131 Wilshire Blvd, Santa Monica. (310) 451-3020. Medically supervised health and fitness center run by Santa Monica Hospital Medical Center. Physiologists, nurses, and behavior specialists on staff. Cardiac rehabilitation and conditioning.

Gold's Gym 4-E4
360 Hampton Dr, Venice. (310) 392-3005. World famous body builder's mecca, still producing prize-wining muscular specimens.

Great Shape, A Woman's Health Club 5-F2
11980 San Vicente Blvd, Brentwood. (310) 820-6602. Strenuous exercise classes.

Jazzercise 4-B4
Call (310) 823-6639 for location nearest you. Choreographed jazz-dance routines. Stamina, posture, flexibility, and cardiovascular fitness are considered. Intense, fun classes.

Kinetic Fitness 1-B2
18402 Ventura Blvd, Tarzana. (818) 342-3676. Analysis and advice on any problem relating to body movement. Computer and high-speed photo analysis. Research library. Personalized programs.

Main Street Fitness, Dance, and Aerobic Center 4-C3
2215 Main St, Santa Monica. (310) 396-4747. Jazz funk, step aerobics, power yoga, African and Brazilian dance to live music.

Physiodynamics 1-D4
3655 Motor Ave, LA. (310) 836-2556. Natural exercise to rid body of problems due to bad posture.

Pritikin Longevity Center 4-D3
1910 Ocean Front Walk, Santa Monica. (310) 450-5433. Pritikin PM Centers in Torrance, Pacific Palisades, and Sherman Oaks. Although the late Nathan Pritikin had no academic qualifications in health care, medicine, or nutrition, his 40 years of experience in changing eating and exercise habits to promote health "from the inside out" brought him fame and fortune. A 26-day, live-in program is strict, strenuous, effective, expensive, and successful. Qualified doctors are on the staff.

Sculptures 6-F2
8330 W. 3rd St, LA. (310) 655-5580. Holistic healing techniques. Chiropractic and body-sculpture treatments, fitness training, yoga, seaweed baths, and body brushing. Whew!

Richard Simmons 5-D8
9306 Civic Center Dr, Beverly Hills. (310) 275-4663. This famous former fatty won the hearts of millions through his lighthearted exercise programs on TV. His studio classes use the same exercise techniques to banish the fat (and guilty) person hidden inside.

Renee Taylor   **1-F4**
3969 Pacific Coast Hwy, Torrance. (310) 316-1916. Yoga, nutrition, and longevity training.

Voight Fitness & Dance Center   **6-D1**
980 N. La Cienega Blvd, LA. (310) 854-0741. An advanced fitness system for all levels that combines yoga with dance. Video analysis, special programs for seniors.

Weight Watchers International   **9-E7**
21800 Sutter St, Suite 300, Concord. (800) 473-3300. Well-known organization. Weekly meetings to change bad eating habits through a flexible food program.

DEPARTMENT STORES

Everyday department stores are located in most shopping malls (see also Shopping Malls*). The following stores are recommended for unusually high-quality merchandise and service.*

I. Magnin   **5-E7**
9634 Wilshire Blvd, Beverly Hills. (310) 271-2131. Six Southern California locations. Prestigious and expensive.

May Company Wilshire   **6-G3**
6067 Wilshire Blvd, LA. (213) 938-4211. The best of many locations, this May Company is at the beginning of the "Miracle Mile" district and was part of that original shopping-district project. A beautifully designed, 1940 streamline building.

Neiman-Marcus   **5-E7**
9700 Wilshire Blvd, Beverly Hills; (310) 550-5900. And 49 Fashion Island, Newport Beach; (714) 759-1900. Dependably high class.

Nordstrom   **5-G6**
Westside Pavilion, Pico Blvd at Westwood Blvd, W. LA; (310) 470-6155. And 21500 Victory Blvd, Woodland Hills; (818) 884-6771. Elegant, spacious, well-planned stores with the most efficient, courteous, and friendly staff anywhere.

Robinson's   **7-C3**
*600 W. 7th St, LA; (213) 488-5522. Eight locations, including 9900 Wilshire Blvd, Beverly Hills (**5-E7**); (310) 275-5464. Full department store. Quality brands only. Fashions, accessories, furniture, appliances, etc. *CLOSED Sun.*

Saks Fifth Avenue   **5-E8**
*9600 Wilshire Blvd, Beverly Hills; (310) 275-4211. And 30 Woodland Hills Promenade, Woodland Hills (**1-B2**); (818) 884-6000. West Coast wings of the famous New York mother store. Super service. Classy designer clothes, sportswear, beauty salon. In-house boutiques. *CLOSED Sun.*

Weller Court   **7-C5**
123 S. Weller St, Little Tokyo. (213) 485-1177. Luxury Japanese department store. Sportswear, fashions, jewelry, furs, and accessories. Oriental restaurants.

CHILDREN'S CLOTHES

See KIDS' LA, Children's Shopping, Clothing.

WOMEN'S CLOTHES
Boutiques

Laura Ashley   **5-F6**
Century Square Shopping Center, 10250 Santa Monica Blvd, Century City; (310) 553-0807. Also in Beverly Hills, Westwood, Redondo Beach, and Woodland Hills. Latest additions to an attractive boutique chain that started in the Welsh countryside. Floral prints, cottons, lace, and country charm. Perfumes, toilet accessories, bridal wear, coordinated home furnishings.

Alan Austin Company   **5-D8**
9533 Brighton Way, Beverly Hills. (310) 275-1162. Classic, tailored outfits expertly made from the purest of fabrics. Up-to-the-minute fashions are cleverly designed to stand the test of time. Quality worth paying for. *CLOSED Sun.*

Camp Beverly Hills   **5-D7**
9640 Little Santa Monica Blvd, Beverly Hills. (310) 274-8317. Zany collection of trendy casual clothes and accessories. Practical work clothes and fun fashions to suit all pocketbooks.

Celine   **5-D8**
460 N. Rodeo Dr, Beverly Hills. (310) 273-1243. Exclusive and expensive. One of Rodeo Drive's finest boutiques, it's filled with a breathtaking collection of wearable treasures. *CLOSED Sun.*

Comme Des Folis   **6-D5**
7384 Melrose Ave, LA. (213) 653-5330. One of the most respected names in Europe for stylish, ready-to-wear fashions. The very latest in head-turning, trendsetting designs. Imported shoes and accessories.

d'Crenza Couture   **6-E3**
7407 Beverly Blvd, W. Hollywood. (213) 937-9555. One and only LA outlet for this famous couturier. But there are benefits—here you can buy d'Crenza originals at a savings. Normal retail prices run into thousands of dollars for one dress, this location sells samples (custom-fit on the premises) at reduced prices. (*By appointment only.*)

French Connection   **6-E1**
8214 Santa Monica Blvd, LA. (213) 654-9393. Silk, cotton, and cashmere. Quality fabrics for up-to-the-minute separates, sportswear, and evening wear. Cacharel, Calvin Klein, Ted Lapidus, and Tahari are among the many labels represented here. *CLOSED Sun.*

Giorgio   **5-E8**
327 N. Rodeo Dr, Beverly Hills. 274-0200. An institution on Rodeo Drive. In-house cocktail bar, pool table, and smiling service—all compliments of the house. Designer fashions for men and women. Shoes, accessories, and gifts. Celebrity clientele. Quite a shopping experience, but expect to pay Beverly Hills prices! *CLOSED Sun.*

Greta's   **5-E8**
141 S. Beverly Dr, Beverly Hills. (310) 274-9217. Well-made imports plus local designer fashions in all sizes. Friendly, unaffected staff. Good selection of shoes (including hard-to-fit sizes) and accessories. *CLOSED Sun.*

Hermes of Paris　　**5-D8**
343 N. Rodeo Dr, Beverly Hills. (310) 278-6440.
Fabulous collection of exclusive creations—at
out-of-this-world prices. *CLOSED Sun.*

Jess　　**5-D8**
9484 Brighton Way, Beverly Hills. (310) 276-
7642. Bright primary colors, mirrors, and sparkling tiles set the stage for popular imported
French fashions and accessories. Fun clothes
that jump in and out of fashion. Prices are reasonable (considering the neighborhood) and the
staff is friendly.

Betsey Johnson　　**6-D4**
7311 Melrose Ave, LA; (213) 931-4490. And
2929 Main St, Santa Monica; (310) 452-7911.
Lively boutiques crammed with Betsey's unique
designs. Fun clothes that are feminine and flat-
tering. Wild prints, unusual combinations of fabrics and textures. Always one step ahead.

Judy's　　**5-F6**
100 Century Square Shopping Center, 10250
Santa Monica Blvd, Century City; (310) 277-
1440. Also in Fox Hills Mall and Santa Monica
Place (*see also* Shopping Malls). Great young
fashions, gifts, and accessories. Latest styles,
from dancewear to frilly party frocks. Shoes and
makeup too. Affordable prices, considerate service.

Le Chateau　　**5-D8**
314 N. Beverly Dr, Beverly Hills. (310) 271-9801.
Their own designer clothes made in Europe plus
other designer labels, including Diane Von Furst-
enberg. Styles range from functional office wear
to silk evening dresses. Great selection of
designer shoes for men and women—at below-
average prices. Fittings and alterations on premises.

Maxfield Bleu　　**6-D2**
8825 Melrose Ave, W. Hollywood. (310) 275-
7007. If you really must have the latest trendsetting togs from France (and have the cash to pay
for them), this is the place for you. Hand-knit
chunky sweaters, spiffy shirts, and clingy
dresses—all hot off the fashion pages. Service is
often unnecessarily arrogant. *CLOSED Sun.*

MGA　　**5-D7**
9520 Santa Monica Blvd, Beverly Hills. (310)
550-6299. Their own designer label "Guess?"
has become a trendy tag for flashy dressers.
Soft suedes are used for blouses and skirts imported from France. Good selection of well-
designed fashions to be noticed in. Men's department also.

NaNa　　**4-C3**
1228 3rd St, Santa Monica. (310) 393-7811.
Small and rock 'n' roll trendy. Inexpensive street
clothes and shoes. Fun socks and accessories.

NEO 80　　**6-D4**
7356½ Melrose Ave, W. Hollywood. (213) 852-
9013. The name stands for neomaniac! Very distinctive one-of-a-kind outfits for ladies who like to
be noticed. Modern designs by Lisa Eliot and
Klaus Wille.

Fred Segal　　**6-D4**
8100 Melrose Ave, LA; (213) 651-4129. And 500
Broadway, Santa Monica (**4-C3**); (310) 393-

4477. High-fashion designer clothing—from eye-
catching daywear to trendsetting sportswear.
Both stores carry designer shoes and accessories.

Suite 101　　**5-D8**
270 N. Canon Dr, Beverly Hills. (310) 276-7143.
Beverly Hills elegance with classic designer
fashions and Beverly Hills prices. Sophisticated
gifts and accessories. *CLOSED Sun.*

St. Laurence Paris　　**6-D2**
8208 Santa Monica Blvd, W. Hollywood. (213)
656-8089. Buyers in New York and Europe send
new shipments every six weeks. Designer fashions for men and women, plus a special lingerie
section upstairs. In-house alterations. *CLOSED
Sun.*

Theodore　　**5-D8**
453 N. Rodeo Dr, Beverly Hills. (310) 276-9691.
Lively fashions for trendier socialites. Good selection of separates sold under the store's own
label (DBA). Excellent designer jewelry counter.
CLOSED Sun.

Weathervane II　　**4-A3**
1209 Montana Ave, Santa Monica. (310) 393-
5344. Warm boutique filled with comfortable
clothing and accessories. Pure Shetland sweaters, plaids, tweeds, Victorian linens, and lace.
Carefully selected items—an obvious emphasis
on craftsmanship and quality materials. Pleasing.

Accessories

Emphasis　　**6-D5**
7361 Melrose Ave, LA. (213) 653-7174. The very
latest in fashionable accessories. Creative ideas
to produce a unique look and clever ideas to
flatter every figure. Clothing by local designers is
also carried.

Ferouchi　　**4-B3**
518 Wilshire Blvd, Santa Monica. (310) 451-
1334. Free wardrobe consultations to ensure that
the right accessories are chosen to complement
tastes and life-style. Belts, bags, "art jewelry,"
silks, and footwear plus classic, versatile clothing. *CLOSED Sun.*

So Much and Company　　**6-D1**
8669 Sunset Blvd, W. Hollywood. (310) 652-
4291. Charming little boutique filled with unique
accessories and gifts. Custom-made jewelry,
delightful evening bags. Belts and beadwork.
CLOSED Sun.

Trappings　　**4-A3**
1621 Montana Ave, Santa Monica. (310) 394-
8782. Designer label accessories include hair
ornaments, belts, purses, shoes, and bags. They
will special order hard-to-find items and give
helpful advice on wardrobe updating. *CLOSED
Sun.*

Vintage Clothing

American Rag Cie　　**6-F4**
150 S. La Brea Ave, LA. (213) 935-3154. European and American vintage clothing, carefully
selected in wool, pure silk, leather, and linen.

Extensive selection of designer and brand names. Every item has been dry-cleaned.

Auntie Mame—Clothes of Fame   6-G2
1102 S. La Cienega Blvd, LA. (310) 652-8430. Here's where to buy that bargain fur coat or evening stole. Full range of vintage clothing plus nearly new items from recent years. Everything is in pretty good condition. The owners will reline and repair flaws (where necessary) in their selection of furs. *CLOSED Sun & Mon.*

Eric & Company   6-E4
6915 Melrose Ave, W. Hollywood. (213) 938-6627. Nostalgic outfits from the 1930s, 1940s, and 1950s, including some World War II military outfits.

La Rue Clothes of Yesterday   9-C4
5320 Lankershim Blvd, N. Hollywood. (818) 762-2072. Superb selection of antique clothes in top-notch condition. Furs, evening gowns, prom dresses, and a full range of daywear. Prices are great considering the high quality.

Palace Museum   4-F5
1239 Abbot Kinney Blvd, Venice. (310) 392-9766. Full range of high-quality vintage and antique clothing with an emphasis on day dresses from 1920 to 1960. Reasonable prices.

Paris 1900   4-D4
2703 Main St, Santa Monica. (310) 396-3477. Beautiful Victorian lace bodices, petticoats, and dresses. Gloves, hats, gowns, capes, and jackets from elegant bygone days. A lovely store that also sells stylish art deco furniture. Everything is thoughtfully selected and presented with care.

Repeat Performance   6-D4
318 N. La Brea, W. Hollywood. (213) 938-0609. Handpicked antique clothing and accessories. Silk pajamas, robes, teddies, dresses, and Hawaiian-style prints. Prices are moderate to high. *CLOSED Sun.*

Time After Time   6-D3
7425 Melrose Ave, LA. 653-8463. Beautiful boutique stocked with quality vintage clothing from the 1930s and 1940s plus an unequaled selection of Victorian garments. Ornate evening wear includes real flapper dresses and lovely beaded outfits. Plenty of antique jewelry too. Party rentals are available.

Sports & Leisure Wear

Dance France   6-G1
2503 Main St, Santa Monica. (310) 396-4924. Complete selection of the latest fashion dancewear and workout wear. Body-hugging comfort clothes in bright colors.

Jaeger Sportswear   5-E7
9699 Wilshire Blvd, Beverly Hills. (310) 276-1062. A world-famous name in superior sportswear. Perfectly fashioned knitwear and separates. Tweeds, plaids, mohair, cashmere, and pure new wool. *CLOSED Sun.*

Kirkpatrick Sales Corp.   1-D4
8592 Washington Blvd, Culver City. (310) 839-6455. Long-established emporium of beachwear and swimwear. Guaranteed satisfaction for ev-

ery age. Dancewear, lounge wear, and cover-ups for all occasions.

Mister Frank   6-E1
8801 Santa Monica Blvd, LA. (310) 657-1023. Unusual active sportswear incorporating imaginative design and a flair for great color combinations makes this a very popular stop for pre-cruise shoppers. Pure wool sweaters, silk blouses, and creative custom jewelry. *CLOSED Sun.*

Modasport   1-C3
2924 Beverly Glen Circle, Bel-Air. (310) 475-3665. High-fashion sportswear imported from Europe's top design houses. Stylish displays and appropriately high prices. *CLOSED Mon.*

Discount

(*See also* Thrift & Surplus Outlets.)

Garment District   7-D4
Downtown LA. A section of South Los Angeles Street, between 7th and 9th streets, contains several excellent discount fashion stores. The following are worth seeking out: **Quality Dress Shop** at 772, **The Candy Store** at 724, **Suzanne's Ladies Wear** at 708, and **Ladies Apparel** at 840. The **Cooper Building** at 860 S. Los Angeles Street contains a concentration of over 20 rooms, all filled with wonderful bargains. Just around the corner (at 210 E. 9th Street) is **Fashion Center**, which contains a dozen discount outlets.

The Garment District is located in a rather dusty area of Downtown, frequented by down-and-outs. Parking is difficult and expensive. Considering these factors, why not carpool or take a bus? **The Shopper's Shuttle** is a service for people living outside central LA. Bus trips are arranged especially for groups traveling to this district. Excursions are daylong and very enjoyable (wine and cheese served en route). For information, call (213) 338-1111.

The Back Room   1-C4
8525 S. Pico Blvd, LA. (310) 652-7141. Women's career fashions and designer sportswear at up to 70% off retail.

Loehmann's   6-F3
6220 W. 3rd St, LA; (213) 933-5675. And 19389 Victory Blvd, Reseda; (818) 873-1155. Trademark name for discounted designer fashions (every fashion-conscious woman is relieved to know there's a Loehmann's close at hand). New shipments arrive daily and prices are at least one-third below retail. All major designers are represented. Clothing, bags, hats, scarves, and leather goods.

Marshall's
Call (800) 627-7425 for the nearest of 14 locations. Large clothing stores offering "'brand names for less." Terrific bargains in latest styles for men and women. Clothing, accessories, and shoes.

Off My Back   4-F6
2308 Abbot Kinney Blvd, Venice; (310) 827-4525. And 1908 Lincoln Blvd, Santa Monica;

(310) 399-6212. Racks of bright, fashionable sportswear at wholesale prices.

Sacks SFO   **4-F4**
114 Washington Blvd, Marina del Rey; (310) 301-2103. Also in Culver City, Studio City, Tarzana, La Brea, West LA, and Hollywood. Top-quality fashions for men and women at huge savings. Raw silk, linen, mohair, and gabardine separates plus a selection of evening wear.

Shelly's   **5-G5**
2083 Westwood Blvd, W. LA. (310) 475-1400. Dance and exercise wear at wholesale prices. First-quality merchandise, brand names. Children's wear, men's wear, and shoes.

Wilson's Outlet Store   **9-D6**
1033 N. Hollywood Way, Burbank. (818) 841-7789. Discount outlet for the Wilson's House of Suede and Leather stores. Incredible values in top-quality leather and suede clothing. Some accessories too.

Ethnic

(*See also* Shopping Centers.)

Oriental Silk Company   **6-E2**
8377 Beverly Blvd, LA. (213) 651-2323. Beautiful hand-embroidered silk blouses and gowns from China. Brocade jackets, painted silk scarves, beaded sweaters. *CLOSED Sun.*

Furs

Edward Borovay   **7-D4**
635 S. Olive St, LA. (213) 622-7809. Manufacturer's showroom offering the largest selection of men's and women's furs on the West Coast. *CLOSED Sun.*

Dicker & Dicker   **5-E8**
400 S. Beverly Dr, 2nd floor, Beverly Hills. (310) 553-9211. Exclusive and expensive "furs by the master." *CLOSED Sat pm & Sun.*

Mannis   **5-E8**
323 S. Robertson Blvd, Beverly Hills. (213) 272-7846. Full-service furrier. Custom designing, restyling, repairs, and storage. *CLOSED Sun.*

Harry Musin Fur Salon   **5-G6**
10747 W. Pico Blvd, Westwood. (310) 475-4544. Manufacturer of handcrafted furs selling direct to the public since 1921. Cold storage vault on premises. Cleaning, remodeling, and repairing. *CLOSED Sun.*

I. Rubin Inc.
(310) 271-5788. Also in Paris and New York. In business for over 60 years, this is the ultimate fur salon (they even have bonded messengers on hand to collect your furs for summer storage). Custom designing, restyling, cleaning, and glazing. Large stock. Fur rentals. *By appointment.*

Somper Furs   **5-E8**
150 S. Rodeo Dr, Beverly Hills. (310) 273-5262. Extensive collection of designer furs. Full service. Good men's selection. *CLOSED Sun.*

Wild Bill's Furs   **6-E1**
534 N. La Cienega Blvd, LA. (310) 657-5151.

Fur coats, jackets, skins, pillows, rugs, you name it. Custom orders and repairs.

Handbags

Beverly Hills Luggage   **5-D8**
404 N. Beverly Dr, Beverly Hills. (310) 273-5885. In business since 1879. Cartier, Atlas, and Louis Vuitton are just a few of the labels here. *CLOSED Sun.*

Gucci   **5-D8**
347 N. Rodeo Dr, Beverly Hills. (310) 278-3451. Need we say more? Everything has that distinctive trademark, acknowledged and flaunted throughout the world. (The doorman at this location is charming, welcoming shoppers and browsers alike.) *CLOSED Sun.*

Lazar's Fine Leather Goods   **1-B3**
14528 Ventura Blvd, Sherman Oaks. (818) 784-1355. Long-established, great selection. Custom work, repairs, gold stamping. Multilingual staff. *CLOSED Sun.*

Weiner's   **4-C3**
Santa Monica Place Mall, Santa Monica; (310) 394-7049. And 75 Bullock's Fashion Square, Sherman Oaks; (818) 981-3380. Authorized dealer for Hartmann, Tourister, French, Lark, etc. Quality service and repairs.

Westwood Luggage   **5-E4**
940 Westwood Blvd, Westwood. (310) 208-7900. All top brands, including Diro, Givenchy, Cardin, and Franco Pugi. Free initials and gift wrapping with every leather purchase.

Lingerie

Frederick's of Hollywood   **6-C5**
6608 Hollywood Blvd, Hollywood. (213) 466-5151. Well worth a visit. This notorious store is filled with imaginative undergarments and sensual stage wear. The best surprise is finding they have a full range of great-fitting undies for everyone. Salespeople are experienced and very helpful. Whether you're looking for a gold Lurex g-string, fishnet stockings, or a basic bra, you'll find it here—and the staff won't bat an eyelid. (Interesting selection of men's loungewear too.)

Juel Park   **6-G1**
17940 Rancho St, Encino. (310) 276-3292. Sheer luxury. Exclusive lingerie, custom-made. French lace and fine silks are used for beautifully handcrafted undergarments, robes, and accessories. *CLOSED Sat & Sun.*

Olga   **1-B3**
15750 Strathern St, Van Nuys. (818) 994-7963. Famous lingerie line. Styles and colors to suit all tastes.

Playmates of Hollywood   **6-C5**
6438 Hollywood Blvd, Hollywood. (213) 464-7636. An eye-popping selection of X-rated undergarments and slinky stage wear. Belly dancer's costumes, garter belts, gem-studded stockings, flimsy baby dolls, scant hotpants, and less!

Private Moments   **5-G6**
10800 Pico Blvd, W. LA (in the Westside Pavilion); (310) 470-8812. Other locations in Topanga and Montclair. Extremely pretty lingerie and underwear. Romantic silks and satins trimmed with antique lace and ribbons. Very feminine.

Trashy Lingerie   **6-E1**
402 N. La Cienega Blvd, LA. (310) 652-4543. Unpretentious, sexy lingerie for the more adventurous woman. Some beautiful fabrics and styles, all guaranteed to make Mother blush. *CLOSED Sun.*

Leather Clothes

Good Old Times American Clothing   **6-D3**
7739 Santa Monica Blvd, W. Hollywood. (213) 654-7103. Good stock of fashionable leatherwear imported from England. Fitted pants, leather jeans, and stylish jackets in unusual colors, for men and women. (Vintage rock 'n' roll clothing too, all dry-cleaned and mended.)

Leatherbound   **5-E4**
1009 Broxton Ave, Westwood; (310) 208-3810. Eight other LA locations including Santa Monica Place and Century City. Successful chain selling a full range of leather clothing for men and women.

North Beach Leather   **6-C1**
8500 Sunset Blvd, Hollywood. (213) 652-3224. High-quality, custom-made leather garments. Unusual styles. Beads, feathers, and appliqués are used to enhance natural suede and leather skins. Exclusive and pricey.

Maternity

Reborn Maternity   **1-B3**
13954 Ventura Blvd, Sherman Oaks. (818) 907-7515. Large selection of contemporary maternity fashions from New York. Silk and velvet evening wear, stylish daywear, and business attire.

Shoes

Bally of Switzerland   **5-E8**
340 N. Rodeo Dr, Beverly Hills. (310) 271-0666. Luxurious shoe salon containing some of the world's finest leather shoes. *CLOSED Sun.*

Bea's Shoe Nook   **1-D3**
3505 Motor Ave, LA. (310) 559-0435. This is the place for those impossible-to-please ladies who drive sales assistants to distraction! Literally hundreds of colors and styles, from evening pumps to thigh-high boots. An added bonus: most shoes are priced below retail.

Birkenstock Footprints   **5-E4**
10912 Le Conte Ave, Westwood; (310) 208-7307. And 8629 Melrose Ave, W. Hollywood; (310) 855-0744. Also 14447 Ventura Blvd, Sherman Oaks; (818) 788-8443. Comfort sandals that mold to your feet, plus clogs and other natural footwear. Elegance is not a prime factor!

Church's English Shoes   **7-D3**
623 W. 7th St, LA; (213) 626-1331. And 9633 Brighton Way, Beverly Hills; (310) 275-1263. Distinctive, expertly crafted shoes for men and women. *CLOSED Sun.*

Erik's   **6-C1**
8673 Sunset Blvd, Hollywood. (310) 655-7732. Large selection of designer shoes and handbags. Beautiful shoe fashions from Europe. Watch for Erik's terrific shoe sales (three pairs for the price of two).

Jay Jordan   **5-F6**
33 Century Square Shopping Center, Century City. (310) 470-6990. Renowned for quality, style, and fit.

Vin Baker   **4-C3**
284 Santa Monica Place Mall, Santa Monica. (310) 394-7054. Dainty imports in bright leathers and suedes. Espadrilles, evening slippers, walking shoes and boots.

Zodiac   **6-D4**
7578 Melrose Ave, LA; (213) 852-0385. Also in Tarzana and Santa Monica. Wild styles for flashy feet. Large inventory of designer shoes and boots that really make a fashion statement.

Unusual Sizes

Chic Shoes   **1-D4**
10746 Washington Blvd, Culver City. (310) 836-2568. Fashionable footwear for extra-wide feet.

The Forgotten Woman   **5-E7**
9683 Wilshire Blvd, Beverly Hills. (310) 859-8829. "Pretty dressing in larger sizes." Evening gowns, day dresses, separates, cocktail dresses, coats, and pants—all made in lovely pure fabrics and fashioned to flatter fuller figures. *CLOSED Sun.*

The Yellow Balloon   **1-E4**
2140 W. Artesia Blvd, Torrance. (310) 538-4257. This store is a delight for both petite and oversized ladies who wish to keep up with fashion trends. Garey Petites, Tomboy, Campus Casuals, and Loubella are all here—and at very affordable prices. *CLOSED Sun.*

MEN'S CLOTHES

Boutiques

Battaglia   **5-E8**
306 N. Rodeo Dr, Beverly Hills. (310) 276-7184. An Italian men's boutique filled with well-tailored, well-fitting, ready-to-wear fashions (as seen in *Gentlemen's Quarterly*). *CLOSED Sun.*

Carroll & Company   **5-D8**
466 N. Rodeo Dr, Beverly Hills. (310) 273-9060. Internationally known and respected for the highest in quality and service, Carroll & Company caters to top executives, statesmen, and (of course) movie stars. There is a ladies department too. *CLOSED Sun.*

Clacton & Frinton **6-E1**
731 N. La Cienega Blvd, LA. (310) 652-2957.
Suits, jackets, pants, and shirts designed by English fashion designer Michael Anderson, who
travels to Europe twice a year to purchase his
fabrics. Off-the-peg and custom-made clothing
in distinctive, easy-to-wear designs. This small
boutique caters to a loyal clientele—some of
whom collect Clacton & Frinton clothes as if they
were paintings.

Cyril's Beverly Hills **5-D8**
370 N. Beverly Dr, Beverly Hills. (310) 278-1330.
European designers—such as Carlo Palazzi,
Valentino, and Michael Axel—are all represented in this distinctive boutique for better-
dressed gentlemen. *CLOSED Sun.*

Giorgio **5-E8**
327 N. Rodeo Dr, Beverly Hills. (310) 278-7312.
Perhaps the most famous fashion house on Rodeo Drive. Assistants will fall over themselves to
please. To add to your comfort while you shop
there's a free bar and a pool table to play at. Oh,
and there's a great selection of quality clothing
and accessories—for that distinctive Giorgio
look. *CLOSED Sun.*

Gucci **5-E8**
347 N. Rodeo Dr, Beverly Hills. (310) 278-3451.
Quality assured—worldwide. Not exactly trendy
but very dependable. Timeless fashions styled
for fit and function. *CLOSED Sun.*

Rudnick's **5-E7**
222 Beverly Dr, Beverly Hills. (310) 278-0155. In
business almost 40 years, Rudnick's is a one-
stop shop for men and boys. Designer labels
abound, and styles will accommodate all tastes.
Accessories include shoes, ties, and even sporting goods. *CLOSED Sun.*

Fred Segal **6-E1**
8100 Melrose Ave, LA; (310) 651-4129. And 500
Broadway, Santa Monica (**4-C3**); (310) 393-
4477. High-fashion designer clothing—from eye-
catching daywear to trendsetting sportswear.
Both stores carry designer shoes and accessories.

Theodore Man **5-D8**
451 N. Rodeo Dr, Beverly Hills. (310) 274-8029.
Trendsetting designer fashions from Europe. An
unpretentious, inviting little store that makes its
own statement here on Rodeo. *CLOSED Sun.*

Weathervane for Men **4-A3**
1132 Montana Ave, Santa Monica. (310) 395-
0397. Country casuals, woven tweeds, and distinctive sportswear by Jaeger, Cacharel, and
Calvin Klein. Everything is of the highest quality
and is presented in a comfortable, unhurried environment. *CLOSED Sun.*

Custom Tailoring

Richard Bennett **6-G1**
3710 S. Robertson Blvd, LA. (310) 836-5682.
Serving the Beverly Hills gentleman for over 35
years. Specialist in made-to-order apparel.
CLOSED Sun.

Executive Tailored Clothes **6-F1**
147 S. Robertson Blvd, Beverly Hills. (310) 657-
8487. Greg Chapman will make up a personal
pattern for each new client to eliminate the need
for continual fittings or further fittings for new garments. (Providing of course you watch your
waistline!) *CLOSED Sat & Sun.*

Rive Gauche Tailoring **6-E1**
8899 Beverly Blvd, Suite 103, LA. (310) 271-
9109. European and American designs to suit
personal tastes. Alterations and restyling.

Tartaglia Bros. **5-E7**
9905 Santa Monica Blvd, Beverly Hills. (310)
553-9475. Custom tailoring using the best in imported fabrics. Guaranteed work and "no pay-
ment until garment is completed." *CLOSED Sun.*

Discount Clothing

The Factory **7-D4**
8060 S. Los Angeles St, LA. (213) 622-7800.
Large selection of quality, up-tempo fashions
and shoes. Flying jackets, blazers, dress slacks,
latest shirts and sweaters plus a good selection
of shoes (some samples).

Rick Pallack **1-B3**
4554 Sherman Oaks Ave, Sherman Oaks. (818)
789-7000. Latest imported fashions from France
and Italy plus top New York designer fashions at
up to 50% below retail.

Sacks SFO **4-F5**
114 Washington Blvd, Marina del Rey. (310)
301-2103. Also in Culver City, Tarzana, Studio
City, and Hollywood. Latest fashions in raw silk,
cotton, and pure wool at bargain prices. Designer labels fill the racks from wall to wall. Emphasis on easy-to-wear fashions.

Hats

The Maddest Hatter **4-C3**
325 Santa Monica Place, Santa Monica. (310)
451-4287. All shapes and sizes plus some truly
mad hats.

Shaunzo's Hat City **1-D4**
4431 S. Crenshaw Blvd, LA. (213) 294-6929.
"One thousand and one hats." Every possible
style for men and women. *CLOSED Sun.*

Vallerio Marc Designs Millinery **5-E7**
9865 Santa Monica Blvd, Beverly Hills. 553-
9177. Exclusive custom millinery. *CLOSED Sun.*

Leather

(*See also* Women's Clothes, Leather Clothes, *for
additional outlets catering to both men and
women.*)

Hart Marc Taylors **5-D8**
9424 Dayton Way, Suite 204, Beverly Hills. (310)
275-5733. High-quality, custom-made leather
and suede apparel. Alterations. *CLOSED Sat &
Sun.*

Jackie Robbin's Leather Waves **1-D1**
3835 S. Cross Creek Rd, Malibu. (310) 456-

8321. Made-to-order leather and suede garments. *CLOSED Sun.*

Rentals

Bruin Tuxedo Shop   **5-E4**
10970 Le Conte Ave, Westwood. (310) 208-8755. Tuxedos, cutaways, tails, and accessories for all formal occasions. *CLOSED Sun.*

House of Uniforms   **5-D8**
334 N. Beverly Dr, Beverly Hills. (310) 273-0700. Morning suits, dinner jackets, tuxedos, and formal accessories. Designer labels available for rental. Resident tailor will make alterations as necessary. *CLOSED Sun.*

Tuxedo Center   **6-C4**
7360 Sunset Blvd, Hollywood; (213) 874-4200. And 250 S. Lake Ave, Pasadena (**8-C4**); (310) 796-4651. Large selection of formal wear always in stock. *CLOSED Sun.*

Shirts—Custom & Ready-to-Wear

Alex Custom Shirtmaker of Paris   **6-F1**
328 N. La Peer Dr, Beverly Hills. (310) 276-3897. Distinguished shirts for those who can afford them. Mr. Alex holds the secret to collars that never wrinkle. *CLOSED Sat & Sun.*

De Mir   **9-F1**
12608 Ventura Blvd, Studio City. (818) 984-1280. Each made-to-measure shirt is individually cut and finished on the premises.

The Shirt Tale   **1-C6**
5128 Valley Blvd, LA. (213) 227-1919. Custom-made shirts from a choice of over 300 fabrics. Personal fittings in home or office, upon request.

Jack Varney   **5-D8**
268 N. Beverly Dr, Beverly Hills. (310) 278-4500. Custom shirt designer with a huge celebrity clientele. Shirts are tailored to suit individuals and need not be outrageously expensive. *CLOSED Sun.*

Barbara Williams Cravats   **6-F3**
Farmer's Market, W. 3rd St at Fairfax Ave, LA. (213) 933-0600. Designer shirts by Dior, Excello, and Countess Mara.

Shoes

Bally of Switzerland   **5-E8**
340 N. Rodeo Dr, Beverly Hills. (310) 271-0666. Guaranteed quality and distinctive styling. *CLOSED Sun.*

Church's English Shoes   **5-E7**
9633 Brighton Way, Beverly Hills. (310) 275-1263. "Considered one of the world's finest quality men's footwear"—and they're right. These shoes are built to last. *CLOSED Sun.*

DiFabrizio Bottega   **6-F2**
8216 W. 3rd St, LA. (213) 655-5248. Custom shoes by champion shoemakers for 20 years. *CLOSED Sun.*

Sportswear & Leisurewear

Banana Republic   **4-E4**
2905 Main St, Santa Monica; (310) 392-8349. Also in Beverly Hills, Pasadena, and South Bay Galleria. "Travel and Safari Clothing." These interesting stores, with their pith-helmeted staff, resemble African hunting lodges. The predominantly khaki clothing is made from the best raw materials and is dependably durable.

Surplus Clothing

Army & Navy Surplus   **1-B3**
6179 Van Nuys Blvd, Van Nuys; (818) 781-3500. And 7116 Reseda Blvd, Reseda (**1-B2**); (818) 344-0237. Great for hard-wearing functional clothes. Socks, hats, gloves, etc. (often 100% wool or cotton), are great for the outdoorsman.

California Surplus Mart   **6-C6**
6263 Santa Monica Blvd, Hollywood. (213) 465-1002. Huge surplus outlet for pants, shirts, down jackets, Western wear, and fashionable army clothing.

Mort's Surplus Mart   **1-B4**
503 N. Victory Blvd, Burbank. (213) 849-3744. Motorcycle apparel, survival equipment, coveralls, jeans, jackets, vests, shoes, and boots. Large inventory of camping and backpacking clothing and equipment.

Ties

Byllee Custom Ties   **6-F2**
8323 W. 3rd St, LA. (213) 653-8648. Ties are made out of fine imported silks to customer specifications. *CLOSED Sun.*

Unusual Sizes

Beverly Hills Big & Tall   **5-D8**
9687 Wilshire Blvd, Beverly Hills. (310) 274-9468. Fashionable designer clothing by Dior, Lanvin, and Donald Brooks.

Joseph's   **7-C5**
238 E. 1st St, LA. (213) 626-1830. Specialists in short and extra-short clothing, including portly sizes. Accessories to complement.

Zeeman's   **1-B5**
215 S. Brand Blvd, Glendale. (818) 244-2726. Catering exclusively to big and tall men. A full range of business and sportswear up to size 60. *CLOSED Sun.*

Western Wear

Falconhead Boots, Belts, and Buckles   5-F2
11191 San Vicente Blvd, Brentwood. (310) 471-7075. Custom-made boots and matching accessories. Ornate buckles and jewelry, clothing.

Howard & Phil's Western Wear   **4-C3**
189 Santa Monica Place Mall, Santa Monica. (310) 395-9015. Large selection of quality boots and Western wear.

King's   **1-B3**
6455 Van Nuys Blvd, Van Nuys. (818) 785-2586. Huge selection of casual Western clothing and

dancewear. Hard-to-find sizes always in stock. Hats, leather jackets, and boots too. *CLOSED Sun.*

FOOD

Baked Goods

The Buttery   **4-E4**
2906 Main St, Santa Monica. (310) 399-3000. Hot croissants, brioches, and crumbly chocolate chip cookies—all fresh from the oven. Homemade pasta, sauces, cheesecakes, and whole grain breads.

Elsyee Boulangerie Patisserie   **5-D3**
1099 Gayley Ave, Westwood. (310) 208-6505. The smell of freshly baked French bread and just-brewed coffee lightens the hearts of Village office workers each morning. A variety of croissants includes cheese, chocolate, and almond. French pastries and cheesecakes too.

Hansen Cakes   **5-E8**
193 S. Beverly Dr, Beverly Hills. (310) 273-3759. Long-established and trusted to create unique cakes in all shapes, sizes, and colors for every possible occasion. Only the very best ingredients are used. *CLOSED Sun & Mon.*

La Mousse   **5-F4**
11162 La Grange Ave, W. LA. (310) 478-6051. Amazing mousse—in every flavor imaginable, from cappuccino and amaretto to pecan and almond fudge. Also available are lemon tortes, pecan pies, New York cheesecakes, and carrot cakes. *CLOSED Sun.*

Le Petit Four   **6-D1**
8654 Sunset Blvd, LA. (310) 652-3863. Gorgeous petit fours, French pastries (splendid Napoleons and eclairs), fruit tarts, and miniature quiches. Good selection of caviars plus imported chocolates and wines.

Miss Grace Lemon Cake Co.   **10-E2**
16571 Ventura Blvd, Encino; (818) 995-1976. And 422 N. Canon Dr, Beverly Hills (**6-G1**); (310) 274-2879. Mousse pies, fudges, luscious desserts, and lemon cakes that defy description. Shipping service. *CLOSED Sun.*

Paris Pastry   **5-F4**
1448 Westwood Blvd, W. LA (310) 474-8888. French breads, pastries, and sumptuous cakes that taste as good as they look. Try their chocolate Grand Marnier cake. *CLOSED Sun.*

Pioneer Boulangerie   **4-D3**
2012 Main St, Santa Monica. (310) 399-1405. A constant flow of customers crowds the counter at this large beachside bakery. Sourdough, French, wheat, and rye loaves come hot from the oven in a variety of shapes and sizes. Excellent pastries, cakes, and truffles are also available. Adjoining wine-and-gourmet shops, restaurant, bar, deli, and large patio cafe.

Michel Richard   **6-G1**
310 S. Robertson Blvd, Beverly Hills. (310) 275-5707. When it became apparent that customers were devouring their purchases before reaching the shop door, Michel Richard installed a few tables to accommodate. Probably the best French pastries on the West Coast. (*See also* RESTAURANTS, Beverly Hills & Century City, French.)

Ethnic Foods

Los Angeles has a truly international population. Immigrants have enriched the city with their customs and exotic fare. The following markets stock authentic and hard-to-find produce.

Chinese
Golden Dragon, 960 N. Broadway, LA. (213) 626-2039.
Hong Kong Low, 943 N. Broadway, LA. (213) 628-6217.
Kowloon Market, 750 N. Hill St, LA. (213) 488-0264.
Kwong on Lung, 680 N. Spring St, LA. (213) 628-1069.
Man Wah Imports, 758 New High St, LA. (213) 628-7490.
La Mexicana Market, 2090 Santa Fe Ave, Long Beach. (310) 432-2715.
Ten Ren Tea, 726 Hill St, LA. (213) 626-8844.

Italian
Bay City Imports, 1517 Lincoln Blvd, Santa Monica. (310) 395-8279.
Claro's Italian Market, 1003 E. Valley Blvd, San Gabriel. (818) 288-2026.
Dominic's, 8301 Santa Monica Blvd, W. Hollywood. (213) 654-1214.
Little Joe's Grocery, 900 N. Broadway, LA. (213) 489-4900.
Sorrento Market, 5518 Sepulveda Blvd, Culver City. (310) 391-7654.

Japanese
Enbun Co., 124 Japanese Village Plaza, LA. (213) 680-3280.
Granada, 1820 Sawtelle Blvd, W. LA. (310) 479-0931.
Mikawaya, 118 E. 1st St, LA. (213) 624-1681.
Modern Food Market, 332 E. 2nd St, LA. (213) 680-9595.
Safe & Save Market, 2030 Sawtelle Blvd, W. LA. (310) 479-3810.
Yaohan, 333 S. Alameda St, LA. (213) 687-6699.

Korean
East-West Market, 3300 W. 8th St, LA. (213) 380-3977.
Far East Oriental Market, 8848 Lankershim Blvd, Sun Valley. (818) 767-1408.
New Market, 19104 S. Norwalk Blvd, Artesia. (310) 860-2931.

Latino
Catalina's, 1070 N. Western Ave, LA. (213) 461-2535. Argentinian.
El Mercado, 3425 E. 1st St, LA. (213) 268-3451. Mexican.
Grand Central Market, 317 S. Broadway, LA. (213) 624-2378. Mexican.

Guatemalan Imports, 2214 W. 7th St, LA. (213) 487-4340. Guatemalan.

La Spanola, 2020 Lomita Blvd, Lomita. (310) 539-0455. Spanish.

Liborio, 864 S. Vermont Ave, LA. (213) 386-1458. South American, Cuban, Guatemalan, and Salvadoran.

Rincon Chileno, 4354 Melrose Ave, LA. (310) 666-6075. Chilean.

Middle Eastern

Al Hilal Market, 3025 S. Vermont Ave, LA. (213) 731-0868.

Bezjian's, 4725 Santa Monica Blvd, LA. (213) 663-1503.

Brashov's, 1301 N. Vermont Ave, LA. (213) 660-0309.

C & K Imports, 2771 W. Pico Blvd, LA. (213) 737-2970.

Islamic Food Mart, 3025 S. Vermont Ave, LA. (213) 731-0868.

Philippines

Filipino Market, 2569 Santa Fe Ave, Long Beach. (310) 426-3509.

Lorenzana Supermarket, 627 N. Vermont Ave, LA. (213) 664-9901.

Phil-Asian Food Market, 3124 W. 8th St, LA. (213) 383-7950.

Philippine Food Center, 1131 W. Temple St, LA. (213) 250-7528.

Thai

Bangkok Market, 4757 Melrose Ave, LA. (213) 662-9705.

Vietnamese

Ai Hoa Supermarket, 860 N. Hill St, LA. (213) 629-8121.

Hoa Fong Market, 22200 Main St, Carson. (213) 513-8031.

Hong Kong Supermarket, 717 New High St, LA. (213) 617-8661.

Gourmet & Specialty Foods

Bit of Sweetland   **6-F1**
8560 W. 3rd St, W. Hollywood. (310) 275-5895. No sugar-blues here! A chocolate paradise oozing with calorie-laden pleasures. Huge selection of homemade and imported chocolate specialties. Fresh-roasted coffee too.

Brentwood Village Market   **5-E2**
11725 Barrington Court, Brentwood. (310) 476-1233. Excellent domestic and imported food and produce. Premium-quality gourmet items including prime poultry and meats.

Chalet Gourmet   **6-C3**
7880 Sunset Blvd, Hollywood. (213) 874-6301. Lovely gourmet market. Huge selection of imported and domestic delicacies to please the palate. Superior wines at reasonable prices. Friendly service.

The Continental Shop   **6-G8**
1619 Wilshire Blvd, Santa Monica. (310) 453-8655. In business over 36 years. European gourmet imports: candies, chocolate, selected groceries. Also books, newspapers, and travel aids.

Farmers Market   **6-F3**
6333 W. 3rd St (at Fairfax Ave), LA. (213) 933-9211. A wondrous collection of shops, market stalls, and restaurants filled with international delights. Among the dozens of special food outlets the following are highly recommended: Mr. K's Gourmet Foods, for fresh-roasted coffee beans and hard-to-find spices; Bisbano's Fruit & Produce, for exotic fruits and fresh herbs; Le Mart Pie Shop for delicious French fruit pies and pastries; Magee's, for homemade relishes and excellent peanut butter. (*See also* Shopping Centers.)

Fireside Market   **4-B3**
1425 Montana Ave, Santa Monica. (310) 451-5743. A neighborhood institution. This small but superior supermarket has catered to Santa Monica's elite for over 30 years. Quality is dependably high. Excellent meat and poultry, fresh produce, and a huge inventory of wines and spirits.

Hugo's Fine Meats   **6-D1**
8401 Santa Monica Blvd, LA. (213) 654-3993. Gourmet groceries and superior meats, including milk-fed veal. Wines, cheeses, and an attractive restaurant.

Irvine Ranch Farmer's Market   **6-E1**
142 S. San Vicente Blvd, LA (in the Beverly Center); (310) 657-1931. Also in Northridge, Woodland Hills, and several Orange County locations. A large, upmarket grocery store where everything is displayed as a work of art. Gourmet grocery items are stacked alongside familiar goods, wines are matched to suitable cheeses. Excellent fresh meats and fish, super-fresh produce.

Le Marmiton   **4-A3**
1327 Montana Ave, Santa Monica. (310) 393-7716. Savor the aroma. A real piece of France to satisfy cravings for just about every taste you remember her by. Rillettes, galantines, celery root remoulade, stuffed crepes, and seasoned salads. Quiches, soups, pastries, desserts, and special daily entrees to take home, heat, and eat. CLOSED Mon.

Pasta Etc.   **6-D1**
8650 Sunset Blvd, LA. (213) 854-0094. Imaginative pasta dishes (hot or cold), roasts, meatballs, seafood salads, imported cheeses, and wonderful desserts. A truly superior outlet for gourmet Italian foods.

Robin Rose   **4-E4**
215 Rose Ave, Venice; (310) 392-4921. Also in Westside Pavilion (**5-G6**), Rodeo Collection (**5-D7**), Garden Grove, and Arcadia. Superlative ice cream—the best in LA (if not the world) and irresistible sorbets. Rich, creamy, homemade indulgences. Not the regular kid's stuff either; they lace their cones with Cointreau, Kahlua, and other liqueurs. Homemade candy plus masterful raspberry chocolate truffles.

Safe and Save Market   **5-G4**
2030 Sawtelle Blvd, W. LA. (310) 479-3810. Oriental food worshipers love this amazing little market filled with imported delicacies from China, Japan, and Hawaii. Traditional fish and meats are cut to order.

Santa Glen Market   **5-F6**
10407 Santa Monica Blvd, W. LA. (310) 474-4317. Beautifully displayed gourmet produce, extensive bakery, fresh flower department, and a deli that sells the world's best barbecued chicken.

Trader Joe's   **1-D4**
10850 National Blvd, W. LA. (310) 470-1917. Also 18 other locations in LA County. Fascinating assortment of gourmet, imported, and discounted items. Great bargains on wine and cheeses. Health food, baked goods, frozen foods, and confections are also carried.

Tudor House British Center   **4-C3**
1403 2nd St, Santa Monica. (310) 451-4107. A real English tearoom serving traditional fare (including pots of tea by the dozen), and a store stuffed with biscuits, jams, marmalades, teas, sauces, puddings, pastries, sausages, cakes, and confectionary. They bake their own bread, pastries, and scones and import real English bacon, beers, china, and collectibles. Newspapers and magazines are usually available. *CLOSED Mon.*

Health Foods

Along with outdoor activities to promote fitness, the number of health food outlets in Los Angeles has grown significantly over the last few years. Most stock organically grown foods, bulk grains, natural dairy products, beauty aids, and a large selection of nutritional supplements. Stores are generally small, with friendly, helpful salespeople; some stores even have a nutrition expert on hand to give advice.

The following stores are particularly recommended.

Erewhon Natural Foods   **6-E3**
7660 Beverly Blvd, LA. (213) 655-5441. Grains, seeds, macrobiotic foods, and produce. Nutritional information, own products.

Mrs. Gooch's Natural Foods Ranch Markets   **4-C7**
3476 Centinela Ave, W. LA; (310) 391-5209. Also in Northridge, (818) 701-5122; Hermosa Beach, (310) 376-6931; Sherman Oaks, (818) 762-5548; Glendale, (818) 240-9350; and Beverly Hills. One-stop health foods. Vitamins, produce, grains, and naturally grown meats, free of hormones and additives. Books and gifts.

Nature Mart   **1-C5**
2080 Hillhurst Ave, LA. (213) 660-0052. Complete selection of purest health foods. Produce direct from farmer; vitamins discounted 10-50%.

One Life Natural Foods   **4-E5**
3001 Main St, Santa Monica. (310) 392-4501. Superior produce, grains, and vitamins. Huge selection of bulk spices, and 335 different herbs.

Quinn's Nutritional Centers   **6-D4**
8468 Melrose Ave, LA. (213) 651-5950. Four locations. Health food supermarket. Excellent produce, vitamins, cosmetics, appliances.

Wines & Spirits

Beverly Hills Liquor Castle   **5-E8**
212 S. Beverly Dr, Beverly Hills. (310) 273-6000. One of the largest selections in the world. Telephone orders taken until midnight. Prompt, free delivery. *CLOSED Sun.*

Duke of Bourbon   **1-A2**
20908 Roscoe Blvd, Canoga Park. (818) 341-1234. Specializing in French Burgundies and rare California wines.

Trader Joe's
See Gourmet & Specialty Foods.

Vendome Liquor & Wine Shops
Several locations. Call (310) 276-9463 for shop nearest you. Reliable and affordable. Always a huge selection at below-average prices.

Wine 'n Liquor Basket   **1-B3**
4454 Van Nuys Blvd, Sherman Oaks. (818) 981-6111. Quite a store; over 1,000 wines, imported beers, and liqueurs. Gourmet gift baskets, engraved bottles.

The Wine Merchant   **5-E7**
9701 Santa Monica Blvd, Beverly Hills. (310) 278-7322. Large selection of domestic and imported wines and spirits, including some notable vintages. Gift baskets, cheeses, free delivery.

HOME

Bath

Altman's Il Bagno   **6-E1**
8919 Beverly Blvd, W. Hollywood. (310) 274-5896. Outstanding range of gorgeous bathroom accessories plus inspiring marble bathtubs, toilets, and bidets. Unusual colors and latest designs. Kitchen fittings too. *CLOSED Sat & Sun.*

China & Housewares

Bobi Leonard   **4-E4**
2801 Main St, Santa Monica. (310) 399-3251. Two locations on Main Street jam-packed with imported and domestic adornments for house and home. Lovely ornaments, vases, wall hangings, unusual baskets, cane chairs, wind chimes, silk flowers, and much more. Interior design service.

Margaret Cavigga Quilt Collection   **6-E1**
8648 Melrose Ave, W. Hollywood. (310) 659-3020. Hundreds of handmade quilts in stock. Custom quilts, appraisals, rentals. American folk art, shawls, and antique quilts. *CLOSED Sun.*

Correia Glass Factory   **4-C3**
711 Colorado Ave, Santa Monica. (310) 394-7300. A renowned studio owned by Steve Correia, whose designs have rapidly become collector's items. Beautiful creations in unusual colors and textures. Studio work and limited editions. *CLOSED Sat & Sun.*

Cottura   **6-D4**
7215 Melrose Ave, LA. (213) 933-1928. Imported, handmade ceramics from Italy, Sicily,

and Portugal. Urns, cachepots, plates, and antique reproductions. Giovanni Desimone collection. Worldwide shipping service.

Frette   5-D8
499 N. Rodeo Dr, Beverly Hills. (310) 273-8540. Finest quality linens from Italy to enhance bedroom, bathroom, and table. *CLOSED Sun.*

Geary's   5-D8
351 N. Beverly Dr, Beverly Hills. (310) 273-4741. Look no further for the perfect wedding gift. Wedgwood, Spode, Royal Doulton, and Limoge are all here—at a price, of course. They also carry quality cookware and unique gadgets. *CLOSED Sun.*

Montana Mercantile   4-B3
1500 Montana Ave, Santa Monica. (310) 451-1418. Large and airy and stocked with the finest cookware from Europe and Asia. This top-notch culinary center also offers (participatory) cooking classes, often with demonstrations by guest chefs. *CLOSED Sun.*

David Orgell   5-D8
320 N. Rodeo Dr, Beverly Hills. (213) 272-3355. Over $1 million worth of china, crystal, glass, and silverware always in stock. *CLOSED Sun.*

Venise Crystal   1-B2
17609 Ventura Blvd, Encino. (818) 907-7755. Extensive selection of fine imported china, silverware, and crystal. *CLOSED Sun.*

Furniture

Mel Brown   1-D5
5840 S. Figueroa St, LA. (213) 778-4444. Huge stock of the very latest in furniture design. Accessories include lighting fixtures and wall coverings.

Danica   5-E8
9244 Wilshire Blvd, Beverly Hills. (310) 275-2503. Beautiful Scandinavian designs that are recognized and acclaimed worldwide.

Fat Chance   6-D3
162 N. La Brea, Hollywood. (213) 930-1960. Designer furniture from the 1930s and 1960s in remarkably good condition.

Hanson Galleries   5-D7
323 N. Rodeo Dr, Beverly Hills. (213) 205-3922. American contemporary artists including Peter Max.

HaRry   6-F4
8639 Venice Blvd, LA. (213) 559-7863. The inspired Harry Segil, who prefers his name spelled HaRry, has a smashing success on this booming part of La Brea. Prepunk plastic kitsch, gawdy tables resembling sputniks, pudgy couches, and everything else imaginable from the fab 50s. *CLOSED Sat & Sun.*

H. U. D. D. L. E.   5-G4
11159 Santa Monica Blvd, W. LA. (213) 479-4769. Great, modular, fun furniture for children. Durable and functional. Compact designs.

Jadis   4-E4
2701 Main St, Santa Monica. (310) 396-3477. Lovely art deco originals (and reproductions). Plush velvets, leather, and brocades. Accessories include period lamps and ornaments. There's even clothing for those who want to dress the part.

Modern Living   4-E7
8125 Melrose Ave, LA. (213) 655-3839. Located next to Modern Props—renowned prop house for futuristic movies. Modern Living is devoted entirely to Driade furniture of Milan, Italy, and is Driade's exclusive distributor in the U.S. Superb designs by Philippe Starck. *CLOSED Sun.*

Pacific Design Center   6-E1
8687 Melrose Ave, W. Hollywood. (310) 657-0800. A big blue palace full of interior design outlets and showrooms. Fine furnishings and accessories, latest innovative styles. (*See also* HISTORIC LA, Buildings & Landmarks.) *CLOSED Sun & Mon.*

Rapport   6-E4
435 N. La Brea Ave, LA. (213) 930-1500. Guaranteed savings on the very latest international styles. Dining, lounging, bedroom, and outdoor furniture, lamps, and accessories. *CLOSED Sun & Mon.*

Rugs

Guity   6-F1
9012 Wilshire Blvd, Beverly Hills. (310) 275-9248. Handwoven oriental rugs. Cleaning and restoration service. *CLOSED Sun.*

Haroonian Oriental Rugs   6-F1
5328 Wilshire Blvd, LA. (213) 938-9191. Direct importer of new and antique rugs, including nomadic pieces.

SPECIALTY SHOPPING

Antiques

Several local shopping districts are known for antique merchants (e.g., Melrose Avenue and Main Street; see also Shopping Centers). *There are too, too many fine antique stores to mention, but for a good selection under one roof, the following locations are recommended.*

Antique Arcade   2-F7
290 N. Harbor Dr, Redondo Beach. (310) 372-8282. Twenty-six antique shops, close to the beach. Free parking.

The Antique Guild   1-D4
880 Venice Blvd, LA. (310) 838-3131. Over 5 acres of antiques from around the world.

Larchmont Japanese Antiques   6-E5
115 N. Larchmont Blvd, LA. (213) 467-0430. Sculpture, paintings, masks, dolls, baskets, lamps, and chests—all from Japan. *CLOSED Sun & Mon.*

The Los Angeles Antique Market—Antiquarius   6-E1
8840 Beverly Blvd, W. Hollywood. (310) 274-0120. Over 90 antique dealers are gathered at this central location. Merchandise ranges from art nouveau to suits of armor. *CLOSED Sun & Mon.*

Memory Lanes Antique Mall **1-F4**
24251 Frampton Ave, Harbor City. (310) 530-8180. One of the nation's largest selections. Over 150 merchants.

Pasadena Antique Center **8-D2**
480 S. Fair Oaks Ave, Pasadena. (818) 449-7706. An attractive mission-style building containing over 60 antique outlets.

Westchester Faire Antique Mall **3-B6**
8655 S. Sepulveda Blvd, LA. (310) 670-4000. Seventy shops cover two floors.

Artist's Materials

The Art Store **6-E4**
7200 W. Beverly Blvd, LA. (213) 933-9284. All major brands. Fine art, drafting, and graphics supplies.

Amsterdam Art **6-E4**
160 S. La Brea Ave, LA. (213) 936-8166. Quality materials for illustration, design, drafting, and fine art.

Continental Art Supplies **1-B2**
7041 Reseda Blvd, Reseda. (818) 345-1044. Full line of supplies for fine art, drafting, engineering, architectural, and graphics. Art books. *CLOSED Sun.*

H. G. Daniels Co. **7-B1**
2543 W. 6th St, LA. (213) 387-1211. Large selection of architectural, engineering, artists, graphics, and audiovisual supplies. *CLOSED Sun.*

M. Flax **5-E4**
10852 Lindbrook Dr, Westwood. (213) 272-5351. Supplies for illustration, architectural design, fine art, and graphics. Framing. *CLOSED Sun.*

Graphaids **1-D3**
3030 S. La Cienega Blvd, Culver City; (310) 204-1212. And 12406 Santa Monica Blvd, Santa Monica; (310) 820-0445. Drafting materials for artists, architects, and engineers. *CLOSED Sun.*

Michael's **6-C5**
1518 N. Highland Ave, Hollywood. (213) 466-5295. Full range of art and drafting supplies. Art books. *CLOSED Sun.*

Mittel's **4-C3**
828 Broadway, Santa Monica. (310) 394-7976. Fine art, engineering, graphic, and drafting supplies. *CLOSED Sun.*

Walser's Art & Photo **1-F4**
22850 Hawthorne Blvd, Torrance. (310) 373-4330. Full line of artist's supplies. Frames, drafting tables, books, and lamps.

World Supply Inc. **9-G5**
3425 W. Cahuenga Blvd, Hollywood. (213) 851-1350. All major brands for artists, engineers, draftsmen, architects, and students. Framing. *CLOSED Sun.*

Zora's Artists Materials **5-F2**
11660 Santa Monica Blvd, W. LA. (310) 477-0451. Domestic and European supplies for fine arts and graphics.

Auctions

Ames Art & Auction Galleries, Inc. **6-F1**
15125 Ventura Blvd, Sherman Oaks. (818) 652-3820. Estate liquidations, fine art, rugs, and antiques. Auctions and private sales. *CLOSED Sat & Sun.*

Christie's **5-D7**
342 N. Rodeo Dr, Beverly Hills. (310) 275-5534. American West Coast branch of the famous London auction house. Sales, held intermittently at local convention centers, include everything from fine art to antique airplanes. *CLOSED Sat & Sun.*

Sotheby Parke Bernet **6-E4**
308 N. Rodeo Dr, Beverly Hills. (310) 274-0340. Originating in London in 1744, this distinguished auction house now conducts sales worldwide. In-house galleries are used for preauction viewings (free). *CLOSED Sat & Sun.*

Automobile Repairs & Service

—Accessories
It is advisable to purchase auto accessories and batteries from department stores, such as Sears, or from specialized retail outlets, such as Pep Boys. Auto repair shops add a substantial markup to parts and accessories.

—Repairs and Service

Mark C. Bloome Co.
Call (714) 632-9660 for location nearest you. General repairs and service. Tire specialists.

Hollywood Sports Cars **6-C7**
5766 Hollywood Blvd, Hollywood. (213) 464-6161. Sales and service for Ferrari, Jaguar, etc. *CLOSED Sat & Sun.*

Martin Cadillac **4-A6**
12101 W. Olympic Blvd, W. LA. (310) 820-3611. Complete Cadillac facility. Sales, service, repairs, bodywork.

Rolls-Royce of Beverly Hills **6-F1**
Sales: 8833 West Olympic Blvd, Beverly Hills; (310) 659-4050. Service: 11401 W. Pico Blvd, W. LA. (**4-A7**); (310) 477-4262.

Books

—General

Chatterton's Bookshop
1818 N. Vermont Ave, LA. (213) 664-3882. Full-line bookstore.

B. Dalton
Over 60 stores in LA, check the Yellow Pages for location nearest you.

Dutton's Books **9-D2**
5146 Laurel Canyon Blvd, N. Hollywood. (213) 877-9222; (818) 769-3866. A complete book and print store. Thousands of paperbacks, new and used reference books, best-sellers, lithographs, and posters.

Fowler Bros.
717 W. 7th St, LA. (213) 627-7846. Full-line bookstore. *CLOSED Sun.*

—Discount

Book Emporium
5539 Stearns, Long Beach. (310) 431-3595. Full-line bookstore.

Cosmopolitan Bookshop   **6-D4**
7007 Melrose Ave, LA. (213) 938-7119. Thousands of used, rare, and out-of-print books at discount prices. CLOSED Sun.

Crown Books   **6-C3**
7916 Sunset Blvd, LA; (213) 851-9183. And 1529 Wilshire Blvd, Santa Monica (**4-B3**); (310) 393-1133. Also 70 other locations in Southern California. Always 35% off every best-seller. Good stock of hardcovers, paperbacks, and magazines (not all are discounted).

Dodd's Book Shops   **1-G6**
4818 E. 2nd St, Long Beach. (310) 438-9948. Full-line bookstore.

—Antique, Old & Used

M. Bernstein Rare Books   **7-C4**
550 S. Grand Ave, LA. (213) 626-9944. Rare books, newspapers, maps, prints, autographs, and documents. Limited editions, sets, and leather bindings. CLOSED Sun.

Book City   **6-C6**
6627 Hollywood Blvd, Hollywood. (213) 466-2525. Over 50,000, mostly used, books stacked on tall shelves, covering every subject imaginable. OPEN Mon-Sat 10am-10pm; Sun 10am-8pm.

Dawson's Bookshop   **6-E6**
535 N. Larchmont Blvd, LA. (213) 469-2186. Rare books, specializing in California history. Art and oriental studies. CLOSED Sun & Mon.

Heritage Book Shop   **6-D1**
8540 Melrose Ave, W. Hollywood. (310) 659-5738. Rare first editions, old travel books, autographs, and manuscripts. CLOSED Sun.

—Special Interest

Acres of Books   **1-G6**
240 Long Beach Blvd, Long Beach. (310) 437-6980. This landmark bookstore, covering half a city block, has been a mecca for bibliophiles since 1934. There are thousands of used books (some dating back to the 17th century) and thousands more on every subject under the sun. CLOSED Sun & Mon.

The Bodhi Tree   **6-E1**
8585 Melrose Ave, W. Hollywood. (310) 659-3227. Mysticism, religion, and psychology. Used books, magazines, and accessories.

Book Circus   **6-D2**
8230 Santa Monica Blvd, Hollywood. (213) 656-6533. A pornographic bookstore with a non-seedy atmosphere. OPEN 6pm-2am.

Larry Edmunds Book Shop   **6-C5**
6644 Hollywood Blvd, Hollywood. (213) 463-3273. Nostalgia. Filled with movie memorabilia; also books, posters, and photographs—all relating to film and theater. CLOSED Sun.

Federal Bookstore   **7-C5**
Federal Building, Flower St, LA. (213) 894-5841. Government publications.

Hennessy & Ingall's   **4-C3**
1254 3rd St Promenade, Santa Monica. (310) 458-9074. Excellent selection of books on every art form, by every known art-book publisher.

Hollywood Book & Poster Co.   **6-C5**
6349 N. Las Palmas Ave, Hollywood. (213) 465-8764. Interesting assortment of new and classic movie material.

Midnight Special Bookstore   **4-C3**
1350 3rd St Promenade, Santa Monica. (310) 393-2923. Quality paperbacks. Politics, feminist, Spanish-language, social services, and children's sections. Radical magazines.

The Museum Bookstore   **6-G3**
Los Angeles County Museum of Art, 5905 Wilshire Blvd, LA. (213) 857-6144. Superior collection of works relating to art and film. CLOSED Mon.

J. Roth Bookseller   **5-F8**
9020 W. Olympic Blvd, Beverly Hills. (310) 557-1848. Jewish interest. Hebrew studies. CLOSED Sat.

Samuel French & Co.   **6-C3**
7623 Sunset Blvd, Hollywood. (213) 876-0570. Plays and productions. CLOSED Sun.

Scene of the Crime   **1-B3**
13636 Ventura Blvd, Sherman Oaks. (818) 981-CLUE. Agatha Christie would have loved it: over 10,000 titles, including rare and out-of-print works, all relating to mystery and detection.

Sisterhood Bookstore   **5-F4**
1351 Westwood Blvd, Westwood. (310) 477-7300. Feminist literature and records. Nonsexist children's section.

The Technical Book Company   **5-G5**
2056 Westwood Blvd, Westwood. (310) 475-5711. Professional—engineering, accounting, medicine, etc. CLOSED Sun.

—Newspapers

See BASIC INFORMATION, Newspapers & Magazines, Newspapers and International Newsstands.

Cleaners

Brown's   **4-B3**
1223 Montana Ave, Santa Monica. (310) 451-8531. Specialists in delicate fabrics, evening wear, beaded and sequined clothing. CLOSED Sun.

Long Cleaners   **5-E2**
142 Barrington Pl, Brentwood. (310) 472-4818. Skillful staff who pay special attention to detail. Trust them with your most delicate clothing. CLOSED Sun.

Magnolia Cleaners   **6-E2**
8410 Melrose Ave, W. Hollywood. (213) 653-0060. Top-quality work by experienced staff who won't ruin your clothes. (Used by Neiman-Marcus and numerous celebrities.) CLOSED Sun.

Security Cleaners   **4-D3**
2005 Main St, Santa Monica. (310) 396-0273.
Small miracles are performed here. Individual
evaluation and attention to detail. Alterations and
repairs. *CLOSED Sun.*

V.I.P. Wardrobe Maintenance   **5-E2**
11701 Wilshire Blvd, LA. (310) 874-3436. Ex-
perts in difficult-to-clean items. Costumes and
beaded gowns are a specialty. Pickup and delivery service—no extra charge. *CLOSED Sun.*

Crafts

Aaron Brothers Art Marts   **6-F1**
364 N. La Cienega Blvd, LA; (310) 657-1168.
And 1645 Lincoln Blvd, Santa Monica (**4-C3**);
(310) 450-6333. Wide selection of quality materials for a variety of arts and crafts.

Artistic Needle   **5-F5**
1541 Westwood Blvd, Westwood. (310) 477-
3640. Rug-making, quilting, needlepoint, knitting, and framing supplies. Antique accessories,
gifts, classes, and workshops. *CLOSED Sun &
Mon.*

The Clayhouse   **4-A5**
2909 Santa Monica Blvd, Santa Monica. (310)
828-7071. Clay, tools, and equipment for pottery. Pottery classes for beginners to advanced
students.

Kit Craft Inc.   **9-F2**
12109 Ventura Pl, Studio City. (818) 984-0780.
Supplies for jewelry-making, flower-making,
trains, models, etc. *CLOSED Sun.*

Nettie's Needlecraft   **5-E7**
9742 Wilshire Blvd, Beverly Hills. (213) 272-
7700. Enormous selection of yarns. Preassem-
bled kits for all forms of needlework and rug-
making. Friendly, helpful staff. Classes. *CLOSED
Sun.*

L'Atelier   **4-A3**
1202 Montana Ave, Santa Monica. (310) 394-
4665. Complete supplies for pillow-making,
needlepoint, knitting, and crocheting. Classes
for all levels. *CLOSED Sun.*

Tandy Leather   **6-G8**
1759½ W. La Palma Ave, Anaheim. (714) 776-
5461. Everything needed for leather crafts. Garment leather and suede skins, leather kits, tools,
snaps, beads, studs, and conchos. *CLOSED
Sun.*

Entertaining

(*See also* Specialty Shopping: Rentals, *and*
KIDS' LA, Children's Entertainment.) *Feeling extravagant, or just wishing to add a dash of dif-
ference to a party? Try some of these.*

Animal Actors
864 W. Carlisle Rd, Thousand Oaks. (805) 495-
2122. Variety of well-trained wild animals for hire.
(Accompanied by experienced handlers.)

Fun Zone Boat Company
700 E. Edgewater Dr, Balboa. (714) 673-0240.
Party boats (accommodating up to 140 people),

complete with bars, food, and stereo music of
your choice.

Hollywood Magic Inc.   **6-C5**
6614 Hollywood Blvd, Hollywood. (213) 464-
5610. A magical array of tricks and illusions, plus
masks, books, cassettes, makeup, and accessories. Everything to make the party fun.
CLOSED Sun.

Lady of the Cloth
(818) 986-2843. Tablecloth and napkin rental for
all occasions. Wide selection. *CLOSED Sat &
Sun.*

Live Wires
(213) 462-3111; (818) 376-6506. Singing telegrams, jugglers, magicians, mime artists,
clowns, and celebrity look-alikes.

Parties Plus
(213) 624-7101. These people do things right!
There's a set designer to create the perfect ambience and a food coordinator who arranges
preparty tastings for hosts. Invitations are taken
care of, suitable entertainment is provided, and
appropriate staff tend to guests' needs.

Porta-Party
(310) 670-3786. Mobile party facility. Set price
includes driver, bartender, and complimentary
cocktails.

Pure Romance   **1-B3**
(818) 508-5026. Everything imaginable for that
romantic occasion can be handled for you—from
limousine picnics with Spode china to society
weddings with horse-drawn carriages. Full custom service.

Vine American Party Store   **6-D7**
5969 Melrose Ave, Hollywood. (213) 467-7126.
Hats, streamers, favors, blowouts, cards, decorations, napkins, noisemakers, candles, cups,
balloons . . . you name it—everything to make
the party swing.

R. Raymond Wolff
(310) 559-9179. A formal butler to greet guests
and supervise the party with discretion and
aplomb.

Ethnic Goods

Buffalo Robe Indian Trading Post   **1-B2**
8415-2 Reseda Blvd, Northridge. (818) 993-
0917. Indian clothing and crafts. Custom-made
moccasins, beads, bags, and books. *CLOSED
Sun & Mon.*

Ethnic Shopping Centers
See Shopping Centers: Chinatown, Farmer's
Market, Little Tokyo, Sawtelle Boulevard, *and*
Solvang; *see also* HISTORIC LA, Main Districts:
Chinatown *and* Little Tokyo.

Indian Art Center of California   **9-F1**
12666 Ventura Blvd, Studio City. (818) 763-
3430. A treasure trove of authentic Indian crafts.
Navajo rugs, Seri ironwood carvings, beautiful
baskets, and pottery. Turquoise, silver, and gold
jewelry. *CLOSED Sun.*

M. Levee and Daughters   **6-F1**
8437 Clinton Ave, W. Hollywood. (310) 855-
0269. Unusual oriental pieces personally se-

lected by the owners, who make frequent trips to China. Carvings, antique porcelains, hand-embroidered silks, lacquerware, and much more.

Flowers & Plants

Cosentino's   **1-D1**
21201 Pacific Coast Hwy, Malibu. (310) 456-3223. A rambling space filled with plants, pottery, and wrought-iron work.

Flower Fashions   **5-E7**
9960 Santa Monica, LA. (213) 272-6063. Outstanding floral arrangements for grand occasions. *CLOSED Sun.*

The Flower Meadows   **6-F1**
9627 Brighton Way, Beverly Hills. (310) 659-8634. Expert floral designs emphasizing a natural look. Plants, grasses, gifts, and party planning. *CLOSED Sun.*

Stanley Kersten Flowers & Service   **7-G4**
734 S. San Julian St, LA. (213) 622-3415. Superior flower service. *CLOSED Sun.*

Maleenee Desert Gallery   **1-B7**
216 S. Rosemead Blvd, Pasadena. (818) 795-2788. One of the largest collections of cacti in America. Indoor and outdoor varieties up to 20 feet high.

Orchids Ltd.   **1-F5**
407 E. Carson St, Carson. (310) 549-7695. Complete selection and supplies for orchid lovers. Care demonstrations and instructions. *CLOSED Tues.*

Yamaguchi Bonsai Nursery   **5-G4**
1905 Sawtelle Blvd, W. LA. (310) 473-5444. Specialists and consultants in bonsai. Complete nursery stock of indoor plants.

Framing

Art Services   **6-D2**
8221 Melrose Ave, W. Hollywood. (213) 653-9033. Every frame is expertly built from scratch. No job too large or small, unusual shapes a specialty. Many mediums. *CLOSED Sun.*

Contemporary Art Framing   **4-D3**
1827 W. Washington Blvd, LA. (213) 731-8846. Custom framing. Hardwood, oriental, gold leaf, welded, sectional, and Plexiglas frames. Rush orders, pickup and delivery service. *CLOSED Sun.*

Gordon Gallery   **4-A3**
1311 Montana Ave, Santa Monica. (310) 394-6545. Museum-quality framing. (Gallery space includes some fine international works.) *CLOSED Sun & Mon.*

Z Gallerie   **4-E4**
2710 Main St, Santa Monica; (310) 392-8369. Also five other locations. Custom framing in all mediums, including chrome and Plexiglas. Large selection of quality poster art.

Gifts

Buddy's California Pottery   **6-D4**
7208 Melrose Ave, W. Hollywood. (213) 939-2419. Interesting collection of American commercial pottery from the 1930s, 1940s, and 1950s.

The Game Keeper   **4-C3**
10800 W. Pico Blvd, Santa Monica. (310) 475-1753. Every conceivable electronic game plus timeless favorites from bridge to chess. Game tables, puzzles, fantasy games, and casino games.

Hammacher Schlemmer   **5-D7**
309 N. Rodeo Dr, Beverly Hills. (310) 859-7255. The most unusual, eccentric, and exclusive gifts imaginable. The store for people who have more than everything. Hammacher Schlemmer has a reputation for being the first with every new gizmo. How about a solar-powered, ventilated pith helmet? They have it!

Homeworks   **4-E4**
2923 Main St, Santa Monica. (310) 396-0101. A busy little store chockablock with interesting goodies, from high-tech tableware to hand-painted baby clothes. There are silk flowers, imported French soaps, enameled brooches, sweatshirts, modular clocks, masks, fans, jackets, toys, socks, stationery, and cards galore.

Moskatel's   **4-C3**
1427 4th St, Santa Monica. (310) 393-9634. Allow at least an hour to browse; the selection is overwhelming. Accessories, toys, party favors, silk flowers, candles, table decorations, seasonal gifts, vases, crafts of all kinds, and a huge selection of stationery.

Palmetto   **4-B3**
1034 Montana Ave, Santa Monica. (310) 395-6687. Gourmet skin and hair care products to pamper and perfect. Natural cosmetics and fragrances, imported soaps and brushes. Expert advice. *CLOSED Sun.*

The Pleasure Chest   **6-D3**
7733 Santa Monica Blvd, Hollywood. (213) 650-1022. Want to get the boss something to make him or her blush? Frivolous gifts, not to everyone's taste but fun for the open-minded. Everything here is inoffensively sex-oriented.

The Sharper Image   **5-D8**
9550 Little Santa Monica Blvd, Beverly Hills. (310) 271-0515. Top of the line executive gifts, games, and status symbols. Latest electronic gadgetry, workout tools, jewelry, and other accoutrements.

So Much and Company   **6-D1**
8669 Sunset Blvd, W. Hollywood. (310) 652-4291. Breathtaking selection of beautiful and unique gifts and accessories. Handmade jewelry in contemporary and antique designs. Purses, combs, beadwork, and handcrafted ornaments. *CLOSED Sun.*

The Soap Plant   **6-D4**
7400 Melrose Ave, Hollywood. (213) 651-5587. Latest ideas in gift giving. Something for everyone, from fragrances to fans, hand-milled soaps, jewelry, dried flowers, hair ornaments, wall hangings, cards, mugs, and much more.

Tottenham Court Ltd.   **9-F1**
12206½ Ventura Blvd, Studio City. (818) 761-6560. An Edwardian chemist's shop filled with

imported European fragrances, toiletries, and personal accessories. Sachets, potpourris, hand-milled soaps, perfume flacons, porcelain table sets, enameled boxes, and enchanting gift baskets. Preserves from Fortnum & Mason in London, Rigaud candles, and Crabtree & Evelyn's line of delightfully fragrant toiletries. Thousands of gift items.

Twigs **4-A3**
1401 Montana Ave, Santa Monica. (310) 451-9934. Tastefully selected gifts with a touch of whimsy here and there. Handcrafted ornaments made from wood burls, brass, and sterling silver. Baskets, silk flowers, antiques. Specialized gift service. *CLOSED Sun.*

Wounded Knee Indian Shop **4-A4**
2413 Wilshire Blvd, Santa Monica. (310) 394-0159. Authentic Indian crafts and gifts. Woven rugs, pottery, sand paintings, beadwork, kachinas, masks, baskets, and jewelry. Specialists in crafts by Northwest Coast Indians. *CLOSED Sun.*

Jewelry

Marcia Caden **5-E8**
(310) 275-2501. One-of-a-kind antique and modern jewelry. High-fashion designs in all precious metals and gems. Antique gifts and accessories also. *By appointment only.*

Frances Klein **5-D8**
310 N. Rodeo Dr, Beverly Hills. (310) 273-0155. Fabulous jewelry salon. Original, nouveau, and art deco pieces; estate jewels; and notable modern pieces. World's finest craftsmen are represented. *CLOSED Sun.*

Morgan and Company **5-E4**
1131 Glendon Ave, Westwood. (310) 208-3377. Domestic and European jewelers. Cartier, Piaget, Seiko, and Ebel are all represented. Antique and estate jewels, repairs, and appraisals. *CLOSED Sun.*

Shanes Jewelry **5-E4**
1065 Broxton Ave, Westwood. (310) 208-8404. Thousands of gold chains, bracelets, and rings—all at below-average prices.

Wm. Stromberg Jewelers **6-C5**
6439 Hollywood Blvd, Hollywood. (213) 465-6115. Catering to a Hollywood clientele since 1920, their specialties are antique watch restoration, diamond jewelry, and jewelry repair. *CLOSED Sun.*

Tiffany & Co **5-E8**
210 N. Rodeo Dr, Beverly Hills. (310) 273-8880. If you really must splash out, here's the place. Perhaps the best-known jewelers in the world. Wondrous gems, some of grand proportions, all of exquisite design, conjure images of royalty and magnificence. *CLOSED Sun.*

Van Cleef & Arpels **5-E8**
300 N. Rodeo Dr, Beverly Hills. (310) 276-1161. Beverly Hills's other prestigious jeweler—and equally popular with the rich and famous. Flawless gems set in precious metals. Custom work

by top designers. Superior service. *CLOSED Sun.*

Libraries—Specialized

Academy of Motion Pictures Arts & Sciences **6-F1**
8949 Wilshire Blvd, Beverly Hills. (310) 247-3000. *CLOSED Sat & Sun.*

Academy of Television Arts & Sciences **9-A8**
5220 Lankershim Blvd, Burbank. (818) 953-7575.

Brand Library **1-B5**
1601 W. Mountain St, Glendale. (818) 956-2051. Distinguished art library. (*See also* HISTORIC LA, Buildings & Landmarks.) *CLOSED Sun & Mon.*

Huntington Library **8-E5**
1151 Oxford Rd, San Marino. (818) 405-2100. Unequaled collection of rare books and manuscripts. (*See also* MUSEUMS & GALLERIES, Museums, General Art.) *CLOSED Mon.*

Jewish Community Library **1-C4**
6505 Wilshire Blvd, LA. (213) 852-1234, ext 3201. Books, periodicals, and films relating to Jewish history. *CLOSED Sat.*

Los Angeles Central Library **7-C4**
433 S. Spring St, LA. (213) 612-3200. Films, recordings, magazines, international newspapers, microfilm library, and over 1.5 million books. (*See also* HISTORIC LA, Buildings & Landmarks.) *CLOSED Sun.*

Mexican Library Casa del Mexicano **7-E8**
2900 Euclid Pl, LA, (213) 267-8527.

Franklin D. Murphy Library **7-C5**
Japanese American Cultural and Community Center, Little Tokyo. (213) 628-2725. Japanese culture and Japanese-American history.

Southern California Genealogical Society **9-A8**
122 S. San Fernando Rd, Burbank. (818) 843-7247.

Theosophical Society International **1-B6**
2416 N. Lake Ave, Altadena. (818) 798-3378.

University Research Libraries **5-D5**
UCLA, 405 Hilgard Ave, Westwood. (310) 825-8301. Specialized subjects from biomedics to oriental studies. Most UCLA libraries are open to the public.

Warner Research Collection **9-A8**
Burbank Central Library, 110 N. Glen Oaks Blvd, Burbank. (818) 953-9743. The most extensive research facility on the motion picture industry to be found on the West Coast. Over 25,000 books plus one million magazine, photo, and newspaper cuttings. *By appointment only (Mon-Fri 10am-5pm). CLOSED Sat & Sun.*

Maps

The Map Shop **1-D4**
12112 W. Washington Blvd, Culver City. (310) 391-1848. Huge variety of maps and charts. *CLOSED Sat & Sun.*

Pets

—Adoption

Pet Adoption Fund
(310) 478-4455. Charity organization caring for strays and unwanted dogs. Ads for adoption run in city newspapers.

Pet Pride
(310) 836-5427. Unwanted cats (spayed and neutered) available for adoption.

—Boarding

Van Nuys Pet Hotel   **1-B3**
7004 Havenhurst Ave, Van Nuys. (818) 787-7232. Luxurious accommodations. Each pet has private patio, bed, and toys. Penthouse suites with personal valet also available. *CLOSED Sun.*

—Burial

Los Angeles SPCA Pet Memorial Park
5068 Old Scandia Lane, Calabasas. (818) 591-7037.

—Emergency Treatment After Hours

Animal Emergency Clinic   **6-D2**
7116 Melrose Ave, LA. (213) 937-5120. *OPEN 24 hours for emergencies.*

Emergency Animal Clinic   **1-B3**
5152 Sepulveda Blvd, Sherman Oaks. (818) 788-7860. *OPEN Mon-Fri 6pm-8am; Sat, Sun & holidays 24 hours.*

Emergency Pet Clinic of South Bay   **1-F4**
2325 Torrance Blvd, Torrance. 320-8300. *OPEN Mon-Fri 6pm-8am; Sat & Sun from noon.*

West Los Angeles Veterinary Medical Group
                                                   5-G4
1559 S. Sepulveda Blvd, W. LA. (310) 473-2951; (310) 477-8001. *OPEN 7 days, 24 hours.*

—Grooming

Bowser Boutique   **6-E1**
610 N. Robertson Blvd, W. Hollywood. (310) 659-0847. Celebrity clientele. Air-conditioned grooming facilities, complete line of pet products and services. *CLOSED Sun & Mon.*

The Pet Dept.   **4-A4**
2828 Wilshire Blvd, Santa Monica. (310) 828-6047. Grooming, baths, and clips for all breeds of cats and dogs.

—Lost & Found

Petfinders
P.O. Box 1904, Studio City. (818) 710-8431. Tracer service, coded tags, placement service. *CLOSED Sun.*

—Services

LA Society for the Prevention of Cruelty to Animals
5026 W. Jefferson Blvd, LA. (213) 730-5300.

Pages Pet Patrol
(818) 998-6148. Pet-sitting service serving the San Fernando Valley area.

—Shelters

Los Angeles Animal Shelter   **7-B5**
320 Lacey St, LA. (213) 222-7138. Several locations. Commonly known as "the pound." Stray, lost, abandoned, and unwanted animals await collection, adoption, or extermination.

—Stores

Animal Farm Pet Shop   **6-E1**
8928 Santa Monica Blvd, W. Hollywood. (310) 659-2498. Puppies, kittens, and birds. Superior pet foods. Supplies and grooming.

Petville USA   **4-D8**
12112 Venice Blvd, Mar Vista. (310) 313-1801. "Animal advocates pet corner," adoptions, grooming, pet-sitting, cat boarding, nutritional care and advice.

—Supplies

The Farmer's Market Pet Shop   **6-F3**
3rd St at Fairfax Ave, LA. (213) 936-8833. Unusual supplies include dog pajamas, sunglasses, and (would you believe) life preservers for dogs that don't swim well.

Pups 'n Pets   **9-A2**
6436 Bellingham Ave, N. Hollywood. (818) 984-1767. Pets and supplies. Individual dog car seats, personalized place mats and bowls, and the usual collars, leashes, etc.

—Training

Hollywood Dog Training School & Kitty City
                                                   9-A4
10805 Vanowen St, N. Hollywood. (818) 762-1262. Varied classes for all ages and abilities. *CLOSED Sun.*

National Institute of Dog Training
(310) 445-4671. At-home obedience training, fully guaranteed. *CLOSED Sun.*

—Travel

Jet Pets   **3-C2**
9014 Pershing Dr, Playa del Rey. (310) 823-8901. Any size animal. Pickup and delivery service Monday to Friday. Will keep pet safely until departure time. Airline-approved containers.

—Treatment

Bel-Air Animal Hospital   **4-A8**
2340 S. Sepulveda Blvd, W. LA. (310) 479-4419. Excellent veterinarians.

Culver City Animal Hospital   **1-D4**
5830 Washington Blvd, Culver City. (310) 836-4551. Highly qualified staff. Latest treatment techniques. *CLOSED Sun.*

Santa Monica Dog & Cat Hospital   **4-B4**
2010 Broadway, Santa Monica. (310) 453-5459. Accomplished doctors. Highly recommended. Appointment preferred. *CLOSED Sun.*

West Los Angeles Veterinary Medical Group
                                                   5-G4
1559 S. Sepulveda Blvd, W. LA. (310) 473-2951. Clinic for domestic pets, reptiles, exotic animals, and birds. Also a 24-hour emergency service.

The West Valley Pet Clinic **1-B2**
22430 Ventura Blvd, Woodland Hills. (818) 348-7160. Respected, qualified veterinarians. *CLOSED Sun.*

Pharmacies

See EMERGENCY SERVICES.

Photographic Equipment & Services

The following stores sell a full line of superior photographic equipment at competitive prices. Sales staffs are knowledgeable and helpful.

A. B. C. Premiums **6-E4**
7266 Beverly Blvd, LA. (213) 938-2724.

Bel-Air Camera & Hi-Fi **5-E4**
1025 Westwood Blvd, W. LA. (310) 208-5150. *CLOSED Sun.*

Miko Photo & Sound **4-C2**
1259 Santa Monica Mall, Santa Monica. (310) 393-9371.

Olympic Camera **7-D3**
828 W. Olympic Blvd, LA. (213) 746-0575. *CLOSED Sun.*

Samy's Camera **6-E2**
8451 Beverly Blvd, LA. (213) 938-2420.

Photographic Processing

Most camera stores offer quality processing, enlargements, and specialty finishing services. For box-brownie lovers, there are dozens of inexpensive outlets where photos can be developed and printed quickly and cheaply. Try **Fromex One Hour Photos** *(call* (310) 479-2237 *for location nearest you).*

Video Supplies
See Specialty Shopping: Video Equipment & Rental.

Records

American Pie **4-D8**
13381 Beach Ave, LA. (310) 821-4005. "Every single single in print"; 45 rpm records from 1930 onward.

Aron's Record Shop **6-D3**
1150 Highland Ave, W. Hollywood. (213) 469-4700. New and used records at huge discounts.

Classical Record Shop **5-C8**
317 S. Robertson Blvd, Beverly Hills. (310) 275-7026. Hard-to-beat selection of classical records. Knowledgeable staff.

Disc Connection Records & Tapes **5-F3**
10970 W. Pico Blvd, W. LA. (310) 208-7211. Specializing in hard-to-find recordings. Libraries, soundtracks, and nostalgia. Appraisals, record rentals. *CLOSED Sun.*

Discoteca Latina **7-E3**
440 S. Broadway, LA. (213) 622-9340. Popular Mexican hits, old and new.

Festival Records **4-B6**
2773 W. Pico Blvd, W. LA. (213) 737-3500. In-ternational folk music; multilingual records and tapes.

Moby Disc **1-B3**
14410 Ventura Blvd, Sherman Oaks; (818) 990-2970. And 3731 E. Colorado Blvd, Pasadena; (818) 793-3475. Large stock of used and discontinued. Good selection of 45s, imports, and independents plus full range of current releases.

National Compact Disc **9-F4**
11392 Ventura Blvd, Studio City. (818) 505-0343. Huge selection of CDs (compact discs) in every musical category.

Rare Records **1-B5**
417 E. Broadway, Glendale. (310) 245-0379. Hard-to-find records, rare sheet music, record-finding service.

Rhino Records **5-F5**
1720 Westwood Blvd, Westwood. (310) 474-8685. Good selection of latest releases and imports at discounted prices.

Tower Classical **6-D1**
8840 Sunset Blvd, Hollywood. (310) 657-3910. Across-the-street annex of Tower Records. Fantastic selection of domestic and imported classical records.

Tower Records **6-D1**
8801 Sunset Blvd, Hollywood; (310) 657-7300. And 1028 Westwood Blvd, Westwood (**5-F4**); (310) 208-3061. Reputedly the world's largest selection. Everything from old wave to New Wave, instrumental to educational. Great import selection. Top-selling albums always discounted.

Vinyl Fetish **6-D4**
7305 Melrose Ave, Hollywood. (213) 935-1300. Almost 90% British imports (albums and 45s). English music papers, magazines, and T-shirts too.

Zed Records **1-G6**
1940 Lakewood Blvd, Long Beach. (310) 498-2757. Great selection of imports and independent-label releases. Adventurous stock, helpful staff.

Rentals

(See also Specialty Shopping: Entertaining *and* Services.)

Cabaret Costume **2-G8**
1302 Kingsdale Ave, Redondo Beach. (310) 370-0098. Costume rentals and sales. Masks, makeup, jewelry, custom designing. *CLOSED Sun & Mon.*

Casino de Paris **1-D5**
9636 Long Beach Blvd, South Gate. (213) 566-1001. Professional gambling equipment and experienced personnel.

Charter Concepts **4-G7**
4051 Glencoe Ave, Suite 7, Marina del Rey. (310) 823-2676. Sailboats and motor yachts, complete with crew and personal chef.

Dreamboats Rent-a-Car **6-F1**
8536 Wilshire Blvd, Beverly Hills. (310) 659-3277. American convertibles from the late 50s

and early 60s, with brand-new interiors, new paint jobs, and FM radios. Reasonable rates.

Ellis Mercantile   **6-E4**
169 N. La Brea Ave, LA. (213) 933-7334. A motion-picture prop company that is open to the public. Rent any hand prop imaginable—from a 50 cents per day plastic pizza to a Zorro sword. *CLOSED Sat & Sun.*

El Monte Rents   **1-C7**
12061 E. Valley Blvd, El Monte. (818) 443-6150. Motor homes for up to six people. Free pickup service.

Gary's Tux Shops
(310) 659-7296. Call for location nearest you. Designer label tuxedos. (*See also* Men's Clothes: Rentals.)

The Postal Center   **6-C2**
8033 Sunset Blvd, Hollywood. (213) 650-0009. Reliable mailbox rentals, message service.

Rent-A-Wreck   **4-B6**
12333 W. Pico Blvd, W. LA. 478-0676. Want to travel incognito? Here's a huge variety of beat-up (and not so beat-up) used cars, all in excellent running order. Some classic cars available. Low rates—of course.

Rent-a-Writer
(818) 985-3250. This lady will expertly compose sharp letters of complaint or polite apologies for those unable to put their thoughts together.

Studio Instrument Rentals
(213) 466-1314 or -3417. Musical rentals, rehearsal studios, sound stages, and storage. Various locations, all in Hollywood.

Western Costume Company   **6-D6**
11041 Van Owen St, N. Hollywood. (213) 469-1451. Famous costume rental outlet. Numerous celebrity costumes. Open since 1912.

Services

(*See also* Complaints & Consumer Services.)
De Forest Library Research Service   **6-D6**
780 Gower St, LA. (213) 469-2271. Unique and acclaimed information service.

Jewish Singles
5870 W. Olympic Blvd, LA. (213) 272-1073. Nonprofit computer service for singles. *CLOSED Sat & Sun.*

Sporting Goods

Big 5 Sporting Goods   **1-D3**
4343 Sepulveda Blvd, Culver City; (310) 397-0645. And over 20 other locations throughout Los Angeles. Sports equipment at reasonable prices.

Bob's Sporting Goods Center   **5-G4**
2003 Sawtelle Blvd, W. LA. (310) 478-2638. Fishing tackle and repair specialists. Fishing information center. *CLOSED Sun & Mon.*

Braun's Sport World   **4-A3**
1610 Montana Ave, Santa Monica. (310) 395-5491. Racquet sports headquarters. All major

brands of clothing and equipment. Restringing and repairs. *CLOSED Sun & Mon.*

Dive 'n Surf Inc.   **2-G7**
504 N. Broadway, Redondo Beach. (213) 372-8423. Diving and surfing supplies.

Foot Locker   **5-F7**
10250 Santa Monica Blvd, Century City; (310) 556-1498. And over 60 other locations citywide. Large selection of footwear for running, tennis, and basketball.

Golden West Billiard Mfg.   **1-B2**
21260 Deering Court, Canoga Park. (818) 888-2300. Supplies for pool and billiards.

The Merchant of Tennis   **6-G1**
1118 S. La Cienega Blvd, LA. (310) 855-1946. Most sports supplies, specializing in tennis. Court rentals. *CLOSED Sun.*

Nike Westwood   **5-E4**
1110 Westwood Blvd, Westwood. (310) 208-6453. Authorized shoe and clothing distributor for Nike brand exclusively.

Offside   **5-G4**
11710 Santa Monica Blvd, W. LA. (310) 473-5192. Soccer and rugby supplies. Clothing and rentals.

Oshman's Sporting Goods   **7-C3**
Broadway Plaza, 700 S. Flower St, LA; (213) 488-9952. And numerous other locations. Wide range of brand-name goods for most sports

Sandy's Ski & Sport   **4-F7**
4110 Lincoln Blvd, Marina del Rey; (310) 822-9203. And 12237 Wilshire Blvd, W. LA. (**5-G2**); (310) 820-8596. Ski equipment rentals, clothing, and supplies. Roller skates. Large sports clothing department.

Santa Monica Ski Haus   **4-A5**
3101 Santa Monica Blvd, Santa Monica. (310) 828-3492. Snow ski and water ski supplies. *CLOSED Sun in summer.*

Scuba Haus   **4-A4**
2501 Wilshire Blvd, Santa Monica. (310) 828-2916. Scuba and skin diving equipment. Rentals.

Soccer West   **10-A1**
6738 Balboa Blvd, Van Nuys. (818) 782-5425. Soccer equipment and clothing.

Southern California Darts Association   **1-D3**
11119 W. Washington Blvd, Culver City. (310) 839-6972. Darts equipment exclusively.

Sportmart   **1-B5**
253 N. Glendale Ave, Glendale; (818) 240-3800. Also in Huntington Beach, Northridge, Redondo Beach, and West Covina. "Over 100,000 name-brand, first-quality items." Discounted sporting goods, clothing, and accessories. Tickets to major sporting events.

Reef Seekers   **6-F1**
8642 Wilshire Blvd, Beverly Hills. (310) 652-4990. Full range of equipment and clothing for diving. Custom-made scuba wear. (Scuba lessons.) *CLOSED Sun.*

The Tennis Place   **6-F4**
5880 W. 3rd St, LA. (213) 931-1715. Full range of tennis equipment. Court rentals and tuition.

Stationery

Aahs **1-B3**
14548 Ventura Blvd, Sherman Oaks; (818) 907-0300. Also in Santa Monica, W. Hollywood, and Westwood. Enormous selection of cards, from Holly Hobbie to high tech. Newest ideas in gift wrappings and stationery supplies. Invitations, place cards, and special-occasion accessories.

The Card Factory **5-G6**
10800 W. Pico Blvd, W Hollywood. (310) 652-0194. Exclusive lines in stationery. Huge variety of cards from arty to risqué.

Robin Caroll **10-E1**
(818) 788-3396. Personalized stationery and invitations. Calligraphy and graphic design, desk accessories. *By appointment.*

Francis-Orr **5-E8**
320 N. Camden Dr, Beverly Hills. (310) 271-6106. Quality, custom-printed personal stationery. Unusual colors to match every mood. *CLOSED Sun.*

McManus & Morgan **7-B1**
2506 W. 7th St, LA. (213) 387-4433. The Neiman-Marcus of stationers. Fabulous supplies for letter writers and artists. Hand-marbled imported papers, sheepskin parchment, unusual sizes, metallics, bookbinding supplies, gold leaf, desk accessories, unusual decals, and much more. *CLOSED Sun.*

Pulp & Hide **5-G1**
13020 San Vicente Blvd, Brentwood. (310) 394-0700. Business and social stationery. Custom invitations, leather desk accessories, quality pens, and executive gifts. *CLOSED Sun.*

Video Equipment & Rental

Advanced Video **6-D3**
6753 Santa Monica Blvd, W. Hollywood. (213) 655-3511. Rentals, repairs, editing, film transfer, and duplications.

Albee's **6-G2**
6305 Wilshire Blvd, LA. (213) 651-0620. Large inventory of video and audiovideo equipment and supplies, plus stereos, cameras, etc., at discount prices.

20 20 Video **5-F3**
11663 Wilshire Blvd, W. LA. (310) 820-2020. Videocassette recorder rentals, with one free movie per month. Over 1,000 titles in stock.

Video 2001 **5-E4**
950 Gayley Ave, Westwood. (310) 824-4737. Video sales, rentals, hookups, games, and computer software.

Vidiots **4-D3**
32 Pico Blvd, Santa Monica. (310) 392-8508. Video rentals. They specialize in works by video artists and independent filmmakers. Good stock of foreign, cult, and classic films plus new releases. *OPEN till midnight Fri & Sat.*

TRANSPORTATION & VACATION INFORMATION

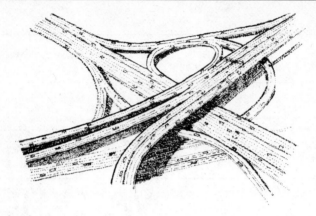

Freeway Stack

PASSPORTS

Phone ahead for required document information and apply for passports at least three weeks prior to departure dates. Call (310) 575-7070 for recorded instructions.
Passport Agencies
11000 Wilshire Blvd, W. LA.   **5-F4**
(310) 209-7075
Terminal Annex Post Office,   **7-F5**
900 N. Alameda St, LA.
Arco Plaza Post Office,   **7-C4**
505 S. Flower St, Level B, LA.
Also at main branches of U.S. Post Offices throughout the city.

VISAS

Intercontinental Visa Service   7-C4
World Trade Center, Suite 185, 350 S. Figueroa St, LA. (213) 625-7175.

INTERNATIONAL DRIVER'S LICENSE

Apply to any office of the Automobile Club of Southern California. Licenses are issued to both members and nonmembers.

INOCULATIONS & VACCINATIONS

Los Angeles County Health Care Centers
Burbank: 1101 W. Magnolia Blvd.

(818) 500–3501   **9–C8**
Central LA: 241 N. Figueroa St. (213)   **7-B4**
974-8203.
East Valley: 5300 Tujunga Ave, N.   **9-D3**
Hollywood. (818) 766-3981.
Hollywood/Wilshire: 5205 Melrose Ave.   **6-D7**
(213) 871-4311.
Inglewood: 123 W. Manchester Blvd.   **1-D4**
(310) 419-5322.
Northeast LA: 2032 Marengo St. (213)   **7-C7**
266-5451.
San Fernando: 604 S. Maclay Ave.   **1-A3**
(818) 365-6341.
San Pedro: 122 W. 8th St. (310)   **1-F5**
519-6060.
Santa Monica: 2509 Pico Blvd. (310)   **4-B5**
315-4500.
South LA: 1522 E. 102nd St. (213)   **1-E5**
563-4060.
Southwest LA: 3834 S. Western Ave.   **1-D4**
(213) 730-3507.
Torrance: 2300 W. Carson St. (310)   **1-F4**
533-6571.
Van Nuys: 17515 Venice Blvd. (818)   **1-B3**
901-3903.
Venice: 905 Venice Blvd. (310) 821-3484.   **4-E6**
W. Hollywood: 621 N. San Vicente Blvd.   **6-E1**
(310) 854-1308.
Whittier: 7643 S. Painter Ave. (310)   **1-D7**
907-3230, ext 260.

FOREIGN EXCHANGE

American Foreign Exchange   7-C4
World Trade Center, Suite 120, 350 S. Flower St, LA. (213) 261-7790.

Thomas Cook   **7-D3**
900 Wilshire Blvd, LA.
(213) 624-4221.
452 N. Bedford Dr, Beverly Hills.   **5-E8**
(310) 274-9176.
301 Del Amo Fashion Center, Torrance.   **1-F4**
(310) 370-6343.
3243 Glendale Galleria, Glendale.   **1-B5**
(818) 242-6883.

TRAVELER'S CHECKS

American Express Travel Service Office
327 N. Beverly Dr, Beverly Hills. (310) 274-8277.
Thomas Cook
452 N. Bedford Dr, Beverly Hills. (310) 274-7051.

CUSTOMS

Information Offices
LA Harbor: (310) 514-6030
Downtown: (213) 894-4749
LA International Airport: (310) 215-2240

IMMIGRATION & NATURALIZATION

Immigration & Naturalization Service   **7-C5**
300 N. Los Angeles St, LA. (213) 894-2119.

TRANSLATION SERVICES

Berlitz Translation Service   **5-D8**
323 N. Beverly Dr, Beverly Hills. (310) 276-1101.
Translation service for all major languages in the world.
Intex Translation Agency   **6-D4**
9021 Melrose Ave, LA. (310) 275-9571. Translation and interpretation into over 20 languages.

TRAVELER'S AID

Traveler's Aid Society   **7-D4**
453 South Spring St, LA. (213) 625-2501.
LA Airport, 400 World Way, Room 275,   **3-D5**
LA. (310) 646-2270.

AUTO RENTAL

Cars can be rented for set daily or weekly rates, either with unlimited mileage or for a set daily rate with additional cost per mile. If you intend to travel extensively it is more economical to rent

with unlimited mileage. The following agencies offer reliable service and fair value for your money.
Avis Rent-A-Car:
(800) 331-1212
Budget Rent-A-Car:
(800) 527-0700
Dollar Rent-A-Car:
(310) 652-2600; (213) 380-5353
Hertz Rent-A-Car:
(800) 654-3131
National Car Rental System:
(800) 328-4567
Rent-A-Wreck:
(See also SHOPPING & SERVICES, Specialty Shopping, Rentals.) (310) 478-0676
Thrifty Rent-A-Car Inc:
(213) 655-9910

LIMOUSINE SERVICES

Professionally chauffeured limousines are a common sight in Los Angeles. Most limousine companies offer 24-hour service and their vehicles have color TV, bar, and telephone—upon request. Some offer bodyguard service.
A-J Limousine Inc.:
(310) 556-2077
Music Express:
(818) 845-1502
Starlight Limousine Service:
(818) 990-1060
White Tie Limousine Service:
(310) 553-6060

TAXIS

Taxicabs are not as abundant in LA as in other large cities, so don't expect to be able to hail a cab in the street. Service is prompt, however, and cabs normally arrive within a few minutes of a telephone request.
Beverly Hills Cab Co.:
(310) 273-6611
Checker Cab Co.:
(213) 481-1234; (213) 482-3456
City Yellow Cab Co.:
(213) 870-3333; (213) 827-2933
Independent Cab Co.:
(310) 659-8294
Checker Cab Co. (LA):
(213) 654-8400

LAX AIRPORT

LA International Airport, often abbreviated LAX, is Southern California's major airport and one of the busiest in the world. Road traffic near the airport is usually congested, so allow plenty of

F.M.

LAX Theme Building

traveling time. When driving toward LAX from West Los Angeles, you can get frequent traffic reports by tuning your radio to 530AM (reports are broadcast between 7am and 11pm). LAX is served by all major air carriers. For general information, call (310) 646-5252.

Los Angeles also has four regional airports: **Hollywood/Burbank**, (818) 840-8847, which is served by American, Alaska, Continental, PSA, and Republic airlines; **Ontario**, (714) 984-1207, served by Air Cal, American, Continental, Delta, PSA, Republic, and United; **Long Beach Municipal Airport**, (310) 421-8295, served by Jet America and PSA; **Orange County Airport**, (714) 252-5006, served by American, Delta, Golden West, Imperial, PSA, and Republic.

For specific flight information always phone the airline direct (see Airlines). Terminal buildings at LAX are clearly numbered and surround a central one-way traffic system. Remember to check for the terminal from which your flight is scheduled. NOTE: West Imperial Terminal is located away from the main terminal area, at the south side of the airport on Imperial Boulevard. (**3-E5**). A complimentary bus service runs between West Imperial Terminal and the central terminals every half hour from 7:30am to 11:30pm.

For information on all airport bus services and parking at LAX, call (818) 247-7678. Free transportation between LAX and local hotels can be obtained by using the "Hotel/Motel" courtesy phones located in baggage claim areas. Airport information aides are on duty between 7am and 11:30pm; to contact an aide use the yellow courtesy phones located in each terminal. A special visitor information line, connecting visitors to multilingual aides, is also available.

Special facilities and services are provided for the handicapped throughout LAX. These include ramps, parking, elevators, telephone booths, rest rooms, wheelchairs, and restaurants. To reserve a wheelchair in advance call the airline company reservation desk. Assistance may also be obtained at airline ticket counters or by contacting an information aide.

Greater Los Angeles has a number of small airports for privately owned aircraft. A pleasant afternoon can be spent plane-watching, as all

are open to the general public. Flying lessons are usually available (see also SPORTS & RECREATION, Sporting Activities, Flying). NOTE: A "(c)" in the following indicates the presence of a control tower.
Chino (c): (714) 597-3910
Compton: (310) 631-8140
El Monte (c): (818) 448-6129
Fullerton (c): (714) 738-6323
Hawthorne (c): (310) 970-7215
Long Beach (c): (213) 421-8293
Santa Monica (c): (310) 390-7606
Torrance (c): (310) 618-2861
Van Nuys (c): (818) 785-8838
Whiteman: (818) 896-5271

Airport Parking at LAX

For general information on airport parking at LAX, call (310) 646-2911.

Large parking lots are situated in and around LAX for short- and long-term parking. To save money and avoid traffic congestion the following are worth noting.

Auto Air Porter   **3-E5**
2222 E. Imperial Hwy, LA. (310) 640-1111. Indoor parking. South side of airport, close to West Imperial Terminal. Moderate daily rates, free transportation to and from all terminals.

Car Barn   **3-D6**
5757 W. Century Blvd, LA. (310) 642-0900. Indoor parking. Close to LAX. Moderate daily rates, free transportation to and from terminals.

Lot C   **3-C6**
96th St, east of Sepulveda Blvd. (310) 646-6402. First two hours free, low daily rates, free transportation to and from airport terminals, special facilities for handicapped passengers. Handicapped van pickup.

Lot VSP   **3-D8**
111th St, between Aviation and La Cienega Blvds. (310) 646-2911. First two hours free, lowest rates, free transportation to and from terminals.

Park Air Express   **3-D6**
6101 W. 98th St, LA. (310) 670-8164. Close to LAX. Hourly and daily rates, free transportation to and from terminals.

Airport Auto Rental (24-hour)

These companies have counters in all terminals at LAX.
Avis:
(310) 646-5600; (800) 331-1212
Budget:
(310) 646-4500; (800) 527-0700
Hertz:
(310) 646-4861; (800) 645-3131

Airport Bus Services

For complete information and tickets, check at booths located next to baggage claim areas.

The Airport Bus
(818) 796-9108; (714) 776-9210. Complete LA and Orange County service from major hotels to LAX and airport-to-airport.

Flyaway Bus Service
(818) 994-5554. 24-hour service. Nonstop between LAX and Van Nuys Bus Terminal. Call for daily information. Also from West LA bus terminal (477-4903).

Super Shuttle
Reservations: (310) 338-1111. Or, no reservation, call collect: (310) 417-8988. Fast service covering LA, Beverly Hills, and south bay area. Wheelchair lift upon request.

Airport Accommodations

See ACCOMMODATIONS, Airport Area.

Emergencies at LAX

NOTE: *Information aides are on duty from 7am to 11:30pm; use the free yellow courtesy phones located in every terminal.*

Airport Security:
(310) 646-6254

Handicapped Van:
(310) 646-6402

Lost and Found:
Check with airline or call (310) 646-4268

Medical:
Call police (310) 646-6254

Multilingual aides:
Information desk, arrival level, Bradley International Terminal (no phone).

Police:
(310) 646-2256

Services for the Handicapped

Handicapped Van:
(310) 646-6402

AIRLINES

Location of Airlines at LAX

Terminal 1
American West
Southwest
USAir
USAir Express

Terminal 2
Air Canada
Avianca
Great American
Hawaiian Air
Key
Northwest
VASP

Terminal 3
Alaska
Mid West Express
TWA

Tom Bradley International—West Terminal
Aero California
Aero Cancun
Aeroquetzal
Aerolineas Argentinas
Aeromexico
Air France
Air Jamaica
Air New Zealand
Alia
Alitalia
ANA (All Nippon)
Asiana
British Airways
Canadian Int'l
Cathay Pacific
China Air
China Eastern
Ecuatoriana
El Al
Garuda
Iberia
Japan Airlines
KLM
Korean Airlines
LACSA
LTU
Lufthansa
MAC
Malaysian
Mexicana
Philippine
Quantas
SAS
Singapore
TACA
Thai
UTA French Airlines
Varig

Terminal 4
American
American Eagle

Terminal 5
Delta

Terminal 6
Continental
Delta
Morris Air
Skywest

Terminal 7
United
United Express
Virgin Atlantic

Imperial Terminal—6661 W. Imperial Hwy.
Air LA
Alpha
Grand Airways
MGM Grand Air
Pacific Coast

Flight Information and Reservations

NOTE: *Use first number for flight information at LAX, second number for reservations.*

Aero California	(310) 322-2644; (310) 322-4222
Aerolineas Argentinas	(310) 646-7181; (800) 333-0276
Aeromexico	(800) 237-6639
AeroPeru	(305) 595-0022
Air Canada	(800) 776-3000
Air France	(310) 646-2621; (310) 274-8381
Air New Zealand	(310) 646-3069; (800) 262-1234
Alaska	(800) 426-0333
Alitalia	(800) 223-5730
America West	(310) 746-6400; (800) 247-5692
American Airlines	(310) 646-6505; (310) 935-6045
Aspen Airways	(800) 241-6522
Avianca	(310) 646-7032; (800) 284-2622
British Airways	(310) 646-7844; (800) 247-9297
Canadian Int'l	(800) 426-7000
Cathay Pacific	(800) 233-2742
Continental Airlines	(310) 772-6000
CPAir	(310) 646-9494; (800) 426-7000
Delta	(310) 386-5510
Ecuatoriana	(310) 627-8844
El Al	(800) 223-6700
Finnair	(800) 221-4300
Japan Airlines	(310) 646-8031; (800) 525-3663
KLM	(310) 646-5584; (800) 777-5553
Korean Airlines	(310) 646-4866; (310) 484-1900
LTU	(310) 640-0269
Lufthansa	(310) 646-7150; (800) 645-3880
Mexicana	(310) 646-0497; (310) 646-9500
Mid West Express	(800) 452-2022
MGM Grand Air	(800) 933-2646
Northwest	(310) 646-7711; (800) 447-4747
Philippine	(800) 435-9725
Qantas	(310) 649-2780; (800) 227-4500
SAS	(310) 646-2180
Singapore	(310) 646-1168; (800) 742-3333
Skywest	(800) 453-9417
Southwest	(310) 485-1221; (800) 854-1221
Thai	(310) 646-3049; (800) 426-5204
TWA	(310) 858-8811; (213) 484-2244; (800) 892-4141
United	(310) 550-1400; (310) 772-2121
United Express	(310) 550-1400
USAir	(310) 646-6897; (800) 428-4322

Varig	(310) 646-2190; (800) 468-2744
Virgin Atlantic	(800) 862-8621

BUS AND METRO RAIL SERVICES

Public transit in Los Angeles has entered a new era with Metro Rail System rail service presently consisting of the 22-mile Blue Line running between Los Angeles and Long Beach, which opened in 1990, and the Red Line in downtown Los Angeles, which began operation in 1993. An important element in the use of the rail system, which will eventually span 400 miles of Los Angeles County, is the connecting bus lines serving the stations along the rail line. The Los Angeles County Metropolitan Transit Authority produces an excellent brochure detailing schedules of rail/bus connections; call (213) 626-4455 for information.

All bus service offices provide free maps and schedules. Special tourist passes are also available. If taking the bus for the first time, call ahead to check on fares. There is usually one set fare, and upon entry correct change must be dropped into a box next to the driver's seat. Los Angeles County Rapid Transport District (RTD) has offices in all major areas. The city of Santa Monica has a particularly good bus service reaching into several districts of Los Angeles. Culver City Municipal bus service covers the southwest area. (See also SIGHTSEEING, Tours.)

Buses

Culver City Municipal Buslines
(310) 559-8310. Frequent service (6am to 10:40pm) to Culver City, Santa Monica, Westchester, West Los Angeles.

Great American Stagelines
(805) 499-4316. Service to Thousand Oaks and Ventura County.

Greyhound Bus Lines
Bus stations in most areas of the city, with connecting services and ticket offices. Tours, charters, and express package service. Call for information on fares and schedules.
    Information: (213) 620-1200
    Package Express: (213) 629-8420
    Customer Service: (213) 629-8430

RTD (24 hours)
Connecting service covering all cities in Greater Los Angeles. Convenient Downtown MiniBus service and Airport Express. Monthly passes for unlimited travel within LA County.
    Information: (213) 626-4455
    Customer Relations: (213) 972-6235
    Passes and Tickets: (213) 972-6000

Santa Monica Municipal Bus Service
(310) 451-5445. Efficient, inexpensive service to Century City, Culver City, Downtown, Westwood, and Marina del Rey. Charters and excursions available.

Trailways Bus System
Intercity and nationwide.
Information: (213) 897-1589
Package Express Service: (213) 742-1269 or
-1251
Charter and tour services: (213) 742-1231

Metro Red Line

Currently only 5 stations have opened on the Red Line of the much anticipated LA subway system. The state-of-the-art stations and trains are an attraction in themselves, especially if you have experienced the New York City subway system. You can travel from Union Station to Westlake/MacArthur Park Station in only 7 minutes. Note: The Metro Red Line is designed to move with the earth and continue operating during small and moderate earthquakes. In the event of a major quake, the line is designed to stop.

Fare $1.10; 55¢ for seniors and disabled. The blind and children under age 5 ride free. Tickets may be purchased at Ticket Vending Machines located in the stations. One-way tickets are valid until the printed expiration time, a maximum of 2 hours after the purchase. Transfers to an RTD bus or the Metro Blue Line require an additional 25¢ fare (10¢ for seniors and the disabled) at the time of purchase of your rail ticket. There are 90¢ discount tokens sold in rolls of 10 for $9, available at RTD Customer Service Centers and monthly passes, sold at authorized Pass Sales Centers. *Hours of operation: 7 days 5am–7pm.* Trains run at 10-minute intervals. Note: Frequency and hours of service may be adjusted to meet demand in the near future.

—Stations

Union Station. Easy access to Chinatown, Olvera Street, Little Tokyo, Amtrak terminals, and Metrolink commuter rail trains.
Tom Bradley Civic Center Station (First & Hill streets). A short walk from the Music Center, City Hall, Times Mirror Square, and the Los Angeles City, County, and State government buildings.
The Pershing Square Station (Fifth & Hill streets). Near the Jewelry Mart, Grand Central

Market, Pershing Square Park, and the shops along Broadway. Transfer point for the Metro Blue Line between Los Angeles and Long Beach.
The Westlake/MacArthur Park Station. Directly across from the park.
The 7th Street/Metro Center Station. Surrounded by Broadway Plaza, Citicorp Plaza/Seventh Market Place, Arco Towers, and the Fine Arts Building.

Metro Blue Line

The riding time for the complete 22-mile Blue Line is 1 hour.

Fare one way $1.10; 55¢ for seniors and disabled. Free for the blind and children under age 5. Transfers are 25¢, seniors and disabled pay 10¢. *Hours of operation: 5am–9pm, 7 days a week between 7th Street/Metro Center (7th & Flower streets) in downtown Los Angeles and the Long Beach downtown Rail Loop at the Transit Mall Station (First & Pine streets).* Trains run every 10 minutes during weekday rush hours morning and evening, every 15 minutes at other times weekdays and on the weekends. Call (213) 626-4455 for more information.

LONG-DISTANCE TRAIN SERVICE

Amtrak
All Amtrak passenger trains leaving from the impressive and historic Union Station (800 N. Alameda Street) travel to such out-of-town points of interest as San Diego, Santa Barbara, and San Francisco. The daylong coastal journey to San Francisco is particularly recommended for scenic beauty as the railroad crosses unspoiled coastal areas not accessible by car. Note: Special rates are available for couples and families. Call (213) 624-0171 for information and reservations.

BOAT SERVICES

For boat chartering, leasing, or renting see SPORTS & RECREATION, Sporting Activities, Sailing & Boating.
Catalina Cruises
(213) 253-9800. From two to 16 trips daily (depending upon weather conditions and time of year) are available to Catalina Island from San Pedro and Long Beach. (*See also* SIGHTSEEING, Tours: Catalina Cruises.)
Catalina Express   **1-G5**
Berth 95, San Pedro. (310) 519-1212. Harbor Blvd exit from Harbor Freeway (11). From three to seven trips daily to Catalina. Fastest fleet to the island—90 minutes one way. Airline-type seating; stewardess service. Reserve in ad-

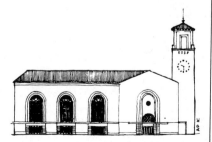

Union Station

vance through Ticketmaster (*see* ENTERTAIN-MENT, Tickets).

CRUISE LINES

Cruise ships leave Los Angeles Harbor for exotic destinations—such as Hawaii, the Far East, Mexico, and Alaska—on a regular basis. The following companies offer a variety of cruises ranging from a few days to a few months.

Carnival Cruise Lines
Contact your travel agent or call (800) 327-9501.
Cunard Line and Cunard Sea Goddess Cruises
Contact your travel agent or call (800) 221-4770.
Holland America Line/Westours
Contact your travel agent or call (800) 426-0327.
Princess Cruises   **5-E7**
2029 Century Park East, Century City. (800) 232-4666.
Royal Cruise Line
Contact your travel agent or call (800) 792-2992.
Royal Viking Line
Contact your travel agent or call (800) 422-8000.
Ships & Trips   **3-F4**
301 Main St, El Segundo. (310) 322-0841.
Western Cruise Lines   **1-G5**
140 W. 6th St, San Pedro. (310) 548-8411.

ANIMALS IN TRANSIT

Jet Pets Inc.   **3-B3**
9111 Falmouth Ave, Playa del Rey. (310) 823-8901. Any size animal. Pickup and delivery Monday to Friday, will keep pet safe until departure time; airline-approved containers.

CONSULATES & FOREIGN TRADE OFFICES

Argentine Embassy   **6-G7**
3580 Wilshire Blvd, Suite 1414, LA (Trade Office). (213) 623-3230.
Australian Consulate   **6-F6**
611 N. Larchmont Blvd, LA. (213) 469-4800.
Austrian Trade Commission   **6-G2**
11601 Wilshire Blvd, Suite 2420, LA.
  (310) 477-9988.
Belgian Consulate   **6-G3**
6100 Wilshire Blvd, Suite 1200, LA.
  (213) 857-1244.
Bolivian Consulate   **7-C3**
3660 Wilshire Blvd, Suite 900.
  (213) 387-5321.
Brazilian Consulate   **6-F2**
8484 Wilshire Blvd, 7th floor, Beverly Hills.
  (213) 651-2664.

British Consulate   **5-E6**
11766 Wilshire Blvd, Suite 400, LA.
  (213) 477-3322.
Canadian Consulate   **1-G4**
300 S. Grand Ave, Suite 1000, LA.
  (213) 687-7432.
Chilean Consulate   **7-C3**
510 W. 6th St, Suite 1204, LA.
  (213) 646-6357.
Chinese Trade Representatives   **6-G7**
3660 Wilshire Blvd, Suite 918, LA.
  (213) 380-3644.
Costa Rican Consulate   **6-G7**
3540 Wilshire Blvd, Suite 404, W. LA.
  (213) 380-7915.
Danish Consulate   **6-G7**
3440 Wilshire Blvd, Suite 904, LA.
  (213) 387-4277.
Ecuadorian Consulate   **7-D4**
548 S. Spring St, Suite 602, LA.
  (310) 628-3014.
El Salvadorian Consulate   **7-C2**
2412 W. 7th St, LA.
  (213) 383-5776.
Finnish Consulate   **5-F7**
1900 Avenue of the Stars, Suite 1025, LA.
  (310) 203-9903.
French Consulate   **5-F5**
10990 Wilshire Blvd, Suite 300, LA.
  (310) 479-4426.
German Consulate   **6-G3**
6222 Wilshire Blvd, LA.
  (213) 930-2703.
Hong Kong Trade Council   **7-C4**
350 S. Figueroa St, Suite 282, LA.
  (213) 622-3194.
Indonesian Consulate   **6-G8**
3457 Wilshire Blvd, LA.
  (213) 383-5126.
Israeli Consulate   **6-G2**
6380 Wilshire Blvd, LA.
  (213) 651-5700.
Italian Consulate   **5-G2**
12400 Wilshire Blvd, Suite 300, LA.
  (310) 820-0622.
Japanese Consulate   **7-C4**
250 E. 1st St, Suite 1507, LA.
  ` (213) 624-8305.
Kenyan Consulate   **5-E8**
9150 Wilshire Blvd, Suite 160, Beverly Hills.
  (310) 274-6635.
Korean Consulate   **6-G8**
3243 Wilshire Blvd, LA.
  (213) 385-9300.
Lebanon Consulate   **6-C4**
7060 Hollywood Blvd, Suite 510, LA.
  (213) 467-1253.
Malay Consulate   **7-C4**
350 S. Figueroa St, Suite 400, LA.
  (213) 621-2991.
Maltese Consulate   **6-E5**
5428 E. Beverly Blvd, LA. (213) 939-5011.

Mexican Consulate 7-B2
2401 W. 6th St, LA. (213) 351-6800.
Netherlands Consulate 6-G7
3460 Wilshire Blvd, LA. (213) 380-3440.
New Zealand Consulate General 5-F4
10960 Wilshire Blvd, Suite 1530, LA.
(310) 477-8241.
Nicaraguan Consulate 7-C2
2500 Wilshire Blvd, LA. (213) 252-1170.
Norwegian Consulate 6-G4
5750 Wilshire Blvd, LA. (213) 933-7717.
Peruvian Consulate 6-G8
3460 Wilshire Blvd, LA. (213) 383-9895.
Philippine Consulate 6-G8
3660 Wilshire Blvd, Suite 900, LA.
(213) 387-5321.
Portuguese Consulate 5-E6
1801 Avenue of the Stars, LA.
(310) 277-1491.
South African Consulate 6-F2
50 N. La Cienega Blvd, Suite 300, Beverly Hills.
(310) 657-9200.
Spanish Consulate 6-G4
6300 Wilshire Blvd, Suite 1630, LA.
(310) 658-6050.
Swedish Trade Council 5-F4
10880 Wilshire Blvd, LA. (310) 475-4501.
Swiss Consulate 6-G8
3440 Wilshire Blvd, LA. (310) 575-1145.
Thai Consulate 6-D4
801 N. La Brea Ave, LA. (213) 937-1894.
Turkish Consulate 6-G4
4801 Wilshire Blvd, Suite 310, LA.
(213) 937-0118.

FOREIGN TOURIST OFFICES

Australian Tourist Commission 5-F6
2121 Ave of the Stars, LA. (310) 552-1988.
Austria 6-G2
11601 Wilshire Blvd, Suite 2480, Brentwood.
(310) 477-3332.
Bahamas 6-G8
3450 Wilshire Blvd, Suite 208, LA.
(213) 385-0033.

Brazil 6-G2
8484 Wilshire Blvd, Beverly Hills.
(213) 651-2664.
France 5-E8
9454 Wilshire Blvd, Beverly Hills.
(310) 271-6665.
Germany 5-E6
11766 Wilshire Blvd, Suite 750, LA.
(310) 575-9799.
Great Britain 7-C4
350 S. Figueroa St, LA. (213) 628-3525.
Greece 1-G4
611 W. 6th St, Suite 2198, LA.
(213) 626-6696.
India 6-G8
3550 Wilshire Blvd, Suite 204, LA.
(213) 380-8855.
Israel 6-G2
6380 Wilshire Blvd, Suite 1700, LA.
(213) 658-7462.
Japan 7-D3
624 S. Grand Ave, Suite 1611, LA.
(310) 623-1952.
Kenya 5-E8
9150 Wilshire Blvd, Suite 160, Beverly Hills.
(310) 274-6635.
Mexico 5-E6
10100 Santa Monica Blvd, Suite 224, LA.
(310) 203-8151.
Philippines 6-G8
3660 Wilshire Blvd, Suite 216, LA.
(213) 487-4525.
Puerto Rico 9-G5
3575 W. Cahuenga Blvd, LA.
(213) 874-5991.
South Africa 6-F2
50 N. La Cienega Blvd, Suite 300, Beverly Hills.
(310) 657-9200.
Spain 6-G8
8383 Wilshire Blvd, Suite 960, LA.
(213) 658-7188.
Tahiti 3-D6
6151 W. Century Blvd, Suite 1024, LA.
(310) 649-2884.
Thailand 6-G8
3440 Wilshire Blvd, Suite 1100, LA.
(310) 382-2353.

SENIOR CITIZENS

The senior citizen population in Los Angeles grows each year. Facilities provided especially for seniors are extensive, and visiting seniors represent a larger proportion of the tourist industry than ever before. The following information should prove useful to senior residents as well as visitors.

SENIOR CITIZEN INFORMATION

City of Los Angeles (general information): (213) 485-4851
Social Security Benefits: (800) 772-1213
Senior Citizens Affairs Dept. (LA County): (213) 738-4236
Lost RTD bus pass information: (213) 626-4455
LA County Dept. of Public Social Services: (213) 738-4236
Senior Citizens *Sentinel* newspaper: (213) 232-3261

ACTIVITY CENTERS

Activity, or recreation, centers can be found in all major areas of Los Angeles. They offer a wide range of classes and pastimes. Classes include painting, yoga, drama, and a variety of workshops. Trips, vacations, and special events are organized frequently. For information on activities and reduced rates for seniors, call (213) 485-4851, or contact any of the following centers.

Crenshaw Senior Citizen Center　　**1-D4**
3929 Santa Rosalia Ave, LA. (213) 296-5220.
Culver City Senior Citizen Center　　**1-D3**
4153 Overland Ave, Culver City. (310) 559-2266.
Fairfax Senior Citizen Center　　**6-D3**
7929 Melrose Ave, LA. (213) 653-1824.
Freda Mohr Multiservice Center　　**6-G3**
330 N. Fairfax Ave, LA. (213) 937-5900.
Hollywood Senior Citizen Multipurpose Center　　**6-D5**
6501 Fountain Ave, Hollywood. (213) 465-3522.
MacArthur Senior Citizen Center　　**7-B2**
607 S. Park View, 4th floor, LA. (213) 383-0496.
Mid-Valley Senior Center　　**10-A4**
14450 Valerio St, Van Nuys. (818) 785-8488.
Santa Monica Senior Recreation Center 4-C3
1450 Ocean Ave, Santa Monica. (310) 394-1227.
Senior Citizen of West Los Angeles Club
　　　　　　　　　　　　　　　　5-G4
11338 Santa Monica Blvd, W. LA. (310) 473-3161; (310) 479-4119.
Watts Senior Citizen Center　　**1-E4**
1660 99th St, LA. (213) 564-9440.
Westminster Senior Center　　**4-F5**
1234 Pacific Ave, Venice. (310) 392-5566.
West Wilshire Senior Citizen Center　**6-E3**
141 S. Gardner St, LA. (213) 939-0275 or -5778.

W.I.F.E. Senior Services　　**4-C3**
1320 Santa Monica Mall, Santa Monica. (310) 394-9871.

NUTRITION

Free or low-cost meals are available at dozens of nutrition centers. Most centers suggest a small donation of less than one dollar. Meals are usually served five days a week, and it is advisable to make reservations. For the nutrition center nearest you, call Senior Line Information Assistance, (213) 857-6411, and tell them your zip code (zip code information [213] 586-1737), or call the Program of Retired Citizens, (213) 851-8449. These people will also give you information on the closest Meals on Wheels service. Normally a daytime service, Meals on Wheels delivers low-cost meals to shut-ins, and they often provide for specialized diets. The Senior Citizen Specialist will provide a list of restaurants offering discounts to seniors, call (310) 278-0840. Mrs. Gooch's Natural Food Store (*see* SHOPPING & SERVICES, Food, Health Food) offers seniors a 10% discount on all vitamins and supplements. Kosher Meals for the Elderly will provide all-kosher meals, call (310) 271-2830.

MEDICAL CARE

In addition to the government free clinic services available to all, specialized services are provided for senior citizens.
Westside Senior Health and Counseling Center　　**4-A4**
2125 Arizona Ave, Santa Monica. (310) 829-4715. Free health services include a complete physical examination with checks on blood pressure, glaucoma, hearing, stress, diet, and nutrition. Free counseling also available.
Didi Hirsch Community Mental Health Center　　**1-D4**
4760 S. Sepulveda Blvd, Culver City. (213) 870-2946. Specialists in problems relating to the elderly.
Internal Medicine Referral for the Senior Citizen
(800) UCLA MD1. This service is operated by trained personnel at UCLA; they provide information on qualified physicians suited to specific needs.
Institute for Rational-Emotive Therapy　**4-D8**
11429 Venice Blvd, Mar Vista. (310) 397-6316. Individual counseling and psychotherapy. Assertiveness training. Seniors get a 25% discount.
Older Adult Counseling Service　　**1-D4**
4760 Sepulveda Blvd, Culver City. (310) 390-6612. Emotional and psychological counseling for seniors.
Senior Health & Peer Counseling Center　　**4-A4**
2125 Arizona Ave, Santa Monica. (310) 829-

4715. Workshops on retirement, sexuality, exercise, nutrition, and health problems.

Hour Glass Eyeglasses   5-G2
12437 Wilshire Blvd, W. LA. (310) 820-6643. Eyeglasses and contact lenses at very low cost with an additional 20% discount to senior citizens.

Nursing Home Information and Referral Service
(213) 974-7779. Service provided by LA County Department of Health Services.

Visiting Nurse Association
(310) 453-0531. In-home health service.

Senior Citizens Health Program
(213) 265-1172.

Cedars-Sinai Hospital
(310) 855-5000.

Freda Mohr Center Jewish Family Services
(213) 937-5900.

TRANSPORTATION

Most nutrition centers provide a transportation service for important appointments and shopping. For information, call (213) 857-6411.

RTD Bus Service
Reduced rates for senior citizens. For information on bus services, call (213) 626-4455. For information on bus passes and tickets, call (213) 972-6000.

Senior Multiservice Center
(310) 394-9871. Shopping and medical appointments.

Trips and Tours for Seniors
(310) 479-4119; (310) 473-3161.

EDUCATION

Emeritus College
(310) 452-9306. Department of Santa Monica College offering a full range of educational and recreational courses designed especially for senior citizens. Most classes are free to residents.

National Council on Aging
(213) 365-0366.

LEGAL AID

LA County Department of Social Services
(213) 974-9237. Information and financial aid in many areas.

Legal Aid Foundation of Los Angeles
(213) 266-6550. Free. Service for those with low income, covering all legal matters except criminal or family law cases.

Neighborhood Justice Center
(310) 451-8192. An organization that brings together disputing parties and resolves differences without expensive court proceedings. Trained mediators are experienced in the fields of law and social services. FREE.

VOLUNTARY WORK

Doves (Dedicated Older Volunteers in Educational Services)
(213) 625-6080.

The Retired Senior Volunteer Program (RSVP)
(213) 938-7239. Seniors are recruited as teachers' aides, office workers, drivers, party organizers, bilingual aides, and many other positions.

RSVP
4153 Overland Ave, Culver City. (310) 559-5088. Volunteer positions for retired people.

USEFUL TELEPHONE NUMBERS FOR SENIORS

California League of Senior Citizens: (213) 386-7771

Casa Maravilla Senior Citizens: (213) 263-9858

Freda Mohr Multiservice Center: (213) 937-5900

National Council on the Aging: (213) 365-0366

Pal-O-Mine Companion Service: (213) 294-4262

Program of Retired Citizens Nutrition and Social Service: (213) 463-7161

Senior Adult: (213) 938-2531

Senior Citizens Association of Los Angeles Inc.: (213) 624-6467

Senior Line Information Assistance: (213) 738-4236

W.I.F.E. Senior Services: (310) 394-9871

Widow-to-Widow Hotline: (818) 990-1049

ALTERNATIVES

Who was it that said, "You cannot conform in LA—there is nothing to conform to"? In this time of the "me" generation, Los Angeles has spawned quite a breed of nonconformist, "new age" liberals. The new consciousness has opened more doors for the women's movement and for the gay community. Holistic healing centers and self-awareness groups spring up daily. Cults, clubs, fraternities, and societies, devoted to every unlikely cause, are now part of LA life.

ALTERNATIVE REMEDIES

(*See also* SHOPPING & SERVICES, Self-Improvement.)

Center for Health   **4-A4**
2105 Wilshire Blvd, Santa Monica. (310) 829-0453. Holistic health care treatments and classes.

Center for Yoga   **6-D7**
230½ N. Larchmont Blvd, LA. (213) 464-1276. LA's oldest yoga center.

Health Integration Center   **1-F4**
3250 W. Lomita Blvd, Suite 208, Torrance. (310) 326-8625. Holistic health and healing center.

Los Angeles Information & Referral Center for Therapy and Growth   **6-D2**
8380 Melrose Ave, Suite 203, LA. (213) 272-1478. Qualified therapists, psychologists, and counselors cover all forms of mind-healing. *CLOSED Sat & Sun.*

Nachis   **1-D3**
10862 Washington Blvd, Culver City. (310) 559-6270. Natural Childbirth Institute. *CLOSED Sat & Sun.*

Physicians Laboratories   **5-E6**
2080 Century Park East, LA. (310) 284-8003. Cytotoxic testing laboratories to test reaction to 150 different foods plus six chemical additives and preservatives. *CLOSED Sat & Sun.*

Planned Parenthood   **7-B7**
Main Office: 1920 Marengo St, LA. (213) 226-0800. There are eight locations in LA County—call for clinic nearest you. Complete reproductive health-care services. Counseling, confidential assistance for at-home teens. *CLOSED Sun.*

Radix Center   **4-C3**
225 Santa Monica Blvd, Santa Monica. (310) 451-8127.

Tao-Healing Arts Center   **4-E4**
2309 Main St, Santa Monica. (310) 396-4877. Acupressure, acupuncture, shiatsu massage school, chiropractic treatments.

Transcendental Meditation Program   **1-C3**
17310 Sunset Blvd, Pacific Palisades. (310) 459-3522. Free public lectures on the program suggested by Maharishi Mahesh Yogi.

The Wholeperson Calendar   **4-B1**
Marina del Rey. (310) 393-5940. A monthly publication with a calendar of Los Angeles events relating to personal growth, both physical and mental.

GAYS

Los Angeles's most active gay community is in, and around, West Hollywood. The following businesses welcome gay clientele, but their inclusion in this section is not intended to indicate the sexual preference of the owners or operators. Listings are in alphabetical order, classified by type of operation.
Abbreviations
GM predominantly gay male clientele.
GF predominantly gay female clientele.

Bars

Detour   **1-C5**
1087 Manzanita St, Silverlake. (213) 664-1189. GM.

Eagle   **6-D3**
7864 Santa Monica Blvd, W. Hollywood. (213) 654-3252. GM.

Limbo Lounge   **6-D2**
In the Four Star Saloon, 8857 Santa Monica Blvd, W. Hollywood. (213) 663-7526. Thursdays only. GM.

The Mother Lode   **6-D1**
8994 Santa Monica Blvd, W. Hollywood. (310) 659-9700. GM.

Numbers   **6-C2**
8029 Sunset Blvd, LA. (213) 656-6300. GM.

The Palms   **6-D1**
8572 Santa Monica Blvd, W. Hollywood. (310) 652-6188. GF.

The Rawhide   **9-C4**
10937 Burbank Blvd, N. Hollywood. (818) 760-9798. GM.

S.S. Friendship   **1-C2**
112 W. Channel Rd, Pacific Palisades. (310) 454-9080. GM.

Spike   **6-D3**
7746 Santa Monica Blvd, W. Hollywood. (213) 656-9343. GM.

Baths

Corral Club Baths   **9-G5**
3747 Cahuenga Blvd, Studio City. (818) 769-6900.

The 8709   **6-F1**
8709 3rd St, W. Hollywood. (Unlisted).

Flex Complex   **6-D8**
4424 Melrose Ave, LA. (213) 663-5858.

The Hollywood Spa   **6-C7**
1650 Ivar St, Hollywood. (213) 463-5169.

Melrose Social Club   **6-D4**
7269 Melrose Ave, W. Hollywood. (213) 937-2122.

Bookstores

A Different Light   **1-C5**
8853 Santa Monica Blvd, W. Hollywood. (310) 854-6601.

National Gay Archives 6-C5
626 N. Robertson Blvd, W. Hollywood. (310)
854-0271.
Sisterhood Bookstore 5-F4
1351 Westwood Blvd, W. LA. (310) 477-7300.
Unicorn Bookstore 6-E1
8940 Santa Monica Blvd, W. Hollywood. (310)
652-6253.

Cinemas

Century Theater 6-C8
5115 Hollywood Blvd, Hollywood. (213) 666-
2822. Sexually explicit gay movies.

Clubs

Apache 9-F3
11608 Ventura Blvd, Studio City. (818) 506-
0404. GM.
Circus Disco 6-D5
6648 Lexington Ave, LA. (213) 462-1219. (*See
also* NIGHTLIFE, Discos & Dance Clubs.) Mixed.
Club 22 9-D4
4882 Lankershim Blvd, N. Hollywood. (818) 760-
9792. GF.
MB Club 6-D8
4550 Melrose Ave, Hollywood. (213) 669-9899.
GM.
Peanuts 6-D3
7969 Santa Monica Blvd, Hollywood. (213) 654-
0280. (*See also* NIGHTLIFE, Discos & Dance
Clubs.) GF.
Probe 6-D5
836 N. Highland Ave, LA. (213) 461-8301. GM.
Rage 6-D2
8911 Santa Monica Blvd, W. Hollywood. (213)
652-7055. GM.
Score 7-C4
107 W. 4th St, LA. (213) 625-7382. GM.
Studio One 6-E1
652 N. La Peer St, W. Hollywood. (213) 659-
0471. (*See also* NIGHTLIFE, Discos & Dance
Clubs.) Mixed.

Community Centers

**Gay Community Center & Lesbian Resource
Program** 6-D5
1213 N. Highland Ave, Hollywood. (213) 464-
7400. Extensive services, including counseling
and referrals.

Counseling

Open Quest
P.O. Box 91446, Pasadena, CA 91109. (213)
664-5000.
Shanti Foundation 6-D1
1616 N. La Brea Ave, LA. (213) 962-8197. Counseling and support for people with AIDS and
those close to them.

Electrolysis

Imre Gordon Electrolysis Inc. 6-D2
7080 Hollywood Blvd, Suite 920, LA. (213) 465-
4111.

Health Clubs

Powerhouse Gym 6-E2
8053 Beverly Blvd, LA. (213) 651-3636.

Medical Help

Aid for AIDS and ARC 6-D3
8235 Santa Monica Blvd, Hollywood. (213) 656-
1107. Financial and medical support for those
with AIDS and ARC. Nutritional programs too.
AIDS Project Los Angeles 6-D3
6721 Romaine St, Hollywood. (213) 962-1600.
Excellent organization that raises funds and co-
ordinates LA County activities.
Ed Edelman Health Center 6-D4
1213 N. Highland Ave, W. Hollywood. (213) 464-
7400. Free, anonymous testing for HTLV III virus.
Counseling.

Publications

The Blue Book 6-C5
1651 Cosmo St, No. 329, LA 90028. Directory to
gay LA.
Centernews 6-D5
1213 N. Highland Ave, Hollywood. (213) 464-
7400. GM and GF.
Compass Magazine
5330 Lankershim Blvd, Suite 201, N. Hollywood.
(213) 874-4383. FREE.
Lesbian News 1-B1
P.O. Box 1430, 29 Palms, CA 92277. (213) 656-
0258, ext 113; (800) 237-0277.
10 Percent 5-D4
406 Kerkoff Hall, 308 Westwood Plaza, Westwood. (310) 825-8500. Gay student union publication.

Radio Programs

IMRU Gay Radio Collective
c/o KPFK, 3729 Cahuenga Blvd W., N. Hollywood, CA 91604. (818) 877-2711. Broadcasts
each Sunday 10pm at 90.7 FM.

Restaurants

French Market Place 6-D3
7985 Santa Monica Blvd, W. Hollywood. (213)
654-0898.
The Golden Bull 4-B1
170 W. Channel Rd, Santa Monica. (310) 454-
2078. (*See* RESTAURANTS, Santa Monica & Marina del Rey, American.)
Rose Tattoo 6-E1
655 N. Robertson Blvd, Hollywood. (310) 854-
4455.

Services

Lesbian Central Resources GLCSC 6-D5
1213 N. Highland Ave, Hollywood. (213) 464-
7400, ext 231.

Whitman-Brooks   **6-D1**
P.O. Box 48320, LA, CA 90048. (213) 650-5752.

Travel

Womantours   **1-D5**
5314 N. Figueroa St, LA. (213) 255-1115.

Unions

Gay Student Union UCLA   **5-D4**
500 Kerkoff Hall, 308 Westwood Plaza, Westwood. (310) 825-8053.
Union of Lesbians and Gay Men
Box 2041, LA, CA 90051.

WOMEN'S ORGANIZATIONS & SERVICES

**Business and Professional Women's
Agency**   **6-G8**
3255 Wilshire Blvd, Suite 1732, LA. (213) 380-8200.
**National Council of Jewish Women,
Women's Center**   **6-E3**
543 N. Fairfax Ave, LA. (213) 651-2930.

National Organization for Women (NOW)
     6-G2
8909 W. Olympic Blvd, Suite 112, Beverly Hills. (310) 657-3894. Task force on political issues, equal rights, lesbian rights, etc.
Rape & Battering Hotline
(310) 392-8381.
Wilshire Club   **6-G7**
607 S. Western Ave, LA, CA 90010. (Unlisted.) Private club for professionals; 85% women. Health spa, fashion salon, cocktail lounge, banquet facilities. Write for membership details.
The Women's Center   **1-C4**
311 S. Spring St, Suite 300, LA; (213) 626-8537. And 901 W. Orengethorpe, Fullerton; (714) 441-0411. Comprehensive health-care centers. Family planning, gynecology, obstetrics.
**Women's Equal Rights Legal Defense &
Education Fund**   **6-G2**
6380 Wilshire Blvd, LA. (213) 653-8087.
Women's Yellow Pages
P.O. Box 66093, LA, CA 90066. (310) 398-5761. Annual publication listing women's businesses plus a survival guide to women's services in LA and surrounding counties. Available by subscription or through bookstores.

EMERGENCY SERVICES

Fire, Police, Ambulance

Dial 911 or operator.

Abortion

Abortion Counseling Service
(213) 388-0077, bilingual.

AIDS

Hotline: (800) 922-AIDS

Air Ambulance

Air Medic
(818) 954-2020

Alcoholism

Al-Anon
(213) 387-3158
Alateen
(213) 387-3158
Alcoholics Anonymous
(213) 387-8316

Ambulance

Los Angeles
Main number: (213) 483-6721. Hearing- and speech-impaired tape: (310) 275-5007.

Animal Emergency Centers

Animal Emergency Center
After-hours emergency care: (213) 937-5120
Animal Emergency Facility
Westwood: (310) 473-1561
West Los Angeles Veterinary Medical Group
(310) 477-8001

Auto Repair (24-hour emergency service)

AAA south of LA Airport
(310) 532-0900
Auto Club of Southern California (AAA)
(213) 937-7411

Battered Women

Help Line
(310) 392-9896 or -8381
Shelters
Central LA: (213) 653-4042 or -4045
Santa Monica: (310) 392-9896
Valley: (818) 887-6589
Pasadena: (213) 681-2626

Call

Community Access Library Line
(800) 372-6641. Multilingual information and referral service.

Child Abuse

Emergency Child Abuse Center
(818) 989-3157
Hotline
(800) 540-4000

Coast Guard

Search & Rescue
(310) 499-5555

Coroner

(213) 343-0506

Dental Emergencies

Dental Society
24-hour emergency referral service: (213) 481-2133
Hollywood Dental Center
(213) 469-1665

Disaster

Los Angeles County Disaster Services
(213) 974-1120

Drug Abuse

Do It Now Help Line
(213) 463-6851
VOA (Volunteers of America)
(213) 627-9000
Narcotics Anonymous
(310) 372-9666

FBI

(310) 477-6565

Fire Department

Los Angeles
Main Number: (213) 384-3131

Flood Control

Los Angeles
Main number: (818) 458-5100

Gambling

Gambling Anonymous
(213) 386-8789

Gays

(*See also* ALTERNATIVES, Gays.)
Gay Community Center & Lesbian Resource Program
(213) 464-7400
Parents & Friends of Gays
(818) 472-8952

Los Angeles
Main number: (213) 736-3374

24-hour emergency services

Brotman Medical Center	**1-D4**

3828 Delmas Terr, Culver City. (310) 836-7000.

Cedars-Sinai Medical Center   **6-E1**
8700 Beverly Blvd, LA. (310) 855-6517.

Centinela Hospital Medical Center   **1-D4**
555 E. Hardy St, Inglewood. (310) 673-4660.

Children's Hospital   **1-C5**
4650 Sunset Blvd, LA. (213) 660-2450.

General Hospital   **7-B7**
1200 N. State St, LA. (213) 226-6707.

Harbor UCLA Medical Center   **1-F4**
1000 W. Carson, Torrence. (310) 533-2345.

La Cienega Medical and Industrial Clinic
1-D4

3344 S. La Cienega Blvd, LA. (213) 870-7666.

Martin Luther King Jr. General Hospital 1-E5
12021 S. Wilmington Ave, LA. (310) 603-4426.

Santa Monica Hospital   **4-B3**
1250 16th St, Santa Monica. (310) 451-1511.

St. John's Hospital   **4-A4**
1328 22nd St, Santa Monica. (310) 829-8212.

UCLA Emergency Medical Center   **5-E4**
10833 Le Conte Ave, Westwood. (310) 825-2111.

USC Medical Center   **7-B7**
1200 N. State St, LA. (213) 226-2622.

Hollywood Lifeline
(213) 463-5433. Crisis help, emergency housing, and transportation for young singles.

Treatment for Sexually Abused Children
(213) 727-4282

North Beaches
(310) 457-2525
Central Beaches
(310) 394-3261
South Beaches
(310) 372-2162

Dick's Lock & Key
(213) 569-0324

Actors & Others for Animals
(818) 985-6263

Marine Mammal Stranding Hotline
(213) 585-5105

Los Angeles
Main number: (213) 262-2111

Passport Agency
(213) 209-7075
See TRANSPORTATION & VACATION INFORMATION, Passports, *and* Foreign Trade Offices *for foreign countries.*

Horton & Converse Pharmacy
6625 Van Nuys Blvd, Van Nuys. (818) 782-6251.
OPEN 8:30am-2am.
Thrifty Drugs
1533 N. Vermont Ave, LA. (213) 664-9854.

Control Center (24 hours)
(213) 484-5151

Los Angeles
Main number: (213) 625-3311

Crisis Unit
(213) 651-5662
Emergency Services
(310) 390-8896
Neurotics Anonymous
(213) 589-3768
USC
(213) 226-5581

Rape & Battering Crisis Hotline
(310) 392-9896
Rape Crisis Center Hotline
(310) 392-8381

Runaway Hotline
(800) 231-6946 (toll-free), confidential help for runaways.

Main number: (213) 627-5571; (213) 774-5399

Senior Citizens

See SENIOR CITIZENS, Useful Telephone Numbers for Seniors.

Suicide Prevention

Suicide Prevention Center
(213) 381-5111

Telegrams

Western Union
Central office: (800) 325-6000

Tel-Med

C.H.I.P.S. (Consumer Health Information and Project Services) Medical information by phone. (English and Spanish) (310) 549-9000.

Toxic Chemicals & Oil Spills

National Response Center
(800) 424-8802

V.D.

V.D. Hotline
(213) 588-5221
V.D. Treatment
(310) 533-2345

Veterans

Veterans Administration
(310) 479-4011

Violence Against Women

Haven House
(213) 681-2626. (*See also* Battered Women.)

Wildlife Rescue

Alliance for Wildlife Rehabilitation & Education
(310) 659-2600

INDEX

Other I LOVE city guides
by Marilyn J. Appleberg

America's most acclaimed urban travel books—
in new, updated editions

I Love Boston
I Love Chicago
I Love New York
I Love San Francisco
I Love Washington